Child Maltreatment

Contemporary Issues in Research and Policy

Volume 7

Series Editors
Jill E. Korbin, Ph.D., Professor of Anthropology, Associate Dean, College of Arts and Sciences, Director, Schubert Center for Child Studies, Crawford Hall, 7th Floor, 10900 Euclid Avenue, Cleveland, OH 44106-7068, USA
jill.korbin@case.edu

Richard D. Krugman, MD, Distinguished Professor of Pediatrics and Dean, University of Colorado, School of Medicine, Room C-1003 Bldg 500, Anschutz Medical Campus, 13001 E. 17th Place, Aurora, CO 80045, USA
richard.krugman@ucdenver.edu

This series provides a high-quality, cutting edge, and comprehensive source offering the current best knowledge on child maltreatment from multidisciplinary and multicultural perspectives. It consists of a core handbook that is followed by two or three edited volumes of original contributions per year. The core handbook will present a comprehensive view of the field. Each chapter will summarize current knowledge and suggest future directions in a specific area. It will also highlight controversial and contested issues in that area, thus moving the field forward. The handbook will be updated every five years. The edited volumes will focus on critical issues in the field from basic biology and neuroscience to practice and policy. Both the handbook and edited volumes will involve creative thinking about moving the field forward and will not be a recitation of past research. Both will also take multidisciplinary, multicultural and mixed methods approaches.

More information about this series at http://www.springer.com/series/8863

Ben Mathews

New International Frontiers in Child Sexual Abuse

Theory, Problems and Progress

Springer

Ben Mathews
Faculty of Law
Queensland University of Technology
Brisbane, QLD, Australia

ISSN 2211-9701 ISSN 2211-971X (electronic)
Child Maltreatment
ISBN 978-3-030-07560-6 ISBN 978-3-319-99043-9 (eBook)
https://doi.org/10.1007/978-3-319-99043-9

Softcover re-print of the Hardcover 1st edition 2019

This Springer imprint is published by the registered company Springer Nature Switzerland AG
The registered company address is: Gewerbestrasse 11, 6330 Cham, Switzerland

Acknowledgements

Some sections of this book are adapted from parts of previously published works. Some of these works were published under Creative Commons licences automatically permitting republication with attribution (CC-BY). Other works were published under other licences requiring permissions or attributions. I am grateful to the publishers for permission to reuse and adapt the materials.

Mathews, B. (2017). Optimising implementation of reforms to better prevent and respond to child sexual abuse in institutions: Insights from public health, regulatory theory, and Australia's Royal Commission, *Child Abuse and Neglect, 74,* 86–98.

Mathews, B., & Collin-Vézina, D. (2017). Sexual Abuse: Towards a Conceptual Model and Definition. *Trauma, Violence, & Abuse,* 1–18.

Mathews, B., Bromfield, L., Walsh, K., Cheng, Q., & Norman, R. (2017). Reports of child sexual abuse of boys and girls: Longitudinal trends over a 20-year period in Victoria, Australia. *Child Abuse & Neglect, 66*, 9–22.

Mathews, B., Collin-Vézina, D. (2016) Child Sexual Abuse: Raising Awareness and Empathy Is Essential To Promote New Public Health Responses, *Journal of Public Health, 37,* 304–314.

Mathews, B., Lee, X., & Norman, R. (2016). Impact of a new mandatory reporting law on reporting and identification of child sexual abuse: A seven-year time trend analysis. *Child Abuse & Neglect, 56,* 62–79.

Mathews, B. (2015). A Theoretical Framework for Designing and Evaluating Strategies to Identify Cases of Serious Child Abuse and Neglect. In B. Mathews and D. Bross (Eds.). *Mandatory reporting laws and the identification of severe child abuse and neglect* (pp. 127–156). Dordrecht: Springer.

Mathews, B. (2013). Legal, cultural and practical developments in responding to female genital mutilation: Can an absolute human right emerge? In C. Sampford, R. Maguire, B. Lewis, (Ed.), *Human Rights and Shifting Global Powers* (pp. 207–227). London: Routledge.

Mathews, B. (2011). Female genital mutilation: Australian law, policy and practical challenges for doctors. *Medical Journal of Australia, 194*(3), 139–141.

Mathews, B., & Kenny, M. (2008). Mandatory reporting legislation in the USA, Canada and Australia: A cross-jurisdictional review of key features, differences and issues. *Child Maltreatment, 13*, 50–63.

I express my sincere gratitude to those whose work has inspired this book. First, thanks to Jill Korbin and Dick Krugman for initiating this series on child maltreatment and for supporting this book. Second, there are scores of researchers around the world, past and present, from whom I have learnt, been inspired, and continue to draw inspiration. Some of these I have been fortunate enough to meet and work with in various capacities. Particular thanks are due to Don Bross, Maureen Kenny, Sandy Wurtele, David Finkelhor, Lil Tonmyr, Elizabeth Letourneau, and Delphine Collin-Vézina. Closer to home, special thanks must go to Michael Dunne, Leah Bromfield, Andrew McGee, and, most of all, professionally and personally, Kerryann Walsh.

I also thank the many survivors with whom I have worked in various professional capacities. The privilege of listening to them, and learning from their experience, has been the most formative experience of my professional career. I hope my work has done them justice. Special mention must go to S, M, H, G, B, and K.

This book is dedicated first and foremost to survivors of child sexual abuse. It is also dedicated to all individuals and institutions who in future can help to prevent it and reduce its effects and in particular to those whose responsibility it is to create change.

Introduction: A Range of Challenges, Cause for Hope, and the Nature of This Book

A Range of Challenges

Recent events across the world highlight multiple diverse challenges for societies in preventing, identifying, and responding to child sexual abuse. A scan of these events demonstrates substantial prevalence, persistent social manifestations and norms and resistance impeding change, prolific offending in institutional settings and systemic failure to respond, and abuse between adolescent peers.

General Prevalence The reported prevalence of CSA continues to be disturbingly high. A recent meta-analysis found high levels of victimisation in most nations for both girls and boys; globally, 1 in 8 children (12.7%) had suffered CSA, with rates of 18% for girls and 7.6% for boys (Stoltenborgh et al. 2011). Even in the USA, where substantial efforts have been dedicated to prevention for several decades, and where there is some evidence to indicate a decline in recent years, the most recent national study found that 21.7% of all 14- to 17-year-olds reported experiencing some form of sexual victimisation in their childhood, and in the past year, 16.4% of girls and 9.4% of boys aged 14–17 reported such an experience (Finkelhor et al. 2015). These data included 12.9% of girls and 5.1% of boys aged 14–17 reporting they had experienced attempted or completed rape. A national study from 2006 in the USA found 4.5% of participants reported experiencing contact CSA by a parent or adult caregiver, before sixth grade (Hussey et al. 2006).

Social Manifestations, Norms, and Resistance Impeding Change

Social norms in many nations, both Western and developing, do not sufficiently proscribe child sexual abuse. Social, legal, health, and educational systems are not equipped to respond to long-established and newly emerging manifestations of child sexual abuse. Attitudes endorsing child sexual abuse, at both the individual and institutional level, are persistent and entrenched. An appreciation of these recent events is important to inform an understanding of the seriousness of the broader situation and the social context and nature of contemporary challenges.

Developing Nations In Yemen, where there are no laws setting an age for marriage or criminalising rape in marriage, families made desperate by war and hunger are selling their daughters as child brides. Child brides are exposed to daily rape and beating (Youssef 2017). The market in China for trafficked and enslaved child brides from other countries such as Myanmar is growing (Baker 2017). Despite recent progress, child marriage remains a massive problem, with an estimated 700 million women alive today being married as a child.

The Philippines is a hub for Internet-based exploitation of children, with the Internet used for the live sexual exploitation of children as young as 2 years old. In 2018, Drew Shobbrook, an Australian, was sentenced to life imprisonment with his Filipino partner Leslie Ann Fernandez, for sexual exploitation of 15 girls in a cybersex ring based in Cebu. More generally, the US Federal Bureau of Investigation estimates that at any given moment, 750,000 child predators are online (Murdoch 2018). More generally, the dark Internet poses a massive challenge for law enforcement. While successful specialised teams exist, such as Task Force Argos in Queensland, Australia, the exploitation of clandestine Internet sites adds a new avenue for some of the worst child sex offenders. In 2015, South Australian man Shannon McCoole was sentenced to 35 years in prison for a range of serious offences against 7 children aged 18 months to 3 years, who he accessed through his job as a carer hired by the South Australian government. His offences included sharing videos and photos of his abuse of the children on a sophisticated global child pornography website with 1000 members; he was also the head administrator of this site (Hancock 2015; Marcus 2016; McGregor and Lim 2015).

Western Nations In Western nations, this problem is exemplified by recent selected events in the USA, France, Australia, and the UK. In the USA, a substantial number of states have amended civil statutes of limitation to give survivors of child sexual abuse a more reasonable amount of time in which to commence civil legal proceedings for compensation for their injuries. However, many other states, including Massachusetts, New York, and Pennsylvania, have resisted reform, influenced by powerful institutions – most notably the Catholic Church and Agudath Israel of America. Some have described the strategies used by the Catholic Church as "mafia-like" (Kirchgaessner 2016). In France in 2018, the government enacted a new law so that a charge of rape would be automatically made out if an adult had sex with a minor aged under 15. This was prompted by public outcry after two cases in which prosecutors judged 11-year-olds to have apparently provided consent to a sexual interaction with men aged 28 and 30. Rape had not been shown under the former law because there was no "coercion, threat, or violence" (Samuel 2018).

In Australia, in the remote Western Australian town of Roebourne, with a population of 2000 and a high concentration of Indigenous Australians, 36 men were charged with 300 offences related to 184 child victims, and there are scores more suspects (Perpitch 2017). Over 90% of the town's school-aged children are thought to be victims (Laurie and Taylor 2018).

England In England, a number of scandals have been revealed regarding organised criminal gangs that have been operating with impunity for years on a mass scale, with a succession of revelations of entire towns being epicentres of CSA. In these cases, the criminal gangs have comprised exclusively or mostly men from British-Asian backgrounds, with this thought to have been one factor influencing authorities' reluctance to intervene due to a fear of being perceived as racially motivated.

The nature of these kinds of offending in England has largely involved the grooming of vulnerable girls, before systematic sexual abuse and trafficking to other areas. Rotherham, a town in South Yorkshire, population 258,000, was the first of these towns to come to light. A report published in 2014 by Professor Alexis Jay found a conservative estimate of at least 1400 children (mostly girls, some as young as 11) were raped and trafficked between 1997 and 2013 (Jay 2014). Police officers and social workers had repeatedly failed to respond to complaints and blamed the girls for being willing participants in child prostitution. Even by the standards of CSA, the offences were extremely serious, often involving gang rapes, trafficking between towns, and appalling violence. Multiple earlier reports as far back as 2002 by a special investigator were ignored. The local council's entire cabinet was eventually forced to resign. In Rochdale, a town of 107,000 in Greater Manchester, police and social workers had been warned dozens of times over a period of years that girls were being sexually abused by a gang of men but repeatedly failed to act; again, the girls were not believed or were judged by social workers to be "making their own choices" (Williams 2012). Nine men were later convicted, but some have maintained the scale of offending is similar to Rotherham (Bunyan et al. 2015). A Member of Parliament attested that she had made direct complaints to the police "virtually every week". Subsequently, a separate criminal gang's activities were the subject of Operation Doublet, a police operation involving 550 officers.

In Oxford, 7 men were imprisoned after being found guilty of offences against 6 girls aged 11–15. The offences were extremely serious and involved grooming, sexual torture, rape, and trafficking. A serious case review published in 2015 concluded that as many as 373 children may have been targeted for sex in Oxfordshire in a 16-year period. Some of the victims had been abused for 8 years despite repeated complaints to police and social welfare authorities. This report found that the girls were disbelieved and were seen by authorities as "precocious and difficult" that authorities had failed to recognise that the girls' ability to "resist" the abuse had been eroded by grooming and violent control (Laville 2015; Oxfordshire Safeguarding Children Board 2015). In Newcastle, Operation Sanctuary identified 700 girls and young women as victims, who again the victims not only of the offenders but of inadequate responses by police (Perraudin 2018; Spicer 2018). Telford, population 170,000, is the latest town to experience the uncovering of child sexual abuse and sex trafficking. Recent estimates, while disputed, have put the number of victims at up to 1000 over a 40-year period (Grierson 2018).

In 2014, Operation Hydrant was launched as a coordinated national police investigation into offending by prominent public figures and in institutions. This strategy was adopted in the wake of an escalating number of separate inquiries as the scope of the problem had rapidly become more apparent. By July 2016, there were 2777 suspects under investigation, including 348 classed as being of "public prominence" (including 99 politicians and 164 media celebrities) and 2358 in child and youth-serving institutions (National Police Chiefs' Council 2016).[1]

Institutional Cases and Concealment and the Catholic Church

A range of child and youth-serving organisations have been shown to facilitate child sexual abuse and knowingly harbour offenders. These revelations have involved the most prominent organisations in society, in numerous countries and settings.

In the UK, in February 2018, the Anglican Church was reported to be facing over 3300 allegations of sexual abuse, with many of these involving CSA. The UK Independent Inquiry into Child Sexual Abuse (IICSA) conducted a hearing into the Anglican Church in March 2018. Amidst revelations of cover-ups and corruption, there are calls for independent oversight and mandatory reporting (Sherwood 2018a, b). In addition, more than 330 football clubs are being investigated by a specialist police unit established after increasing numbers of revelations of CSA since November 2017. The unit, named Operation Hydrant, is now examining over 2000 individual referrals in sporting organisations, with the great majority of these involving football (Steinberg 2018). The Football Association is also conducting an independent inquiry, which commenced in 2016. The epicentre of the CSA in football expose is former football coach and talent spotter Barry Bennell, who was sentenced in February 2018 to 30 years in prison for hundreds of offences involving children who played football at numerous clubs where Bennell was employed (Taylor 2018a). Bennell had hundreds of victims, many of whom he abused hundreds of times (Taylor 2018b, c). One club, Crewe Alexandra, had ignored police advice in the late 1980s that they may be employing a paedophile (Taylor 2018d). Manchester City, another of his employers, was also warned by one of its coaches in the 1970s that it was "general knowledge" he was a risk to children (Taylor 2018e). Crewe has since rejected calls for an independent inquiry (Halliday 2018).

Allegations of child sexual abuse by UN peacekeepers in multiple countries have plagued the UN for decades (Grady 2016). A recent Associated Press inquiry found almost 2000 allegations of various sexual assaults have made against UN peacekeepers, with 300 of these against children in numerous countries (Dodds 2017). The UN has recognised the problem of "peacekeeper babies" since 2005 but has

[1] In October 2012, Operation Yewtree was launched into the prolific offending of media personality Jimmy Savile and other high-profile offenders. This Operation was initiated after numerous victims made allegations to police in the wake of a TV documentary named Exposure: The Other Side of Jimmy Savile, in which several victims made allegations about abuse by Savile.

still not taken effective action (Sieff 2016). Whistle-blowers, such as Anders Kompass, have been sacked. Recent plans have been criticised as inadequate (McGeough 2017).

Larry Nassar, the USA Gymnastics physician, was convicted of multiple criminal offences against scores of girls. He was sentenced to at least 40 years in prison and up to 175 years. He had previously pleaded guilty to abusing seven girls and had been convicted of other pornography offences and sentenced to 60 years in federal prison. Over 150 young women spoke out publicly about their experiences of his abuse. He maintained his innocence (Cacciola 2018). While employed for around 20 years at a Michigan State University clinic, Nassar was the subject of repeated complaints by girls who had attended the clinic for medical care. Despite these complaints, MSU did not respond appropriately. In May 2018, Michigan State University was reported to have reached a $500 million settlement with 332 women who Nassar had abused while employed there (Smith and Hartocollis 2018). This settlement easily exceeds the Penn State agreement of $109 million to 30 plaintiffs and is believed to be eclipsed only by a 2007 settlement by the Roman Catholic Church Archdiocese in Los Angeles of around $650 million.

The Catholic Church Faced with known high levels of offending in the Church, and a history of concealment and corruption, Pope Francis initiated promising efforts at reform early in his papacy, including the establishment of the Pontifical Commission for the Protection of Minors, but these efforts have floundered in the face of substantial political opposition. As well, while touring Chile in 2018, Pope Francis accused Chilean victims of CSA of slander and was met with disbelief and outrage. They had been abused by a notorious paedophile, Fernando Karadima, and had complained in 2002 to the Bishop, Juan Barros. The Bishop – who survivors claimed knew about the abuse and had even seen it – had not believed them and did nothing to prevent the abuse continuing. Subsequently, the victims launched public action in 2010; the Vatican investigated and sentenced Karadima in 2011 to a lifetime of penance and prayer, and Bishop Barros only then apologised for not believing them. Yet, Pope Francis accused the survivors of calumny unless there was proof that the Bishop had covered up the crimes committed by Karadima (Franklin and Kirchgaessner 2015).

Research conducted by the Australian Royal Commission into Institutional Responses to Child Sexual Abuse (Australian Government 2017a) found there were 4445 proven or accepted claims made against the Church between 1 January 1980 and 28 February 2015, involving over 2000 offenders of whom 90% were male. On the basis of these data – the tip of the iceberg, given these were only those cases disclosed, made the subject of a formal complaint, and accepted as proven – analysis by the Royal Commission conservatively calculated that of all Australian Catholic authorities with priest members in the period 1950–2010, 7% of priests were offenders. The Catholic Church was involved in 37% of the 6302 individual sessions heard by the Royal Commission.

In March 2018, 3 months after the Australian Royal Commission into Institutional Responses to Child Sexual Abuse delivered its Final Report, former Commissioner

Robert Fitzgerald eviscerated the Catholic Church for still failing to fully accept its responsibility for the abuse and for inadequate responses to abuse survivors. Part of this criticism related to the Church's failure to commit to participate in the Australian federal government's redress scheme, an informal out-of-court scheme to provide compensation to survivors of institutional abuse (Schneiders et al. 2018). In addition, the Church had misled the Royal Commission by grossly undervaluing its property portfolio; a media investigation found the Church held more than $30 billion in property and assets in Australia (Millar et al. 2018). After continued delays, the Prime Minister of Australia, Malcolm Turnbull, wrote personally to the Catholic Church, and other churches, to urge their immediate commitment to the scheme (Koziol et al. 2018).

Sexual Abuse by Adolescent Peers

In the UK, a report by the House of Commons Women and Equalities Select Committee (WESC) found endemic sexual violence against girls in schools. The WESC Report reinforced earlier research by the BBC in 2015, which found that in a 3-year period to July 2015, there were 5500 sexual offences on school grounds reported to police, including 600 rapes. The government's failure to respond a year after receiving the WESC report led to calls for the Secretary of the Department for Education to be charged with breach of statutory duty under the Equality Act s. 149, which requires her to have due regard for the need to eliminate discrimination against girls in school and to advance equality of opportunity. These reported offences of course represent a mere fraction of the true incidence: a 2010 YouGov poll of 16- to 18-year-olds found that one third of all girls experienced unwanted sexual touching at school (Okolosie 2016; Weale 2017).

Research in Europe has found substantial proportions of teenage girls age 14–17 are coerced into sexual acts by their intimate partners, with reported rates in England (41%), Italy (35%), Norway (28%), Bulgaria (21%), and Cyprus (17%) (Barter et al. 2018). In Australia, health service providers perceive some sexual practices, most notably anal sex, are becoming increasingly common between adolescents and are believed influenced by exposure to violent pornography (McNally 2015).

In numerous elite Australian grammar schools, a series of scandals have been revealed involving systematic cultures of degradation of females and serious criminal sexual offending. Examples include male students creating a "young sluts" Instagram account and a Dropbox folder containing nude images of girls from the school. In the case of St Paul's College at the University of Sydney, the oldest college in the country, a pro-rape Facebook page was established in 2009 (at Australian universities, students in first year are mostly aged 17). These scandals have been judged as especially concerning given graduates from these schools commonly proceed to occupy positions of leadership in Australian politics and in corporate and professional sectors (Gilmore 2017). The Vice Chancellor of the University of Sydney condemned St Paul's College for its ingrained culture of "deep contempt for women" (Singhal 2017). The endemic culture of sexual and gender-based violence and its effect on those entering the environment have been astutely pinpointed (James 2017). Other research in Australia involving 3000 young people aged 12–24 found 1 in 4 who thought it was normal for men to pressure women into sex (Margetts 2017).

Cause for Hope

However, there are glimmers of hope and developments indicating both social and governmental commitment to take child sexual abuse more seriously and to create new methods of identification of cases, prevention, and better responses. These are discussed later in this book, especially in Chap. 5; here we can note in summary:

- In the Democratic Republic of the Congo, a trial commenced in November 2018 to prosecute 18 alleged members of an armed militia who over a period of years abducted and raped 46 children in the village of Kavumu. The accused include a politician, and the alleged victims include some children who were as young as 1 year old when they were raped. The accused have been charged with crimes against humanity based on an organised endeavour, with the military prosecutor supported by the NGO Physicians for Human Rights.
- Child marriage laws, including those that allow a rapist to escape punishment if he marries his child victim, are gradually being repealed in numerous countries (Sengupta 2017). Other progress is also notable: in India, where the legal age of marriage is 18, the Supreme Court ruled that sexual intercourse with an unlawfully married child aged 15–18 constitutes rape (Aziz 2017).
- Ongoing efforts to eliminate female genital cutting (FGC) – often called female genital mutilation (FGM) – including increased legal prohibitions, have led to an overall decline in the last 30 years (UNICEF 2016). Nigeria, the most populous country in Africa, and a politically powerful nation, outlawed FGM in 2015 (Topping 2015). There are now laws against FGC in 26 countries in Africa and the Middle East and in 33 other countries with migrant populations from countries that have traditionally practised FGC (World Health Organization 2018).
- In Ireland, on 11 December 2017, Section 14 of the Children First Act 2015 commenced. This law creates a mandatory reporting law for child sexual abuse and a legal obligation for organisations providing services to children to prepare and publish a Child Safeguarding Statement.
- In Australia, criminal committal proceedings commenced in March 2018 against Cardinal George Pell. Cardinal Pell is the third most senior member of the Roman Catholic Church and is the highest ranking Vatican official ever to be personally charged with criminal sexual offences against children. The charges include multiple alleged offences against multiple complainants (Davey 2018), with clusters of alleged offending in different towns and cities from the 1970s to

the late 1990s when he was Archbishop of Melbourne (Younger 2018a).[2] He has consistently denied all charges. On 2 May 2018, the Magistrate delivered her judgement in the committal and found that roughly half of the charges had sufficient substance to warrant committal to full trial. Cardinal Pell will now be formally tried for a range of criminal offences involving alleged sexual offending at a swimming pool in Ballarat in the 1970s and at Melbourne's St. Patrick's Cathedral in the 1990s when he was Archbishop of Melbourne (Younger 2018b).

- Also in Australia, in 2015, Archbishop Philip Wilson became the most senior Catholic clergyman in the world to be charged with knowingly concealing a serious child sex offence, under the New South Wales Crimes Act 1900 s. 316 (McCarthy 2015). Wilson has since appealed three times to have the charge dismissed, but each appeal was dismissed, and he was convicted in May 2018. Cardinal Pell has not yet been proved to have committed a criminal offence, and he is entitled to the presumption of innocence. However, what is significant in both these prosecutions, as demonstrated by the testimony of survivors, is their upholding of the rule of law and the restoration of belief in the public that even eminent and powerful figures can be held accountable by the legal system.
- In Canada, in December 2017, Quebec joined other provinces in making sex education compulsory from elementary school onwards; it will be taught for 5–15 h per school grade (Alphonso 2017).
- The Australian Royal Commission into Institutional Responses to Child Sexual Abuse (the Royal Commission) delivered its Final Report in December 2017 (Australian Government 2017b). This is the single most extensive inquiry of its type ever undertaken. It made over 400 recommendations for legal, policy, and practical reforms. Many of these are already beginning to be translated into criminal law and civil law. Examples include the following:
  - The enactment of "child safe standards" legislation, requiring child and youth-serving organisations to take measures to improve prevention and response mechanisms[3]
  - The enactment of "reportable conduct schemes", which create tighter requirements for organisations to respond to alleged cases and which improve external oversight of the responses made by organisations in these cases[4]
  - The enactment of legislation removing time limitation periods for civil compensation claims against individuals and institutions responsible for child sexual abuse,[5] meaning that survivors can commence a civil lawsuit at any time after the event

[2] See also Milligan (2017) and Marr (2014).

[3] See, for example, Victoria's Child Wellbeing and Safety Act 2005 Part 6; and see Chap. 5.

[4] See, for example, Victoria's Child Wellbeing and Safety Act 2005 Part 5A; and see Chap. 5.

[5] See generally Chap. 5.

- The passing of special laws to prevent the Catholic Church exploiting a technical legal loophole and evading liability for the acts of its clergy and non-clergy offenders[6]
- A new criminal offence of grooming a child for sexual abuse[7]
- A new criminal offence for any adult to fail to report a reasonable belief that a sexual offence has been committed against a child[8]
- A new criminal offence for a person in a position of authority in an organisation, who knows of the risk of abuse of a child by an adult associated with the organisation, to fail to reduce or remove the risk[9]

Cause for hope can also be found in the increasing attention given by scholars from philosophy, and particularly feminist scholars, to issues directly or indirectly connected to child sexual abuse, sexual misconduct, problems of masculinity and aggression, and social and gender inequality more generally. These scholars have substantial and growing influence in multiple societies including but well beyond the West. Martha Nussbaum, arguably the world's leading philosopher, is increasingly engaged with issues of children's rights (Nussbaum 2011; Dixon and Nussbaum 2012). Renowned feminist writers like Chimamanda Ngozi Adichie (2014, 2017) and Rebecca Solnit (2017) are also incisively exposing problems of gender inequality and sexual politics, which are at a broader level inextricably entwined with child sexual abuse, given its disproportionate impact on girls.

In addition, journalists, and especially female journalists and investigative teams, are increasingly engaged with child sexual abuse. The power of the media is an essential tool to focus attention on major social problems and inequities and to shift social norms. The extraordinary work in 2002 by the *Boston Globe*'s Spotlight team in exposing the corruption in the Catholic Church in the archdiocese of Boston was the spark for major exposure of that and other scandals in the USA. This work had stunning resonance in creating further sensitisation about institutional CSA across societies in the wake of popular and critical acclaim, through both the Pulitzer Prize (The Investigative Staff of the Boston Globe 2016) and the Academy Award-winning film *Spotlight*. Since then, journalists in many countries have played a major role in holding governments and institutions accountable for CSA occurring in institutional settings. In particular, substantial works have been published about the Catholic Church (e.g. Berry and Renner 2004; Podles 2008; Robertson 2010).

[6] See generally Chap. 5.

[7] Crimes Act 1958 (Vic) s. 49M.

[8] Crimes Act 1958 (Vic) s. 327.

[9] Crimes Act 1958 (Vic) s. 49O.

The Nature of This Book

In societies across the world, multiple issues exist regarding child sexual abuse, in both private and institutional contexts. There are challenges in how to prevent it, how to detect it, and how best to respond to it. These challenges confront a range of social systems including legal systems, educational systems, and health systems. New social norms, technological communication modes, and shifting social contexts present new challenges in designing justifiable and effective systems of prevention, detection, and response. Some specific challenges arise in technology-rich societies; other challenges arise in developing countries. All these questions arise at the interface of multiple disciplines and demand consideration informed by diverse bodies of knowledge and theory.

This book examines a selection of key contemporary issues and challenges in child sexual abuse, and is relevant for diverse audiences of researchers, legislators, policymakers, and societies worldwide. The book draws from bodies of knowledge including history, law, social science, political philosophy, public health, bioethics, and medicine. It takes a multidisciplinary approach to issues confronting societies and considers the legal duties and ethical responsibilities held by institutional and individual actors. These actors comprise the state; child and youth-serving organisations (e.g. educational sectors, other organisations providing health, welfare, sporting, arts, and recreational and cultural activities to children and youth); civil legal systems; criminal legal systems; other social systems including the medical sector and corporations; civil communities; individual adults; and individual children. The book also considers recent legal and regulatory measures that have been taken in an effort to better respond to child sexual abuse, detect it, and prevent it, in different institutional and other settings. These measures draw heavily on Australian developments, partly because this is where I live but also because Australia has arguably witnessed more of these developments in recent years than any other nation, due in large part to the ground-breaking Royal Commission Into Institutional Responses to Child Sexual Abuse from 2012 to 2017.

Part I (Chaps. 1 and 2) sets the context for the book. In Chap. 1, I draw together the best current evidence about the nature, prevalence, contexts, consequences, and causes of child sexual abuse. In Chap. 2, I discuss the challenge of defining the concept of child sexual abuse, drawing heavily on a recently published conceptual model and definition. Part II (Chaps. 3 and 4) deals with theory. In Chap. 3, I explore new theoretical understandings of children's rights and other key theories including public health, Martha Nussbaum's Capabilities Approach, and Charles Foster's concept of human dignity, due to their relevance to child sexual abuse prevention and responses. In Chap. 4, I discuss the role of legal systems in preventing, detecting, and responding to child sexual abuse. Part III (Chaps. 4 and 5) deals with problems and progress. This part details a selection of the most pressing contemporary problems in child sexual abuse in institutional settings and non-institutional contexts (Chap. 5) and contemporary and emerging cultural and technological challenges (Chap. 6). It also notes significant progress in dealing with these problems and remaining challenges. Chap. 7 makes some observations on future directions and urgently needed change.

Contents

Part I
The Context

Chapter 1
The Context of Child Sexual Abuse, and Points of Departure

Abstract This chapter sets out the context of child sexual abuse and marks out several points of departure from which the rest of the book proceeds. It first defines the concept of child sexual abuse. Then, it reviews the best literature on the prevalence of child sexual abuse both generally, and in specific contexts, around the world. It reviews other important epidemiological features, referring to evidence about gender, age of onset, the relationship between those who inflict abuse and the child, frequency of offending, factors influencing offending, and theories of offending. It notes the common health and behavioural consequences of child sexual abuse. Significantly, it then reviews literature on the common non-disclosure of child sexual abuse by both girls and boys: a critical feature of this context. The chapter than shows that the gravity of child sexual abuse should be and is recognised in international policy and in most social norms. An appropriately nuanced approach is then urged, in recognition of a spectrum of cases that demand appropriately differentiated responses. Finally, the chapter explains that the book also proceeds on the basis that in any civilised society, individuals, institutions and broader social systems and nation states have a deep ethically-based duty to prevent and identify child sexual abuse, and to respond appropriately to it after it occurs. These ethical duties are consistent with bodies of political and public health theory, the Capabilities Approach, and human dignity informing the book's entire conceptual approach.

Keywords Child sexual abuse · Prevalence · Nature · Non-disclosure · Health and behavioural consequences · Recognition by international and social norms · Ethical duty of prevention possessed by individuals, institutions and societies

Science and Social Norms: Points of Departure

This book takes as a point of departure several well-established bodies of knowledge which lay the scientific foundation for further consideration of key issues. At various points in the book, these bodies of knowledge will be referred to again. However, to inform the discussion in the subsequent chapters, it is necessary at the outset to draw attention to several central facts about the nature and sequelae of

B. Mathews, *New International Frontiers in Child Sexual Abuse*, Child Maltreatment 7, https://doi.org/10.1007/978-3-319-99043-9_1

child sexual abuse, to clearly disavow some common myths; and to explain the sense of the term "child sexual abuse" in which I use it.

In sum, the broad base of departure involves the following scientifically established facts and ethical norms:

- The concept of "child sexual abuse" must be appropriately defined; the definition should not be so narrow as to be incongruent with scientific and ethical principles, but nor should it be unjustifiably wide.
- The prevalence of child sexual abuse must be recognised and taken seriously, drawing on a range of studies
- Other important epidemiological features of CSA must be recognised and taken seriously, drawing on scientific evidence of the age of onset, the gender of victims and abusers, the settings of offending, the relationships between offenders and children
- The consequences of child sexual abuse for the child's health, behaviour and functioning must be acknowledged and taken seriously
- Typical delays in disclosure, and non-disclosure, and partial disclosure, must be recognised and taken seriously
- International agencies' embedding of social norms and standards must be taken seriously.

These important concepts each need some further elaboration.

Definition of the Concept

In Chap. 2, I will cover in much more detail the complex problem of defining the term "child sexual abuse". It is a contested concept, and different definitions have been used in research, policy, epidemiology and law. Child sexual abuse is generally understood at a minimum to include a range of acts covering penetrative abuse, masturbation, oral sex, fondling, and involvement in pornography, and other acts to sexually gratify the abuser in circumstances where the child cannot or does not give true consent. The World Health Organization (1999, 2006) states child sexual abuse occurs when the child is involved "in sexual activity that he or she does not fully comprehend, is unable to give informed consent to, or for which the child is not developmentally prepared and cannot give consent, or that violate the laws or social taboos of society".

However, even these generally accepted approaches leave room for debate. For example, at what age, or under what circumstances, is an individually properly seen as a "child"? When is an act "sexual"? What makes an act or a series of acts "abuse" rather than "assault" or "harassment"? Must the offender be an adult, or several years older than the child, to have inflicted child sexual abuse, or can an adolescent or a similarly-aged peer, or even a younger peer, also inflict CSA? Under what circumstances can a child provide genuine consent to a sexual act? Can sexual abuse be constituted by non-contact acts? Being able to differentiate "child sexual abuse" from other concepts such as assault and harassment and unwanted experiences is important. While most instances of "child sexual abuse" will also at the same time comprise a specific type of sexual assault, and may also meet the technical legal definition of sexual harassment, some may not; and moreover, the characterisation of something as child sexual abuse has important consequences for research, law, policy, clinical treatment, ethics and social norms. Especially in analysing hard cases that are neither clearly child sexual abuse, nor clearly not child sexual abuse, it is necessary to have nuanced and legitimate understandings of the relevant concepts.

Based on a recently published extensive multidisciplinary and conceptual analysis (Mathews and Collin-Vézina 2017), I will here consider "child sexual abuse" to be present when *all* of the following conditions are met:

1. **The individual must be a child**. In general, all individuals aged under 18 should be understood as being a child for this purpose. However, the concept of "child" should be analysed from dual perspectives of individual developmental capacity and legal chronological age of adulthood. This becomes especially significant when dealing with complex cases (e.g., sexual activity between adolescent peers of equal power, or cases where an individual is aged under 18 but older than a society's low age of adulthood).
2. **No capacity to provide true consent, or capacity present but not given**. In general, individuals aged under 18 should be understood as possessing either no or diminished capacity to provide true consent to sexual activity. This diminished capacity begins at zero from birth, continues to be at this level through early childhood, and only gradually increases with sufficient age and developmental maturity in the particular individual's case, and even in these cases is further dependent on the circumstances of each individual interaction. Even in cases where the child has any level of capacity to provide consent in the abstract, the concept of consent and its application in the specific case must be considered at both face validity of apparent surface consent, and experientially by asking whether true consent exists, which requires full, free, voluntary and uncoerced participation in all the circumstances.
3. **Acts are sexual in a range of circumstances involving either or both the person's gratification, and or the child's experience**. The concept of "sexual" should embrace contact and non-contact acts done for the purpose of seeking or obtaining physical or mental sexual gratification, whether immediate or deferred temporally or spatially, as well as the child's experience of the act. This is significant for several reasons including the insistence that an act does not have to involve physical contact between offender and child to constitute child sexual abuse.
4. **Acts constituting abuse will usually also constitute an assault; however, the concept of "abuse" contains a heightened wrongfulness**. The term "abuse" possesses a heightened wrongfulness derived from the unconscionability of the acts, which flows from four indicia: the presence of a relationship of power; the child being in a position of inequality; the child's vulnerability being exploited to her or his detriment; and absence of true consent. One significant consequence of this understanding of the term is that child sexual abuse can be inflicted by a wider range of persons than simply parents, caregivers and other adults.

Recognition of Prevalence – Generally, and in Specific Contexts

Epidemiological studies have used different definitions of child sexual abuse and have therefore found significantly different prevalence. The meta-analysis of 55 studies by Barth et al. (2013) found overall rates of CSA ranged from 0% to 69% for girls, and 0% to 47% for boys. Bolen and Scannapieco (1999) pointed to this same problem, finding divergence in rates of 0–62%. The question of appropriate definition of the concept of CSA has been referred to briefly above, and will be returned to in depth in Chap. 2. Further difficulties in arriving at reliable rates of child sexual abuse are presented by studies using a range of different methodologies, with different clinical and non-clinical samples, and participants of different ages.

Nevertheless, despite these challenges, drawing on a range of robust, reliable studies demonstrates without doubt that child sexual abuse is widespread. Population-wide prevalence studies have been conducted in many countries. While different methodologies have been used, many studies have captured data with sufficiently large random samples of the population, obtaining prevalence rates through self-reported experiences, and these studies are the most reliable. These kinds of studies avoid biases inherent in clinical or convenience samples, and data from self-report studies is far more accurate than data from sentinel studies or government administrative data. While recall bias may affect results both positively and negatively, it has been convincingly shown that people are able to report reliably even experiences were long ago, and non-response analyses have further supported the reliability of data obtained from those who participate in such studies compared with those who do not (Finkelhor et al. 2015). In addition, even the most rigorous approaches are likely to underestimate true prevalence, since no participant can recall events before a certain age of childhood, and others are susceptible to reframing of adverse sexual experiences, and some may not respond truthfully due to feelings of shame or embarrassment (Finkelhor et al. 2014). In addition, given the difficulty of reaching hard-to-reach subpopulations who are likely at higher risk of CSA, such as those who are in prison, homeless, or in out-of-home or other formal care facilities, prevalence rates in otherwise robust studies are probably more likely to underestimate prevalence than to overestimate it.

A summary of important studies which have used relatively sound definitions, and which have gathered evidence using self-report studies to generate reliable data, demonstrates the prevalence of child sexual abuse. Reference to global meta-analyses and major national and regional studies is instructive.

Global Meta-Analyses CSA has been shown to be a widespread phenomenon in all societies, although some report higher prevalence than others (Stoltenborgh et al. 2011). Meta-analyses of prevalence studies of child sexual abuse indicate high levels of victimisation in most nations for both girls and boys. The overall rates generated by these studies can be useful to indicate the general scale and significance of the problem.

Three recent meta-analyses have made similar findings. The first of these, by Pereda et al. (2009), analysed pooled results from 65 studies regarding children aged under 18. They found CSA rates of 19.2% for girls and 7.4% for boys. In the second, Stoltenborgh et al. (2011) analysed pooled results from 217 studies regarding children aged under 18. In total, they found that one in eight children (12.7%) had suffered CSA, and found rates of 18% for girls and 7.6% for boys. Stoltenborgh et al. also found varying rates by region, with lower rates in Asian countries. The third meta-analysis, by Barth et al. (2013), concluded that on the basis of its category of "mixed CSA", prevalence in girls was 15% and in boys was 8%. These three studies have therefore arrived at very similar rates for both girls and boys, at the global level. From these three studies, it is reasonable to provide an overall estimated international prevalence rate for girls of 15–20%, and for boys of 5–10%.

However, while these broad rates are useful for short-hand purposes, their nuances require attention. The finer detail in meta-analyses, and in other national and provincial studies, provide much greater illumination of the scale and nature of the prevalence of CSA. This is because the nature of CSA must not be too narrowly circumscribed or it will exclude many cases from recognition; in addition, some specific kinds of CSA are far more likely to have more severe consequences, and to call for certain kinds of responses.

Barth et al. (2013) analysed pooled results from 55 studies regarding children aged under 18. They generated results in four different categories: non-contact abuse (inappropriate sexual solicitation, indecent exposure); contact abuse (touching/fondling, kissing); forced intercourse (oral, vaginal, anal, attempted); mixed CSA (different types of abuse had been inquired about, but only one rate was reported, or the type of abuse was not specified). Combined, they found rates of contact CSA of 13% for girls and 6% for boys. In subcategories of CSA, stratified by gender, they found the following rates:

- girls: non-contact CSA was experienced by 31% of girls; contact CSA was experienced by 13%; forced intercourse was experienced by 9%; and mixed CSA was experienced by 15%.
- Boys: non-contact CSA was experienced by 17% of boys; contact CSA was experienced by 6%; forced intercourse was experienced by 3%; and mixed CSA was experienced by 8%.

National Analyses

North America

USA In the USA, repeated national studies have been conducted by David Finkelhor and his colleagues. A study in 1990 found CSA throughout their childhood reported by 27% of women and 16 of men (Finkelhor et al. 1990). A series of four national studies then obtained data directly from children aged 10 to 17, and from the parents of children aged under 10. These overall prevalence rates give conservative estimates of childhood prevalence given that the respondents were still themselves children who had not reached adulthood, and the breakdown of rates by child age group are instructive. In 2005, the Developmental Victimization Survey, which was the first study to use the Juvenile Victimization Questionnaire, identified rates in the preceding year rather than lifetime rates. It found 8.2% of all children experienced some form of sexual victimization in the preceding study year, comprising 9.6% of girls and 6.7% of boys (Finkelhor et al. 2005).

The first National Study of Children's Exposure to Violence (NATSCEV) found a past year rate of sexual victimization of 6.1%, and 9.8% in their lifetime (Finkelhor et al. 2009). Children aged 14–17 reported substantially higher prevalence across childhood of 27.8%. The second and third NATSCEV studies, published in 2013 and 2015, also found substantial rates. The collation of these three studies also shows some interesting trends over time (Table 1.1).

Furthermore, a subsequent pooled analysis of participants aged 15, 16 and 17 in the three NATSCEV studies examined the experience of specific kinds of child sexual abuse which were measured the same way in each study. The four items encompassed forced and unwanted contact sexual acts with anyone including inappropriate contact sexual acts with adults (Finkelhor et al. 2014).[1] This resulted in analysis of responses from 781 15-year-olds, 804 16-year-olds, and 708 17-year-olds. Pooled

[1] Finkelhor, D., Turner, H., Shattuck, A., & Hamby, S. (2014). The Lifetime Prevalence of Child Sexual Abuse and Sexual Assault Assessed in Late Adolescence. Journal of Adolescent Health, 55, 329e333.

The authors stated that (p. 331): "Family offenders comprise immediate and extended family members including uncles, cousins, and grandparents. Acquaintance perpetrator refers to anyone who was not categorized by the respondent as a stranger or family member. Juvenile perpetrator refers to offenders who were also under 18 and adult perpetrators refer to offenders who were 18 and older." The items were expressed as follows:

S1 At any time in your life, did a grown-up you know touch your private parts when they should not have or make you touch their private parts? Or did a grown-up you know force you to have sex?

S2 At any time in your life, did a grown-up you did not know touch your private parts when they should not have, make you touch their private parts, or force you to have sex?

S3 Now think about other kids, like from school, a boy friend or girl friend, or even a brother or sister. At any time in your life, did another child or teen make you do sexual things?

S4 At any time in your life, did anyone TRY to force you to have sex, that is sexual intercourse of any kind, even if it did not happen?

Table 1.1 Child sexual abuse prevalence rates from national studies in the USA by Finkelhor et al.

Study	All children	Girls	Boys	Age 14–17
Finkelhor et al. 1990	n.a	**Lifetime: 27%**	**Lifetime: 16%**	n.a
Developmental Victimization Survey (Finkelhor et al. 2005)	Past year: 8.2%	Past year: 9.6%	Past year: 6.7%	n.a
NATSCEV 1 (Finkelhor et al. 2009)	Past year: 6.1%	Past year: 7.4%	Past year: 4.8%	All children, lifetime: 27.8%
	Lifetime: 9.8%	**Lifetime: 12.2%**	**Lifetime: 7.5%**	
NATSCEV 2 (Finkelhor et al. 2013)	Past year: 5.6%	Past year: 7.5%	Past year: 3.8%	Past year: girls 22.8%; boys 10.3%
	Lifetime: 9.5%	**Lifetime: 11.4%**	**Lifetime: 7.8%**	**Lifetime**: all children aged 14–17: 27.4% (girls 34.9%; boys 20.2%)
NATSCEV 3 (Finkelhor et al. 2015)	Past year: 5.0%	Past year: 5.9%	Past year: 4.1%	Past year: girls 16.4%; boys 9.4%
	Lifetime: 8.4%	**Lifetime: 9.6%**	**Lifetime: 7.4%**	**Lifetime**: all children aged 14–17: 21.7%

analysis revealed that 26.6% of 17 year old girls and 5.1% of 17 year old boys had experienced sexual abuse or sexual assault during their childhood.

This study is extremely useful because it provides nuanced data for both girls and boys about the prevalence rates at different ages (including near the end of childhood), and by different perpetrator type. The data on sexual abuse involving penetration also provides some information about severity. Below, some of the data from Table 1.1 of this study is reproduced (p. 331; bolding by this author).

Type of perpetrator; gender of victim	Lifetime experience of sexual abuse or sexual assault, by age of participant		
	Age 15	Age 16	**Age 17**
All perpetrators			
Females	16.8	21.7	**26.6**
Males	4.3	3.3	**5.1**
Adult perpetrators			
Females	6.1	7.7	**11.2**
Males	1.0	0.6	**1.9**
Juvenile perpetrators			
Females	12.1	13.4	**17.8**
Males	3.3	2.6	**3.1**
Family perpetrators			
Females	3.3	2.3	**5.5**
Males	0.0	0.4	**0.6**

(continued)

Type of perpetrator; gender of victim	Lifetime experience of sexual abuse or sexual assault, by age of participant		
	Age 15	Age 16	**Age 17**
Acquaintance perpetrators			
Females	14.2	15.4	**19.6**
Males	2.3	1.8	**3.1**
Stranger perpetrators			
Females	0.6	2.3	**3.0**
Males	0.7	0.3	**1.4**
With penetration			
Females	2.4	4.8	**6.1**
Males	0.7	0.4	**0.6**

Another USA Study Restricted to Contact CSA by Parents and Caregivers Using a different approach and a much more restrictive definition of CSA, the national study by Hussey et al. (2006) analysed self-report data from the National Longitudinal Study of Adolescent Health. It asked only one question, which defined CSA very narrowly in this way: "How often had one of your parents or other adult care-givers touched you in a sexual way, forced you to touch him or her in a sexual way, or forced you to have sexual relations". The study found that of 10,046 respondents aged 18–26, 4.5% reported that they experienced contact CSA by a parent or adult care-giver, before 6th grade. Of these, 233 (2.4%) said they experienced it once; 76 (0.5%) said they experienced it twice, and 170 (1.6%) said they experienced it 3 or more times.

Canada In Canada, no national studies have been conducted. However, in the province of Quebec, Hébert et al. (2009) found that 22.1% of girls and 9.7% of boys aged under 18 had experienced unwanted sexual touching or intercourse by an adult or by a child at least 3 years older.

In another study in the province of Ontario, MacMillan et al. (1997) found 12.8% of girls and 4.3% of boys had experienced any form of CSA, and 11.1% of girls and 3.9% of boys had experienced "severe" CSA. "Any CSA by an adult" was defined as including any of the following: experiencing exposure more than once; threatened to have sex with you; touched the sex parts of your body; tried to have sex with you or actually attacked you. In contrast, "severe CSA" by an adult was defined as experiencing any one or more of the last three listed experiences, therefore excluding exposure).

Europe

Nordic Nations Kloppen et al. (2016) conducted a meta-analyses of studies in five Nordic nations, (Finland, Iceland, Norway, Denmark, Sweden: 26 studies). They found that:

- for girls, the prevalence rate for all CSA experienced before age 18 ranged from 11.2% to 35.6%; for contact CSA, from 5.5% to 29.9%; and for penetrative CSA, from 1.1% to 13.5%. The contact CSA rate when peer-inflicted CSA was included was up to 29.9%, but when limited to CSA by those aged at least 5 years older was up to 14.4%.
- for boys, the prevalence rate for all CSA experienced before age 18 ranged from 3.1% to 22.5%; for contact CSA, from 1.2% to 11.9%; and for penetrative CSA, from 0.3% to 6.8%. The contact CSA rate when peer-inflicted CSA was included was up to 11.9%, but when limited to CSA by those aged at least 5 years older was up to 5.7%.

Balkan Nations A group of researchers conducted a study of children aged 11, 13 and 16 to examining children's experiences of maltreatment including sexual abuse in nine countries in the Balkans (Albania, Bosnia and Herzegovina, Bulgaria, Croatia, Former Yugoslavian Republic of Macedona, Greece, Romania, Serbia and Turkey) (Nikolaidos et al. 2018). This study is known as the Balkan Epidemiological Study of Child Abuse and Neglect (BECAN). The study used the definition of child sexual abuse from the ICAST-C instrument. This covered five questions about non-contact sexual abuse and contact sexual abuse, as follows[2]:

> Sometimes people do sexual things or show sexual things to children and adolescents. Thinking about has anyone familiar to you or an unknown person ever made you feel bad or uncomfortable by doing any of these things to you?
>
> 41. Made you upset by speaking to you in a sexual way or writing sexual things about you?
> 42. Made you watch a sex video or look at sexual pictures in a magazine or computer when you did not want to?
> 43. Made you look at their private parts or wanted to look at yours?
> 44. Touched your private parts in a sexual way, or made you touch theirs?
>
> 45A. Made a sex video or took photographs of you alone, or with other people, doing sexual things?
>
> 46. Tried to have sex with you when you did not want them to?

Nikolaidis et al. (2018) reported that children's self-reported exposure to contact sexual violence ranged from 2.1% to 7.7% for the previous year, and 3.5% to 9.8% across the lifespan. Interestingly, the study found that in some categories, boys experienced sexual abuse at a level comparable to or higher than girls: boys in

[2] Note that for 11 year olds, the question about sex videos was not asked.

Albania, Bosnia and Herzegovina, Former Yugoslavian Republic of Macedona, Greece, Romania and Serbia all reported higher levels of contact sexual violence exposure compared to girls. Lifetime prevalence of any sexual abuse ranged from 7.9% (Romania) to 18.6% (Bosnia). Lifetime prevalence of contact sexual violence ranged from 3.6% (Romania) to 9.8% (Bosnia). Further breakdowns by age were not reported by this study.

Croatia In the earlier, more comprehensive report of the Croatian study, Ajduković et al. (2013) reported their findings regarding Croatian children aged 11, 13 and 16 as part of this wider study in the Balkans. The authors found that 10.8% of all children experienced some kind of sexual abuse in their lifetime (13.0% of girls and 8.6% of boys), and 7.7% reported experiencing sexual abuse in the previous year. Of the respondents aged 16 years old, 16.5% reported experiencing child sexual abuse in their lifetime (20.4% of girls and 12.5% of boys). Of the 16 year olds, contact sexual abuse was reported by 9.4% of girls and 7.5% of boys.

Ireland In Ireland, McGee et al. (2011) found rates stratified by type of CSA, as follows:

Form of child sexual abuse	Girls (%)	Boys (%)
Any CSA	30.4	23.5
Indecent exposure	9.2	4.7
Exposure to pornography or involvement in pornography	0.8	2.7
Touching breasts or genitals	14.9	11.2
Contact abuse	12.8	12.0
Attempted penetration	2.0	1.5
Penetration or oral sex	5.6	2.7

Africa

The Violence Against Children Studies The CDC conducted a series of seven studies, covering children aged under 18 in five nations in Africa, one in South-East Asia (Cambodia), and one in the Caribbean (Haiti) (Sumner et al. 2015). Sexual violence was relatively narrowly defined to include contact experiences only, and was broadly categorized into two categories of any sexual violence, and pressured or forced penetrative acts.[3] These studies revealed the following rates:

[3]The broader concept of "sexual violence" was defined as: "unwanted touching, unwanted attempted sex, pressured/coerced sex, and forced sex" with "sex" defined as vaginal/anal penetration by the penis, hands, fingers, mouth, or objects, or oral penetration by the penis". There were slightly different definitions used in Swaziland: (penetration of vagina/anus by penis only) and Malawi (oral, vaginal, or anal sex or vaginal/anal object insertion).

Country	Girls	Boys
Swaziland	Any CSA: 37.6%	Not studied
	Penetrative CSA: 17.5%	
Zimbabwe	Any CSA: 32.5%	Any CSA: 8.9%
	Penetrative CSA: 13.5%	Penetrative CSA: 1.8%
Malawi	Any CSA: ~22%	Any CSA: ~15%
	Penetrative CSA: 6.7%	Penetrative CSA: 1.9%
Tanzania	Any CSA: ~26%	Any CSA: ~12%
	Penetrative CSA: 6.1%	Penetrative CSA: 2.7%
Kenya	Any CSA: ~32%	Any CSA: ~17%
	Penetrative CSA: 11.8%	Penetrative CSA: 3.6%
Haiti	Any CSA: 25.7%	Any CSA: 21.2%
	Penetrative CSA: 9.0%	Penetrative CSA: 7.6%
Cambodia	Any CSA: 4.4%	Any CSA: 5.6%
	Penetrative CSA: 1.5%	Penetrative CSA: 0.2%

Asia

The Middle East Relatively few national studies have been conducted in the Middle East. However, several substantial and methodologically robust studies indicate that sexual abuse is also significant in this region. In Palestine, Haj-Yahia and Tamish (2001) examined prevalence of child sexual abuse using a list of 13 contact and non-contact acts. This study found rates of CSA by a family member of 18.6%; by a relative of 36.2%; and by a stranger of 45.2%.

In Kuwait, Al-Fayez et al. (2012) surveyed 4467 high school students, using the definition from MacMillan's Ontario study. The mean age of participants was 16.9 years. They found that:

- 8.6% reported someone had sexually attacked them (9.1% of females and 8.0% of males);
- 5.9% reported someone threatened to have sex with them (5.5% of females and 6.4% of males);
- 17.4% reported someone touching their sexual parts (14.0% of females and 21.1% of males); and
- 15.3% reported unwanted sexual exposure (8.9% of females and 22.5% of males).

In discussing the unusual finding about boys experiencing as much or more sexual abuse as girls, the authors posited that strict sexual segregation in Arab cultures may have been influential.

In Saudi Arabia, Al-Eissa et al. (2015) conducted a study of 2043 participants aged 15–18, using the ICAST instrument and its six items on sexual abuse. Like the study in Kuwait, this study also found substantial prevalence in both boys (15.2%) and girls (13.1%).

China In China, Chen et al. (2004) conducted a study across four provinces, using the same definition used in Dunne et al. (2003). They found the following rates for girls, boys, and all children, aged under 16: "any CSA" was experienced by 16.7% of girls, and 10.5% of boys; contact CSA was experienced by 8.9% of girls, and 5.0% of boys; and non-contact CSA was experienced by 12.9% of girls, and 8.8% of boys. A meta-analysis of 24 Chinese studies by Ji et al. (2013) found a pooled estimate for females of 15.3% (any CSA), 9.5% (contact CSA), and 1% (penetrative CSA). For boys, the rates were 13.8% (any CSA), 8.0% (contact CSA), and 0.9% (penetrative CSA). Ji et al. (2013) considered the contact and penetrative CSA rates particularly relevant, given that the "total CSA" rate was likely inflated by questions about circumstances not generally seen as constituting CSA, and because the comparative international rates they extracted from Stoltenborgh et al. (2011) were as follows:

- Females: 19.1% (any CSA), 21.2% (contact CSA), and 15.1% (penetrative CSA).
- Males: 7.0% (any CSA), 10.7% (contact CSA), and 6.9% (penetrative CSA).

Taiwan In Taiwan, Feng et al. (2015) surveyed adolescents aged 12–18 about their experience of child sexual abuse using the ICAST-CH instrument, where sexual abuse was defined as experiencing any of the following events: someone talked to you in a sexual way; showed you pornography; looked at your private parts or made you look at theirs; touched your private parts or made you touch theirs; made a sex video of you; forced sex behaviours. The mean age of respondents was 14.5 years. The study found 15% of all children reported past year prevalence of child sexual abuse, and 19.8% reported lifetime prevalence. Interestingly, males reported higher prevalence than females, reporting 17.4% in the past year compared with females 12.5%, and 21.8% in their lifetime compared with 17.7% of females. These trends were evident even for categories of more severe sexual abuse. For example, more males than females reported past year touching of private parts (7.7% compared to 2.1%), past year forced sex behaviours (1.6% compared to 0.6%), lifetime touching of private parts (10.7% compared to 4.4%) and lifetime forced sex behaviours (2.2% compared to 1.4%). Shedding further light on these experiences, the study found that apart from the sex video category, at least half the perpetrators were teenagers; as well, the overwhelming majority of offenders were either very well known to the child, or somewhat known. Taken together, these findings indicate a high level of offending by adolescent acquaintances.

South Korea In South Korea, a national study by Kim and Kim (2005) of 1672 adolescents found 3.7% reported experiencing incest, where this was narrowly defined to include only "at least one incident of unwanted sexual penetration of a bodily orifice by an older blood relative occurring either by threat or force."

Australasia

Australia In Australia, a nationwide study found that before age 16, 33.6% of women and 15.9% of men experienced non-penetrative CSA, and 12.2% of women and 4.1% of men experienced penetrative CSA (Dunne et al. 2003). Dunne et al. (2003) included a list of experiences within the definition used.[4] A meta-analysis by Moore et al. (2015) found prevalence in children aged under 16 of 14.1% for girls and 5.5% for boys. A study in the state of Victoria found 14.0% of girls and 4.6% of boys reported contact CSA (Moore et al. 2010). A study in the Australian Capital Territory found 2.0% of girls and 0.1% of boys reported contact CSA by a parent or caregiver (Rosenman and Rodgers 2006).

New Zealand In New Zealand, Fanslow et al. (2007) conducted a nationwide study of women aged 18–64. They found child sexual abuse was reported by 23.5% of women in urban areas and 28.2% in rural areas. Further, they found Maori women reported higher prevalence. One quarter reported that the abuse happened "a few times" and almost one quarter reported that the abuse happened "multiple times". The reported median age of onset was 9 years old, and the reported median age of the offender was 30 years old.

Recognition of Other Important Epidemiological Features of CSA

Gender In general, girls are at least twice as likely to be victimized. There is a clear gender-based vulnerability where girls. However, although girls are reported by most studies to be more frequently victimized than boys, in some nations the studies show that boys' experience of sexual abuse may be as high as or even higher than girls' experience. Moreover, in general, even when victimised to a lower extent than girls, most studies indicates boys' experience of CSA is substantial. It is also relevant that in some specific contexts, especially in some religious institutions, and even in some sporting organisations, boys may be more frequently victimized than girls (John Jay College of Criminal Justice 2004; Parent and Bannon 2012; Parkinson et al. 2010).

Age of Onset The age of onset has been found to be approximately 9–10 years for both girls and boys (Finkelhor et al. 1990; Fleming 1997; Goldman and Goldman 1988). Most CSA commences when the child is aged under 13. Finkelhor et al. (1990) found that 78% of women and 69% of men were aged 12 years or under at

[4] In paraphrased form, this included: Exposure of genitals to child; masturbation in front of child; tried to sexually arouse the child; touched or fondled the child's body including breasts or genitals; made the child touch their body in a sexual way; rubbed their genitals against their body in a sexual way; touched the child's genitals with their mouth; made the child touch the perpetrator's genitals with their mouth; attempted or actual intercourse; attempted or actual anal intercourse.

onset of abuse, and the median age of onset was 9.6 and 9.9 years respectively. Australian studies have found mean ages at first episode of 10.0 (Fleming 1997) and 10.8 (Dinwiddie et al. 2000). CSA may be more likely at particular ages in some cultures (Fry 2011; Haj-Yahia and Tamish 2001).

Relationship of the Person Inflicting the Abuse to the Child, and the Settings in Which Sexual Abuse Occurs While studies rarely pinpoint the identity of offenders and the precise settings within which CSA occurs, data indicates most CSA is inflicted by known family members, non-family members and adolescents, in private familial settings and general community settings (e.g., Finkelhor et al. 1990, 2014; Hussey et al. 2006; Smallbone and Wortley 2001).

Much child sexual abuse also occurs in religious, school and other institutional settings, as shown in countries including Australia, the USA, Ireland and Germany (Australian Government Royal Commission into Institutional Responses to Child Sexual Abuse 2017a, b; Boston Report 2003; Commission to Inquire into Child Abuse 2009; Rassenhofer et al. 2015). Accumulated data over extensive time periods have shown conservative estimates of the proportion of Catholic priests who have sexually abused children of 5% in the U.S.A (Terry et al. 2011) and 7% in Australia (Australian Government Royal Commission Into Institutional Responses to Child Sexual Abuse 2017b).

While comprehensive data is lacking, there is evidence that CSA is also common in other organizational settings where children and youth services are provided. These cover sports, recreational arts and cultural bodies. Approximately 9.6% of children have been found to experience sexual abuse in educational settings (Shakeshaft 2004), and other studies have also found frequent victimisation in schools (Young et al. 2009). Prevalence of 10.0% has been found in sporting contexts (Leahy et al. 2002), and an annual incidence of 9.5% has been found in juvenile detention settings (Beck et al. 2010).

Frequency of Offending A significant proportion of perpetrators victimize multiple children (Smallbone and Wortley 2001). Often, children are abused multiple times over a substantial period of time (e.g., Easton et al. 2014; Fanslow et al. 2007), even when the perpetrator is a parent or caregiver (Hussey et al. 2006). In institutional settings, children can be especially vulnerable to repeated, continuous abuse by authority figures who exert significant and sometimes total power over the child. This can occur in religious settings contexts where the child's vulnerability is magnified by deep spiritual beliefs, commitment and fear. It can also occur in competitive sporting settings where the child's athletic prospects are highly dependent upon the favour of adult authority figures.

Factors Influencing Offending Multiple factors at individual, institutional and societal levels influence the perpetration, concealment and continuance of child sexual abuse. At the individual level, while more research has investigated adult offenders, it has been found that those who inflict child sexual abuse have poorly developed socio-emotional skills, attitudinal and cognitive distortions (Seto et al.

2015; Whitaker et al. 2008), and possess similar attributes to sex offenders against adult women,(Whitaker et al. 2008), namely a sense of sexual entitlement, empathy deficits, a construction of masculinity emphasizing sexual performance and dominance, and a history of childhood victimisation (Abbey et al. 2006; Jewkes et al. 2013).[5] Amongst adolescent offenders, the meta-analysis by Seto and Lalumiere (2010) of 59 studies comparing male adolescent sex offenders with male adolescent non-sex offenders broadly found that the evidence provides support for the influence of a sexual abuse history, exposure to sexual violence, other abuse or neglect, social isolation, early exposure to sex or pornography, atypical sexual interests, anxiety, and low self-esteem. Based on effect size, the largest differences were produced by atypical sexual interests, followed by sexual abuse history, criminal history, antisocial associations, and substance abuse.[6]

At the institutional level, such as in schools and religious institutions, child sexual abuse is more likely to occur, be covered up, and continue, in settings characterised by a rigid power hierarchy, a culture of silence protecting the institution's reputation, and a lack of protective regulatory mechanisms including robust organisational policy, codes of conduct, incident reporting processes, and staff education (Mathews 2017; Smith and Freyd 2013; Wurtele 2012). At the societal level, child sexual abuse is enabled when children's rights are not recognised, laws and policies do not prohibit sexual offending, social norms against sexual violence are weak, gender inequality is pervasive, constructions of masculinity emphasise aggression and sexual dominance (Jewkes et al. 2015), there is ignorance about sex and sexual violence, and society's leaders lack the will to act.

Theories of Offending Various theories have been posited as explaining child sexual abuse, with the most widely accepted of these being generally accepted as being broadly congruent with the factors found to be associated with child sexual abuse. Three of the most significant are briefly mentioned here. On Finkelhor's model (1984) four preconditions are required for child sexual abuse to occur, with

---

[5] There may be differences between intrafamilial and extrafamilial offenders: see for example the meta-analysis by Seto et al. (2015), which found that intrafamilial offenders were significantly lower on variables reflecting antisocial tendencies (e.g., criminal history, juvenile delinquency, impulsivity, substance use, and psychopathy) and atypical sexual interests (e.g., pedophilia, other paraphilias, and excessive sexual preoccupation). Intrafamilial offenders also scored lower on offense-supportive attitudes and beliefs, emotional congruence with children, and interpersonal deficits, and did not differ from extrafamilial offenders on most indicators of psychopathology. However, intrafamilial offenders were more likely to have experienced sexual abuse, family abuse or neglect, and poor parent-child attachments. See further: Seto (2008). Pedophilia and sexual offending against children: Theory, assessment, and intervention. Washington, DC: American Psychological Association.

[6] The evidence did not support explanations for adolescent sexual offending focusing on general antisocial tendencies (since adolescent sex offenders had much less extensive criminal histories, fewer antisocial peers, and fewer substance use problems compared with non-sex offenders). Nor did it provide support for the influence of attitudes and beliefs about women or sexual offending, family communication problems, poor parent-child attachment, exposure to nonsexual violence, social incompetence, conventional sexual experience, and low intelligence.

each occurring in a temporal sequence. First, the offender had to be motivated to sexually abuse a child (this required the male finding a child sexually arousing – arousal; and finding that sex with a child met an emotional need – emotional congruence; and being unable to have their sexual needs met in other appropriate ways – blockage). Second, the offender had to overcome any internal inhibitions to offending, which could occur through various means such as rationalising socially entrenched patriarchal attitudes, through individual factors such as impulse disorder or severe stress, or through behavioural factors such as the influence of alcohol. Third, the offender had to overcome any external inhibitors to offending (e.g., exploiting lack of parental supervision, familial social isolation, or unusual sleeping conditions). Fourth, the offender had to overcome a child's resistance to the abuse, which could be done by force, or by more subtle means such as grooming, desensitizing a child to sex, or establishing emotional dependence.

In 2002, Tony Ward and Richard Siegert presented the Pathways Model (Ward and Siegert 2002; Ward 2003; Ward and Beech 2006) as a psychological theory positing that a number of pathways facilitate the infliction of child sexual abuse. As summarised by Ward and Beech (2006, p. 60):

> the Pathways Model suggests that the clinical phenomena evident among child molesters are generated by four distinct and interacting psychological mechanisms: intimacy and social skill deficits; distorted sexual scripts; emotional dysregulation; and cognitive distortions. Each mechanism depicts a specific offense pathway with different psychological and behavioral profiles, and separate etiologies and underlying deficits. The number and type of etiologies will vary depending on a pathway's particular developmental trajectory.

On this model, all these mechanisms interact to cause sexual offending. The source for a pathway is a group of clinical problems in the individual's psychology, namely:

- difficulties in identifying and controlling emotional states;
- social isolation, loneliness and dissatisfaction;
- offence-supportive cognitions (e.g., a belief that children are not harmed by abuse)[7]; and
- deviant sexual fantasies.

Ward has since presented an integrated theory of sexual offending which seeks to move beyond isolation of the surface-level factors influencing behaviour, to articulate underlying causal mechanisms of offending (Ward and Beech 2006). These underlying causes include biological, ecological and neuropsychological factors that continuously interconnect. Factors in brain development (e.g., persistently high levels of sex hormones), neuropsychological functioning (e.g., defects in the individual's motivational/emotional system) and the ecological environment (e.g., living or working in settings of higher access to children, and where children are at higher risk or greater vulnerability). These interact with and produce clinical symptomatology via four clusters of problems or symptoms typically found among adults who sexually abuse children: emotional regulation problems; cognitive distortions;

[7] For further analysis of cognitive distortions, see Burn and Brown (2006), and Ward et al. (1997).

social difficulties; and deviant sexual arousal. The authors go on to argue that "genes, social learning, and neuropsychological systems interact to generate the clinical problems evident in offenders, i.e., deviant arousal, offense related thoughts and fantasies, negative/positive emotional states, and social difficulties. These state factors … lead to sexually abusive actions." (2006, p. 50).

The Social-Ecological Model These theories are generally consistent with a social-ecological model which posits that factors in multiple interconnected dimensions of social life influence individual attitudes and behaviour (Quadara et al., 2015). At the individual level, factors in the person's own history influence the likelihood of an individual either becoming or not becoming a victim or perpetrator of sexual abuse. These factors include, for example, alcohol and substance abuse, attitudes and beliefs that support sexual interaction with children, impulsive and other antisocial tendencies, hostility towards women, and a childhood history of sexual abuse or other family violence. At the interpersonal relationship level, factors affect risk as a product of relationships with peers, intimate partners and family members, who can reinforce positive or negative attitudes that in turn influence the individual's experiences and behaviour. At the community level, factors in the community environment influence risk and protective factors through shaping an individual's experiences in key social institutions such as schools. At the societal level, broad social structural factors also influence attitudes and behaviours, including laws and policies connected with sexual behaviour, gender relations, and social norms.

Recognition of Sequelae

A vast body of research has demonstrated the substantial psychological, behavioural and physical harms in victims of CSA, and that these consequences occur in both the short-term, continue through adolescence, and endure through the lifespan (Chen et al. 2010; Dube et al. 2005; Gilbert et al. 2009; Paolucci et al. 2001; Putnam 2003; Spataro et al. 2004; Trickett et al. 2011). The consequences to health, behaviour and functioning vary for each individual, and are moderated by a range of factors. There is evidence that child sexual abuse of longer duration and severity, and abuse by a family member or similarly trusted authority figure, are more likely to have significant consequences (Chen et al. 2010; Edwards et al. 2012; Trickett et al. 2011). When abuse occurs within institutional settings, effects are often exacerbated by the institution's failure to prevent the abuse or to respond appropriately after its occurrence (Goldsmith et al. 2014; Smith and Freyd 2013, 2014).

Children of both genders experience similar adverse physical and mental health sequelae of CSA (Maikovich-Fong and Jaffee 2010; Paolucci et al. 2001; Rhodes et al. 2011). Typical sequelae include post-traumatic stress disorder (Boney-McCoy and Finkelhor 1995; Dubner and Motta 1999; Trickett et al. 2011; Trowell et al. 1999), depression and low self-esteem (Spataro et al. 2004), often continuing through adulthood (Chen et al. 2010; Cutajar et al. 2010a; Spataro et al. 2004). Also common are dissociative disorders, involving a radical involuntary cognitive disconnection with the events as a way of coping with the extreme trauma (van der Kolk 2014). These kinds of response demonstrate the intense fear and utter terror produced in these instances.

Consequential effects on behaviour and social functioning are substantial: coping mechanisms include alcohol abuse and the use of illicit drugs (Simpson and Miller 2002). Some effects are particularly acute at certain life stages. Adolescents are susceptible to suicidal ideation and behaviour (Cutajar et al. 2010b; Wozencraft et al. 1991), alcohol abuse, substance abuse and running away from home (Dube et al. 2006; Simpson and Miller 2002). In contrast to children of much earlier ages, adolescents are more likely to have a fuller understanding of what has been done to them, and to experience more comprehensive injury to the psyche. All these effects also have a major adverse impact on intellectual, academic and personal achievement (Daignaut and Hebert 2009; Perez and Widom 1994), flowing through into adult economic wellbeing (Currie and Widom 2010). In addition, child sexual abuse can have intergenerational effects (Trickett et al. 2011). The costs to society are immense, including the economic burden (Fang et al. 2012, 2015; Letourneau et al. 2018).

Post-traumatic Stress Disorder Is Particularly Significant One of the most significant psychological injuries is post-traumatic stress disorder (PTSD), which is a common consequence of child sexual abuse, especially when the abuse is in the more severe range. A large body of literature has examined the presence of PTSD after child sexual abuse, establishing its commonality and manifestations (Boney-McCoy and Finkelhor 1995; Deblinger et al. 1989; Dubner and Motta 1999; Lindberg and Distad 1985; McLeer et al. 1988, 1992, 1994, 1998; Trowell et al. 1999; Wolfe et al. 1994). Post-traumatic stress disorder is a trauma-related disorder recognized in the *Diagnostic and Statistical Manual of Mental Disorders V* (American Psychiatric Association 2013). It is highly significant that the latest iteration of the DSM acknowledges that sexual violation (including sexual abuse) is a specific phenomenon that commonly causes PTSD. Post-traumatic stress disorder is particularly relevant to many legal, policy and practical issues related to identification and response to child sexual abuse. This disorder is a trauma- or stress-related disorder, triggered by exposure to actual or threatened death, serious injury or sexual violation. It causes clinically significant distress or impairment in the person's social interactions, working capacity, and related areas of functioning in life that last for at least 1 month and can continue for years. Broadly, there are four types of symptoms: first, re-experiencing/intrusive memories (spontaneous memories, flashbacks); second, avoidance; third, negative cognitions and mood (distorted sense of self; self-blame); and fourth, arousal (sleep disturbance, hypervigilance, reckless/self-destructive behaviour). Of these, the avoidance symptom is particularly significant. A person with PTSD persistently avoids trauma-related stimuli, and has numbed general responsiveness, as shown by factors including: avoiding thoughts, feelings or conversations concerned with the event; avoiding activities, people or places that recall the event; and an inability to remember an important feature of the event. This condition therefore *inherently compromises* a person's capacity to disclose the abuse, discuss it, revisit the events, and do other things related to the events.

Recognition of Non-disclosure, Delayed Disclosure, and Veracity of Disclosure

One of the most significant features of this context is that child sexual abuse is a hidden phenomenon that is often not disclosed by the child for many years and even decades after the events. Child sexual abuse occurs in private, unwitnessed by others, and frequently does not leave clearly noticeable signs of its occurrence so that it is difficult for others to detect. Most significantly, there are a range of factors which naturally inhibit the child from being able to tell anyone about the abuse. This tendency towards nondisclosure and continued silence often lasts for years, frequently endures for decades, and in a significant proportion of cases the silence continues through the survivor's entire life. The reasons for the silence surrounding child sexual abuse is critical to understand for any proper consideration of appropriate responses by social systems. Such an understanding can overcome inappropriate disbelief of those who disclose some time after the events, and can nullify inappropriate expectations that a child should tell someone about the experience immediately or very soon after the events. This understanding is also necessary so that one can appreciate why a child may not disclose even in cases where abuse continues over weeks, months or years. A scientifically based understanding of the temporal and contextual features of disclosure is also necessary to inform the development of appropriate responses by health, clinical and legal systems.

Secrecy and Nondisclosure by Individual and Institutional Offenders Child sexual abuse occurs in private, clandestine situations. This means that only the child and the offender are aware of what has happened. The acts constitute criminal offences as well as fundamental transgressions of social norms, and the welfare of the child is not considered meaningful by those who inflict the abuse, and by others who may have enabled or assisted the abuse, or concealed it. Those who inflict abuse will tend to prefer their own interests in ensuring it remains concealed. Institutions have additional motivations for concealing offending that occurs within their settings, due to the damage to their public image, reputation, and potential legal liability and financial cost. As a result, wrongdoers rarely disclose their own conduct to social agencies such as law enforcement or health institutions. In the USA, for example, data shows that only 0.1% of substantiated cases are identified by perpetrator disclosure (U.S. Department of Health and Human Services 2009).

The Fact of Non-disclosure and Delayed Disclosure by the Child Child sexual abuse is inherently difficult to disclose because it involves acts of profound violation of not only a person's body, but their privacy, sexuality, emotions and psyche. It involves a multiform abuse of power in which the adult or more powerful person exploits their superiority in a number of dimensions: physical, sexual, cognitive, emotional, social and economic. Transgressions of a person's sexual integrity are particularly invasive, because sexuality is such an integral part of one's self. Individual research studies and systematic reviews have found that nondisclosure and delayed disclosure is typical (Alaggia et al. 2017; Easton 2013; Jonzon and

Lindblad 2004; Kogan 2004; McElvaney 2013; Paine and Hansen 2002; Smith et al. 2000; Ungar et al. 2009). Findings from these studies demonstrate the length of time it can take many survivors to be able to disclose their experience to anyone, and it should further be noted that most disclosures are to trusted individuals rather than social agencies:

- Smith et al. (2000): in a study of 288 women who were raped as a child, 28% of study respondents had never disclosed before participating in the study and 58% took between 1 year and 5 years to disclose.
- Jonzon and Lindblad (2004): in a study of 122 Swedish women who were sexually abused as a child, with an average duration of 7 years, and all of whom had in fact disclosed, 68% of study respondents had not disclosed until adulthood.
- Easton (2013): in a study of 487 men whose mean age of onset of child sexual abuse was 10.3 years, on average, it took participants 21 years to tell someone, and the mean age at the time of first telling was 32.
- The Australian Government Royal Commission into Institutional Responses to Child Sexual Abuse (2014, p. 6) found it took an average of 22 years for those who disclosed institutional CSA to be able to do so.
- In their review of studies, London et al. (2007) found that 60–70% of adult survivors of child sexual abuse said they did not disclose their abuse during childhood.

Multiple Factors Influence Non-disclosure Research studies, systematic reviews and conceptual analyses have found that there are multiple factors increasing the likelihood of nondisclosure, and delayed disclosure (Alaggia et al. 2017; Collin-Vézina et al. 2015; Lemaigre et al. 2017). The child may be preverbal or very young, and may not recognise or understand the nature of the acts. Slightly older children may be deceived into thinking the acts are normal. More generally, the child who understands that what is being done to them is wrong will be overwhelmed by feelings of shame, guilt, self-blame and embarrassment, and may internalize responsibility (Berliner and Conte 1990). Non-disclosure is more likely where the offender is known to the child, and especially if they are a known and trusted authority figure (Kogan 2004). This is all the more powerful where the authority figure has the ability to determine the child's future, as in the situation of elite schooling or competitive sports; here the child may be completely dependent on the abuser for ongoing support and patronage. Abusive situations involving societal authority figures such as police also exhibit the highest levels of deterrence of disclosure.

Another major factor influencing nondisclosure is the presence of threats, and fear of reprisals against the child, another child, or the child's family (Palmer et al. 1999), and sometimes even fear of punishment of the offender (Mian et al. 1986). Perpetrators clothed with religious authority have an additional insidious source of power affecting nondisclosure (Parkinson et al. 2010). This spiritual abuse can be exceptionally powerful and itself can take many forms. The child may be convinced they will go to hell or suffer eternal damnation if they disclose the abuse. The child may know that if she or he discloses to their devout parent, the parent would not believe them, would shun the child, would themselves be psychologically annihilated, or that the disclosure would catalyse a disintegration of the family.

Especially in more severe cases, the child may adopt extreme coping mechanisms such as dissociation (Herman 1997), and may experience severe psychological injuries including post-traumatic stress disorder, anxiety, and depression; these conditions also inherently compromise the ability to disclose. Post-traumatic stress disorder is especially likely to compromise capacity to disclose, since its core symptoms prevent the individual from being able to discuss and revisit the events.

Boys and Non-disclosure Boys are known to be unlikely to disclose child sexual abuse for the same reasons as girls, including fear, embarrassment, and guilt (Fontes and Plummer 2010; Ullman and Filipas 2005). However, factors specific to males mean boys may be even less likely to disclose than girls, both proximate to the events and in later self-report studies (Ullman and Filipas 2005). Male self-disclosure is inhibited by feelings of extreme anger, shame, withdrawal, and suppression, often accompanied by later drug use (Dhaliwal et al. 1996; Romano and De Luca 2001; Spataro et al. 2001), and fear of being perceived as a potential perpetrator (Fontes and Plummer 2010). In particular, the power and durability of gender norms and social stereotypes of masculinity prevent men sharing their experiences, even with those closest to them. Admitting victimisation undermines images of masculine strength, heightening shame at inability to prevent the abuse. Revealing abuse by a male can cause fear of being perceived as homosexual, and revealing abuse by a female subverts an idealised construction of masculine power, which is elevated by any sexual interaction with females (Alaggia 2005, 2010; Dorahy and Clearwater 2012; Easton 2013, 2014; Fontes and Plummer 2010; Gagnier and Collin-Vézina 2016; Holmes and Slap 1998; O'Leary and Barber 2008; Romano and De Luca 2001). Victimisation in religious and institutional contexts by perpetrators possessing additional power further inhibits males' disclosure (Parkinson et al. 2010). Disclosures by boys may be less likely to be believed or taken seriously, partly because the sexual abuse of boys has historically received less scientific attention and social awareness than the abuse of girls (Dhaliwal et al. 1996; Holmes and Slap 1998; Violato and Genuis 1993). Relative to girls, the sexual abuse of boys is less well detected and reported, and receives less serious responses (Holmes and Slap 1998; Peake 1989; Spataro et al. 2001). Amongst the general community, awareness of boys and their experience of sexual abuse is likely lower even than for girls.

Cultural Factors Inhibiting Disclosure Disclosure is further inhibited by cultural, religious, familial and institutional forces, and by societal taboos around sex and stigma attaching to victims (Collin-Vézina et al. 2015; Feiring et al. 2009; Fontes and Plummer 2010). Non-disclosure is magnified in cultures where the existence and severity of CSA is silenced or minimized. There are powerful cultural reasons which can deter disclosure by children and their parents, and potentially also by professionals who encounter cases. Fontes and Plummer (2010) synthesised literature on a range of cultural norms and values that subvert disclosure:

- Shame (central in many cultures, influenced also by religion, and often accompanied by other illicit activity such as drinking alcohol);

- Taboos/modesty (non-exhaustive examples provided included these values in Arab cultures, Spanish cultures, and India);
- Sexual scripts (different sex roles ascribed to males and females often reinforce the ideas of boys or men not being to blame for offending; of girls being to blame for such offending; and of boys not being able to be victimized);
- Virginity (in many cultures, a girl losing her virginity before marriage – even through abuse – is not only shameful, but destroys her family's honour and her own marriageability);
- Women's status (includes ideas that boys are not to be blamed for their actions whereas girls are required to bear whatever acts they experience);
- Honour, respect and patriarchy (non-exhaustive examples provided included these values in South Asian and East Asian communities, especially filial piety which can excuse father-child incest and disclosure of other abuse where the father forbids it).

Other studies powerfully show the overwhelming force of cultural factors in suppressing disclosure. In Palestine, Shalhoub-Kevorkian (1999) interviewed 19 assorted professionals. The study's overall purpose was to elicit information about reasons leading to girls' disclosure of child sexual abuse, the social reaction to disclosure, and personal and social outcomes. It was found that the main reasons motivating disclosure were to terminate pregnancy, respond to loss of virginity, and gain expert advice about whether virginity had been lost (the concern being breaking of the hymen). Shalhoub-Kevorkian (1999) engaged in a detailed discussion of social and cultural factors which in the context of Palestinian society are exceptionally powerful deterrents to disclosure by the child, parents and other social agents. These deterrents include death (honour killing), being forced to marry one's rapist, banishment, home imprisonment, or institutionalisation in orphanages or centers for broken families. The research acknowledges the exceptionally powerful concepts of family honour and family shame in this society, with revelation of abusive sexual acts perpetrated against a girl being perceived as devastating and even terminal to a family's honour and its individuals' reputations.

Abu-Baker (2013) reported findings from a study of Arab-Palestinian families who were already receiving clinical therapy after having disclosed child sexual abuse. The study explored parental reactions to four categories of perpetrator of child sexual abuse of their child: incest; member of extended family; known non-kin; stranger. While different strategies were adopted, all tended to involve reliance on family and community networks rather than agents not social control. These families were generally found to condemn the sexually abusive behaviour, and to be committed to a solution which promoted the best interest of the entire family unit. The study also found that initial parental reactions to the child sexual abuse differed; if the family was functional (defined as one which knows how to balance the needs of the victim's mental health with the needs of the family and its relationship with the community) then the reaction was likely to help the victim recover and to help the family cope with the crisis. However, if the family was dysfunctional (described as positioning the child's needs as secondary to those of the family and its relation to the community, lack tools to cope with the abuse, and minimize the suffering caused to the child, and blaming the child) then the reaction was likely to cause secondary trauma and long-term problems. Again, concepts of family honour and family shame are exceptionally powerful.

Systematic Reviews and Conceptual Analyses Collin-Vézina et al. (2015) conceptualised the barriers to disclosure using a tripartite ecological model comprising factors related to the individual, to others, and to the social world. A single factor can silence the child, and multiple factors can amplify the power of this silencing effect. This tripartite model comprises:

- first, barriers from within (those related to the individual, e.g. self-protection; internalizing blame; lack of cognitive development and skills enabling disclosure);
- second, barriers in relation to others (relational power dynamics; fear of consequences; silence induced by threats; feared impact of disclosure on others); and
- third, barriers in relation to the social world (societal and cultural forces including the taboo of sexuality, stigma attaching to victims due to social ignorance, and general lack of cultural consciousness).

Similarly, Alaggia et al. (2017) reviewed and analysed 33 studies published since the year 2000. They found five major themes (2017, p. 17–21):

- Disclosure is not a single clear event, but is often an ongoing iterative and interactive process.
- Current conceptual models of disclosure of child sexual abuse are premised on a social–ecological, person-in-environment perspective, to understand the complex interplay of individual, familial, contextual, and cultural factors involved in disclosure.
- Age and gender are strong predictors for delaying or withholding disclosure with trends showing fewer disclosures by younger children and boys (in addition, abuse within families and family-like relationships also further inhibit disclosure).
- the body of evidence lacks a cohesive life-course perspective, limiting understandings of disclosure trends at different stages of life.
- there is more information about barriers to disclosure than facilitators of disclosure; and shame, self-blame and fear are uniformly shown to be deterrents to disclosure.

Research studies and systematic reviews have found that there are factors increasing the likelihood of disclosure, and of prompt disclosure (Alaggia et al. 2017; Collin-Vézina et al. 2015; Lemaigre et al. 2017). These factors include the child being older; the offender being a stranger; and the availability of a trusted confidante (Collin-Vézina et al. 2015).

Recognition of Gravity of Child Sexual Abuse in International Policy and Social Norms

Several major international policy bodies and instruments recognise the seriousness of CSA, and promote a variety of measures to respond to it. These measures recognise that acts of child sexual abuse simultaneously constitute:

- criminal acts, which can be prosecuted by the state
- civilly actionable acts, which can be the subject of lawsuits by the individual, against both individual and organisational wrongdoers
- a matter of child protection law and family law, in cases concerning CSA by parents, caregivers, siblings or other family members, and sometimes in cases of failure by parents to protect the child from other CSA
- a public health concern.

Legislatures in countries all around the globe have made acts of CSA criminal offences (World Health Organization 2018). More broadly, international and national communities have acknowledged the urgent need for governments and policymakers to do more to prevent, identify and respond appropriately to child sexual abuse. The United Nations' (2015) Sustainable Development Goals has set an agenda for global human development efforts from 2015 to 2030 (United Nations General Assembly 2015).[8] Significantly, these Goals have added two new targets acknowledging child abuse as a fundamental obstacle to health, demanding concerted action. Target 16.2 aims to end abuse and exploitation of children, and Target 5.2 aims to eliminate all forms of violence against women and girls, including sexual exploitation. Governments are required to report on progress against these targets.

The United Nations Convention on the Rights of the Child (UNCRC) contains several articles relevant to the context of child sexual abuse. Article 19 requires nations to take all appropriate legislative, administrative, social and educational measures to protect children from sexual abuse while in the care of parents and caregivers, and article 34 requires measures to be taken to protect the child from sexual exploitation in all circumstances. The most relevant articles from the UNCRC are detailed below:

Article 3(1): In all actions concerning children, including by public or private social welfare institutions and administrative authorities, the best interests of the child shall be a primary consideration

Article 3(2): States Parties shall take all appropriate legislative and administrative measures to ensure the child such protection and care as is necessary for his or her well-being, taking into account the rights and duties of his or her parents

Article 12: States Parties shall assure to the child who is capable of forming his or her own views the right to express those views freely in all matters affecting the child, the view of the child being given due weight in accordance with the age and maturity of the child

[8] United Nations General Assembly. (2015) Transforming Our World: The 2030 Agenda for Sustainable Development. United Nations General Assembly; Seventieth Session. September 18, 2015; New York, NY. https://sustainabledevelopment.un.org/post2015/transformingourworld.

Article 19(1): States Parties shall take all appropriate measures to protect the child from all forms of violence, injury or abuse, including sexual abuse, while in the care of parent(s), legal guardian(s) or any other person who has the care of the child.

Article 19(2): Such protective measures should include effective procedures for the establishment of social programmes to provide necessary support for the child and for those who have the care of the child, as well as for other forms of prevention and for identification, reporting, referral, investigation, treatment and follow-up of instances of child maltreatment.

Article 24: States Parties recognize the right of the child to the enjoyment of the highest attainable standard of health and to facilities for the treatment of illness and rehabilitation of health.

Article 34: States Parties undertake to protect the child from all forms of sexual exploitation and sexual abuse. For these purposes, States Parties shall in particular take all appropriate national measures to prevent (a) the inducement or coercion of a child to engage in any unlawful sexual activity; (b) the exploitative use of children in prostitution or other unlawful sexual practices; (c) the exploitative use of children in pornographic performances and materials.

Article 39: States Parties shall take all appropriate measures to promote physical and psychological recovery and social reintegration of a child victim of any form of neglect, exploitation or abuse.

The **Committee on the Rights of the Child** has reinforced these Convention rights and has made declarations providing more substantive insights into the nature of the abstract rights. In 2011, in its General comment No. 13 on the right of the child to freedom from all forms of violence, the Committee elaborated on the meaning of "sexual abuse" for the purpose of interpreting and applying article 19 (the right to freedom from violence), stating (p. 10)[9]:

> Sexual abuse and exploitation includes:
>
> (a) The inducement or coercion of a child to engage in any unlawful or psychologically harmful sexual activity;
> (b) The use of children in commercial sexual exploitation; and
> (c) The use of children in audio or visual images of child sexual abuse;
> (d) Child prostitution, sexual slavery, sexual exploitation in travel and tourism, trafficking (within and between countries) and sale of children for sexual purposes and forced marriage. Many children experience sexual victimization which is not accompanied by physical force or restraint but which is nonetheless psychologically intrusive, exploitive and traumatic.
>
> Sexual abuse comprises any sexual activities imposed by an adult on a child, against which the child is entitled to protection by criminal law. Sexual activities are also considered as abuse when committed against a child by another child, if the child offender is significantly older than the child victim or uses power, threat or other means of pressure. Sexual activities between children are not considered as sexual abuse if the children are older than the age limit defined by the State party for consensual sexual activities.

The inclusion of forced marriage is a significant, and will be discussed in Chaps. 2 and 6, along with other complex categories.

[9] Committee on the Rights of the Child. General comment No. 13 (2011) on the right of the child to freedom from all forms of violence.

Recognition of a Spectrum of Cases Demanding Appropriately Differentiated Responses

Child sexual abuse in its various forms constitutes criminal offending and causes substantial injuries to victims who because of their individual qualities are extremely vulnerable. The hidden nature of child sexual abuse means the child is vulnerable to further abuse and harm. Because of the gravity of these events, the child's vulnerability, and the likelihood of nondisclosure by both perpetrator and child, there are major challenges for society in

- how to prevent child sexual abuse occurring in the first place;
- how to identify cases of child sexual abuse at an early stage so as to stop the abuse continuing;
- responding to the child including through rehabilitation, and support for the child's family; and
- responding to the offender.

Taken together, these challenges can be understood as those of prevention, identification and response. Multiple groups are faced with these challenges, including legislatures, law enforcement authorities, educational institutions, regulatory bodies, policy-makers in CYSOs, individual professionals and practitioners who work with children, and clinicians.

These challenges are all complex, and are further complicated because there are different manifestations of child sexual abuse. These may be envisaged as cases of various types and seriousness on a spectrum, depending on the characteristics of the offending, the characteristics of the offender, the characteristics of the victim, the setting in which abuse occurs, the nature of the harms done, the nature of the continuing risk, and the level of culpability for offending (blameworthiness).

- *Offending* ranges from a single more minor event involving, for example, exposure by a peer at school, to daily rape by a caregiver or abduction and systematic severe abuse by an organised criminal gang.
- *Offenders* may be other children; parents and caregivers; non-familial but known adults; clergy or other figures in church institutions; teachers; authority figures in other child and youth-serving organisations; members of organised crime groups.
- *Victims* range from neonates through to those who are nearly 18.
- *Settings* of offending include the home, the school, the premises of a CYSO, the offender's home, other premises controlled by the offender, organised prostitution premises, societies beyond the offender's jurisdiction of residence, and cyberspace.
- *Harms* to the child range from minimal or no actual harm, through to extremely severe physical injuries and life-threatening psychological injuries.
- *The continuing risk* to the child, and to other children, may range from zero to certainty; in addition, the current stage of offending will normally involve cases where the abuse has already occurred, but may also involve cases where the child is being groomed for abuse without abuse having yet occurred).

- *Culpability* for offending may vary from low (e.g., a first-time 12 year old offender with a troubled background committing a low level act of sexual abuse) to very high (e.g., systematic serious abuse by a group of powerful adult offenders in an institution whose leaders also conceal the offending).

While there may be baseline priorities common to cases across the spectrum, this spectrum of cases requires appropriately differentiated responses. Robust and justifiable legal and policy responses will need to adopt strategies that discriminate appropriately between different kinds of case. This applies to legal, regulatory and practical strategies adopted by the following social systems:

- Legal systems, in domains of civil law, criminal law, child protection law, and family law.
- Educational systems, especially school settings.
- Religious institutions, especially those who to have particularly high levels of offending.
- Other child and youth-serving organisations.
- Health systems.

Ethical Engagement

This book also proceeds on the basis that in a civilised society, individuals, institutions and broader governing social systems possess an ethical responsibility to prevent and respond appropriately to child sexual abuse. The central theoretical premise of the book is that fundamental ethical principles animate the obligations of the individual, the institution or other child and youth-serving organisation, and the state, to prevent, identify, and respond appropriately to child sexual abuse.

First and foremost, these ethical principles are centred around duties that are *other-directed*. The individual, the institution and the state owe duties to protect the rights and welfare of vulnerable children. In this sense, this ethical posture urges a deontological approach as the legitimate basis for action in this context: the substance of laws, policies, regulatory frameworks and actions should be made so as to be congruent with performing one's duties and protecting the rights of others. However, since any analysis and argument for reforms must appeal to pragmatic interests as well as to principles, it is also important to note that this ethical approach can be understood as promising self-oriented payoffs for each of these actors. This is because the adoption of this ethical posture can also be seen as promoting *self-directed* interests, both pragmatic and principled.

For the individual, these ethical duties may be conceived as promoting:

- *other-directed* ethical duties not to injure others through inflicting sexual abuse directly, to take steps to protect children when knowing of their abuse by others, and not to further enable and assist infliction by others of child sexual abuse by concealing it and protecting offenders; and

- *self-serving* interests in avoiding criminal and civil legal liability, avoiding reputational damage, maintaining a clear conscience, acting with temperance and self-control, securing dignity and integrity, behaving honourably, and the inherent self-serving good of virtue being its own reward.

For the institution, these ethical duties may be conceived as promoting:

- *other-directed* ethical duties to take appropriate preventative steps to protect the children in its care from experiencing sexual abuse, to take appropriate steps to identify cases at an early stage, to respond appropriately when becoming aware of sexual abuse occurring, to forbid the concealment of known or suspected sexual abuse; and
- *self-serving* interests in demonstrating to the public its commitment to protecting children, enhancing the institution's reputation and maintaining profitability by elevating its child-safe credentials, promoting the professionalisation of the workforce, creating an environment that will attract excellent staff and clientele, eliminating reputational damage and financial cost from avoidable scandals, avoiding criminal and civil legal liability, and the inherent self-serving good of virtue being its own reward).

For the state, these ethical duties may be conceived as promoting:

- *other-directed* ethical and political duties to take appropriate preventative steps to protect vulnerable children from experiencing sexual abuse, to take appropriate steps to identify cases at an early stage, to minimise injury when sexual abuse has occurred, and to otherwise respond appropriately when becoming aware of it; and
- *self-serving* interests in reducing the socio-economic cost of child sexual abuse, increasing the stock of human capital, avoiding criminal and civil legal liability, demonstrating to the public and the international community that it has discharged its duty and acted honourably, creating a legacy of social progress, and the inherent good of fulfilling the essential role of the state as protector of vulnerable citizens.

Ethical Duties Consistent with Bodies of Theory, the Capabilities Approach, and Human Dignity All these duties can be understood as consistent with bioethical principles of justice, beneficence (to do good), non-maleficence (not to do harm), and autonomy (self-rule) (Beauchamp and Childress 2013). They are congruent with principles of social justice and public health (Krieger 2005, 2011). They are also consistent with fundamental principles of liberal society and the responsibilities of the state and of the individual as properly understood, discussed further in Chap. 3.

In addition, they are also a manifestation of Nussbaum's Capabilities Approach, which is fundamentally concerned with requiring the state to secure, protect and foster certain capabilities in each individual citizen, as without a certain level of these capabilities, it is not possible for an individual to lead a life of sufficient equality, dignity, autonomy and freedom (Nussbaum 2011). In particular, Nussbaum is especially concerned to protect those in asymmetrical power relationships, and her further concern to afford *special priority* to children, because of their special vulnerability and dependence (Dixon and Nussbaum 2012). For Nussbaum, the truly liberal state should focus on supporting forms of capability that are most fertile, and on eliminating those forms of disadvantage that are most corrosive, especially in relations of significant power asymmetry involving particularly vulnerable individuals, including children. Here, the protection of the child from sexual abuse promotes multiple capabilities, going well beyond simple bodily inviolability, due to the frequent experience of substantial psychological injury and other sequelae affecting the individual's future capacity to flourish as a human being. Consideration of Nussbaum's approach within this context is novel, and will be discussed further in Chap. 3. It also affords a greater focus on the "non-physical" dimension of this context. While sexual abuse does have physical consequences, it is the psychological and emotional sequelae that are most damaging for mental health, behaviour and functioning, and further consequences on social participation and freedom that fundamentally compromise one's opportunity to have a decent and fulfilling life.

Finally, and importantly, as will be argued in Chap. 3, these principles are consistent with an approach based on the concept of human dignity as understood by the leading scholar Charles Foster (2014, 2015). On Foster's understanding of the concept, human dignity is concerned with the broad question of human thriving or flourishing. This concept provides additional insights beyond the more conventional application of ethical principles, and may be particularly helpful in analysing difficult normative questions, in challenging deeply embedded social practices that produce injustice, and in developing responses to new phenomena.

Regarding the individual, the institution and the state, these ethical responsibilities and an approach based on human capabilities and dignity may sometimes coincide with the nature of existing law, regulation and practice. However, the introduction to this book has shown the devastating continuance of CSA in diverse settings, and major problems in social and legal responses and institutional behaviour. Accordingly, it is clear that in many settings, these three categories of actors are not currently subject to sufficient legal, regulatory or policy measures.

In considering future reforms, the scientific evidence about the nature of CSA, together with ethical principles, Nussbaum's capabilities approach and Foster's concept of dignity, as applied to individuals, institutions and the state, should together inform the kinds of measures required to be adopted by legal and social systems to identify, prevent and respond to CSA. In sum, an understanding of the scientific context, allied with sound ethical principles and philosophical approaches, should inform the design of appropriate policies and laws, which in turn work to embed social norms. These structures and norms are directed towards protecting vulnerable children, and increasing human thriving through reducing suffering, and increasing respect, equality and dignity, and the opportunity for a decent life.

References

Abbey, A., Parkhill, M., BeShears, R., Clinton-Sherrod, A., & Zawacki, T. (2006). Cross-sectional predictors of sexual assault perpetration in a community sample of single African American and Caucasian men. *Aggressive Behavior, 32*, 54–67.

Abu-Baker, K. (2013). Arab parents' reactions to child sexual abuse: A review of clinical records. *Journal of Child Sexual Abuse, 22*, 52–71.

Adichie, C. N. (2014). *We should all be feminists*. New York: Random House.

Adichie, C. N. (2017). *Dear Ijeawele, or a feminist manifesto in fifteen suggestions*. London: 4th Estate.

Ajduković, M., Susac, N., & Rajter, M. (2013). Gender and age differences in prevalence and incidence of child sexual abuse in Croatia. *Croatian Medical Journal, 54*, 469–479.

Alaggia, R. (2005). Disclosing the trauma of child sexual abuse: A gender analysis. *Journal of Loss and Trauma, 10*(5), 453–470.

Alaggia, R. (2010). An ecological analysis of child sexual abuse disclosure: Considerations for child and adolescent mental health. *Journal of the Canadian Academy of Child and Adolescent Psychiatry, 19*, 32–39.

Alaggia, R., Collin-Vézina, D., & Lateef, R. (2017). Facilitators and barriers to child sexual abuse (CSA) disclosures: A research update (2000-2016). *Trauma, Violence & Abuse, 21*, 1–26.

Al-Eissa, M. A., AlBuhairan, F. S., Qayad, M., Saleheen, H., Runyan, D., & Almuneef, M. (2015). Determining child maltreatment incidence in Saudi Arabia using the ICAST-CH: A pilot study. *Child Abuse and Neglect, 42*, 174–182.

Al-Fayez, G. A., Ohaeri, J. U., & Gado, O. M. (2012). Prevalence of physical, psychological, and sexual abuse among a nationwide sample of Arab high school students: Association with family characteristics, anxiety, depression, self-esteem, and quality of life. *Social Psychiatry and Psychiatric Epidemiology, 47*, 53–66.

Alphonso, C. (2017, December 14). Quebec becomes latest province to make sex education compulsory. *The Globe and Mail*.

American Psychiatric Association. (2013). *Diagnostic and statistical manual of mental disorders – Fifth edition (DSM-V)*. Arlington: American Psychiatric Association.

Australian Government Royal Commission Into Institutional Responses to Child Sexual Abuse. (2014). *Interim report*. Sydney: Commonwealth of Australia http://www.childabuseroyalcommission.gov.au/about-us/our-reports.

Australian Government Royal Commission Into Institutional Responses to Child Sexual Abuse. (2017a). *Analysis of claims of child sexual abuse made with respect to Catholic Church Institutions in Australia*. Sydney: Commonwealth of Australia http://www.childabuseroyalcommission.gov.au/policy-and-research/our-research/published-research.

Australian Government Royal Commission into Institutional Responses to Child Sexual Abuse. (2017b). *Final report*. Sydney: Commonwealth of Australia https://www.childabuseroyalcommission.gov.au/final-report.

Aziz, S. (2017, October 11). Indian court rules sex with minor wife is rape. *Al Jazeera*.

Baker, N. (2017, October 8). The child bride trade is booming in Myanmar as the gender gap bites in China. *ABC News*.

Barter, C., et al. (2018). *The safeguarding teenage intimate relationships (STIR) project*.

Barth, J., Bermetz, L., Heim, E., Trelle, S., & Tonia, T. (2013). The current prevalence of child sexual abuse worldwide: A systematic review and meta-analysis. *International Journal of Public Health, 58*, 469–483.

Beauchamp, T. L., & Childress, J. F. (2013). *Principles of biomedical ethics*. New York: Oxford University Press.

Beck, A. J., Harrison, P. M., & Guerino, P. (2010). *Sexual victimization in juvenile facilities reported by youth, 2008–09*. Bureau of Justice Statistics.

Berliner, L., & Conte, J. R. (1990). The process of victimization: The victims' perspective. *Child Abuse and Neglect, 14*, 29–40.

Berry, J., & Renner, G. (2004). *Vows of silence: The abuse of power in the Papacy of John Paul II*. New York: Free Press.

Bolen, R., & Scannapieco, M. (1999). Prevalence of child sexual abuse: A corrective meta-analysis. *Social Service Review, 73*, 281–313.

Boney-McCoy, S., & Finkelhor, D. (1995). Prior victimization: A risk factor for child sexual abuse and for PTSD-related symptomatology among sexually abused youth. *Child Abuse & Neglect, 19*, 1401–1421.

Boston Report. (2003). *The sexual abuse of children in the Roman Catholic Archdiocese of Boston – A report by the Attorney General*. Boston: Office of the Attorney-General, Commonwealth of Massachusetts.

Bunyan, N., & Weaver, M. (2015, March 13). Police apologise to Rochdale child sex abuse victims. *The Guardian*.

Burn, M., & Brown, S. (2006). A review of the cognitive distortions in child sex offenders: An examination of the motivations and mechanisms that underlie the justification for abuse. *Aggression and Violent Behavior, 11*, 225–236.

Cacciola, S., & Mather, V. L. N. (2018, January 24). Larry Nassar sentencing: I just signed your death warrant. *The New York Times*.

Chen, J. Q., Dunne, M. P., & Han, P. (2004). Child sexual abuse in China: A study of adolescents in four provinces. *Child Abuse and Neglect, 28*(11), 1171–1186.

Chen, L. P., Murad, M. H., Paras, M. L., Colbenson, K. M., Sattler, A. L., Goranson, E. N., Elamin, M. B., Seime, R. J., Shinozaki, G., Prokop, L. J., & Zirakzadeh, A. (2010). Sexual abuse and lifetime diagnosis of psychiatric disorders: Systematic review and meta-analysis. *Mayo Clinic Proceedings, 85*(7), 618–629.

Collin-Vézina, D., De La Sablonniere-Griffin, M., Palmer, A., & Milne, L. (2015). A preliminary mapping of individual, relational and social factors that impede disclosure of childhood sexual abuse. *Child Abuse and Neglect, 43*, 123–134.

Commission to Inquire into Child Abuse. (2009). *Final report*. Dublin: Government Publications Retrieved from: http://www.childabusecommission.ie/rpt/.

Committee on the Rights of the Child. (2011) General comment no. 13 on the right of the child to freedom from all forms of violence. Child Abuse & Neglect, v35 n12: 967–969.

Currie, J., & Widom, C. (2010). Long-term consequences of child abuse and neglect on adult economic Well-being. *Child Maltreatment, 15*, 111–120.

Cutajar, M., Mullen, P., Ogloff, J., Thomas, S., Wells, D., & Spataro, J. (2010a). Psychopathology in a large cohort of sexually abused children followed up to43 years. *Child Abuse & Neglect, 34*, 813–822.

Cutajar, M., Mullen, P., Ogloff, J., Thomas, S., Wells, D., & Spataro, J. (2010b). Suicide and fatal drug overdose in child sexual abuse victims: A historical cohort study. *Medical Journal of Australia, 192*(4), 184–187.

Daignaut, I., & Hebert, M. (2009). Profiles of school adaptation: Social, behavioural and academic functioning in sexually abused girls. *Child Abuse & Neglect, 33*, 102–115.

Davey, M. (2018, March 8). Cardinal George Pell: Committal hearing begins into sexual offence charges. *The Guardian*.

Deblinger, E., et al. (1989). Post-traumatic stress in sexually abused, physically abused, and nonabused children. *Child Abuse and Neglect, 13*, 403–408.

Dhaliwal, G., Gauzas, L., Antonowicz, D., & Ross, R. (1996). Adult male survivors of childhood sexual abuse: Prevalence, sexual abuse characteristics, and long-term effects. *Clinical Psychology Review, 16*, 619–639.

Dinwiddie, S., Heath, A. C., Dunne, M. P., & Bucholz, K. K. (2000). Early sexual abuse and lifetime psychopathology: A co-twin-control study. *Psychological Medicine, 30*(1), 41–52.

Dixon, R., & Nussbaum, M. (2012). Children's rights and a capabilities approach: The question of special priority. *Cornell Law Review, 97*, 549–594.

Dodds, P. (2017, April 12). UN child sex ring left victims but no arrests. *AP News*.

Dorahy, M., & Clearwater, K. (2012). Shame and guilt in men exposed to childhood sexual abuse: A qualitative investigation. *Journal of Child Sexual Abuse, 21*(2), 155–175.

Dube, S., Anda, R., Whitfield, C., Brown, D., Felitti, V., Dong, M., & Giles, W. (2005). Long-term consequences of childhood sexual abuse by gender of victim. *American Journal of Preventive Medicine, 28*(5), 430–438.

Dube, S. R., Miller, J. W., Brown, D. W., Giles, W. H., Felitti, V. J., Dong, M., & Anda, R. F. (2006). Adverse childhood experiences and the association with ever using alcohol and initiating alcohol use during adolescence. *Journal of Adolescent Health, 38*(4), 444 e1-444.e10.

Dubner, A., & Motta, R. (1999). Sexually and physically abused foster care children and posttraumatic stress disorder. *Journal of Consulting and Clinical Psychology, 67*, 367–373.

Dunne, M., Purdie, D., Cook, M., Boyle, F., & Najman, J. (2003). Is child sexual abuse declining? Evidence from a population-based survey of men and women in Australia. *Child Abuse & Neglect, 27*, 141–152.

Easton, S. (2013). Disclosure of child sexual abuse among adult male survivors. *Clinical Social Work Journal, 41*(4), 344–355.

Easton, S. (2014). Masculine norms, disclosure, and childhood adversities predict long-term mental distress among men with histories of child sexual abuse. *Child Abuse & Neglect, 38*, 243–251.

Easton, S. D., Saltzman, L. Y., & Willis, D. G. (2014). Would you tell under circumstances like that? Barriers to disclosure of child sexual abuse for men. *Psychology of Men & Masculinity, 15*(4), 460–469.

Edwards, V., Freyd, J., Dube, S., Anda, R., & Felitti, V. (2012). Health outcomes by closeness of sexual abuse perpetrator: A test of betrayal trauma theory. *Journal of Aggression, Maltreatment & Trauma, 21*, 133–148.

Fanslow, J., Robinson, E., Crengle, S., & Perese, L. (2007). Prevalence of child sexual abuse reported by a cross-sectional sample of New Zealand women. *Child Abuse & Neglect, 31*(9), 935–945.

Fang, X., Brown, D., Florence, C., & Mercy, J. (2012). The economic burden of child maltreatment in the United States and implications for prevention. *Child Abuse & Neglect, 36*, 156–165.

Fang, X., Brown, D., Mercy, J., Dunne, M., Butchart, A., Corso, P., et al. (2015). The burden of child maltreatment in the East Asia and Pacific region. *Child Abuse & Neglect, 42*, 146–162.

Feiring, C., Simon, V. A., & Cleland, C. M. (2009). Childhood sexual abuse, stigmatization, internalizing symptoms, and the development of sexual difficulties and dating aggression. *Journal of Consulting and Clinical Psychology, 77*(1), 127–137.

Feng, J. Y., Chang, Y. T., Chang, H. Y., Fetzer, S., & Wang, J. D. (2015). Prevalence of different forms of child maltreatment among Taiwanese adolescents: A population- based study. *Child Abuse and Neglect, 42*, 10–19.

Finkelhor, D. (1984). *Child sexual abuse: New theory and research*. New York: The Free Press.

Finkelhor, D., Hotaling, G., Lewis, I., & Smith, C. (1990). Sexual abuse in a national survey of adult men and women: Prevalence, characteristics, and risk factors. *Child Abuse & Neglect, 14*, 19–28.

Finkelhor, D., Ormrod, R. K., Turner, H. A., & Hamby, S. L. (2005). The victimization of children and youth: A comprehensive, national survey. *Child Maltreatment, 10*, 5–25.

Finkelhor, D., Turner, H., Ormrod, R., & Hamby, S. L. (2009). Violence, abuse, and crime exposure in a national sample of children and youth. *Pediatrics, 124*, 1411–1423.

Finkelhor, D., Ji, K., Mikton, C., & Dunne, M. (2013). Explaining lower rates of sexual abuse in China. *Child Abuse & Neglect, 37*(10), 852–860.

Finkelhor, D., Turner, H., Shattuck, A., & Hamby, S. (2014). The lifetime prevalence of child sexual abuse and sexual assault assessed in late adolescence. *Journal of Adolescent Health, 55*, 329–333.

Finkelhor, D., Turner, H., Shattuck, A., & Hamby, S. (2015). Prevalence of childhood exposure to violence, crime, and abuse. *JAMA Pediatrics, 169*(8), 746–754.

Fleming, J. (1997). Prevalence of child sexual abuse in a community sample of Australian women. *Medical Journal of Australia, 166*, 65–68.

Fontes, L., & Plummer, C. (2010). Cultural issues in disclosures of child sexual abuse. *Journal of Child Sexual Abuse, 19*(5), 491–518.

Foster, C. (2014). Dignity and the ownership and use of body parts. *Cambridge Quarterly of Healthcare Ethics, 23*, 417–430.
Foster, C. (2015). Human dignity in bioethics and law. *Journal of Medical Ethics, 41*, 935.
Franklin, J., & Kirchgaessner, S. (2015, March 18). Pope's promise to tackle abuse tested by appointment of Chilean bishop. *The Guardian*.
Fry, E. (2011). *A systematic review of research on child maltreatment in the East Asia and Pacific Region*. United Nations Children's Fund.
Gagnier, C., & Collin-Vézina, D. (2016). The disclosure experiences of male child sexual abuse survivors. *Journal of Child Sexual Abuse, 25*, 221–241.
Gilbert, R., Widom, C., Browne, K., Fergusson, D., Webb, E., & Janson, S. (2009). Burden and consequences of child maltreatment in high-income countries. *Lancet, 373*(9657), 68–81.
Gilmore, J. (2017, September 6). How shocking sexism becomes normal in 'elite' environments. *The Age*.
Goldman, R., & Goldman, J. (1988). The prevalence and nature of child sexual abuse in Australia. *Australian Journal of Sex, Marriage & Family, 9*(2), 94–106.
Goldsmith, R., Martin, C., & Smith, C. (2014). Systemic trauma. *Journal of Trauma & Dissociation, 15*, 117–132.
Grierson, J. (2018, March 12). Up to 1,000 children may have been victims in worst UK abuse ring. *The Guardian*.
Haj-Yahia, M., & Tamish, S. (2001). The rates of child sexual abuse and its psychological consequences as revealed by a study among Palestinian university students. *Child Abuse and Neglect, 25*(10), 1303–1327.
Halliday, J. (2018, March 3). Crewe reject calls for inquiry into Barry Bennell sexual abuse. *The Guardian*.
Hancock, J. (2015, August 7). The capture of Shannon Grant McCoole: How police tracked his crimes from Denmark to Australia. *ABC News*.
Hébert, M., Tourigny, M., Cyr, M., McDuff, P., & Joly, J. (2009). Prevalence of childhood sexual abuse and timing of disclosure in a representative sample of adults from Quebec. *Canadian Journal of Psychiatry, 54*(9), 631–639.
Herman, J. (1997). *Trauma and recovery: The aftermath of violence, from domestic abuse to political terror*. New York: Basic Books.
Holmes, W., & Slap, G. (1998). Sexual abuse of boys: Definition, prevalence, correlates, sequelae, and management. *JAMA Pediatrics, 280*(21), 1855–1862.
Hussey, J., Chang, J., & Kotch, J. (2006). Child maltreatment in the United States: Prevalence, risk factors, and adolescent health consequences. *Pediatrics, 118*(3), 933–942.
James, C. (2017, June 1). I spent one night at St Paul's College. I didn't sleep because I was genuinely scared. *The Guardian*.
Jay, A. (2014). *Independent inquiry into child sexual exploitation in Rotherham (1997–2013)*.
Jewkes, R., Fulu, E., Roselli, T., & Garcia-Moreno, C. (2013). On behalf of the UN multi-country cross-sectional study on men and violence research team. Prevalence of and factors associated with non-partner rape perpetration: Findings from the UN multi-country cross-sectional study on men and violence in Asia and the Pacific. *The Lancet Global Health, 1*(18), 208–218.
Jewkes, R., Flood, M., & Lang, J. (2015). From work with men and boys to changes of social norms and reduction of inequities in gender relations: A conceptual shift in prevention of violence against women and girls. *Lancet, 385*, 1580–1589.
Ji, K., Finkelhor, D., & Dunne, M. P. (2013). Child sexual abuse in China: A meta-analysis of 26 studies. *Child Abuse & Neglect, 37*, 613–622.
John Jay College of Criminal Justice. (2004). *The nature and scope of sexual abuse of minors by Catholic priests and deacons in the United States, 1950–2002*. Washington, DC: United States Conference of Catholic Bishops www.jjay.cuny.edu/churchstudy/main.asp.
Jonzon, E., & Lindblad, F. (2004). Disclosure, reactions, and social support: Findings from a sample of adult victims of child sexual abuse. *Child Maltreatment, 9*, 190–200.
Kim, H., & Kim, H. (2005). Incestuous experience among Korean adolescents: Prevalence, family problems, perceived family dynamics, and psychological characteristics. *Public Health Nursing, 22*, 472–482.

Kirchgaessner, S. (2016, June 17). Catholic Church accused of using 'mafia-like' tactics to fight sex abuse bill. *The Guardian.*

Kloppen, K., Haugland, S., Svedin, C. G., Mæhle, M., & Breivik, K. (2016). Prevalence of child sexual abuse in the Nordic countries: A literature review. *Journal of Child Sexual Abuse, 25*(1), 37–55.

Kogan, S. (2004). Disclosing unwanted sexual experiences: Results from a national sample of adolescent women. *Child Abuse & Neglect, 28*, 147–165.

Koziol, M. (2018, March 23). Malcolm Turnbull blasts 'indifference and resistance' by churches in child sex abuse letter. *Sydney Morning Herald.*

Krieger, N. (2005). Researching critical questions on social justice and public health: An ecosocial perspective. In B. Levy & V. Sidel (Eds.), *Social injustice and public health* (pp. 460–479). New York: Oxford University Press.

Krieger, N. (2011). *Epidemiology and the people's health: Theory and context.* New York: Oxford University Press.

Laurie, V., & Taylor, P. (2018, June 8). Pilbara man jailed for filming sex with girls. *The Australian.*

Laville, S. (2015, March 2). Serious case review slams police failure in serial abuse of Oxford girls. *The Guardian.*

Leahy, T., Pretty, G., & Tenenbaum, G. (2002). Prevalence of sexual abuse in organised competitive sport in Australia. *Journal of Sexual Aggression, 8*(2), 16–36.

Lemaigre, C., Taylor, E. P., & Gittoes, C. (2017). Barriers and facilitators to disclosing sexual abuse in childhood and adolescence: A systematic review. *Child Abuse and Neglect, 70*, 39–52.

Letourneau, E., Brown, D., Fang, X., Hassan, A., & Mercy, J. (2018). The economic burden of child sexual abuse in the United States. *Child Abuse & Neglect, 79*, 413–422.

Lindberg, F., & Distad, L. (1985). Post-traumatic stress disorders in women who experienced childhood incest. *Child Abuse and Neglect, 9*, 329–334.

London, K., Bruck, M., Ceci, S., & Shuman, D. (2007). Disclosure of child sexual abuse: A review of the contemporary empirical literature. In M.-E. Pipe, M. Lamb, Y. Orbach, & A.-C. Cederborg (Eds.), *Child sexual abuse: Disclosure, delay, and denial* (pp. 11–39). New York: Routledge.

MacMillan, H. L., Fleming, J. E., Trocmé, N., Boyle, M. H., Wong, M., Racine, Y. A., Beardslee, W. R., & Offord, D. R. (1997). Prevalence of child physical and sexual abuse in the community. *Results from the Ontario Health Supplement, 278*(2), 131–135.

Maikovich-Fong, A., & Jaffee, R. (2010). Sex differences in childhood sexual abuse characteristics and victims' emotional and behavioural problems: Findings from a national sample of youth. *Child Abuse & Neglect, 34*, 429–437.

Marcus, C. (2017, January 28). Families SA got many warning signs on paedophile carer Shannon McCoole, SA royal commission told. *ABC News.*

Margetts, J. (2017, March 31). The line domestic violence campaign targets young attitudes towards relationships, sex. *ABC News.*

Marr, D. (2014). *The prince: Faith, abuse & George Pell.* Melbourne: Black, Inc.

Mathews, B. (2017). Optimising implementation of reforms to better prevent and respond to child sexual abuse in institutions: Insights from public health, regulatory theory, and Australia's Royal Commission. *Child Abuse and Neglect, 74*, 86–98.

Mathews, B., & Collin-Vézina, D. (2017). Child sexual abuse: Toward a conceptual model and definition. *Trauma, Violence, & Abuse, 21*, 1–18.

McCarthy, J. (2015, March 18). Archbishop Philip Wilson becomes world's most senior Catholic charged with concealing child abuse. *Sydney Morning Herald.*

McElvaney, R. (2013). Disclosure of child sexual abuse: Delays, non-disclosure and partial disclosure. *Child Abuse Review, 24*, 159–169.

McGee, H., Garavan, R., Byrne, J., O'Higgins, M., & Conroy, R. (2011). Secular trends in child and adult sexual violence – One decreasing and the other increasing: A population survey in Ireland. *European Journal of Public Health, 21*(1), 98–103.

McGeough, P. (2017, July 6). Sexual abuse and exploitation by peacekeepers: New UN plan met with scorn.

McGregor, K., & Lim, J. (2015, August 7). Families SA paedophile Shannon McCoole sentenced to 35 years in jail for horrific sexual abuse of children in care. *The Advertiser.*

McLeer, S., et al. (1988). Post-traumatic stress disorder in sexually abused children. *Journal of the American Academy of Child and Adolescent Psychiatry, 27*, 650–654.

McLeer, S., et al. (1992). Sexually abused children at high risk for post-traumatic stress disorder. *Journal of the American Academy of Child and Adolescent Psychiatry, 31*, 875–879.

McLeer, S., et al. (1994). Psychiatric disorders in sexually abused children. *Journal of the American Academy of Child and Adolescent Psychiatry, 33*, 313–319.

McLeer, S., et al. (1998). Psychopathology in non-clinically referred sexually abused children. *Journal of the American Academy of Child and Adolescent Psychiatry, 37*, 1326–1333.

McNally, L. (2015, May 29). Pornography, violence and sexual entitlement: An unspeakable truth. *ABC News*.

Mian, M., Wehrspann, W., Klajner-Diamond, H., et al. (1986). Review of 125 children 6 years of age and under who were sexually abused. *Child Abuse & Neglect, 10*, 223–229.

Millar, R., Schneiders, B., & Vedelago, C. (2018, February 12). Catholic Inc. What the Church is really worth. *The Age*.

Milligan, L. (2017). *Cardinal: The rise and fall of George Pell*. Melbourne: Melbourne University Press.

Moore, E., Romaniuk, H., Olsson, C., Jayasinghe, Y., Carlin, J., & Patton, G. (2010). The prevalence of childhood sexual abuse and adolescent unwanted sexual contact among boys and girls living in Victoria, Australia. *Child Abuse and Neglect, 34*, 379–385.

Moore, S., Scott, J., Ferrari, A., Mills, R., Dunne, M., Erskine, H., et al. (2015). Burden attributable to child maltreatment in Australia. *Child Abuse and Neglect, 48*, 208–220.

Murdoch, L. (2018, Feburary 21). Australian businessman sentenced in Philippines for child sex crimes. *Sydney Morning Herald*.

National Police Chiefs' Council. (2016). *Operation hydrant statistics: Breakdown of live investigations as at 1 July 2016*. http://www.npcc.police.uk/FreedomofInformation/OperationHydrant/Statistics.aspx.

Nikolaidos, G., Petroulaki, K., Zarokosta, F., et al. (2018). Lifetime and past-year prevalence of children's exposure to violence in 9 Balkan countries: The BECAN study. *Child Adolescent Psychiatry and Mental Health, 12*, 1.

Nussbaum, M. (2011). *Creating capabilities*. Cambridge, MA: Harvard University Press.

O'Leary, P., & Barber, J. (2008). Gender differences in silencing following childhood sexual abuse. *Journal of Child Sexual Abuse, 17*(2), 133–143.

Okolosie, L. (2016, April 20). Sexual violence at schools is endemic. The Government can't ignore it any longer. *The Guardian*.

Oxfordshire Safeguarding Children Board. (2015). *Serious case review into child sexual exploitation in Oxfordshire: From the experiences of children A, B, C, D, E, and F*. http://www.oscb.org.uk/case-reviews/.

Paine, M., & Hansen, D. (2002). Factors influencing children to self-disclose sexual abuse. *Clinical Psychology Review, 22*, 271–295.

Palmer, S. E., Brown, R. A., Rae-Grant, N. I., & Loughlin, M. J. (1999). Responding to children's disclosure of familial abuse: What survivors tell us. *Child Welfare, 78*, 259–282.

Paolucci, E., Genuis, M., & Violato, C. (2001). A meta-analysis of the published research on the effects of child sexual abuse. *The Journal of Psychology, 135*(1), 17–36.

Parent, S., & Bannon, J. (2012). Sexual abuse in sport: What about boys? *Children and Youth Services Review, 34*, 354–359.

Parkinson, P., Oates, K., & Jayakody, A. (2010). Breaking the long silence: Reports of child sexual abuse in the Anglican Church of Australia. *Ecclesiology, 6*, 183–200.

Peake, A. (1989). Issues of underreporting: The sexual abuse of boys. *Educational and Child Psychology, 6*, 42–50.

Pereda, N., Guilera, G., Forns, M., & Gomez-Benito, J. (2009). The international epidemiology of child sexual abuse: A continuation of Finkelhor (1994). *Child Abuse & Neglect, 33*(6), 331–342.

Perez, C., & Widom, C. (1994). Childhood victimization and long-term intellectual and academic outcomes. *Child Abuse & Neglect, 18*(8), 617–633.

Perpitch, N. (2017, August 30). The heart in the darkness. *ABC News*.
Perraudin, F. (2018, February 23). *Police appeared to punish victims of Newcastle grooming gangs, review finds*.
Podles, L. (2008). *Sacrilege: Sexual abuse in the Catholic Church*. Baltimore: Crossland Press.
Putnam, F. (2003). Ten-year research update review: Child sexual abuse. *Journal of the American Academy of Child & Adolescent Psychiatry, 42*, 269–278.
Quadara, A., Nagy, V., Higgins, D., & Siegel, N. (2015). *Conceptualising the prevention of child sexual abuse*. Melbourne: Australian Institute of Family Studies.
Rassenhofer, M., Zimmer, A., Sprober, N., & Fegert, J. (2015). Child sexual abuse in the Roman Catholic Church in Germany: Comparison of victim-impact data collected through church-sponsored and government-sponsored programs. *Child Abuse and Neglect, 40*, 60–67.
Rhodes, A. E., Boyle, M. H., Tonmyr, L., Wekerle, C., Goodman, D., Leslie, B., Mironova, P., Bethell, J., & Manion, I. (2011). Sex differences in childhood sexual abuse and suicide-related Behaviors. *Suicide and Life-threatening Behavior, 41*(3), 235–254.
Robertson, G. (2010). *The case of the pope: Vatican accountability for human rights abuse*. Camberwell: Penguin.
Romano, E., & De Luca, R. (2001). Male sexual abuse: A review of effects, abuse characteristics, and links with later psychological functioning. *Aggression and Violent Behaviour, 6*, 55–78.
Rosenman, S., & Rodgers, B. (2006). Childhood adversity and adult personality. *Australian and New Zealand Journal of Psychiatry Banner, 40*, 482–490.
Samuel, H. (2018, March 6). France to set age of consent at 15 after outrage over cases involving sex with 11-year-old girls. *The Telegraph*.
Schneiders, B., Millar, R., & Vedelago, C. (2018, March 10). Catholic Church fails to confront tragedy of 'epic proportions'. *The Age*.
Sengupta, S. (2017, July 22). One by one, marry-your-rapist laws are falling in the Middle East. *The New York Times*.
Seto, M. (2008). *Pedophilia and sexual offending against children: Theory, assessment, and intervention*. Washington, DC: American Psychological Association.
Seto, M., & Lalumiere, M. (2010). What is so special about male adolescent sexual offending? A review and test of explanations through meta-analysis. *Psychological Bulletin, 136*(4), 526–575.
Seto, M., Babchishin, K., Pullman, L., & McPhail, I. (2015). The puzzle of intrafamilial child sexual abuse: A meta-analysis comparing interfamilial and extrafamilial offenders with child victims. *Clinical Psychology Review, 39*, 42–57.
Shakeshaft, C. (2004). *Educator sexual misconduct: A synthesis of existing literature*. Washington, DC: U.S. Department of Education.
Shalhoub-Kevorkian, N. (1999). The politics of disclosing female sexual abuse: A case study of Palestinian society. *Child Abuse and Neglect, 23*(12), 1275–1293.
Sherwood, H. (2018a, March 24). Child abuse inquiry: 'Collusion and cover-up' rife among C of E clergy. *The Guardian*.
Sherwood, H. (2018b, March 23). C of E facing 3,300 sexual abuse claims, figures reveal. *The Guardian*.
Sieff, J. (2016, February 27). Members of a U.N. peacekeeping force in the Central African Republic allegedly turned to sexual predation, betraying their duty to protect. *Washington Post*.
Simpson, T., & Miller, R. (2002). Concomitance between childhood sexual and physical abuse and substance abuse problems: A review. *Clinical Psychological Review, 22*, 27–77.
Singhal, P. (2017, May 31). St Paul's has deep contempt for women: Sydney University's vice-head Michael Spence. *Sydney Morning Herald*.
Smallbone, S. W., & Wortley, R. K. (2001). Child sexual abuse: Offender characteristics and modus operandi. *Australian Institute of Criminology, 193*, 1–6.
Smith, C., & Freyd, J. (2013). Dangerous safe havens: Institutional betrayal exacerbates sexual trauma. *Journal of Traumatic Stress, 26*, 119–124.
Smith, C., & Freyd, J. (2014). Institutional betrayal. *American Psychologist, 69*, 575–587.
Smith, M., & Hartocollis, A. (2018, May 16). Michigan state's $500 million for Nassar victims Dwarfs other settlements. *New York Times*.

Smith, D., Letourneau, E., Saunders, B., Kilpatrick, D., Resnick, H., & Best, C. (2000). Delay in disclosure of childhood rape: Results from a national survey. *Child Abuse & Neglect, 24*(2), 273–287.

Solnit, R. (2017). *The mother of all questions: Further feminisms*. London: Granta.

Spataro, J., Moss, S., & Wells, D. (2001). Child sexual abuse: A reality for both sexes. *Australian Psychologist, 36*(3), 177–183.

Spataro, J., Mullen, P., Burgess, P., Wells, D., & Moss, S. (2004). Impact of child sexual abuse on mental health: Prospective study in males and females. *British Journal of Psychiatry, 184*, 416–421.

Spicer, D. (2018). *Joint serious case review concerning sexual exploitation of children and adults with needs for care and support in Newcastle upon Tyne*. www.newcastle.gov.uk.

Steinberg, J. (2018, March 29). FA sexual abuse inquiry head ready to investigate any clubs who fail to cooperate. *The Guardian*.

Stoltenborgh, M., Van Ijzendoorn, M., Euser, E., & Bakermans-Kranenburg, M. (2011). A global perspective on child sexual abuse: Meta-analysis of prevalence around the world. *Child Maltreatment, 16*(2), 79–101.

Sumner, S., Mercy, J., Saul, J., Motsa-Nzuza, N., Kwesigabo, G., Buluma, R., & Hillis, S. (2015). Prevalence of sexual violence against children and use of social services–seven countries, 2007-13. *Morbidity and Mortality Weekly Report, 64*, 565–569.

Taylor, D. (2018a, February 20). Barry Bennell branded 'sheer evil' as he is sentenced to 30 years. *The Guardian*.

Taylor, D. (2018b, February 15). Barry Bennell: The predatory Pied Piper who made stars and shattered lives. *The Guardian*.

Taylor, D. (2018c, February 16). 'There will be hundreds more,' says player Bennell abused on Maine Road pitch. *The Guardian*.

Taylor, D. (2018d, February 28). Crewe ignored police advice in late 1980s to 'move on' Barry Bennell. *The Guardian*.

Taylor, D. (2018e, February 16). Manchester City 'ignored warnings' and key Barry Bennell in youth set-up. *The Guardian*.

Terry, K., Smith, M., Schuth, K., Kelly, J., Vollman, B., & Massey, C. (2011). *Causes and context of the sexual abuse crisis in the Catholic Church*. Washington, DC: United States Conference of Catholic Bishops.

The Investigative Staff of the Boston Globe. (2016). *Betrayal: The crisis in the Catholic Church – The findings of the investigation that inspired the major motion picture spotlight* (Updated ed.). London: Profile Books.

Topping, A. (2015, May 30). Nigeria's female genital mutilation ban is important precedent, say campaigners. *The Guardian*.

Trickett, P., Noll, J., & Putnam, F. (2011). The impact of sexual abuse on female development: Lessons from a multigenerational, longitudinal research study. *Development and Psychopathology, 23*, 453–476.

Trowell, J., Ugarte, B., Kolvin, I., et al. (1999). Behavioural psychopathology of child sexual abuse in schoolgirls referred to a tertiary centre: A North London study. *European Journal of Child and Adolescent Psychiatry, 8*, 107–116.

Ullman, S., & Filipas, H. (2005). Gender differences in social reactions to abuse disclosures, post abuse coping, and PTSD of child sexual abuse survivors. *Child Abuse & Neglect, 29*, 767–782.

Ungar, M., Tutty, L. M., McConnell, S., Barter, K., & Fairholm, J. (2009). What Canadian youth tell us about disclosing abuse. *Child Abuse & Neglect, 33*, 699–708.

UNICEF. (2016). *Female genital mutilation/cutting: A global concern*. New York: UNICEF https://data.unicef.org/resources/female-genital-mutilationcutting-global-concern/.

United Nations. (2015). *Sustainable development goals*. Geneva. http://www.un.org/sustainabledevelopment/.

United Nations General Assembly. (2015). *Transforming our world: The 2030 Agenda for sustainable development*. United Nations General Assembly; Seventieth session. September 18, 2015; New York, NY. https://sustainabledevelopment.un.org/post2015/transformingourworld.

U.S. Department of Health and Human Services. (2009). Child maltreatment 2007. Accessed at http://www.acf.hhs.gov/programs/cb/resource/childmaltreatment-2007

Van der Kolk, B. (2014). *The body keeps the score*. New York: Penguin.

Violato, C., & Genuis, M. (1993). Problems of research in male child sexual abuse. *Journal of Child Sexual Abuse, 2*, 33–54.

Ward, T. (2003). The explanation, assessment and treatment of child sexual abuse. *International Journal of Forensic Psychology, 1*(1), 10–25.

Ward, T., & Beech, A. (2006). An integrated theory of sexual offending. *Aggression and Violent Behavior, 11*, 44–63.

Ward, T., & Siegert, R. J. (2002). Toward and comprehensive theory of child sexual abuse: A theory knitting perspective. *Psychology, Crime & Law, 9*, 319–351.

Ward, T., Hudson, S. M., Johnston, L., & Marshall, W. L. (1997). Cognitive distortions in sex offenders: An integrative review. *Clinical Psychology Review, 17*(5), 479–507.

Weale, S. (2017, September 15). Greening could face legal action over failure to protect raped pupils. *The Guardian*.

Whitaker, D., Le, B., Hanson, R., Baker, C., McMahon, P., Ryan, G., Klein, A., et al. (2008). Risk factors for perpetration of child sexual abuse: A review and meta-analysis. *Child Abuse and Neglect, 32*, 529–548.

Williams, R. (2012, September 27). Rochdale police and council 'repeatedly warned' about sex abuse risk in town. *The Guardian*.

Wolfe, D., Sas, L., & Wekerle, C. (1994). Factors associated with the development of post-traumatic stress disorder among child victims of sexual abuse. *Child Abuse and Neglect, 18*, 37–50.

World Health Organization. (1999). *Report of the consultation on child abuse prevention*. Geneva: World Health Organization.

World Health Organization. (2018). *Female genital mutilation: Fact sheet.* http://www.who.int/mediacentre/factsheets/fs241/en/

World Health Organization, & International Society for Prevention of Child Abuse and Neglect. (2006). *Preventing child maltreatment: A guide to taking action and generating evidence*. Geneva: World Health Organization.

Wozencraft, T., Wagner, W., & Pellegrin, A. (1991). Depression and suicidal ideation in sexually abused children. *Child Abuse & Neglect, 15*, 505–511.

Wurtele, S. (2012). Preventing the sexual exploitation of minors in youth-serving organizations. *Children and Youth Services Review, 34*, 2442–2453.

Young, A., Grey, M., & Boyd, C. (2009). Adolescents' experiences of sexual assault by Peers: Prevalence and nature of victimization occurring within and outside of school. *Journal of Youth and Adolescence, 38*(8), 1072–1083.

Younger, E. (2018a, March 30) George Pell: The pool, the cinema and the cathedral – What we learned at the committal. *ABC News*.

Younger, E. (2018b, May 2). Cardinal George Pell pleads not guilty to historical sexual offence charges after being committed to stand trial. *ABC News*.

Youssef, N. (2017, October 9). 2 paths for Yemen's war-scarred children: Combat, or marriage. *The New York Times*.

Chapter 2
Issues in Defining Child Sexual Abuse

Abstract This chapter provides a brief historical overview of the social context of child sexual abuse, focusing on themes of ignorance, recognition and suppression. It relates these themes to recent and current debates about the nature of child sexual abuse. It reviews international policy and prevalence study approaches to the definition of child sexual abuse, identifying different interpretations of the concept and focusing on three major dimensions of variance. It then analyses the concept of child sexual abuse and provides a recommended conceptual model and definition. The key message from this Chapter is that child sexual abuse should be considered to exist when: (1) the person is a child (from either or both developmental and legal standpoints); (2) there is no true consent (due either to lack of capacity to provide consent, or presence of capacity but lack of consent in fact); (3) the acts are sexual (being contact or non-contact acts done to seek or obtain physical or mental sexual gratification, whether immediate or deferred in time or space, or otherwise legitimately experienced by the child as a sexual act); and (4) the acts constitute abuse (due to the presence of a relationship of power, the child's position of inequality, and the exploitation of the child's vulnerability).

Keywords Child sexual abuse · Historical overview · Ignorance, suppression and recognition · Contemporary problems in definition · International policy definitions · Prevalence study definitions · A rigorous conceptual model and definition

Introduction

A growing number of societies are now appearing to take child sexual abuse more seriously.

Efforts continue to measure the prevalence of child sexual abuse and the nature of its consequences, and to create policies and practices that can prevent it. Laws are created to identify it, facilitate personal safety, provide financial compensation, and make criminal court processes more child-friendly. Clinicians work on optimal ways to identify it and treat it. Community efforts play a part in building awareness.

B. Mathews, *New International Frontiers in Child Sexual Abuse*,
Child Maltreatment 7, https://doi.org/10.1007/978-3-319-99043-9_2

Public inquiries seek to uncover it, identify the conditions which enabled it to flourish, and make recommendations for reform of law, policy and practice. All these responses aim to build a culture more conducive to prevention and appropriate responses. Internationally, policy statements are made at the highest level encouraging all nations to take action. The prevalence and severe harms of child sexual abuse, together with cross-cultural recognition of its moral unjustifiability, has contributed to its inclusion as a specific target for action and prevention in the United Nations Sustainable Development Goals, Targets 5.2 and 16.2 (United Nations General Assembly 2015).

However, as seen in Chaps. 1, 5 and 6 of this book, individuals, institutions and societies continue to exhibit a persistent and concerning tendency to ignore and minimise child sexual abuse, to blame the child for it, to excuse offenders, and to fail to hold accountable those who had the power and responsibility to intervene. Despite pockets of progress, rates of prevalence continue to be substantial, and governmental inertia in failure to respond adequately is characteristic of most societies. Efforts to respond face multiple challenges.

One of these is the inherent, surprisingly complex challenge in defining what we understand as "child sexual abuse". Different definitions of the concept are used in epidemiological studies, international policy documents and laws. This creates major challenges for research, knowledge formation, and prevention efforts. Possibly most importantly, it undermines the creation of defensible social norms, which are essential if the problem is to be tackled effectively. Sufficient agreement on what we understand to constitute "child sexual abuse" is necessary if we wish to advance and prioritize efforts at prevention and identification, and to inform appropriate responses in legal systems and institutions. The need to develop a sound definition possessing a sufficiently high level of consensus has been recognised for decades by leading researchers, and by the World Health Organization (2006), but has remained elusive (Mathews and Collin-Vézina 2017).

This chapter discusses the major issues in defining child sexual abuse, illustrates the key dimensions of variance in different definitions, and presents a conceptual model and operational definition of the concept. In doing so, it draws on a recently published comprehensive analysis and model (Mathews and Collin-Vézina 2017). In addition, to situate the argument presented here about how child sexual abuse should best be conceptualised and defined, it is necessary to briefly consider some historical background. While a comprehensive historical treatment is not possible or necessary, an overview of influential features of the historical context is essential. Awareness of societal dispositions to sexual behaviour with children is needed to understand what has gone before and why, and to illuminate the structural forces and attitudes that need to be confronted to properly re-cast an understanding of what types of acts constitute "child sexual abuse". This understanding is necessary to then isolate what should justifiably be understood as constituting "child sexual abuse" and to be able to distinguish this from other behaviour.

A Brief Historical Overview: Ignorance, Suppression, and Recognition

Incest and other forms of child sexual abuse have occurred in all societies throughout human history (Bolen 2001; Brundage 1987; Conte 1994; De Mause 1976; Lascaratos amd Poulakou-Rebelakou 2000; Olafson et al. 1993; Rush 1980; Walker 2013).

Often, endemic sexual abuse has been rhetorically rationalised as a cultural practice, and no or little attention has been given to the pain and suffering of its child victims, or of their denigration as mere objects for the use of others. This posture has been facilitated by a long-standing denial to children of individual human rights, juridical status, meaningful social standing, and realistic avenues of assistance. This is exemplified by children's historical status across virtually all societies as mere chattels, able to be sold, enslaved, placed into forced labour, abandoned and killed; and for females, further denigration simply by virtue of sex (Borkowski 1986; Eisenberg 1981; Gardner 1986; McGillivray 2011; Pinker 2011; Ten Bensel et al. 1997). Despite the frequency of child sexual abuse in all eras and places, it is only since the late 1970s and early 1980s that it has been more broadly and formally recognised in societal institutions as a phenomenon of significant concern, and even then, this recognition has been beset with challenges and confined to some societies.

Before this recent period of recognition, those who tried to bring society's attention to it faced implacable opposition. The French physician Ambroise Tardieu was one of the first medical professionals to document cases of child sexual abuse and to advocate for social reforms to protect children (Labbé 2005). Tardieu was the most painstaking of several French physicians in the mid-nineteenth century to examine child sexual abuse, preceded by Toulmouche in 1856, and accompanied by other work from Bernard and Lacassagne (Olafson et al. 1993). Tardieu's 1857 book, a medico-legal study of offences against morals, analysed 632 cases of sexual abuse of girls. This extensive study covered cases that were intra-familial and extra-familial, cases with and without clinical signs, and cases with and without penetration. He focused on the physical consequences of sexual abuse, but also discussed a range of its consequences for psychological health. He also analysed 302 cases of pederasty and sodomy, which included a large number of cases of adults abusing young boys. This work established clearly that the problem was widespread, that children were truthful, that sexual abuse was not confined by social class, and that sexual abuse often left no clear signs. Over the next several decades, Tardieu's book was published in seven successive editions, and was translated into German (Labbé 2005). Yet, reflecting the culture at the time, Tardieu's colleagues and successors refused to believe children were being truthful, and instead dismissed children's allegations as the product of children's natural inventiveness.

Non-recognition and Repression Much has been written about the reasons for societal non-recognition of child sexual abuse (Bolen 2001; De Mause 1976; Herman 1997; Miller 1998; Rush 1980), and of cycles of its recognition and suppression (Collings 2009; Conte 1994; Myers 2004; Olafson et al. 1993). A particularly important cycle of repression occurred from the end of the nineteenth century through the first seven decades of the twentieth century. Some progress was made in this period, including the work of late nineteenth century feminists and reformers, the early twentieth century work of Ferenczi, and occasional significant studies (Gagnon 1965; Landis 1956). However, in general in this period, the insights developed by Tardieu and his colleagues were systematically undermined, especially by psychiatrists, through the marginalisation, mitigation, and minimalisation of child sexual abuse (Collings 2009; Herman 1997; Olafson et al. 1993).

The Freudian Coverup The most influential force in this modern repression of reality was Sigmund Freud. Freud's discovery of sexual abuse of girls by their fathers and his subsequent retreat from this finding has been discussed by many. Arguably the most instructive, insightful and riveting accounts appear in "The Freudian Coverup", the landmark analysis by Florence Rush (1977), and the historical analysis by Judith Lewis Herman (1997, pp. 10–20). These accounts must be considered essential classical texts in this setting, and they have informed the summary provided here.

Freud knew of Tardieu's work, and owned a copy of this book (Labbé 2005). His early work on the nature of hysteria had been influenced by the French pioneer and neurologist Jean-Martin Charcot, but also Freud's contemporary and rival Pierre Janet (Herman 1997). Both Freud and Charcot conducted extensive consultations where they listened to women relate their experiences. Freud worked closely with his colleague Joseph Breuer in Vienna, while Janet worked in France. Both reached similar conclusions, that the women's "hysteria" was a product of psychological trauma related to extremely distressing events.

In 1896, as a result of his extensive work conducting what he would later term "psycho-analysis" with female patients who had symptoms of "hysteria", he reached the conclusion that the cause of the symptoms exhibited by the women was sexual abuse during childhood by the father. This conclusion was presented in a collection of three papers entitled "The Aetiology of Hysteria", informed by an analyses of 18 cases where women had experienced child sexual abuse. He declared that "at the bottom of every case of hysteria there are one or more occurrences of premature sexual experience [in] the earliest years of childhood", although in this public forum he did not name the father as the offender. This finding was especially significant because Freud's practice was in well-to-do Vienna, not in poverty-stricken women in Paris. Herman (1997) interprets the tenor of Freud's finding as indicating his awareness of a signal breakthrough. In private letters, most prominently to his colleague Willhelm Fliess, he was unequivocal, both about sexual abuse being the cause of anxiety and other symptoms, and of the girls' fathers being the offenders (Rush 1977, p. 266). Freud related anecdotes of the fathers' abuse, and stated that "I have come to the opinion that anxiety is to be connected, not with a mental, but with a physical consequence of sexual abuse...primary sexual experience (before puberty) accompanied by revulsion and fright" (Rush 1977, p. 266).

However, Freud's commitment to this extraordinary discovery was short-lived. Within a year, Freud had performed an extraordinary about face. The theory of "seduction" by the girl's father had been inverted and replaced by the utterly non-empirical artifice of the "Oedipal complex". In resiling from the radical implications of his findings, Freud now reassigned blame to a range of other parties, consciously minimising and excluding fathers' responsibility. Blame was placed on the mother (for originally awakening in her daughter pleasurable genital sensations, even if unintentionally) and offenders were suddenly recast not as the father (as reported by the women), but as opposite-sex children (especially siblings), nurses, governesses, maids, teachers, and relatives (Rush 1977). Most important of all, blame was firmly placed on the girl herself. On Freud's new interpretation, the girl herself possessed an incestuous desire for the father, had fantasised the events, and her symptoms were borne of frustration, anxiety, guilt and penis envy (Rush 1977). Having himself performed such a bizarre, extraordinary act of fantasy must rank as one of history's great ironies.

Many have concluded Freud's about face was influenced primarily by a need for professional self-preservation, given the professional and cultural climate at the time and that he would have faced both professional exile and personal annihilation if he was to persist with his thesis after its only public airing in 1896 (Herman 1997; Rush 1977). Herman (1997) notes Freud's correspondence with Fliess at this time, indicating the emergent ostracism by his peers: "the word has been given out to abandon me, and a void is forming around me". However, it has also been posited that his intellectual contortions were partly caused by being overwhelmed at understanding the nature and prevalence of paternal abuse, and by being thrown into a personal psychological crisis as a result of his own childhood experiences and unresolved feelings towards his mother and father (Rush 1977).

In essence, Freud was faced with a choice about whether to remain faithful to his findings form hearing his patient's stories, or to retreat from this empirical evidence, succumb to the forces of patriarchy and culture, and conform with professional convention. Herman (1997) notes that Janet had maintained his commitment to his traumatic theory of hysteria and had paid the price, being with his work slipping into obscurity. Freud chose the path of retreat. Rush (1977) concludes that, for several reasons, Freud chose to perform a series of "mental acrobatics", including the frank alteration of information, for the primary reason of protecting fathers. Ultimately, she interprets the "Freudian coverup" as "the refusal to name the offender" (1977, p. 274) and the accompanying attribution of culpability to the girl, who therefore is compelled to remain silent. The girl [correctly] fears that if she does complain, she will be blamed; the patriarchal distortions have established "a system of foolproof emotional blackmail: if the victim incriminates the abuser, she also incriminates herself. The sexual abuse of the child is therefore the best-kept secret in the world." (Rush 1977, p. 275.)

Effect of the Coverup: Repression and Continuing Mythologies The cumulative effect of these events, patriarchal dominance, societal features and historical influences was that the nature and prevalence of child sexual abuse was covered up during this period. Instead, it was consigned to a phenomenon at the periphery of society, involving only the morally and pathologically degenerate, and not "normal" or "respectable" men. Where it was acknowledged as having occurred, the responsibility and culpability for child sexual abuse was sheeted home to the child – and especially to the female child - and the child's mother through a panoply of rationalisations and denials; the males who actually inflicted the acts were absolved of responsibility.

These mythologies entered public discourse and have proved remarkably resilient, being reinforced by Freud's successors and supported by the continuing patriarchal culture (Armstrong 1978, 1994; Rush 1977, 1980, 1996). The marginalisation myth manifested in people thinking child sexual abuse, where it existed, was perpetrated by strange old men in trench-coats, rather than by fathers, relatives and trusted social figures. The mitigation myth manifested in the belief that the child was a manipulative sexual delinquent, "wanted it" or instigated the events, or was mentally ill; alternatively, the child's mother was responsible through any of a range of failings. The minimisation myth manifested in the belief that child sexual abuse was not damaging, and may even be beneficial for the child. These postures were enabled and reinforced by non-empirical pseudoscience, fundamental entrenched attitudes about the supremacy of the male (and especially the father), the inferiority of the female, and the lowly moral status of the child. Most of all, they were enabled by the basic view that treated children and females as inferior, and not as individuals worthy of dignity, respect, equality and rights to bodily inviolability. In society and law, the adult male held all the power. The child was considered a chattel, a non-individual, an entity without juridical, social or political standing, and without rights. This position of radical inequality was exacerbated by fundamental inequalities of gender, class, colour and ethnicity.

Florence Rush and Other Feminist Pioneers: Recognition, Outrage and Mobilisation Several factors and events coalesced to catalyse the change in awareness. The most important was the emergence of courageous, articulate feminist work on both child sexual abuse, and on rape and sexual assault of women more generally. In 1971, Florence Rush delivered a coruscating oration at the New York Radical Feminist Conference about child sexual abuse. Rush drew on her personal and professional experiences (1974, 1980). As a child, when aged 7, she had first been sexually abused by her family's dentist. She told her mother immediately, who was initially disturbed but then told Florence that she was lying and had made up the story to avoid future dental visits. Aged 10, she was molested by the father of a boy she secretly loved. Aged 13, her uncle repeatedly fondled her. In addition, she had been abused by adult male strangers in cinemas and other public spaces, at the time a regular occurrence for her and her female friends. In Rush's words, she and her friends were "addicted to the movies but discovered we that we could scarcely get through a double feature without finding the hand of some strange man up our skirts

… [we] compared techniques on how to ward off being touched, grabbed at or even mauled in buses and subways, and created strategies for extricating ourselves from uncomfortable and even dangerous situations" (1980, p. xii).

Professionally, she drew on her experiences with dependent and neglected girls as a social worker at the Society for the Prevention of Cruelty to Children (1974, 1977). She had also worked in an institution for these girls, and discovered that every single girl she worked with there had been sexually abused. Rush wanted to listen to and validate the child's experience, and to reassure her she had done nothing wrong and that it was the offender who was to blame. However, she had been instructed by her supervisor to follow the Freudian line by maintaining the girl's shame was a result not of the experience, but of her unconscious incestuous desire for her father (Rush 1977). Rush had also worked in an orphanage, where the director would regularly abuse girls.

Her oration in 1971 galvanised other intellects, awakening in them a sense of recognition, outrage and resolve. Rush was unequivocal in declaring there was a connection between child sexual abuse and the cultural and private atmosphere which enabled and authorised sexual violence against women. She insisted that "sexual abuse of children … is an unspoken but prominent factor in socializing and preparing the female to accept a subordinate role: to feel guilty, ashamed, and to tolerate through fear, the power exercised over her by men." She decried Kinsey's minimisation (1953), where he had said "It is difficult to understand why a child, except for its cultural conditioning, should be disturbed by having its genitalia touched" and instead blamed parental and social reactions for psychological sequelae. Rush eviscerated this, isolating not only the attitudinal and structural problems that still impede many societies today, and the continued rhetorical minimisation of sexual abuse, but the failure of empathic imagination at the heart of obliviousness and cruel responses (1974, p. 70):

> With the usual male arrogance, the author cannot imagine that a sexual assault on a child constitutes a gross and devastating shock and insult, so he blames everyone but the offender. The fact is that sexual offenses are barely noticed except in the most violent and sensational instances. Most sex offenses are never revealed; when revealed, most are either ignored or not reported; if reported, a large percentage are dismissed for lack of proof, and when proof is established many are dropped because of the pressure and humiliation forced on the victim and family by the authorities.

Then, in 1980, in *The Best Kept Secret*, Rush published her excoriating critique of patriarchy's culpability for child sexual abuse across cultures, time periods, and media industries. This book, together with her 1971 oration and other published work through the 1970s (Rush 1972, 1974, 1977), surgically dissected and demolished the pretentions and denials of the Freudian movement. Florence Rush's sensitive insights and formidable critiques would form a touchstone for the growing movement against sexual abuse of children, and sexual violence against women, and the patriarchal forces enabling it. Rush not only urged immediate recognition and action in response to child sexual abuse; she related it to deeper patriarchal forces of society-wide suppression and victimisation of women: one of her concluding points in her 1971 oration was that "sexual abuse of children is permitted because it is an unspoken but prominent factor in socializing and preparing the female to accept a subordinate role; to feel guilty, ashamed, and to tolerate, through fear, the power exercised over her by men" (1974, p. 73–74). This was not at all overstating the case; one only need consider the fact that in the USA, it was only in the mid 1970s that marital rape began to be criminalized, and similarly in England, the law did not prohibit marital rape until 1991.[1] Other work criticising Freud received significant notice, but Kitzinger (1996) insists it was Rush's work that irrevocably shifted the terrain of social understanding. Similarly, Segal (1996) declared that "Rush's essay was part of a profound and abiding cultural consciousness-raising around the criminal extent and obscene neglect of child sexual abuse".

Around this time, feminist work was building momentum about sexual violence against women generally, insisting on the malign influence of patriarchal structures. In 1975, Susan Brownmiller published her magisterial study of rape. Louise Armstrong's landmark study of 183 incest survivors also was a defining work and added critical weight to this movement (Armstrong 1978). Scholars and activists began to mobilise against sexual violence against women in the private sphere, and in the workplace. Catharine MacKinnon (1979) condemned sexual harassment of women in the workplace, conceiving this form of sexual violence – spanning non-physical transgressions such as sexual comments, and leering, through to sexual touching and rape – as injuring not only the individual woman, but women as a whole through violence against gender.[2]

A number of women presented articulate accounts of their childhood experiences, giving voice to what previously had been silenced. Louise Armstrong had related her own experience of incest in her 1978 work *Kiss Daddy Goodnight*. Another earlier account was by the actor, playwright and activist, Maya Angelou. Her 1969 book, *I Know Why the Caged Bird Sings*, related her sexual abuse and rape by her mother's boyfriend, when she was 8 years old. She told her brother, who told the rest of their family. The man was charged and found guilty, but was imprisoned for only 1 day. Shortly after his release, he was murdered, thought to be by Angelou's uncles. After this, Angelou became mute for almost 5 years, because, as she recalled, "I thought, my voice killed him; I killed that man, because I told his name. And then I thought I would never speak again, because my voice would kill anyone" (Lupton 1998).[3]

All of these developments also built on the courageous efforts of black American women in exposing endemic sexual violence against girls and women by white men, especially in the South, assisted by police cover-ups and failure to act.

---

[1] R v R [1991] 4 All ER 481.

[2] Early theoretical work about sexual harassment animated its recognition in US jurisprudence in Meritor Savings Bank v Vinson, 477 U.S. 57 (1986), where the Supreme Court held sexual harassment can create a "hostile working environment" constituting unlawful discrimination under the Civil Rights Act 1964.

[3] Biographers posited that this forced period of silence was the background to Angelou developing a love of literature, and an exceptional ability to listen and observe the world (Gillespie et al., 2008).

McGuire's magisterial historical analysis shows how the brave testimony of women, and mobilisation as a political force, eventually led to landmark criminal prosecutions and shifts in attitudes and social norms (McGuire 2011). Amongst the catalogue of examples McGuire relates is that of Fannie Lou Hamer, whose mother bore 23 children, 20 of whom were the products of rape. Fannie Lou's mother would pack a gun in her lunch box so she could protect herself and her daughters from being attacked while working in the cotton fields. Hamer's mother and grandmother taught her that in the South, a black woman's body was never hers alone. Hamer would go on to become one of many courageous advocates for social reform.

Gathering Momentum: Scientific Analysis The momentum for scholarship and advocacy regarding child sexual abuse gathered pace in the late 1970s and early 1980s. Contributions came from diverse disciplinary fields, including psychology, sociology, law enforcement, medicine, and social work. Early work included articles and comprehensive books focusing on incest (Armstrong 1978; Butler 1978; Herman and Hirschman 1976; Herman 1981; Russell 1984a, 1986; Sgroi 1975), as well as articles about its clinical treatment (Adams-Tucker 1981; Giarretto 1977; Jorné 1979). Significantly, nearly all of this work was by women, perhaps influenced by the feminist work on sexual violence against women more generally, their ability to relate to the issues based on their experiences of discrimination and sexism, their heightened empathy, and their commitment to social justice and equality.

A broad body of research grew to examine other manifestations of sexual abuse (Burgess et al. 1978; Finkelhor 1979a, b, 1984, 1986; Kempe and Kempe 1984; Rush 1974; Russell 1983, 1984b; Steele and Alexander 1981; Wyatt 1985). Clinical work and theoretical analysis helped to develop a deeper understanding of the phenomenon (e.g., Summit 1983). By the late 1970s, medical professionals and social work practitioners were unequivocally declaring sexual abuse to be a major problem. Summit and Kryso (1978, p. 250) described child sexual abuse as "the most concealed, most distressing, and most controversial form of child abuse." In 1978, Colorado paediatrician Henry Kempe, most renowned for his earlier work on child physical abuse and the concept of "Battered-child Syndrome" (Kempe et al. 1962), publicly recognised sexual abuse. He defined it as "The involvement of dependent, developmentally immature children and adolescents in sexual activities that they do not fully comprehend, to which they are unable to give informed consent or that violate the social taboos of family roles." (p. 382). Kempe insisted that whatever other priorities there were, including in detecting offenders, the primary priority was to provide assistance to the child: "The child deserves a chance at therapy just as much as if there were by other insult to development" (1978, p. 389). Kempe also observed that underreporting was "massive" and that the true incidence must far exceed those cases that come to the attention of health authorities.

In the next few years, prevalence studies by sociologists David Finkelhor and Diana Russell found evidence of the true scale of child sexual abuse. Finkelhor's survey of 796 New England college students (530 women and 266 men) found 19.2% of women and 8.6% of men reported being sexually victimized as children

(Finkelhor 1979a). There had been earlier studies, such as the 1969 work by Vincent De Francis, which also helped to lay the foundation for community sensitisation to the problem. De Francis published his analysis of interviews with 250 families of abused children from New York City, in the first US study of the incidence of child sexual abuse and the consequences for mental health and personality development. His report, entitled *Protecting the Child Victim of Sex Crimes Committed By Adults* (De Francis 1969), concluded the prevalence of child sexual abuse was probably larger than that of physical abuse, that two thirds of the children were emotionally harmed, and that these children are "a community's least protected children".

However, the studies by Finkelhor and Russell were significant because of their scientific rigour and detail, substantial samples of participants, and more formal publication of results. Following Finkelhor's first study, Diana Russell (1983) surveyed 930 women in San Francisco. She found 16% reported intra-familial sexual abuse before age 18 (and 12% before age 14), and 31% reported extra-familial abuse before age 18 (and 20% before age 14). In total, Russell also found that only 2% of the cases of intra-familial cases, and 6% of the extra-familial cases, were ever reported to police. Russell (1984b) further analysed the cases of intra-familial abuse, examining abuse by biological fathers and stepfathers where these men were primary caregivers in the girl's first 14 years. She found 17% of the respondents who had a stepfather as one of the primary people with whom she resided up to age 14 had been sexually abused by him before age 14, compared with approximately 2.5% of the biological fathers. Russell also found that the step-fathers committed more serious kinds of sexual offences than the biological fathers.

Historical Forces Persist: The Need to Name and Conceptualise Child Sexual Abuse

Despite this growing evidence base and emerging movement to recognize child sexual abuse and grant it the attention it deserved, the deep currents of historical forces would continue to pervade social discourse, even in societies where it was beginning to be taken more seriously. Often, children would be accused of lying, and simply not believed, as shown by survivors' accounts in public inquiries (Royal Commission 2017), public attitudes to children's veracity (Cromer and Goldsmith 2010; Fontes and Plummer 2010; McGee et al. 2011; Shackel 2008), in police refusing to take complaints seriously (Jay 2014), or in parental custody cases in family law (Nichols 2014; O'Donohue et al. 2016).[4] Frequently, where believed, it would be minimized as not damaging. In other cases, it would be mitigated, with the child

[4]The so-called "parental alienation syndrome" centred around this falsehood causes particular damage. While scientifically discredited, it continues to have pernicious effects, where considered by misinformed family court judges. These problems have been extensively documented: see Clemente & Padilla-Racero, 2016; Dallam & Silberg, 2016; Geffner, 2016; Kleinman, 2016; Nichols, 2014; O'Donohue et al., 2016).

blamed for wanting it, as epitomised by the scandals in England,[5] and famously by Anglican Archbishop Peter Hollingworth, the Australian Governor-General, being forced to resign in 2003, largely because he had publicly blamed a victim for instigating her own abuse. Child sexual abuse would be marginalized, with people being unable to believe that a trusted figure could sexually abuse a child, and the child victims themselves knowing they would not be believed: just one of the powerful protections enjoyed by prolific offenders like Jimmy Savile, Barry Bennell, and Jerry Sandusky.

Essential preconditions for reform and action would include the demonstration that child sexual abuse in diverse forms was both ethically wrong, and often harmful to the child's health and behavior. This required ethical analysis, and scientific analysis of the prevalence and etiology of child sexual abuse, and reliable studies of its effects on psychological health, behavior and social functioning. If these bodies of evidence were established, reforms of fundamental social structures would have to occur, so that measures could be designed and implemented to respond to child sexual abuse after the event, identify it and interrupt it in ongoing cases, and prevent it where possible before it began. Legal principles would have to be reframed to enable better protection of children's rights. There would need to be sufficient civil and criminal causes of action available to survivors, which would require recognition of all acts which should be considered as child sexual abuse and therefore as acts and experiences which should be regarded as legitimate bases for legal claims; whereas acts outside these would have to be excluded. Broader social norms around what is considered acceptable and unacceptable personal and sexual behavior would have to be recalibrated.

But to do all these things, child sexual abuse, in all its forms, had to be *named*, conceptualized, defined, and enumerated. Fundamental to all of these activities was the challenge of conceptualising the nature of child sexual abuse. This complex challenge had multiple dimensions. Who is a child? Who can be an abuser? What acts can constitute abuse, and under what circumstances? While the most blatant form of child sexual abuse – being penetrative rape by a man's penis of a girl's vagina – may have been somewhat more readily accepted and recognized, much work had to be done to explore the conceptual nature and many manifestations of what should be considered as child sexual abuse. A normatively justified conceptual understanding of child sexual abuse was needed, that could attract sufficient consensus among scientists, advocates and policymakers, which could be the basis of laws, social norms, policy and practice. If this was not developed, then nor could a full taxonomy of acts constituting child sexual abuse. Partial, distorted and illegitimate approaches to what was perceived as "child sexual abuse" would leave many survivors of what was in fact child sexual abuse, excluded from social recognition, protection, early intervention and assistance. Acts not recognized as sexual abuse would be justified as normative and acceptable, rather than fundamental breaches of

---

[5] See Chap. 1.

children's human rights that also often cause multiple kinds of psychological and behavioural damage.

Florence Rush recognised this danger of failing to recognize the full spectrum of cases of child sexual abuse when she lamented the facts that only the most violent and sensational cases receive recognition, whereas the whole panoply of sexual abuse needed to be taken seriously and prohibited. As we will now see, the problem of conceptualising and defining child sexual abuse has continued from the 1970s to the present day.

Relevance to Recent and Current Debates About the Nature of Child Sexual Abuse

In 1988, David Finkelhor and Jill Korbin declared that child sexual abuse should be classed as one of three domains of maltreatment demanding a "focus for concerted international action and attention" (1988, p. 16). When they made this statement, they acknowledged that human cultures have historically possessed different behavioural practices, yet maintained that even on the most culturally sensitive and respectful approach, there are some universal standards of human behaviour that can and should be set about what is acceptable. Yet, some 30 years later, the international community is still grappling with the absence of a shared understanding of what acts do and do not constitute "child sexual abuse", and why.

The problems in defining child sexual abuse, and the need to generate a justified definition of the concept, have been noted since the 1970s (Finkelhor and Korbin 1988; Giovannoni and Becerra 1979; Haugaard 2000; Holmes and Slap 1998; Ondersma et al. 2001; Wyatt and Peters 1986). The World Health Organization also identified this need when it stated (2006, pp. 3–4): "The various sectors involved in addressing child maltreatment need to develop a common conceptual definition of child maltreatment and common operational definitions to enable case identification and enumeration". Despite these repeated exhortations, lack of progress has prompted many in more recent years to repeat these calls for a conceptually robust definition (Barth et al. 2013; Trickett 2006; Veenema et al. 2015).

There are good reasons for this call for better conceptualisation and definition, since variance in definitions of child sexual abuse presents many serious problems. The lack of a justified model, and of a shared understanding of what different experiences should be called, and why, can distort or limit the capacity of researchers, clinicians, legislators, policymakers and communities to appropriately measure, treat, prevent, interrupt and respond to child sexual abuse. Problems are caused for research and knowledge formation, legal systems, prevention efforts, policy development, and establishment of social norms. In social science, public health, law and public policy, the appropriate characterisation of acts and experiences as child sexual abuse as opposed to another conceptual category, can carry enormous significance. It is instructive to briefly summarise each of these problems.

Problems for Research and Knowledge Formation Different definitions of child sexual abuse in research into prevalence, etiology, and sequelae have led to substantial variance in findings about ostensibly the same phenomenon (Barth et al. 2013). This means knowledge of prevalence cannot be developed, or traced over time. Different definitions also create the potential for both overestimation and underestimation of health sequelae and socio-economic cost. In contrast, research using precise definitions produces more reliable outcomes. One such program of research has analyzed the exact nature, duration and frequency of the acts, the use of force or threats, age of onset, and the abuser's identity, enabling a sophisticated association between specific types of CSA and sequelae (Negriff, et al. 2014; Trickett, et al. 2001, 2011; Trickett 2006). Lack of sound definitions means we cannot generate or chart trends in prevalence; therefore, we cannot reliably measure whether interventions are having a positive effect. In this sense, the absence of a robust definition undermines a society's entire effort to reduce child sexual abuse, and to respond to it.

Problems for Legal Systems Laws play a central role in identifying, responding to and preventing child sexual abuse, and in setting and enforcing social norms. Different areas of law prohibit specified acts and provide remedies for breaches, therefore also setting norms of conduct. In civil law, people who have experienced child sexual abuse can claim financial compensation for their injuries and economic loss. In criminal law, the state can prosecute offenders, enabling punishment, incapacitation, deterrence and community norms. In child protection law, the state can intervene in cases where a child is being sexually abused to interrupt the abuse and ensure the child is made safe. In constitutional law, the boundaries of free speech can be circumscribed by prohibiting people from creating, distributing or consuming material about child sexual abuse. In all these domains, appropriate definition of what is child sexual abuse - and what is not - is necessary to soundly define the scope of the law and its protection. Unwarranted exclusion of acts from the legal definition of child sexual abuse will deny survivors of the capacity to seek civil compensation, will deny the state the ability to prosecute, and will enable people to engage in behaviour which should be prohibited. Equally, unwarranted inclusion of an act as child sexual abuse may result in unjust outcomes, creating civil liability where it should not exist, and exposing individuals to criminal sanctions without appropriate justification.

Laws have often evaded the challenge of defining the concept of child sexual abuse. This can clearly lead to problems of uncertainty, and the potential for unduly narrowing the scope of the application of the law; also, it creates the prospect that the law could be interpreted in an unduly wide manner. For example, in many jurisdictions including the USA, Canada, Australia, and Ireland, mandatory reporting laws require designated persons to report known or suspected child sexual abuse to protect the child. "Sexual abuse" is often simply undefined, or is defined vaguely to include "molestation" or "explicit conduct", or "sexual abuse" and "sexual assault" without further detail; and sometimes it is limited to acts by parents, caregivers, or family members (Mathews and Kenny 2008). Clearly, cases falling outside the legally defined scope will not activate the duty to report, meaning that at least in theory, children experiencing sexual abuse not characterised as such by the law may not have their circumstances reported. A further example is that some jurisdictions have passed special laws removing the civil statute of limitations for personal injury claims in cases of child sexual abuse (see further Chap. 5). Yet, where this is done, child sexual abuse is sometimes not defined, or is expressed in a vague and ambiguous way. British Columbia and Ontario define it as "misconduct of a sexual nature"; Manitoba defines it as "assault of a sexual nature", and New Brunswick uses the term "act of a sexual nature". Accordingly, an unduly restrictive interpretation of these concepts would rule out plaintiffs who have experienced acts not deemed to fall within their scope; whereas a careful, theoretically justified, robust and comprehensive approach to the definition of the concept would ensure such injustices could not occur.

Problems for Prevention and Treatment Prevention programs have proliferated, with diverse targets: children (Walsh, et al. 2015); offenders (adolescents and adults) (Hanson and Bussière 1998; Ward and Beech 2006); parents (Mendelson and Letourneau 2015); and institutions (e.g., schools, churches) (Letourneau, et al. 2016; Wurtele 2012). Yet, depending on what is included in the concept of child sexual abuse, such approaches may have different levels of theoretical soundness and will vary in their likelihood of practical success. Depending on its conceptualisation and operational definition, prevention and policy approaches will require different content and mechanisms. In addition, for clinicians, and for other professionals who deal with children on a daily basis like teachers, diagnosing a child as having experienced sexual abuse or not clearly has significant consequences for whether therapeutic responses can be made available, and which responses are actually provided.

Problems for International and National Policy Development and Implementation Authoritative professional bodies like the World Health Organization (2006), the Centres for Disease Control (Basile et al. 2014), and others at the international and national levels, have immense influence. Their approaches to prevention can achieve substantial gains. It is essential that their policy efforts be driven by a sound definition of child sexual abuse.

Problems for Establishment of Social Norms Perhaps most importantly, a theoretically justifiable definition of child sexual abuse is required to inform the development of norms of acceptable behaviour. Lack of a sound reference point against which to evaluate conduct facilitates continuance of harmful practices infringing children's human rights. These rights are sourced in the liberal canon, such as the rights to bodily inviolability, sexual integrity and choice, equality, dignity and healthy sexual development, and in the Convention on the Rights of the Child (United Nations 1989), to which 196 nations are parties (United Nations 2016). The most damaging consequence of absence of a sound definition is the exploitation of this uncertainty by those individuals, groups or even cultures who would wish to justify certain categories of child sexual abuse on grounds that are specious, yet which are difficult to expose without a powerful and theoretically based conceptual model. A sound conceptual model with sufficient consensus can act as a bulwark against such claims, constitute a reference point for future discussion, and enable future progress.

Current Examples of Different Interpretations of the Concept of Child Sexual Abuse: Three Major Dimensions of Variance

The concept of child sexual abuse is complex and contested, and is therefore subject to multiple interpretations. Accordingly, it has been defined differently in international policy instruments, prevalence studies, legislation, and national policy documents. Often, the concept is expressed in abstract terms; in other cases, it is articulated through a series of more concrete expressions. A brief review of some of the major definitions used, both by international organisations, and in major prevalence studies, illustrates these differences (Mathews and Collin-Vézina 2017). Analysis of the differences shows there are three major dimensions of variance which must be considered by any attempt to create a sound conceptual model and definition. These are[6]:

- First, the definition of the *construct* of child sexual abuse (in particular, variance in the child's age, the relationship between child and abuser/limiting abuse to adult abusers only, and whether an element of sexual gratification is present);
- Second, definition of the *acts* and experiences which constitute child sexual abuse (in particular, variance in whether the acts are limited to contact acts only, or also include non-contact acts and if so which); and
- Third, definition of *consent* (in particular, variance in whether the concept of consent is present, and if so, how it is expressed).

Definitions Used by International Organisations Different approaches can be seen in definitions used by international bodies. Several examples show these dimensions of variance regarding the construct of child sexual abuse, the acts included in the concept of child sexual abuse, and the approach to consent. In 1999, the World Health Organization (1999, pp. 15–16) defined child sexual abuse as:

> the involvement of a child in sexual activity that he or she does not fully comprehend, is unable to give informed consent to, or for which the child is not developmentally prepared

[6] Bolen and Scannapieco (1999) identified three aspects in which definitions varied: an upper age limit at which sexual abuse occurred (varying from 15 to 17); the level of contact qualifying an incident as child sexual abuse (ranging from penetrative acts only, through a broad spectrum to whether the respondent experienced "unwanted acts" or "sexual things"); and whether the study restricted child sexual abuse to acts by a person of a set age difference (ranging from no restriction, to offenders aged at least 3–5 years older, to adults only). They did not consider different approaches to consent.

and cannot give consent, or that violates the laws or social taboos of society. Child sexual abuse is evidenced by this activity between a child and an adult or another child who by age or development is in a relationship of responsibility, trust or power, the activity being intended to gratify or satisfy the needs of the other person. This may include but is not limited to:

- the inducement or coercion of a child to engage in any unlawful sexual activity;
- the exploitative use of a child in prostitution or other unlawful sexual practices;
- the exploitative use of children in pornographic performance and materials.

In 2006, the World Health Organization (p. 10) stated that child sexual abuse is:

> the involvement of a child in sexual activity that he or she does not fully comprehend, is unable to give informed consent to, or for which the child is not developmentally prepared, or else that violates the laws or social taboos of society. Children can be sexually abused by both adults and other children who are – by virtue of their age or stage of development – in a position of responsibility, trust or power over the victim

Then, in 2011, the United Nations Committee on the Rights of the Child (2011) elaborated on the meaning of "sexual abuse" for the purpose of interpreting and applying the Convention on the Rights of the Child article 19 (the right to freedom from violence). It stated (p. 10):

> Sexual abuse and exploitation includes:
>
> (a) The inducement or coercion of a child to engage in any unlawful or psychologically harmful sexual activity;
> (b) The use of children in commercial sexual exploitation;
> (c) The use of children in audio or visual images of child sexual abuse;
> (d) Child prostitution, sexual slavery, sexual exploitation in travel and tourism, trafficking (within and between countries) and sale of children for sexual purposes and forced marriage.
>
> Many children experience sexual victimization which is not accompanied by physical force or restraint but which is nonetheless psychologically intrusive, exploitative and traumatic. Sexual abuse comprises any sexual activities imposed by an adult on a child, against which the child is entitled to protection by criminal law.
>
> Sexual activities are also considered as abuse when committed against a child by another child, if the child offender is significantly older than the child victim or uses power, threat or other means of pressure. Sexual activities between children are not considered as sexual abuse if the children are older than the age limit defined by the State party for consensual sexual activities.

Of these definitions, the approach in 2011 by the United Nations Committee on the Rights of the Child is clearly the most detailed. It combines abstract concepts and concrete examples. Among other things, it makes it clear that child sexual abuse is present where:

- Inducement or coercion can be physical or non-physical, violent or non-violent;
- Sexual abuse may be legally prohibited, but is present whenever there is psychological harm;
- Non-contact and contact abuse is included (for example, involvement in audio and visual images may not always involve contact between abuser and child);
- Traditional cultural practices are not exempt and will constitute child sexual abuse (forced marriage);

- Other historical practices, even if commonly practiced in extreme circumstances, remain child sexual abuse (e.g., trafficking and sale);
- In this definition, there is no express use of the concept of consent; instead the focus; is on coercion and its implicit breach of true consent;
- In this definition, there is no requirement for sexual gratification;
- Other children can commit child sexual abuse, with abuse of power for coercion being the defining feature;
- Consensual sex between children over the age of consent in the jurisdiction is not considered sexual abuse.

This United Nations Committee definition is overall very sound in its approach to the construct, to the acts which can constitute child sexual abuse, and to the nature of consent. However, for reasons I provide below, *genuinely consensual* sex between children who are aged *under* a jurisdiction's lawful age of consent should also be understood as not being abusive.

Definitions Used in Epidemiological Studies Similarly, different approaches to the concept of child sexual abuse can be seen in definitions used in epidemiological studies, even those by leading international figures. Several examples show these dimensions of variance in the construct, the acts, and the approach to consent.

The Construct of Child Sexual Abuse: The Child's Age Studies have expressed the age of the "child" or of "childhood" differently. Most studies, including many across cultures, have defined childhood as including all those aged under 18, or aged up to 18, therefore including all children including those aged 17 and excluding those aged 18 and over (Dube et al. 2005; Finkelhor et al. 2015; Ji et al. 2013; Radford et al. 2013; Sumner et al. 2015). However, some have used a cut-off of 17 (i.e., limiting experiences to those occurring before turning 17, rather than 18: McGee et al. 2002). Others have used a cut-off of 16, limiting experiences to those occurring before turning 16 (Denholm et al. 2013; Dunne et al. 2009; Rosenman and Rodgers 2006). While some jurisdictions use 16 as the lawful age at which a child can provide consent to sex, this is not especially relevant to studies attempting to gauge the prevalence of child sexual abuse.

The Construct of Child Sexual Abuse: Acts by Adults Only, by Those Several Years Older, or by Anyone Some studies limit their scope by asking about acts by adults only (e.g., MacMillan et al. 1997). Others include both adults, and other children or adolescents aged at least a specified number of years older than the child (e.g., Dube et al. 2005). Many others include adults and any other adolescents or children (Finkelhor et al. 2015; McGee et al. 2002).

The Acts Which Constitute Child Sexual Abuse: Contact Sexual Abuse Only Several studies have limited the measurement of sexual abuse to events involving contact abuse only. For example, in the multi-country Violence Against Children Studies (Sumner et al. 2015), sexual violence was relatively narrowly defined to include contact experiences only, and was broadly categorized into two categories of any sexual violence, and pressured or forced penetrative acts. The broader concept of "sexual violence" was defined as: "unwanted touching, unwanted attempted sex, pressured/coerced sex, and forced sex" with "sex" defined as vaginal/anal penetration by the penis, hands, fingers, mouth, or objects, or oral penetration by the penis". There were slightly different definitions used in Swaziland: (penetration of vagina/anus by penis only) and Malawi (oral, vaginal, or anal sex or vaginal/anal object insertion). Similarly, the Adverse Childhood Experiences Study (USA) (Dube et al. 2005) adapted questions from the earlier study by Wyatt and Peters (1986). The question was introduced and had four dimensions as follows:

> Some people, while they are growing up in their first 18 years of life, had a sexual experience with an adult or someone at least 5 years older than themselves. These experiences may have involved a relative, family friend, or stranger. During the first 18 years of life, did an adult, relative, family friend, or stranger ever:
>
> (1) touch or fondle your body in a sexual way,
> (2) have you touch their body in a sexual way,
> (3) attempt to have any type of sexual intercourse with you (oral, anal, or vaginal), or
> (4) actually have any type of sexual intercourse with you (oral, anal, or vaginal)?

The Adverse Childhood Experiences International Questionnaire (ACE-IQ) adopts the same approach with slight wording changes.[7] These definitions also restrict the concept of the abuser to adults or others aged at least 5 years older, therefore excluding other children and adolescents.

The Acts Which Constitute Child Sexual Abuse: Contact and Non-contact Sexual Acts In contrast, many studies include contact and non-contact acts. The Balkan Epidemiological Study of Child Abuse and Neglect (BECAN) used the definition of child sexual abuse from the ICAST-C instrument. This covered questions about non-contact sexual abuse and contact sexual abuse; however, curiously, the instrument does not expressly ask a question about having any kind of sexual intercourse. The questions are framed as follows (Nikolaidos et al. 2018):

> Sometimes people do sexual things or show sexual things to children and adolescents. Thinking about yourself, has anyone familiar to you or an unknown person ever made you feel bad or uncomfortable by doing any of these things to you?
>
> 41. Made you upset by speaking to you in a sexual way or writing sexual things about you?
> 42. Made you watch a sex video or look at sexual pictures in a magazine or computer when you did not want to?
> 43. Made you look at their private parts or wanted to look at yours?
> 44. Touched your private parts in a sexual way, or made you touch theirs?
> 45A. Made a sex video or took photographs of you alone, or with other people, doing sexual things?
> 46. Tried to have sex with you when you did not want them to?

[7] The ACE-IQ asks four questions, as follows: 1. Did someone touch or fondle you in a sexual way when you did not want them to? 2. Did someone make you touch their body in a sexual way when you did not want them to? 3. Did someone attempt oral, anal, or vaginal intercourse with you when you did not want them to? 4. Did someone actually have oral, anal, or vaginal intercourse with you when you did not want them to? Accessible at: http://www.who.int/violence_injury_prevention/violence/activities/adverse_childhood_experiences/en/

Similarly, the Juvenile Victimization Questionnaire (the JVQ) contains contact and non-contact sexual acts. The JVQ is the instrument designed by David Finkelhor, the most experienced researcher in this field. The JVQ has been used in repeated national studies in the USA, and in studies in other countries. It has gone through several iterations, with questions being refined and added over time. Regarding sexual abuse, the latest version of the JVQ asks a series of eight items as follows, with three other items about internet harassment (Finkelhor et al. 2015):

S1) Sexual Assault by Known Adult: At any time in your life, did a grown-up you know touch your private parts when they shouldn't have or make you touch their private parts? Or did a grown-up you know force you to have sex?

S2) Sexual Assault by Unknown Adult: At any time in your life, did a grown-up you did not know touch your private parts when they shouldn't have, make you touch their private parts or force you to have sex?

S3) Sexual Assault by Peer/Sibling: Now think about other kids, like from school, a boy friend or girl friend, or even a brother or sister. At any time in your life, did another child or teen make you do sexual things?

S4) Forced Sex (Including attempts): At any time in your life, did anyone try to force you to have sex; that is, sexual intercourse of any kind, even if it didn't happen?

S5) Flashing/Sexual Exposure: At any time in your life, did anyone make you look at their private parts by using force or surprise, or by "flashing" you?

S6) Verbal Sexual Harassment: At any time in your life, did anyone hurt your feelings by saying or writing something sexual about you or your body?

S7) Statutory Rape & Sexual Misconduct: At any time in your life, did you do sexual things with anyone 18 or older, even things you both wanted?

S8) Has anyone ever had sex or tried to have sex with you when you didn't want it, when you were very high, drunk, or drugged?

Like the JVQ, the Sexual Abuse and Violence in Ireland study instrument (McGee et al. 2002) used a list of 12 specific questions, covering both contact and non-contact acts. The scale was introduced to participants as being about "prevalence of unwanted sexual experiences in childhood, i.e. prior to age 17":

1. Did anyone ever show you or persuade you to look at pornographic material (for example, magazines, videos, internet etc.) in a way that made you feel uncomfortable?
2. Did anyone ever make you or persuade you to take off your clothes, or have you pose alone or with others in a sexually suggestive way or in ways that made you feel confused or uncomfortable in order to photograph or video you?
3. Did anyone expose their sexual organs to you?
4. Did anyone masturbate in front of you?
5. Did anyone touch your body, including your breasts or genitals, in a sexual way?
6. Did anyone try to have you arouse them, or touch their body in a sexual way?
7. Did anyone rub their genitals against your body in a sexual way?
8. Did anyone attempt to have sexual intercourse with you?
9. Did anyone succeed in having sexual intercourse with you?
10. Did anyone, male or female, make you or persuade you to have oral sex?
11. Did anyone, male or female, make you or persuade you to have anal sex?
12. Did anyone put their fingers or objects in your vagina or anus?

Consent Various bodies of knowledge align in setting a high threshold for true consent, incorporating at least some of these insights. The WHO policy definitions (2006, 1999) include three situations where consent is not present: sexual activity the child does not fully comprehend, is unable to give informed consent to, or for which the child is not developmentally prepared. Finkelhor (1979b) posited that the essence of child sexual abuse lies in the inability of the child to provide full informed consent and the lack of true freedom to accept or decline participation.[8]

Epidemiological studies vary in whether the concept of consent is included, and how it is expressed. Some make no reference to the concept of consent. Others do refer it, sometimes using terminology asking whether the experience was "wanted", or that engendered feelings of discomfort or distress or confusion. The use of these terms is intended to exclude developmentally normal play and consensual peer-peer acts from the concept of child sexual abuse. However, these approaches may not be sufficient to capture acts and experiences that are abusive and non-consensual. The international policy documents adopt a broader concept of consent, making it clear that consent turns on not only the child's subjective experience, but also developmental concepts such as the child not fully comprehending the act, being unable to give informed consent to it, or not being developmentally prepared for it. Neither policy includes specific details of circumstances under which a child's consent would be absent.

Similar to the policy approach, but with further helpful qualification, criminal laws in many jurisdictions set a high threshold for consent. For example, in Canada, the Criminal Code makes clear that not only must true consent be fully, freely and voluntarily given; it will be void if obtained by threat, intimidation or abuse of authority, and it will also be voided if consent was initially given but then withdrawn by words or conduct (RSC 1985, c C-46, s 273). This more nuanced approach is consistent with philosophical understandings of the concept of consent (Archard 1998; Beyleveld and Brownsword 2007; Miller and Wertheimer 2010; Wertheimer 2003). In terms of consent being "fully" given, medical law indicates the level of knowledge required to constitute full consent. To be lawfully entitled to give her or his own consent to medical treatment, a child must possess sufficient understanding and intelligence to fully understand what is proposed (AC v Manitoba 2009 SCC 30; Secretary, Department of Health and Community Services v JWB (1992) 175 CLR 218).

Articulation of the Challenge in Interpreting the Concept of Child Sexual Abuse The preceding discussion has shown that even the more generally accepted approaches in key epidemiological studies and policy documents, and in legal principles, there are important differences creating plenty of room for debate. Overall, there are three major dimensions of variance and conceptual dispute, summarised in Table 2.1. These three major dimensions of conceptual variance will be focus points for attention and conceptual analysis in the next section, and must be accommo-

[8]Ondersma et al. (2001, p. 711) seemed to accommodate individual variance in capacity to consent by resorting to the bedrock assumption that there are societal beliefs that children do not possess the maturity to provide true consent, and require protection from those who would exploit that vulnerability.

dated by any conceptual model of child sexual abuse. It is useful to summarise these differences, point to the important conceptual and normative questions they raise, and indicate what conclusions will be reached by the subsequent analysis, before presenting the more comprehensive analysis.

Construct of Child Sexual Abuse First, there are different definitions of the construct of child sexual abuse, with particular variance in the child's age, the relationship between the child and the abuser, and the element of sexual gratification. Variance in this dimension raises several questions about how the construct of child sexual abuse should best be conceptualised.

- At what age, or under what circumstances, is an individually properly seen as a "child"? Can a 17 year old be a victim of child sexual abuse? Approaches to age not only differ by the age specified, but are limited by chronological age and do not consider individual developmental stage or attributes, which may be problematic.
- Must the offender be an adult, or several years older than the child, to have inflicted child sexual abuse, or can an adolescent or a similarly-aged peer, or even a younger peer, also inflict child sexual abuse? Some studies have limited their examination of child sexual abuse to acts by an adult; others have limited the concept to acts by someone at least 5 years older; others do not apply any restriction to the age of the person.

A nuanced examination of the construct of child sexual abuse must therefore consider two aspects of this dimension. Regarding the first question, it is not a simple matter to settle on an "age of childhood" and an "age of adulthood" for these purposes. Despite this, there are good reasons to conclude that the age at which childhood should best be considered to end is 18, rather than 16 or 17. However, in complex factual scenarios, as will be shown, it may be necessary to also consider a particular child's psychosocial capacities as well as her or his chronological age, to be able to conclude whether "sexual abuse" has occurred; this is particularly relevant in cases of peer-to-peer consensual activity. On the second question, the analysis presented below will show there is no scientific, logical or ethical reason to limit acts of sexual abuse to those by adults, or by other children aged a certain number of years older than the child.

The Acts that Constitute Child Sexual Abuse Second, there is variance in definitions of the acts which constitute child sexual abuse. There is some common ground, such as the inclusion of intercourse between adults and young children. However, epidemiological studies vary in whether non-contact acts are included, and in which non-contact acts qualify as child sexual abuse. Policy documents appear to encompass a broader range of acts as child sexual abuse, including any sexual act that violates a society's laws; this, together, with a normally broad range of criminal law offenses covering a multiplicity of sexual acts both contact and non-contact, ostensibly enables inclusion of many more kinds of acts within CSA. However, non-contact acts may be excluded by a jurisdiction's laws, and some epidemiological studies have also excluded them from consideration.

Table 2.1 Dimensions of conceptual variance in definitions of child sexual abuse in epidemiological studies, policy definitions, and legal frameworks

Dimension of variance	Epidemiological studies	Policy documents	Legal frameworks
Dimension 1: Definition of the construct of CSA use of the child's age use of the relationship between the child and the person who abuses the child use of an element of sexual gratification	the defined upper age of the child varies (e.g., before 18; before 17; before 16) the defined relationship varies (e.g., anyone of any age; anyone at least 5 years older; any adult, relative, family friend or stranger at least 5 years older; adult only) definition of an element of sexual gratification normally not present; sometimes incorporated by stating "in a sexual way"	the child's age is never stipulated the defined relationship is always expressed to include any adult, and any child (or any child who is older or uses "power, threat or other pressure", or who is in a "position of responsibility, trust or power") definition of an element of sexual gratification normally not present, with one exception	in criminal law, the child's age is always stipulated but can vary; the defined relationship is always expressed to include anyone; and sexual gratification is normally not present in civil law, the child's age is always stipulated but can vary; the defined relationship varies (e.g., anyone; a person in a position of authority); and sexual gratification is normally not present in child protection law, the child's age is always stipulated but varies; the defined relationship varies; and sexual gratification is normally not present
Dimension 2: The definition of the acts which constitute CSA	definition of acts constituting CSA varies in detail (e.g., long list of 12 specific acts; shorter list of 4–6 specific acts; intercourse only) definition of acts constituting CSA varies in nature (e.g., contact acts only; contact acts and non-contact acts)	definition of acts constituting CSA varies in detail (e.g., longer list of acts described conceptually; single, shorter conceptual description) definition of acts constituting CSA varies in nature (more detail; less detail)	in criminal law, the term "CSA" is typically not used, but there is a wide range of different sexual offences which specify acts in civil law, the term "CSA" is typically not defined in child protection law, the definition of acts constituting CSA varies (e.g., not defined; limited to criminal acts)

(continued)

Table 2.1 (continued)

Dimension of variance	Epidemiological studies	Policy documents	Legal frameworks
Dimension 3: Consent whether the concept of consent is present in the definition if present, the way the concept of consent is defined	definition of consent varies in presence (i.e., not stated explicitly; stated explicitly) definition of consent varies in nature (e.g., when you did not want to; when they should not have; when you did not want them to; were you ever forced)	definition of consent varies in presence (i.e., not stated explicitly; stated explicitly) definition of consent is consistent when present ("does not fully comprehend, is unable to give informed consent to, or for which the child is not developmentally prepared")	in criminal law, the definition of consent is consistent in both presence and nature (requiring full, free and voluntary agreement and absence of threat, intimidation and abuse of power) in civil law, the concept of consent is not defined or stated explicitly in child protection law, the concept of consent is not defined or stated explicitly

- Can sexual abuse be constituted by non-contact acts? If so, what is it about the acts that makes them both sexual, and abusive?
- What qualities make an act sexual?
- Is an element of sexual gratification required at the time of the act, and if so, of whom?
- Does the child have to experience immediate harm, discomfort or distress to qualify the acts as sexual abuse?
- Are acts of grooming "sexual acts" if they are not inherently sexual, but are done for the purpose of cultivating a relationship in which the sexual abuse can take place?
- Are cultural practices, like child marriage and female genital cutting, properly considered species of child sexual abuse, and if so, why?
- Is it significant to differentiate between "abuse", and other terms like "assault" and "harassment", and if so, why?

A nuanced examination of the acts that can constitute child sexual abuse will show that it is illogical to limit "sexual acts" to those involving physical contact. This most prominent aspect of variance can therefore be finally resolved. Careful examination will also elaborate on the other questions noted here, to present a coherent analysis of what acts should, and should not, be regarded as constituting child sexual abuse.

Consent Third, there is variance in the presence and nature of the concept of consent. The requirement that an individual has the power to provide or withhold consent to certain kinds of acts in relation to her or his body is a hallmark of all free societies. In matters regarding one's own body, and how it is used, consent embodies political principles of liberty and equality, and the ethical principle of autonomy (self-rule), the breach of which is the basis for a range of legal entitlements. Whether an individual in fact has the capacity to provide consent to a sexual act depends on whether she or he possess a range of cognitive and psychosocial attributes; if she or he does not have these attributes, they cannot provide genuine consent and any argument to the contrary is simply logically, ethically and legally incoherent. On the other hand, if a particular individual does possess these attributes which endows them with the capacity to provide consent, the secondary question then concerns the nature of the circumstances required to demonstrate that they have in fact provided genuine consent to specific sexual acts under certain conditions of fairness. In sum, the core questions arising here are:

- Under what circumstances, if any, might a child have capacity to provide genuine consent to a sexual act?
- Under what circumstances might a particular individual child who possesses the capacity to provide genuine consent, actually provide consent?

A nuanced examination of the dimension of consent will show that it is incoherent and simply wrong to claim that all children possess the capacity to provide consent to all kinds of sexual acts, and to claim that all children possess the capacity to provide consent to any particular kind of sexual act. Similarly, most children will not have the capacity to in fact provide consent. At the same time, careful analysis will also show that – especially when the context involves any adult, or any other individual who is in a position of power over the child – even an older individual child with the capacity to provide consent, may not be able to actually provide genuine consent, because of the abuse of power involved, and the absence of circumstances of sufficient fairness.

A Conceptual Model and Definition

The analysis in this section presents a conceptual model of child sexual abuse that considers and responds to each of the three dimensions of variance identified in the literature, and key questions presented by the manifestations of these variations. The conceptual model has four components, which equate to four conditions, all of which must be present for an act or experience to be categorised as child sexual abuse. The model presented here draws on extensive analysis set out in a recently published article (Mathews and Collin-Vézina 2017).

This model can also be used in reverse. If one is considering whether a specific phenomenon should be classed as a species of child sexual abuse, the four conditions can be considered in turn to see if they are present in cases of that type as a whole (for example, all cases where a father rapes his 10 year old daughter), or, in some more complex instances, in a particular case which may have distinctive characteristics that differ from other cases in that category (some cases of female genital cutting may differ from others).

The dimensions of variance and the model conditions which respond to them are as follows.

Dimension of variance / dispute	Conceptual model conditions/components, and brief summary
Dimension 1: Definition of the construct of child sexual abuse	Condition 1 The individual must be a child
Variance in the child's age	All individuals aged under 18 should be understood as being a child for this purpose. However, the concept of "child" should be analysed from dual perspectives of individual developmental capacity and legal chronological age of adulthood. This becomes especially significant when dealing with complex cases.
Dimension 1: Definition of the construct of child sexual abuse	Condition 4 When an act is "abuse"
Variance in the age of the abuser and/or their identity or relationship to the child	Acts constituting abuse will usually also constitute an assault; however, the concept of "abuse" contains a heightened wrongfulness which flows from four indicia: the presence of a relationship of power; the child being in a position of inequality; the child's vulnerability being exploited to her or his detriment; and absence of true consent. One significant consequence of this understanding of the term is that child sexual abuse can be inflicted by persons including but not limited to parents, caregivers and other adults.
Dimension 1: Definition of the construct of child sexual abuse	Condition 3 When is an act "sexual"
Variance in whether sexual gratification is included	Acts are sexual in a range of circumstances involving either or both the person's gratification, and or the child's experience. The concept of "sexual" should embrace contact and non-contact acts done for the purpose of seeking or obtaining physical or mental sexual gratification, whether immediate or deferred temporally or spatially, as well as the child's experience of the act.
Dimension 2: Definition of the acts which constitute child sexual abuse	Condition 3 When is an act "sexual"
Contact acts only, or contact acts and non-contact acts	Acts are sexual in a range of circumstances involving either or both the person's gratification, and or the child's experience. The concept of "sexual" should embrace contact and non-contact acts done for the purpose of seeking or obtaining physical or mental sexual gratification, whether immediate or deferred temporally or spatially, as well as the child's experience of the act.
	Condition 4 When an act is "abuse"
	Acts constituting abuse will usually also constitute an assault; however, the concept of "abuse" contains a heightened wrongfulness which flows from four indicia (see above)
Dimension 3: Consent	Condition 2 No capacity to provide true consent, or capacity present but not given.

(continued)

Dimension of variance / dispute	Conceptual model conditions/components, and brief summary
Variance in whether consent is present in the definition, and if so, how defined	In general, individuals aged under 18 should be understood as possessing either no or diminished capacity to provide true consent to sexual activity. This diminished capacity begins at zero from birth, continues to be at this level through early childhood, and only gradually increases with sufficient age and developmental maturity in the particular individual's case, and even in these cases is further dependent on the circumstances of each individual interaction. Even in cases where the child has any level of capacity to provide consent in the abstract, the concept of consent and its application in the specific case must be considered at both face validity of apparent surface consent, and experientially by asking whether true consent exists, which requires full, free, voluntary and uncoerced participation in all the circumstances.

A Summary of the Model

The conceptual analysis and model of child sexual abuse designed by Mathews & Collin-Vézina (2017) concluded that "child sexual abuse" is present when four conditions are met. This model was informed by a multidisciplinary review and conceptual analysis, and I have drawn on it here in this chapter. The model is also underpinned by a recognition of the scientific evidence about the prevalence and etiology of child sexual abuse, its consequences for health and behaviour in various different forms, and the lived experience of children who experience sexual abuse. It is also animated by a commitment to dignity and individual human rights including liberty, equality and bodily inviolability, and ethical values of autonomy, beneficence, non-maleficence and justice. It also takes the view that a conceptual model of "child sexual abuse" that does not recognise this scientific evidence, and that does not recognise and seek to protect these values, is simply irrational in any meaningful sense and is therefore invalid.

The four conditions are as follows.

1. **The individual must be a child**. In general, all individuals aged under 18 should be understood as being a child for this purpose. However, the concept of "child" should be analysed from dual perspectives of individual developmental capacity and legal chronological age of adulthood. This becomes especially significant when dealing with complex cases (e.g., sexual activity between adolescent peers of equal power, or cases where an individual is aged under 18 but older than a society's low age of adulthood).

2. **No capacity to provide true consent, or capacity present but not given**. In general, individuals aged under 18 should be understood as possessing either no or diminished capacity to provide true consent to sexual activity. This diminished capacity begins at zero from birth, continues to be at this level through early childhood, and only gradually increases with sufficient age and developmental maturity in the particular individual's case, and even in these cases is further dependent on the circumstances of each individual interaction. Even in cases where the child has any level of capacity to provide consent in the abstract, the concept of consent and its application in the specific case must be considered at both face validity of apparent surface consent, and experientially by asking whether true consent exists, which requires full, free, voluntary and uncoerced participation in all the circumstances.
3. **Acts are sexual in a range of circumstances involving either or both the person's gratification, and or the child's experience**. The concept of "sexual" should embrace contact and non-contact acts done for the purpose of seeking or obtaining physical or mental sexual gratification, whether immediate or deferred temporally or spatially, as well as the child's experience of the act. This is significant for several reasons including the insistence that an act does not have to involve physical contact between offender and child to constitute child sexual abuse.
4. **Acts constituting abuse will usually also constitute an assault; however, the concept of "abuse" contains a heightened wrongfulness**. The term "abuse" possesses a heightened wrongfulness derived from the unconscionability of the acts, which flows from four indicia: the presence of a relationship of power; the child being in a position of inequality; the child's vulnerability being exploited to her or his detriment; and absence of true consent. One significant consequence of this understanding of the term is that child sexual abuse can be inflicted by a wider range of persons than simply parents, caregivers and other adults.

The Methodology of Conceptual Analysis and the Nature of a Conceptual Model

Child sexual abuse is both a composite concept, and contains three constituent concepts: "child"; "sexual"; and "abuse". To avoid being arbitrary, developing a conceptual model requires a sound methodology. The methodology adopted here is conceptual analysis, informed by evidence from social science, ethics and the child's experience. The model also draws on law and developmental psychology in analysing the concept of "child"; considers CSA involving sexual gratification and non-gratification in analysing when an act is "sexual"; and considers etymological distinctions and the legal concept of unconscionability in analysing what constitutes "abuse".

Conceptual analysis aims to clarify complex concepts whose meaning is contested (Wittgenstein 1968). The complex concept must be broken down into its constituent parts to more precisely understand the issues, and to enable a formulation of more robust interpretations of them (Beaney 2015). A conceptual model should describe the fundamental features of the phenomenon. It should provide a clear and reasoned basis to interpret a complex phenomenon that is otherwise prone to ambiguity and inconsistency in instrumentalisation. The model should integrate a range of concepts to assist in understanding the subject matter from a sound theoretical standpoint. In this way, a conceptual model can better isolate and integrate the relevant components of a multiform concept. Applied here to the concept of child sexual abuse, a well-reasoned conceptual model can enable clearer, more precise, shared communication about its meaning and scope, informed by both normative and diagnostic perspectives. It can then be a clearer subject of research, prevention, legal and policy responses, and social norm formation.

Therefore, the conceptual analysis rests on the sub-concepts of "child", "sexual" and "abuse", and integrates analysis of the three dimensions of conceptual variance: the construct of child sexual abuse (including elements of the "child", the relationship between the child and the person inflicting the abuse, and the element of sexual gratification); definitions of the acts constituting CSA; and consent. This approach takes the primary unit of analysis as the child's subjective experience of the acts (experiential validity); however, our analysis will also be informed by objective consideration of whether an act should be considered to be child sexual abuse, and why or why not (face validity). This analytical process also enables identification of "central cases" of child sexual abuse (i.e., those with which all rational people can agree), and "peripheral cases" (i.e., those on which rational people may disagree). For illustrative purposes regarding specific concepts, we use examples of core cases (those that are definitely child sexual abuse), clearly excluded cases (those that are definitely not child sexual abuse), and more complex cases.

A Conceptual Model of Child Sexual Abuse

On this model, the presence of all four conditions is required for an act or experience to be conceptualised as "child sexual abuse", and all four must therefore be considered together.

Condition 1. The Person Must Be a Child This condition will clearly be satisfied in many cases. In all societies it is uncontentious that a person under a low age is a "child", and therefore acts of sexual abuse inflicted on that person will be committed against a child. It is impossible to make a rational case, for example, that any infant or other young or pre-pubertal individual is not a child. These are core cases of child sexual abuse.

However, there are complexities. Is a person a "child" because of their legal status alone, their developmental status (cognitive, psychosocial), or both? Suppose a society's law set an unusually low age of 12 as the age of adulthood. Based on all we know from the social science evidence of the nature and sequelae of child sexual abuse, and of children's lived experience of sexual abuse, we would maintain that a child in that society (or any other) who is 12, 13, 14, 15, 16 or 17 years old can be a victim of child sexual abuse. So, the status of childhood cannot rest solely on a legal principle about the legal age of adulthood. While different cultures have different standards of expected child conduct, and hence have different chronological ages of legal adulthood, what seems a sounder theoretical basis for our purposes is that the person's status as a child should be sourced in her or his developmental state and capacity to provide true consent to the acts, *as well as* her or his status in law based simply on chronological age.

We should acknowledge at this point the scientific literature which has shown that adolescents of around age 15 to 16 are generally able to exhibit adult-like cognitive processing ability, but are still in the early stages of developing the psychosocial capacity to understand long-term consequences and regulate conduct (Albert and Steinberg 2011). In particular, adolescents' capacity to withstand social and emotional pressures is still developing (Albert and Steinberg 2011; Steinberg, et al. 2017). In decision-making contexts, adolescent cognitive capacity may generally be considered as "adult-like", but adolescent behavioral decisions tend to be directed by still-developing self-regulatory capacity and the emotional and social rewards offered by the context (Casey et al. 2008).

The significance of this is that legal rules about the status of the individual in society (the legal age of adulthood or majority) and about the individual's ability to participate in sexual activity (the legal age at which a child may provide consent) are relevant, but not always solely determinative. Further, while a society's laws may set the same age of adulthood and sexual consent, they may set a different, lower age at which a child may give sexual consent than for adulthood in general; but for our purposes here, we are primarily concerned with the individual's general status as a child. Similarly, one's status as a child cannot rest solely on developmental capacity: an adult with impaired capacity who experiences sexual assault has not experienced "child sexual abuse"; rather, she or he is an adult with impaired capacity who experienced assault.

One difficulty this position presents is that individuals have different developmental capacities, so a child who is developmentally advanced or "adult-like" may not be perceived as a "child" despite being younger than the age set by a legal or social norm. A resolution of this difficulty is that a child who has in fact attained adult-like developmental capacity, but whose age is under the legal threshold of adulthood, should still be classed legally and socially as a child, and an individual who interacts sexually with that person should be held to have breached a legal and social norm. So, a 15 year old of "advanced" or "adult-like" psychosocial development, in a society where the legal age of adulthood is 16, should still be classed as a child for this purpose.

A second difficulty this position presents would arise in a society with an unusually low legal age of majority. The developmentally advanced 15 year old in a society where the legal age of majority is unusually low, e.g., 14, seems to meet both criteria for adulthood, and this is an example of a complex case. In general, it is evident that the complex cases of defining childhood in the broader endeavour of conceptualising child sexual abuse arise most prominently when a person is in the teenage years; she or he is no longer clearly a child, nor clearly an adult. The inherent challenges produced by the developmental phase of adolescence will arise again in considering other concepts below.

Overall, this first condition can be presented as the question: Is the person *either* developmentally a child, *or* considered a child at law or by the society's norms? On this basis:

- *core cases* (i.e., where the individual is clearly a "child") exist wherever a person is both developmentally a child (and so cannot provide true consent), *and* is below the legal age of adulthood;
- *core cases* (i.e., where the individual is clearly a "child") will also exist wherever a person is *either* developmentally a child (and so cannot provide true consent), *or* is below the legal age of adulthood;
- *clearly excluded cases* (i.e., where the individual is clearly not a "child") exist where a person is *both* developmentally not a "child" (due to their psychosocial development and ability to provide true consent), *and* is above the legal age of adulthood in that particular society, *and* is considered by the society's norms not to be a child;
- *complex cases* (i.e., where the individual is neither clearly a "child", nor clearly an "adult") exist where a hypothetical 15 year old of "advanced" psychosocial development lives in a society with a legal age of adulthood higher than 15.

As should be clear from this analysis, the more nuanced characterisation of who should be considered a child can repel the kinds of rhetorical arguments favoured by those who inflicted abuse, or who would seek to do so, that the victim is "not a child" or "is old enough" or "is old enough to know what she is doing".

Condition 2. True Consent Must Be Absent The condition of consent overlaps with the condition of "abuse", and should be considered with that concept. Here, though, we can explain why the concept of consent is important, and articulate its nature. We can also isolate examples of core cases where consent is absent, of clearly excluded cases where consent is present, and of complex cases where it is more difficult to conclude whether consent is present or absent. It may seem redundant to articulate whether consent is absent in cases of child sexual abuse. Indeed, at the outset we can point out that in the great majority of cases, it will be very clear that the child does not have the capacity to provide consent, and so cannot in fact provide consent, and does not provide consent; and that in other cases even where a child may have capacity to consent, she or he does not in fact provide consent. However, to develop a conceptual model, it is necessary to articulate the reasoning behind conclusions, to isolate the nature of consent and its operationalisation, and distinguish between cases where consent is clearly absent, others where it may be present, and others where it is more difficult to conclude. It is also necessary because it assists in identifying any situations where a child may have capacity to provide consent to sexual activity, and therefore may in limited circumstances be able to in fact provide consent; this is important in identifying what will and will not be abusive, which is related to a child's rights to expression and autonomy, and which is relevant to the legitimate boundaries of legal and moral prescriptions.

The concept of consent is important because it so central to this entire context. The presence or absence of consent to sexual activity is relevant to whether child sexual abuse has or has not occurred. In this sense, the centrality of consent to legitimise sexual activity is just as important here – although arguably more so, due to children's relative position of inequality and vulnerability on multiple dimensions – as it is to interactions involving adults. If true consent is absent, a key condition for demonstrating that a sexual act is abusive will be satisfied. However, if true consent is present, then a condition required to show that a sexual act is abusive will not be met.

The concept of consent is important because it embodies fundamental political principles of liberty and equality, and the ethical principle of autonomy (self-rule), in matters regarding one's own body. A breach of these principles constitutes morally wrongful conduct by the person inflicting the abuse, and is the basis for conferring on the victim a range of legal entitlements.[9] Whether an individual in fact has the capacity to provide consent to a sexual act depends on whether she or he possess a range of cognitive and psychosocial attributes. The primary question in analysing a particular case then is first to ask whether the individual possesses these attributes. If she or he does *not* have these attributes, they cannot provide genuine consent and any argument to the contrary is simply logically, ethically and legally incoherent. On the other hand, if a particular individual *does* possess the cognitive and psychosocial attributes and therefore has the general capacity to provide consent, the principles of liberty and equality mean that in general, this individual should be entitled to provide consent to sexual acts, and should not be punished for engaging in non-harmful sexual behavior. The secondary question, for an individual child who has the capacity to provide consent, then concerns the nature of the circumstances required to demonstrate that she or he in fact provided genuine consent to specific sexual acts under certain conditions of fairness.

The Nature of Consent, and the Capacity to Provide Consent To answer the first question of whether it is possible that a child may have capacity to provide genuine consent to a sexual act, in specific circumstances, we must articulate the nature of consent. Philosophical understandings of what is required for an individual to provide genuine consent to an interaction, and to a sexual interaction, evince agreement on several requirements around cognition, freedom or voluntariness, and lack of coercion (Archard 1998; Beyleveld and Brownsword 2007; Miller and Wertheimer 2010; Wertheimer 2003). In sum:

- for an individual child to have capacity to provide true consent to a sexual act, she or he must fully comprehend the nature of the acts. This comprehension clearly has a cognitive dimension, in that the child must understand the nature of

[9] There are of course exceptions to this, such as emergency medical treatment, and unavoidable incidental bodily contact in society, e.g., brushing against a person in a crowded train.

the acts. However, it may on a broader interpretation also have a psychosocial application, in that the child must have an affective understanding the consequences of the acts, at least in understanding their short-term and long-term consequences);
- for an individual child who has capacity to provide consent, to in fact provide true consent, the consent must be freely and voluntarily given. In particular, for consent to be "true" or "genuine", it must not be coerced in any sense. Coercion can take any one or more of multiple forms. Coercion can occur through threats, intimidation, manipulation or pressure, and can be manifested physically, emotionally, psychologically, cognitively, spiritually, or economically, or by abuse of any kind of authority).

Informed by these insights, and by an understanding of child development, we can draw some conclusions:

- At the broadest level, we can conclude that it is incoherent and simply wrong to claim that all children possess the capacity to provide consent to all kinds of sexual acts, and to claim that all children possess the capacity to provide consent to any particular kind of sexual act. As a consequence, most children, and especially those of more tender years and nascent psychosocial capacity, will not have any capacity to provide consent.
- In general, individuals aged under 18 should be understood as possessing either no or diminished capacity to provide true consent to sexual activity, such that they cannot provide consent.
- This diminished capacity is completely absent at birth, and continues to be so through early childhood.
- This diminished capacity will only gradually increase with developmental maturity in the particular individual's case, and even in these cases is further dependent on the circumstances of each individual interaction.
- Even in cases where a more developmentally advanced and usually older child has any level of capacity to provide consent to sexual activity in the abstract, the concept of consent and its application in the specific case must then be considered at both face validity of apparent surface consent, and experientially by asking whether true consent exists, which requires full, free, voluntary and uncoerced participation in all the circumstances.

If a Particular Child Has the Capacity to Provide Consent, Under What Circumstances Might She or He Actually Provide Genuine Consent? As a result of the analysis above, it should be clear that capacity to provide consent to sexual acts requires a suite of cognitive attributes, and arguably some psychosocial attributes as well. Further, the factual giving of true consent can only occur in circumstances where there is genuine circumstantial equality and fairness, and no coercion of any kind. This has the result that when the context involves individual who is in a position of sufficient power over the child – whether physical, emotional, psychological, cognitive, spiritual, or economic, even an older individual child with the capacity to provide consent will not be able to in fact provide genuine consent. This will generally include any adult,[10] because of the inherent abuse of power involved, and the absence of circumstances of sufficient equality and fairness.

Overall, this condition can be presented as the question: Is the child unable to give true consent to the acts due to lack of capacity, *or* did the child have capacity but not in fact give true consent to the acts? On this basis:

- *core cases* in which true consent is absent would include those in which a child *either* does not have capacity to give consent, *or* has capacity but does not in fact give true consent to the sexual acts due to one or more of the vitiating factors. In most cases, because of their developmental stage, a child will not have the capacity to provide true consent to sexual acts; accordingly, any child lacking the necessary comprehension or developmental capacity cannot give true consent. In other cases, even where a child has the capacity to consent to a sexual act because of her or his advanced psychosocial state, true consent to the specific acts with the specific person will in fact be lacking due to clear coercion, force or pressure.
- *clearly excluded cases* – that is, cases where true consent is present – are those where the child *both* has capacity to give consent, *and* actually does give consent to the specific acts with the specific person at the specific time, and there are no factors vitiating true consent. Such cases would include two developmentally mature children who have capacity to consent, who in fact provide full, free and voluntary consent to the acts in which they engage, and where there are no factors vitiating consent including any aspect of coercion.
- *complex cases* arise where it is not clear whether the child possesses capacity, or in fact provides consent.
  - It may be difficult to determine whether an individual child has capacity to provide consent. My view - and this has been proposed elsewhere (Wertheimer 2003) - is that in these situations, a conservative view is generally to be preferred, given the gravity of the consequences of concluding incorrectly that a child does in fact have capacity.
  - It may be difficult to determine if consent is vitiated by coercion or not, in complex cases where it may be difficult to conclude if participation is truly consensual or is a product of coercion, or some kind of social or economic pressure. Is true consent present where a psychosocially advanced child engages in transactional sex to survive (Lalor 2004; Williams et al. 2012), or is this "consent" voided by abuse of authority? Is true consent present if a child captured in combat allies herself with a captor to avoid violation by other soldiers and survive life-threatening danger (Denov 2006)? In such cases, different interpretations of the nature of consent and coercion will produce different conclusions about whether true consent is present. Arguably,

[10] There are potential exceptions to this; for example, a developmentally advanced adolescent girl who is about to turn 18, who is in a relationship with a young man who has just turned 18, where the girl is as or more cognitively, emotionally, psychosocially and sexually advanced than the man.

these are circumstances of "constrained choice", regarding a matter of such gravity that the choice made by the child in such a situation is not truly free, and is coerced by the person inflicting the abuse and by the accompanying circumstances. A broader interpretation of the nature of consent, as provided above, would hold that these situations do in fact involve breach of true consent.

As should be clear from this analysis, the more nuanced characterisation of what is required to give true consent can repel the kinds of rhetorical arguments favoured by those who inflicted abuse, or who would seek to do so, that she or he "wanted it", "consented", "asked for it", or "knew what he was doing". However, they can also repeal simplistic arguments that adolescents are not able to have genuinely consensual sex under certain quite stringent circumstances of equality, and absence of coercion and any other vitiating factor.

Condition 3. The Acts Must Be Sexual Consistent with epidemiological, policy and legal approaches, the nature of the act must concern sex. A sexual act may directly involve the child when conscious, or when unaware (e.g., voyeurism, filming). While in most cases the child will perceive the acts as sexual (exemplifying subjective experiential validity), this is not required to qualify the acts as such (e.g., the child may be asleep, preverbal, or acculturated to the "normalcy" of the acts, exemplifying objective face validity). On our analysis, non-contact acts can clearly be sexual, including photography, filming, exposure, and voyeurism, being of or related to sex, and can very clearly involve sexual gratification. As well, it is clear that non-contact acts can cause significant harm. It is therefore simply neither logical nor accurate to limit the concept of child sexual abuse to contact acts only (e.g., Violato and Genuis 1993).

A related aspect of this condition is whether sexual gratification is required to qualify an act as "sexual". Sexual gratification may be intended either directly for the abuser, or the victim, or both. It may be intended indirectly through other acts, such as the production or supply of child pornography for others' gratification. Is sexual gratification required to constitute an act as "sexual", and if so, must the gratification be immediate, and must it be related to the primary abuser?

The WHO (1999) definition requires intent to gratify the abuser, and some epidemiological definitions refer to acts done "in a sexual way", implicitly embodying gratification. On our analysis, sexual gratification is a clear marker of a sexual act; we would add that sexual gratification may be mental or physical, and may be immediate or deferred in time and space. Moreover, consistent with some studies (e.g., McGee et al. 2002), we would include as "sexual acts" some non-contact acts which may not themselves be inherently "sexual", but which are undeniably done *for the purpose* of having sex, such as verbal demands and other forms of coercive manipulation to engage in sex or attempts to do so. Many acts of grooming will also fall into this category, especially where the act – whether inherently sexual or not; e.g., exposure to pornography, compared with giving a child a gift – is done with the clear intention to groom the child, and where the person seeks or obtains mental or physical sexual gratification from the act. This analysis is consistent with some of the non-contact questions used in prevalence studies (e.g., McGee et al. 2002; Zolotor et al. 2009).

Finally on this point, it is possible that some acts may not clearly be related to obtaining sexual gratification, but they may be inherently related to sex and may be legitimately perceived by the child as a sexual act, whether at the time or retrospectively. One example of this is female genital cutting (FGC). While not typically conducted to obtain sexual gratification for any person, it sometimes is, and in all cases is inherently related to sex (Barstow 1999; Toubia 1994). The complex question of whether FGC should be considered as constituting child sexual abuse will be further discussed in Chap. 6. However, at this point, we can observe that while FGC takes different forms and has different sequelae, a particular individual could legitimately perceive it as a sexual act because of its primary focus on sexual function and its impact on physical and psychological sexual capacity.

On this analysis, three categories of act should be interpreted as being "sexual":

1. any act where the person inflicting the abuse seeks or obtains any level of mental or physical sexual gratification, whether immediate or deferred in time and space;
2. any act where the person seeks sexual gratification for another person (e.g., the child victim, or a third party who is directly involved in the abuse of the child, or a third party who is involved more distally such as a consumer of child pornography);
3. any other act, which may not meet either of the sexual gratification categories, but which is legitimately experienced by the child as a sexual act.

Overall, this condition can be presented as the question: Is the act done to seek any degree of physical or mental sexual gratification for the abuser or for another person, or is the act otherwise legitimately experienced by the child as a sexual act?

On this basis:

- *core cases* of "sexual acts" would include all acts of sexual intercourse and any other contact or non-contact act where the person seeks or obtains sexual gratification for any person, and acts done expressly to groom a child with any level of mental or physical sexual gratification.
- *core cases* of "sexual acts" would also include non-contact verbal or written requests or demands for sexual acts, and other communication of sexual writing or imagery transmitted in person or electronically (e.g., sexting between romantic partners, and the sharing of sexual imagery).
- *clearly excluded cases* (i.e., acts that are not "sexual") include developmentally normal play between children involving mere curiosity about bodily functions; other acts involving no sexual gratification and not experienced by the child as sexual (e.g., parental bathing with young children).
- *complex cases* include ostensibly non-sexual acts done without a clear purpose of either gratification or grooming, *and* which are not clearly experienced by the child as sexual. One example is a grandfather touching his grandson's genitals as

a gesture of pride, found acceptable by some but not all members of a cultural group (Ahn and Gilbert 1992).

As should be clear from this analysis, the more nuanced characterisation of what constitutes a sexual act can repel rhetorical arguments favoured by those who inflicted abuse, or who would seek to do so, that the acts are not sexual, or are legitimate cultural practices.

Condition 4. The Acts Must Constitute Abuse What features make an act constitute abuse compared to a different concept like assault? This is an important question, partly because many widely understood examples of child sexual abuse do not involve physical contact, so exclusive use of the term assault will exclude many experiences from the concept of child sexual abuse.

In the conceptual model, Mathews and Collin-Vézina (2017) considered the term "abuse" to be a broader and more distinctively wrongful concept than other concepts like assault. This is not to minimise the seriousness of assaults and we expressly accept that many assaults, ranging from less severe to extremely severe incidents, will simultaneously constitute abuse and therefore will be just as wrongful. As well, we agreed with Ondersma et al. (2001) that physical or psychological harm is not *required* to qualify an act as abuse, and hence as child sexual abuse. Sexual abuse experiences will usually involve harm, but may not always (Finkelhor 1979b). Different experiences will involve different levels of harm; they may also last for a limited time (Ondersma et al. 2001), or be latent (Negriff et al. 2014). A different kind of harm characterises all manifestations of child sexual abuse, namely, the breach of the individual child's rights to bodily inviolability, and of rights to autonomy, freedom and dignity.

There are areas of conceptual overlap between the terms abuse and assault, but there is also a distinctive quality to the concept of abuse. It is instructive to consider etymological differences. The concept of "assault' is defined as a physical attack (Oxford English Dictionary 2016). Similarly, in criminal law, assault is defined to mean actual or threatened application of force to another's body. The focus is on application of physical force. Accordingly, there is an immediate problem with studies which merely use the term "assault" to capture the full spectrum of child sexual abuse experiences. This is because many accepted forms of child sexual abuse like voyeurism, exhibitionism, or an adult stimulating themselves while not touching the child, are not "assaults" in either a linguistic or legal sense, and would be excluded.

In contrast, the concept of "abuse" means the improper use, misuse, or wrongful taking advantage of (Oxford English Dictionary 2016). The first consequence of this is that because "abuse" is *not* limited to acts of physical contact, the concept of abuse is much wider than assault, as it embraces a broader range of experiences. So, sending pornographic images to a child, or sending such images of a child, can be sexual abuse, even if not sexual assault.

The second consequence is that it supports the contention there is something distinctive about the concept of "abuse" pointing to its higher degree of moral wrongfulness compared with the concept of assault, and the problematic term "unwanted" experience, which implies some abusive experiences are "wanted". Again, accepting that many sexual assaults will also constitute sexual abuse, the concept of "abuse" connotes an act which will often but not always involve a physical sexual assault, but which because of its improper nature, context and wrongful exploitation of an imbalance of power, is more serious than an assault. Significantly, the term "abuse" captures the power dynamics at play in the experience of events constituting of child sexual abuse. Accordingly, the term child sexual abuse encompasses various forms of sexual abuse experiences ranging in severity, power disparities, relational components and social determinants. On this theoretical basis, child sexual abuse can and should be perceived as an overarching term incorporating an array of specific experiences of sexual abuse (e.g., rape as a form of child sexual abuse; fondling as a form of child sexual abuse; exposure to pornography as a form of child sexual abuse, etc).

On this view, the heightened wrongfulness of sexual "abuse" derives from its distinctive feature of *unconscionability*. This unconscionability is a product of four indicia, which are recognised by special legal remedies developed to recognise interpersonal circumstances of oppression, pressure, or other vulnerability (Miglin v Miglin 2003 SCC 24).

First, abuse occurs within *a relationship of power*. There is something distinctive about sexual acts inflicted within a context of a relational power dynamic, as opposed to a context where there is no such relationship. "Abuse" occurs within a relationship of power involving closeness or dependence between offender and victim. This is consistent with definitions of CSA in civil law and in policy (WHO 2006, 1999). However, it contrasts with some epidemiological studies, which apply a narrower range of potential power relationships by excluding adolescent peers or romantic partners (Dube et al. 2005). Without seeking to be exhaustive, our analysis would maintain that the relational dynamic of power may exist, and be exploited, where the wrongdoer is in a position of power through a familial relationship (e.g., parent, adult family member, sibling); an institutional relationship (e.g., teacher, sports coach, clergy member); an economic relationship (e.g., employer); and a psychological relationship (e.g., a peer or romantic partner with greater psychological power). Arguably, there are two other, more generalised power dynamics: first, the dynamic between most adults and most children, based on differences in age, psychosocial development and social power; and second, the dynamic between female children and males, whether adolescent or adult, based on deep and long-held socio-cultural practices and dispositions concerning gender roles and sexism. Although experienced by girls and boys, and sometimes perpetrated by females, it is very clear that in most countries, child sexual abuse remains a profoundly gendered phenomenon.

The importance of the power dynamic is that it connects most immediately and deeply with a harm extending beyond the physical, to psychological and emotional violation. The breach of the power dynamic endows it with a deeper psychological or emotional force, giving it added gravity. On this conception, depending on the acts and the relationship between wrongdoer and child, most cases of sexual abuse will involve a sexual assault, but there may be cases of sexual assault that do not reach the level of abuse.

Second, abuse involves a *position of inequality*. Further elucidating the first element, this indicia is met when the abused child is in a position of fundamental disadvantage in relation to the person inflicting the abuse. Inequality can exist in several senses: age; physical, cognitive and psychological capacity; cultural inequality (e.g., caste); and gender inequality. The question of age differential is important. In a large proportion of cases, the offender is an adult, with inequality being clear in age, cognition, and other aspects. Other situations of abuse by a child on another child will also possess clear inequality, often by age, and physical, psychological and cognitive inequality. However, whereas some studies use an age differential to qualify an abuser on the implicit basis of inequality (Dube et al. 2005), on our analysis, age difference is not a precondition for inequality. Rather, abuse can be inflicted by a child of the same age, or by a younger child, if another condition of inequality and the power relationship are met. So, a sibling who commits incest against his (older or younger) sibling can occupy a relationship of power (familial, gender, physical, or psychological) and can be in a position of superiority through his victim's inequality; this would be abuse, rather than only assault. In contrast, a non-consensual sexual act by a peer on another peer, where the primary actor holds no superiority or relational power, could be sexual harassment, but not "abuse". A 13 year old girl who does not hold any relational superiority or power over a mature and self-possessed 17 year old boy at school, and who playfully slaps his bottom, does not exploit inequality or a power differential, but could be sexually harassing him.

Third, abuse involves *exploitation of vulnerability*, with the person taking advantage of the child's vulnerability and using their superior position to their benefit and to the child's detriment. An aspect of exploitation in this sense is that it degrades the child as a human being (Wood 1995). So, for example, a priest who commits sexual acts on a boy, and an authority figure who exposes a boy to pornography to groom him, each exploit the child's vulnerability and degrade him in a profound way. In contrast, the 13 year old girl's action with the 17 year old boy is likely not exploiting vulnerability or degrading him in a profound way.

Fourth, abuse involves an *absence of true consent*, in the senses discussed above. These indicia combine to create an overarching unconscionability, which in terms of sequelae can have resonance beyond the physical nature of the acts. Our contention about the significance of this unconscionability, and of "abuse", finds support in the growing evidence about heightened psychological injury from abuse by persons in relationships of power, responsibility and superiority (Edwards et al. 2012; Trickett et al. 2011; Trickett 2006).

Overall, this final condition about whether the act constitutes "abuse" can be presented as the question: Is the act marked by indicia of a relationship of power; the victim being in a position of inequality; exploitation of the victim's vulnerability; and absence of true consent? On this basis:

- *core cases* of abuse would include: any sexual act, whether involving physical contact or not, by any adult including authority figures e.g., teachers, clergy, coaches or supervisors in sports, cultural, arts or religious groups;

- *core cases* of abuse would also include any non-consensual sexual acts by another child who is in a superior position in a relationship of power and inequality;
- *clearly excluded cases* would include sexual acts between peers who each have capacity and who each provide genuine consent;
- *clearly excluded cases* would also include those where a non-consensual yet playful non-serious sexual act is committed by a peer who does not hold a superior position in any kind of power dynamic with the victim, where the victim does not have a meaningful position of inequality, and where the victim is not genuinely exploited;
- *complex cases* include those where a non-consensual sexual act is committed but is not clearly seriously improper or wrongful, and is done within a romantic relationship between peers where the power dynamic is generally equal, with no clear inequality or exploitation of vulnerability.

As should be clear from this analysis, the more nuanced characterisation of what constitutes abuse can repel rhetorical arguments favoured by those who inflicted abuse, or who would seek to do so, that the acts are lesser assaults, or are otherwise minimal physical transgressions.

Summary Definition

Any effort to develop a conceptual model of CSA must recognise not only its complexity, but the sensitivity of the topic and the potential significance of the model's influence on theory, research, policy, law and practice. This model does not in any way legitimise or minimize the seriousness of impermissible acts falling outside its parameters. Acts not characterised on this model as CSA can still involve violence and serious consequences requiring strong responses. Nevertheless, there is a clear need to improve shared understandings of the concept of CSA, for multiple domains of research, law, policy, prevention, and the establishment of social norms.

The analysis and theoretical grounding for this model promotes a deep, nuanced focus on the key concepts in this context. The analysis in Mathews and Collin-Vézina (2017) concluded that the concept of "child" should be analysed from dual perspectives of developmental capacity and legal chronological age of adulthood. The concept of consent must be considered at face validity of apparent surface consent, and experientially by asking whether true consent exists, which we argue requires full, free, voluntary and uncoerced participation. The concept of when acts are "sexual" should embrace contact and non-contact acts done for the purpose of seeking or obtaining physical or mental sexual gratification, whether immediate or deferred temporally or spatially, as well as the child's experience of the act. Finally, the term "abuse" is distinctive in possessing a heightened wrongfulness derived from the unconscionability of the acts, which in turn flows from four indicia: a relationship of power; the child being in a position of inequality; the child's vulnerability being exploited to her or his detriment; and absence of true consent.

On this approach, while instances of sexual assault and harassment will also often (but not always) constitute abuse, these understandings of the concepts individually and collectively constituting "child sexual abuse" distinguish the overarching it as a concept from others such as assault, harassment and victimization, and illustrate when and why an act or experience is more legitimately understood as child sexual abuse.

Child sexual abuse will always exist when:

1. the person is a child (from either or both developmental and legal standpoints);
2. there is no true consent (due either to lack of capacity to provide consent, or presence of capacity but lack of consent in fact);
3. the acts are sexual (being contact or non-contact acts done to seek or obtain physical or mental sexual gratification, whether immediate or deferred in time or space, or otherwise legitimately experienced by the child as a sexual act); and
4. the acts constitute abuse (due to the presence of a relationship of power, the child's position of inequality, and the exploitation of the child's vulnerability).

So, for example, a 9 year old girl will be a "child", unable to give true consent, and will experience sexual abuse in situations of incest, rape, and all other contact and non-contact acts that are done to seek physical or mental sexual gratification for any person, whether immediate or deferred in time or space, where those acts occur in a relationship of power, with the girl in an unequal position, with her vulnerability exploited in a profound way to the benefit of the other person and to her detriment. Accordingly, this would also include as child sexual abuse all acts done in relation to a child to create child pornography, involve the child in sex trafficking, prostitution or the sex trade. It would also include many instances of child marriage, and may extend to some instances of female genital cutting.

References

Adams-Tucker, C. (1981). A socioclinical overview of 28 sex-abused children. *Child Abuse and Neglect, 5*, 361–367.

Ahn, H., & Gilbert, N. (1992). Cultural diversity and sexual abuse prevention. *Social Service Review, 66*, 410–427.

Albert, D., & Steinberg, L. (2011). Judgment and decision making in adolescence. *Journal of Research on Adolescence, 21*(1), 211–224.

Angelou, M. (1969). *I know why the caged bird sings*. New York: Random House.

Archard, D. (1998). *Sexual consent*. Boulder: Westview Press.

Armstrong, L. (1978). *Kiss daddy goodnight: A speak-out on incest*. New York: Pocket Books.

Armstrong, L. (1994). *Rocking the cradle of sexual abuse*. New York: Addison-Wesley.

Barstow, D. (1999). Female genital mutilation: The penultimate gender abuse. *Child Abuse & Neglect, 23*, 501–510.

Barth, J., Bermetz, L., Heim, E., Trelle, S., & Tonia, T. (2013). The current prevalence of child sexual abuse worldwide: A systematic review and meta-analysis. *International Journal of Public Health, 58*, 469–483.

Basile, K., Smith, S., Breiding, M., Black, M., & Mahendra, R. (2014). Sexual violence surveillance: Uniform definitions and recommended data elements, version 2.0. *Atlanta: National Center for Injury Prevention and Control* Centers for Disease Control.

Beaney, M. (2015). Analysis. In: E. Zalta (Ed.), *The Stanford encyclopedia of philosophy*. Accessed on 1 Feb 2016 at http://plato.stanford.edu/archives/spr2015/entries/analysis

Beyleveld, D., & Brownsword, R. (2007). *Consent in the law*. Oxford: Hart Publishing.

Bolen, R. (2001). *Child sexual abuse: Its scope and our failure*. New York: Kluwer.

Bolen, R., & Scannapieco, M. (1999). Prevalence of child sexual abuse: A corrective meta-analysis. *Social Service Review, 73*(3), 281–313.

Borkowski, A. (1986). *Textbook on Roman law*. London: Blackstone Press.

Brownmiller, S. (1975). *Against our will: Men, women and rape*. New York: Simon & Schuster.

Brundage, J. (1987). *Law, sex, and Christian Society in medieval Europe*. Chicago: University of Chicago Press.

Burgess, A., Groth, A., Holmstrom, L., & Sgroi, S. (1978). *Sexual assault of children and adolescents*. Lexington: Lexington Books.

Butler, S. (1978). *Conspiracy of silence: The trauma of incest*. San Francisco: Volcano Press.

Casey, B. J., Jones, R. M., & Hare, T. A. (2008). The adolescent brain. *Annals of the New York Academy of Science, 1124*, 111–126.

Clemente, M., & Padilla-Racero, D. (2016). When courts accept what science rejects: Custody issues concerning the alleged "parental alienation syndrome". *Journal of Child Custody, 13*(2–3), 126–133.

Collings, S. (2009). See no evil, hear no evil: The rise and fall of child sexual abuse in the 20th century. *PINS, 38*, 61–73.

Committee on the Rights of the Child. (2011). *General comment No. 13 on the right of the child to freedom from all forms of violence*. Accessed on 1 Nov 2016 at http://www.ohchr.org/EN/HRBodies/CRC/Pages/CRCIndex.aspx

Conte, J. (1994). Child sexual abuse: Awareness and backlash. *Future of Children, 4*, 224–232.

Cromer, L. D., & Goldsmith, R. E. (2010). Child sexual abuse myths: Attitudes, beliefs, and individual differences. *Journal of Child Sexual Abuse, 19*(6), 618–647.

Dallam, S., & Silberg, J. L. (2016). Recommended treatments for "parental alienation syndrome" (PAS) may cause children foreseeable and lasting psychological harm. *Journal of Child Custody, 13*(2–3), 134–143.

De Francis, V. (1969). *Protecting the child victim of sex crimes committed by adults*. Denver: American Humane Association, Children's Division.

De Mause, L. (1976). *The history of childhood*. London: Souvenir Press.

Denholm, R., Power, C., Li, L., & Thomas, C. (2013). Child maltreatment and household dysfunction in a British birth cohort. *Child Abuse Review, 22*, 340–353.

Denov, M. (2006). Wartime sexual violence: Assessing a human security response to war-affected girls in Sierra Leone. *Security Dialogue, 37*(3), 319–342.

Dube, S., Anda, R., Whitfield, C., Brown, D., Felitti, V., Dong, M., & Giles, W. (2005). Long-term consequences of childhood sexual abuse by gender of victim. *American Journal of Preventive Medicine, 28*(5), 430–438.

Dunne, M., Zolotor, A., Runyan, D., Andreva-Miller, A., Choo, W.Y, Dunne, S., & Youssef, R. (2009). ISPCAN child abuse screening tools retrospective version (ICAST-R): Delphi study and field testing in seven countries. Child Abuse & Neglect, 33, 815–825.

Edwards, V., Freyd, J., Dube, S., Anda, R., & Felitti, V. (2012). Health outcomes by closeness of sexual abuse perpetrator: A test of betrayal trauma theory. *Journal of Aggression, Maltreatment & Trauma, 21*, 133–148.

Eisenberg, L. (1981). Cross-cultural and historical perspectives on child abuse and neglect. *Child Abuse & Neglect, 5*, 299–308.

Finkelhor, D. (1979a). *Sexually victimized children*. New York: The Free Press.

Finkelhor, D. (1979b). What's wrong with sex between adults and children: Ethics and the problem of sexual abuse. *American Journal of Orthopsychiatry, 49*(4), 692–697.

Finkelhor, D. (1984). *Child sexual abuse: New theory and research*. New York: The Free Press.
Finkelhor, D. (1986). *A sourcebook on child sexual abuse*. Beverly Hills: Sage.
Finkelhor, D., & Korbin, J. (1988). Child abuse as an international issue. *Child Abuse & Neglect, 12*, 3–23.
Finkelhor, D., Turner, H., Shattuck, A., & Hamby, S. (2015). Prevalence of childhood exposure to violence, crime, and abuse: Results from the national survey of children's exposure to violence. *JAMA Pediatrics, 169*(8), 746–754.
Fontes, L., & Plummer, C. (2010). Cultural issues in disclosures of child sexual abuse. *Journal of Child Sexual Abuse, 19*(5), 491–518.
Gagnon, J. (1965). Female child victims of sex offenses. *Social Problems, 13*, 176–192.
Gardner, J. (1986). *Women in Roman law and society*. London: Routledge.
Geffner, R. (2016). Editor's note about the special section. *Journal of Child Custody, 13*(2–3), 111–112.
Giarretto, H. (1977). Humanistic treatment of father-daughter incest. *Child Abuse and Neglect, 1*, 411–426.
Gillespie, M., Butler, R., & Long, R. (2008). *Maya Angelou: A glorious celebration*. New York: Random House.
Giovannoni, J., & Becerra, R. (1979). *Defining child abuse*. New York: Free Press.
Hanson, R. K., & Bussière, M. T. (1998). Predicting relapse: A meta-analysis of sexual offender recidivism studies. *Journal of Consulting and Clinical Psychology, 66*(2), 348–362.
Haugaard, J. (2000). The challenge of defining child sexual abuse. *American Psychologist, 55*(9), 1036–1039.
Herman, J. L. (1981). *Father-daughter incest*. Cambridge, MA: Harvard University Press.
Herman, J. L. (1997). *Trauma and recovery*. New York: Basic Books.
Herman, J. L., & Hirschman, L. (1976). Father-daughter incest. *Signs: Journal of Women in Culture and Society, 2*, 735–756.
Holmes, W., & Slap, G. (1998). Sexual abuse of boys: Definition, prevalence, correlates, sequelae, and management. *JAMA Pediatrics, 280*(21), 1855–1862.
Jay, A. (2014). *Independent inquiry into child sexual exploitation in Rotherham (1997–2013)*. http://www.rotherham.gov.uk/downloads/file/1407/independent inquiry case in Rotherham.
Ji, K., Finkelhor, D., & Dunne, M. P. (2013). Child sexual abuse in China: A meta-analysis of 26 studies. *Child Abuse & Neglect, 37*, 613–622.
Jorné, P. (1979). Treating sexually abused children. *Child Abuse and Neglect, 3*, 285–290.
Kempe, C. (1978). Sexual abuse, another hidden pediatric problem: The 1977 C. Anderson Aldrich Lecture. *Pediatrics, 62*, 382–389.
Kempe, R., & Kempe, C. (1984). *The common secret: Sexual abuse of children and adolescents*. New York: Freeman.
Kempe, C., Silverman, B., Steele, B., Droegemuller, W., & Silver, H. (1962). The battered-child syndrome. *Journal of the American Medical Association, 181*, 17–24.
Kinsey, A., et al. (1953). *Sexual behavior in the human female*. New York: Pocket Books.
Kitzinger, C. (1996). The Freudian coverup: A reappraisal. *Feminism & Psychology, 6*, 251–259.
Kleinman, T. G. (2016). Ethics on trial: A comment. *Journal of Child Custody, 13*(2–3), 147–153.
Labbé, J. (2005). Ambroise Tardieu: The man and his work on child maltreatment a century before Kempe. *Child Abuse & Neglect, 29*, 311–324.
Lalor, K. (2004). Child sexual abuse in sub-Saharan Africa: A literature review. *Child Abuse & Neglect, 28*, 439–460.
Landis, J. (1956). Experiences of 500 children with adult sexual deviation. *Psychiatric Quarterly Supplement, 30*, 91–109.
Lascaratos, J., & Poulakou-Rebelakou, E. (2000). Child sexual abuse: Historical cases in the Byzantine empire (324–1453 A.D). *Child Abuse & Neglect, 24*, 1085–1090.
Letourneau, E., Nietert, P., & Rheingold, A. (2016). Initial assessment of stewards of children program effects on child sexual abuse reporting rates in selected South Carolina counties. *Child Maltreatment, 21*, 74–79.

Lupton, M. (1998). *Maya Angelou: A critical companion*. Westport: Greenwood Press.
MacKinnon, C. (1979). *Sexual harassment of working women*. New Haven: Yale University Press.
MacMillan, H. L., Fleming, J. E., Trocme, N., Boyle, M. H., Wong, M., Racine, Y. A., Beardslee, W. R., & Offord, D. R. (1997). Prevalence of child physical and sexual abuse in the community. Results from the Ontario health supplement. *JAMA Pediatrics, 278*(2), 131–135.
Mathews, B., & Collin-Vézina, D. (2017). Child sexual abuse: Toward a conceptual model and definition. *Trauma, Violence, & Abuse, 21*, 1–18.
Mathews, B., & Kenny, M. (2008). Mandatory reporting legislation in the USA, Canada and Australia: A cross-jurisdictional review of key features, differences and issues. *Child Maltreatment, 13*, 50–63.
McGee, H., Garavan, R., de Barra, M., Byrne, J., & Conroy, R. (2002). *The SAVI report: Sexual abuse and violence in Ireland*. Dublin: Liffey Press.
McGee, H., O'Higgins, M., Garavan, R., & Conroy, R. (2011). Rape and child sexual abuse: What beliefs persist about motives, perpetrators, and survivors? *Journal of Interpersonal Violence, 26*(17), 3580–3593.
McGillivray, A. (2011). Children's rights, paternal power and fiduciary duty: From Roman law to the supreme court of Canada. *International Journal of Children's Rights, 19*, 21–54.
McGuire, D. (2011). *At the dark end of the street – Black women, rape and resistance*. New York: Vintage Books.
Mendelson, T., & Letourneau, E. (2015). Parent-focused prevention of child sexual abuse. *Prevention Science, 16*, 844–852.
Miller, A. (1998). *Thou shalt not be aware*. New York: Farrar, Straus and Giroux.
Miller, F. G., & Wertheimer, A. (2010). *The ethics of consent: Theory and practice*. Oxford: Oxford University Press.
Myers, J. (2004). *A history of child protection in America*. XLibris.
Negriff, S., Schneiderman, J., Smith, C., Schreyer, J., & Trickett, P. (2014). Characterizing the sexual abuse experiences of young adolescents. *Child Abuse & Neglect, 38*, 261–270.
Nichols, A. M. (2014). Toward a child-centered approach to evaluating claims of alienation in high-conflict custody disputes. *Michigan Law Review, 112*(4), 663–668.
Nikolaidos, G., Petroulaki, K., Zarokosta, F., et al. (2018). Lifetime and past-year prevalence of children's exposure to violence in 9 Balkan countries: The BECAN study. *Child and Adolescent Psychiatry and Mental Health, 12*, 1–15.
O'Donohue, W., Benuto, L. T., & Bennett, N. (2016). Examining the validity of parental alienation syndrome. *Journal of Child Custody, 13*(2–3), 113–125.
Olafson, E., Corwin, D., & Summit, R. (1993). Modern history of child sexual abuse awareness: Cycles of discovery and suppression. *Child Abuse and Neglect, 17*, 7–24.
Ondersma, S., Chaffin, M., Berliner, L., Cordon, I., Goodman, G., & Barnett, D. (2001). Sex with children is abuse: Comment on rind, Tromovitch, and Bauserman (1998). *Psychological Bulletin, 127*(6), 707–714.
Oxford English Dictionary. (2016). Accessed on 5 Jan 2017 at http://www.oed.com/
Pinker, S. (2011). *The better angels of our nature: The decline of violence in history and its causes*. London: Allen Lane.
Radford, L., Corral, S., Bradley, C., & Fisher, H. (2013). The prevalence and impact of child maltreatment and other types of victimization in the UK: Findings from a population survey of caregivers, children and young people and young adults. *Child Abuse & Neglect, 37*, 801–813.
Rosenman, S., & Rodgers, B. (2006). Childhood adversity and adult personality. *Australian and New Zealand Journal of Psychiatry, 40*, 482–490.
Rush, F. (1972). The myth of sexual delinquency. *Women: A Journal of Liberation, 3*(3), 38–39.
Rush, F. (1974). The sexual abuse of children: A feminist point of view. In N. Connell & C. Wilson (Eds.), *Rape: The first source book for women* (pp. 64–75). New York: Plume.
Rush, F. (1977). The Freudian cover-up. *Chrysalis, 1*, 31–45.
Rush, F. (1980). *The best kept secret: Sexual abuse of children*. Englewood Cliffs.

Rush, F. (1996). The words may change but the melody lingers on. *Feminism & Psychology, 6*(2), 304–313.

Russell, D. (1983). The incidence and prevalence of intra-familial and extra-familial sexual abuse of female children. *Child Abuse and Neglect, 7*, 133–146.

Russell, D. (1984a). The prevalence and seriousness of incestuous abuse: stepfather's vs biological fathers. *Child Abuse and Neglect, 8*, 15–22.

Russell, D. (1984b). *Sexual exploitation: Rape, child sexual abuse, and sexual harassment*. Beverly Hills: Sage.

Russell, D. (1986). *The secret trauma: Incest in the lives of girls and women*. New York: Basic Books.

Segal, L. (1996). Freud and feminism: A century of contradiction. *Feminism & Psychology, 6*(2), 290–297.

Sgroi, S. (1975). Sexual molestation of children: The last frontier in child abuse. *Children Today, 4*, 18–21.

Shackel, R. (2008). The beliefs commonly held by adults about children's behavioral responses to sexual victimization. *Child Abuse & Neglect, 32*, 485–495.

Steele, B., & Alexander, H. (1981). Long-term effects of sexual abuse in childhood. In P. Mrazek & C. Kempe (Eds.), *Sexually abused children and their families* (pp. 223–234). Oxford: Pergamon.

Steinberg, L., Icenogle, G., Shulman, E., Breiner, K., Chein, J., Bacchini, D., & Takash, H. (2017). Around the world, adolescence is a time of heightened sensation seeking and immature self-regulation. *Developmental Science, 21*(2).

Summit, R. (1983). The child sexual abuse accommodation syndrome. *Child Abuse and Neglect, 7*, 177–193.

Summit, R., & Kryso, J. (1978). Sexual abuse of children: A clinical spectrum. *American Journal of Orthopsychiatry, 48*, 237–251.

Sumner, S., Mercy, J., Saul, J., Motsa-Nzuza, N., Kwesigabo, G., Buluma, R., & Hillis, S. (2015). Prevalence of sexual violence against children and use of social services–seven countries, 2007–2013. *Morbidity and Mortality Weekly Report, 64*, 565–569.

Ten Bensel, R., Rheinberger, M., & Radbill, S. (1997). Children in a world of violence: The roots of child maltreatment. In M. Helfer, R. Kempe, & R. Krugman (Eds.), *The battered child* (5th ed., pp. 3–28). Chicago: University of Chicago Press.

Toubia, N. (1994). Female circumcision as a public health issue. *New England Journal of Medicine, 331*(11), 712–716.

Trickett, P. (2006). Defining child sexual abuse. In M. Feerick, J. Knutson, P. Trickett, & S. Flanzer (Eds.), *Child abuse and neglect: Definitions, classifications and a framework for research* (pp. 129–149). Baltimore: Brookes.

Trickett, P., Noll, J., Reiffman, A., & Putnam, F. (2001). Variants of intrafamilial sexual abuse experience: Implications for long term development. *Development and Psychopathology, 13*, 1001–1019.

Trickett, P., Noll, J., & Putnam, F. (2011). The impact of sexual abuse on female development: Lessons from a multigenerational, longitudinal research study. *Development and Psychopathology, 23*, 453–476.

United Nations. (1989). *Convention on the rights of the child*. New York: General Assembly of the United Nations. Accessed on 31 Mar 2016 at https://treaties.un.org/

United Nations. (2016). Convention on the Rights of the Child: Status as at 30 March 2016. United Nations Treaty Collection. Accessed on 31 Mar 2016 at https://treaties.un.org/

United Nations General Assembly. (2015). *Transforming our world: The 2030 agenda for sustainable development*. New York: United Nations. Accessed on 31 Jan 2016 at https://sustainabledevelopment.un.org/post2015/transformingourworld.

Veenema, T., Thornton, C., & Corley, A. (2015). The public health crisis of child sexual abuse in low and middle income countries. *International Journal of Nursing Studies, 52*(4), 864–881.

Violato, C., & Genuis, M. (1993). Problems of research in male child sexual abuse. *Journal of Child Sexual Abuse, 2*, 33–54.

Walker, G. (2013). Sexual violence and rape in Europe, 1500–1750. In S. Toulalan & K. Fisher (Eds.), *The Routledge history of sex and the body, 1500 to the present* (pp. 429–443). London/New York: Routledge.

Walsh, K., Zwi, K., Woolfenden, S., & Shlonsky, A. (2015). School-based education programmes for the prevention of child sexual abuse. *Cochrane Database of Systematic Reviews, 16*(4), CD004380.

Ward, T., & Beech, A. (2006). An integrated theory of sexual offending. *Aggression and Violent Behavior, 11*, 44–63.

Wertheimer, A. (2003). *Consent to sexual relations*. Vermont: Cambridge University Press.

Williams, T., Binagwaho, A., & Betancourt, T. (2012). Transactional sex as a form of child sexual exploitation and abuse in Rwanda: Implications for child security and protection. *Child Abuse & Neglect, 36*, 354–361.

Wittgenstein, L. (1968). *Philosophical investigations* (3rd ed.). Oxford: Blackwell.

Wood, A. (1995). Exploitation. *Social Philosophy and Policy, 12*, 136–158.

World Health Organization. (1999). *Report of the consultation on child abuse prevention*. Geneva, WHO. Accessed on 3 Mar 2016 at http://apps.who.int/iris/handle/10665/65900

World Health Organization and International Society for Prevention of Child Abuse and Neglect. (2006). *Preventing child maltreatment: A guide to taking action and generating evidence*. Geneva: WHO. Accessed on 3 Mar 2016 at http://www.who.int/violence_injury_prevention/publications/violence/child_maltreatment/

Wurtele, S. (2012). Preventing the sexual exploitation of minors in youth-serving organizations. *Children and Youth Services Review, 34*, 2442–2453.

Wyatt, G. (1985). The sexual abuse of afro-American and white American women in childhood. *Child Abuse & Neglect, 10*, 231–240.

Wyatt, G., & Peters, S. (1986). Issues in the definition of child sexual abuse in prevalence research. *Child Abuse & Neglect, 10*, 231–240.

Zolotor, A., Runyan, D., Dunne, M., Jain, D., Peturs, H., Ramirez, C., & Isaeva, O. (2009). ISPCAN child abuse screening tools Children's version (ICAST-C): Instrument development and multi-national pilot testing. *Child Abuse & Neglect, 33*, 833–841.

Part II
Theory: Multidisciplinary Understandings of Child Sexual Abuse and Regulatory Responses

Chapter 3
Political Theory and Public Health Theory

Abstract This chapter examines political theory, social justice, human rights and the responsibility of the state, incorporating a discussion of Locke, Mill, Rawls and the rights of children. It then focuses on Martha Nussbaum, her Capabilities Approach, and its incorporation of a special priority for children, and notes its implications for public policy about child sexual abuse. The chapter then explores public health theory, drawing on the origins of public health, and considering public health and its connected concepts of social justice and human rights, with reference to leading theorists. Then, it discusses public health law and its multidimensional capacity and role in this context, applying public health theory to child sexual abuse. Importantly, this chapter then discusses the concept of human dignity as articulated and defended by Charles Foster, concluding that dignity is an important useful concept in this context, in addition to the traditional ethical concepts and political theory as proposed by the Capabilities Approach. The key message of this chapter is that this broad range of theoretical concepts provide insights and justifications for a range of legitimate public policy and legal strategies to prevent, identify, and respond to child sexual abuse.

Keywords Child sexual abuse · Theoretical approaches concerning the role of the state and organisations · Political theory · Public health theory · Public policy · Social justice · Human rights · Children's rights · Human dignity · Capabilities approach · Marth Nussbaum · Rosalind Dixon · John Rawls · John Stuart Mill · John Locke · Richard Rorty · Charles Foster · The origins of public health · Cantemporary public health theory · Nancy Krieger · James Mercy · Lawrence Gostin

In human affairs, normative questions about what should be done, and the reasons it should be done, are unable to be finally settled to the satisfaction of every person. Any theoretical account moves from certain points of departure and must adopt certain values and philosophical preferences and reject or ascribe less priority to others. It is not possible to set down a theory that resists every alternative theory. Other perspectives adopting different social, philosophical and economic preferences would privilege other goals and outcomes. In this context, the theory I support is animated

B. Mathews, *New International Frontiers in Child Sexual Abuse*,
Child Maltreatment 7, https://doi.org/10.1007/978-3-319-99043-9_3

by the principles inherent in liberal theory, and in particular, an approach which prioritises children's rights to bodily inviolability and to protection from child sexual abuse and associated rights to autonomy and sexual dignity. My view is that societal structures that do not possess similar notions of rights do not bestow children with essential human qualities and entitlements as ends in themselves worthy of social and legal protection; and this creates an absence of fundamental protections and heightens children's vulnerability, both in theory and in practice. Other approaches inconsistent with the principles of liberalism and just societies must account for that incompatibility and its consequences for children in the context of sexual abuse.

As a theoretical construct, the idea that children have rights is a recent development, and remains contested in different societies and schools of thought. For the purposes of this book, I subscribe to the following ideas, which are shared by many (e.g., Brighouse 2002; Freeman 2007). First, children as individual humans should and do possess rights, because they have fundamental interests that need to be protected by rights. Prominent among these are interests in safety and bodily inviolability; sometimes referred to as welfare rights, or rights to protection. Underpinning this is the idea that recognition of one's rights also recognises one's dignity, essential humanity; this connects with the Kantian principle that individuals are ends in themselves, and are not means to others' ends. Second, possession of rights in a theoretical sense is a logical precondition to the conferral by legal and social systems of rights in an instrumental sense (i.e., rights that can be realised, protected and enforced). Third, these rights are important in that they provide a means to protect fundamental interests that children have (e.g., to safety, health, and education). This chapter discusses major principles from both classical liberal political philosophy, and leading political philosophers from the twentieth century and the first part of the new millennium.

Political Theory, Social Justice, Human Rights and the Responsibility of the State

The conceptual basis for any law or policy in human affairs in a liberal democratic state must be to promote the key principles with which a liberal polity is concerned. The fundamental principle is that individuals, including children, are free and equal and have rights to bodily inviolability and personal security and safety. They should also have equal opportunities which are not unfairly limited by chance, or by the typical dimensions of personhood which have historically been used to discriminate against people and perpetrate injustice and undesirable power imbalances: gender, race, religion, and class. The essence of the modern liberal project is to promote fundamental ideals of equality, freedom, dignity and autonomy, and in an applied sense to do this by creating social conditions that better advance these priorities. Social and legal measures can be devised to help create conditions of lived experience so that these goals are more likely to be achieved for more individuals, and especially those in traditional dimensions of vulnerability, overcoming the natural imbalances in opportunity bestowed by chance at birth. The creation of better opportunities for those born into less equal conditions translates to provision to these individuals of a higher chance of attaining core attributes of personal security, equality of opportunity, autonomy, and dignity. The benefits of creating such opportunities flow to individuals and broader society.

Liberal Thought Generally Liberal thought prioritises the idea that individuals have ultimate value, such that individuals' entitlements will prevail over those of groups or institutions. Liberal thought also insists that all human beings possess rights simply because they are human, regardless of cultural context. The value of equality posits that individuals should not be discriminated against, such as on grounds of race, gender or class. The idea of meliorism proposes that human reason can indefinitely enhance society and its institutions. Classical liberalism as espoused by Enlightenment philosophers including Locke, Kant and Mill, revolves around the defence of individual liberty and autonomy. The individual has freedom to pursue their own conception of their own good in their own way, and is entitled to be free from State interference. Liberty is the cornerstone of true freedom: of conscience, thought, expression, preferences, pursuits, and association. Kant viewed law as indispensable to securing individual freedom, ideally both in their relations with government and individuals within nations, and as between nations (Stacy 2009). Liberalism freed the individual from the untrammelled power of the monarch and instead gave individuals the right to develop their own worldview and personal plan of action that warranted protection unless it caused harm to others.

The conception of human existence that came to dominate was of the individual's rights and freedoms holding moral priority over the interests of society. Locke founded the idea of individual rights as occurring naturally simply by being human, and so honours the rights to life, liberty and property. Kant placed individuals at the top of a social hierarchy, being intrinsically possessed of dignity and equal worth, as being rational and autonomous individuals who exist as ends in themselves and not as a means to any collective goal. Mill's defining proposition was that the only purpose that justifies either the State or the populace interfering with an individual's acts is to prevent that person from harming others. The crucial value of individuality is that it promotes the quality of humanity. Individuality promotes richness, diversity, value to self and others, and development of human life. The private sphere is the province of individual autonomy, which was generally to be free from State interference.

While promulgated by Enlightenment theorists as applying in principle to all individuals, the application of such principles was often circumscribed. Some early theorists and political instruments conceived these rights as worthy of conferral only on white adult males, especially where they were property owners (Hunt 2007; Moyn 2011). This meant that in practice, for example, the atrocity of slavery remained tolerated, and the systematic racial and ethnic cruelties perpetrated in the name of colonialist expansion were endorsed. Women and children were also excluded from these early conceptions of rights-bearers. These limits were transposed to early formal declarations of rights, and their effects on social systems arguably reverberate to this day.

Opposition to these limits eventually gathered pace, but this took a long time. In the case of women, this was exemplified in scholarly work as early as Mary

Wollstonecraft's *A Vindication of the Rights of Woman* (1792), and continued through the 1860s by Mill in *The Subjection of Women* (1869). Significantly, on Hunt's account (Hunt 2007), this sensitization to others and an acceptance of a broadening of human rights was further enabled by literacy, the publication and reading of novels about individuals' suffering, and the development in readers of empathy for the suffering of individuals different to themselves, including women and children. For Hunt, an empathic connection with others, including those in previously excluded groups, assisted in expanding the liberal polity's circle of human concern.

In the mid-twentieth century, with the United Nation Declaration of Human Rights in 1948 and multiple instruments created in the 1960s, a body of international human rights law promoted the idea of human dignity and fundamental human rights considered essential for individual security and human flourishing, and protection from unjust state coercion and interference. These instruments had their genesis in the work of Enlightenment philosophers including Locke, Kant and Mill. Conceptually, they built upon the original declarations and bills of rights created in England in 1688, and in the US and France in the late 1700s, which were influenced by the politicians and writers who inspired them, including Jefferson, Paine, Wollstonecraft, and Montesquieu (Hunt 2007). As will be further discussed in Chap. 4, some of the twentieth century documents recognised children's needs and interests, although it would not be until 1989 that an international instrument dedicated to would transpire, with the United Nations Convention on the Rights of the Child.

Through the 1970s, further theoretical discussions of individuals' rights developed, with landmark works including John Rawls' *A Theory of Justice* (Rawls 1971), discussed below, and Ronald Dworkin's *Taking Rights Seriously* (Dworkin 1977) viewing rights as moral trumps over other interests. Henry Kempe (1977) echoed Wollstonecraft in his 'Vindication of the Rights of Children', focusing on methods to promote children's health from infancy through adolescence, advocating a range of measures to make health services widely accessible; perhaps reflecting the time, this recognition of children's rights did not appear to gain traction. Mirroring the political ignorance of children's rights, eminent philosophers in the 1970s and 1980s such as Dworkin and Okin barely considered the rights of children when they were deliberating about the nature and scope of individual rights (Freeman 2007). Rawls initially also ignored children, although as we will see, he was forced to reconsider this.

Subsequently, some significant developments occurred. UNESCO named 1979 as The Year of the Child, intending to draw attention to fundamental rights of children that needed urgent attention, such as the rights to education and malnutrition. The UNCRC was drafted over 10 years, was signed in 1989, and was soon ratified by almost every nation. Around this time, some began to consider the nature of children's rights in more detail, often in the context of legal systems and developments, but sometimes more in a theoretical sense (Archard 1993, 2004; Eekelaar 1986, 1992; Freeman 1980, 1983). In 2011, the Capabilities Approach to human development was proposed by arguably the world's leading philosopher, Martha

Nussbaum (2011). Following this, Dixon and Nussbaum (2012) declared that children's rights constitute a fourth frontier of justice.

In the broader arc of human experience, these developments are quite a sudden outpouring of a new understanding of children's rights within the liberal project. It can be useful to appreciate this when faced with natural frustration at the apparent lack of theoretical and practical progress in children's lives, and the. These concepts have taken too long to coalesce and there is much significant work that remains to be done. This is especially poignant when it can be seen that, while the earlier leading liberal theorists had not paid much attention to the experience or political position of children the crucial concepts animating an approach to children's rights and interests can be perceived in the both their candid comments and applied concepts. Nussbaum provides a most recent and relevant account, and I will discuss this shortly. However, core ideas and ideals animating a children's rights approach can be found in prominent thinkers from liberal thought. While children's rights and welfare have not explicitly occupied a great deal of time in these writings, both classical and more recent, there are sufficient acknowledgments of children's place in this theory on which we can construct an applied framework. While the theorists discussed below expound various principles over a timespan of several centuries, a common strand uniting their ideas is evident: a genuinely liberal society must not ignore wrongs committed against children by adults and by others, including by parents and caregivers. Notions of parental liberty should not be unduly privileged over children's rights to personal security. A just society must include measures to address the vulnerability of children to abuse and neglect, and to promote children's rights to dignity, security, egalitarian treatment, and to a decent opportunity in life.

John Locke: Children Have Rights to Life, Liberty and Security in a Liberal Society, and Parental Power Is Limited John Locke's Second Treatise of Government (1690) has as a starting point that people are born free and equal, meaning not that this is so in reality, but that a legitimate government must promote this value. For Locke, the legitimacy of government in a political society rested on its central concern to secure individuals' 'property', with 'property' embracing not only goods and realty, but the individual's life, liberty and security. The very reason for government's existence was to protect and secure the rights of the individual. This purpose of government marked the justifiable parameters of State action.

Within the family context, Locke stated that parental power extended only to govern children for their own "help, instruction, and preservation" (Locke 2003, p. 176); it did not extend to life, or death, or the child's liberties. The child's rights were acknowledged: 'The power of the father doth not reach at all to the lives, liberties and estates of the child, which is only in [the child's] own disposing.' Parental guardianship was conditional on being appropriately exercised, and so could be forfeited. These principles were ground-breaking at the time, given the social realities of children's lived experience (see Chap. 4), and given that on a broader scale, an institution as fundamental as education did not become compulsory in England until the 1880s. However, the principle of the child's liberty and right to security of the person – while often breached – can be seen as a logical and long-articulated principle in the liberal framework.

John Stuart Mill: Liberalism Must Protect Children in the Family Sphere The next prominent and influential proponent of children's rights was the influential theorist and campaigner John Stuart Mill. In 1859, in his famous work *On Liberty*, Mill demanded the protection of children from external injury (Mill 1998, p. 14). Significantly, despite all the other contexts in which children suffered various depredations – workplaces such as mines and factories, the street for the homeless and destitute, and other institutions such as orphanages – Mill identified the family sphere as the most important domain requiring State control to prevent abuse of power (Mill 1998, p. 116). Mill recognised the link between a distorted sense of parental claims over their children's bodies and lives, and the State's neglect to secure children's safety (Mill 1998, p. 116). These principles were consistent with Mill's harm principle, in which he demarcated the limit of the State's justifiable sphere of action, and the individual's sphere of protected activity. Mill's harm principle posited that the State may not intervene in an individual's behaviour provided it is only self-regarding and causes no harm to others. For Mill, the State could intervene to respond to a parent's behavior that harmed her or his child, but not in relation to behavior that did not. The parameters of what can constitutes sufficient 'harm' are slippery, and the methods of State intervention are numerous and may involve measures which are supportive as well as coercive. However, but one example Mill provides relates to the parental duty to ensure their child is educated (the reason being that the child has a right to be provided by their parent with an education and hence an opportunity to succeed in life; society also has a right not to have to support an uneducated child). If a parent could not pay for their child's education, this should be subsidized by the State.

John Rawls: The Fundamental Conditions of a Just Society John Rawls is widely viewed as the most significant political philosopher of the twentieth century. In A Theory of Justice (Rawls 1971), Rawls devised the tool of a thought experiment, using the twin concepts of the original position and a veil of ignorance, as a means of contemplating and arriving at the fundamental conditions of a society which would provide its citizens with a reasonable chance of equality and human flourishing. Rawls posited that if a group of rational people were placed in the 'original position' of having to design the fundamental characteristics of the society into which they were born, with these persons being situated behind a 'veil of ignorance' such that they did not know any of their personal or familial attributes on being born – such as their race, gender, creed, wealth, or class – then they would choose organizing political and economic principles for that society which would ensure equal basic liberties for all citizens (on Rawls' conception, confined to civil and political rights), equality of opportunity, and the 'difference principle': that social and economic inequalities are only just if they produce compensating benefits for all, and especially for the least advantaged members of society.

The benefit of Rawls's theory is that it aims to reveals some of the essence of what a just society must contain, stripped of self-serving motivations and vested interests produced by advantages conferred by birth. However, the actors in Rawls's original position are assumed to be in a position of physical and cognitive equality, and to be adults possessing rationality and agency. While they are contemplating what features a just society should possess to enable each rational agent to flourish to a minimal level, these actors do not contain those without moral or prudential rationality, and the task originally set by Rawls did not include the requirement to ensure justice and equality for those who lack these attributes. The 1971 theory reflected its author and time, with those in the original position stated to be 'heads of families', a major limiting factor which has been criticized (Okin 2004). As well, sex was not a characteristic placed behind the veil of ignorance, so that issues of gender equality and oppression were neither acknowledged nor considered by Rawls. Furthermore, and arguably even more problematically, Rawls initially stated that those who cannot enter agreements or contracts, including children, are not owed political justice. Where does this leave children generally, and in particular, children who suffer maltreatment, including sexual abuse? While it may be reasonable to conclude that this limited group of actors in the original position would choose principles of social organization which neither permit child sexual abuse nor allow it to go unaddressed, this gap in Rawls's model presented a conundrum that others would challenge (Okin 1989, 2004). Rawls was strongly criticised for simply assuming that family relations are just (Okin 1989, 2004).

Rawls's Revised Theory Acknowledges Children's Rights These criticisms prompted Rawls to consider some but not all familial injustices and power asymmetries. In *The Idea of Public Reason Revisited* (1999), Rawls acknowledges that the family is part of the basic structure of society to which the core principles of justice apply. This was because a central role, and therefore a duty, of parents is to raise and care for their children, and to ensure their moral development and education so that they can develop into responsible adult citizens. Rawls claimed that while political principles do not apply directly to the internal life of the family, they 'impose essential constraints on the family as an institution and so guarantee the basic rights and liberties, and the freedom and opportunities, of all its members…by specifying the basic rights of equal citizens who are the members of families. The family as part of the basic structure cannot violate these freedoms' (1994, p. 159). Significantly, Rawls explained that (1994, pp. 159–61):

> These principles do not inform us how to raise our children, and we are not required to treat our children in accordance with political principles…Surely parents must follow some conception of justice (or fairness) and due respect with regard to their children, but, within certain limits, this is not for political principles to prescribe. Clearly the prohibition of abuse and neglect of children, and much else, will, as constraints, be a vital part of family law…Just as the principles of justice require that wives have all the rights of citizens, the principles of justice impose constraints on the family on behalf of children who as society's future citizens have basic rights as such…the principles of justice still put essential restrictions on the family…adult members of families [are] equal citizens first…No institution or association in which they are involved can violate their rights as citizens…The equal rights

of women and the basic rights of their children as future citizens are inalienable and protect them wherever they are…If the so-called private sphere is alleged to be a space exempt from justice, then there is no such thing.'

These statements indicate that Rawls had come to accept that children possessed fundamental rights both within and beyond the family, and that it was important to recognize this. His statements about children's rights within the family, including the right to be free from abuse and neglect, are particularly notable. They show beyond any doubt that on his approach, there were fundamental limits on what parents were permitted to do in relation to their children, and that abuse and neglect should neither be permitted nor allowed to go unaddressed.[1]

Other theorists identified issues with the mechanics of Rawls's approach, while supporting its overall usefulness as a device for identifying principles of social justice. Okin (2004) herself defended liberalism as the organizing framework for society, arguing that 'liberalism properly understood, with its radical refusal to accept hierarchy and its focus on the freedom and equality of individuals, is crucial to feminism…consistent and fully developed liberalism, quite radically revised so as to include women, has great potential for feminism' (p 1546). Similarly, Nussbaum (2009) observed that, rather than being too focused on the individual, liberalism needed to pay more attention to the individuals within the family sphere.

Martha Nussbaum's 'Capabilities Approach' to Social Justice and Human Development, a Fourth Frontier of Children's Rights, and Special Priority for Children

The American pragmatist philosopher Richard Rorty had declared that (Rorty 1999, p. xxix): "What matters for pragmatists is devising ways of diminishing human suffering and increasing human equality, increasing the ability of all human children to start life with an equal chance of happiness." For Rorty, this approach required an ability to sympathise with others' pain, to have sensitivity to that pain, and to feel we owe a moral obligation to those who endure that pain.

This sensitivity to others' pain is echoed by Martha Nussbaum's 'Capabilities Approach' to social justice and human development (Nussbaum 2011). Nussbaum is arguably the world's leading contemporary political philosopher. At its core, her Capabilities Approach is concerned with ensuring that government secures, protects and fosters certain capabilities in each individual citizen, because without a certain level of these capabilities, it is not possible for an individual to lead a life of sufficient equality, dignity, autonomy and freedom. This approach also seeks to overcome

[1] In one respect, Rawls's revised outlook must be modified. Where Rawls refers to children's rights as future citizens, the reference should be to children as citizens. Children have status as citizens, being entitled to protection by the laws of their country, and being bound by legal duties themselves. Children's duties and entitlements do not accrue on majority, but are present throughout childhood. Legal principles recognise this, and often confer some rights before birth.

entrenched social inequalities embedded through unjust constructions favouring those in one group over another. The core duty of a legitimate government is to generate the circumstances under which these capabilities are created for all, and including for children.

Nussbaum's approach is substantially consistent with much of Rawls in its concern with a just ordering of society to overcome the inequalities and the injustices created by the accident of birth. In this sense, it is of the same liberal lineage in its concern to overcome traditional divisions of reality and opportunity based on class, gender, race and religion, and instead to enable a fairer conferral of opportunity to obtain meaningful values inherent to a dignified human life. However, Nussbaum moved beyond Rawls's consensus approach to the social contract, by being concerned with inequality generally, and by being more explicitly and consciously concerned with several dimensions of inherent inequality, including those in which there is a clear asymmetry of power. This attention took her beyond issues which are not commonly central to the liberal project.

Nussbaum's expansion of the circle of human concern is highly significant because it clearly embraces not only the interests of those with cognitive impairments; it also embraces a clear consideration of children's interests. In 2012, with her colleague Rosalind Dixon, she explicitly identified children's rights as a new fourth frontier of justice, after the three she had identified in 2006 (Dixon and Nussbaum, 2012).

The basis for this was children's special vulnerability, and the fact that the social contract model does not adequately cater for theorising entitlements in domains characterized by marked power asymmetry; children's special vulnerability means they are not the free independent and equal agents in the social contract model; their 'unusual vulnerability and powerlessness' requires a new approach to basic rights. Accordingly, the fundamental inequalities that may subsist within core societal structures such as the family must be addressed. An example of this is that to the extent that a traditional patriarchal family and the actions occurring within it cannot be reconciled with attainment by individuals within the family of the capabilities, then that structure must be radically re-assessed and its adverse effects remedied. Within the family context, Nussbaum maintains, like Mill, that any views which seek to preserve parental authority causing injustice are inconsistent with true liberalism, and must be remedied by a just society (Nussbaum 2011).

The Capabilities Approach, Children's Rights and Child Maltreatment At the core of Nussbaum's Capabilities Approach is a striving to nurture each individual's potential as a human being by ensuring the protection of a sufficient amount of the core capabilities required for each individual to deploy those attributes in their own life. The way the individual uses those capabilities is determined by their own choice; the prior concern is therefore to arrange social policy to ensure that all individuals have an adequate 'set of opportunities, or substantial freedoms' (Nussbaum 2011, p. 18) to exercise genuine autonomy and live a decent life.

For Nussbaum, there are ten core capabilities which are seen as necessary for an individual to live a decent life. The attainment of these capabilities does not require an equal measure of each capability across all individuals in society. Rather, it requires a minimum measure of each capability for each individual, without which the individual's dignified existence and capacity to flourish is compromised. Significantly, consistent with the Kantian ideal, each person is seen as an end in themselves, and is not a means to an end. The consequence of this is that social policy must primarily be focused on the needs of the individual, rather than, for example, the interests of the parents or the broader social group. This focus on the individual person's needs is required precisely because the group-based structures within society may in fact be the context and cause of individual injustice and suffering. The ten capabilities are, in summary form (Nussbaum 2011, pp. 33–34):

1. Life: being able to live a life of normal length
2. Bodily health: being able to have good health, nourishment and shelter
3. Bodily integrity: being able to be secure against violent assault including sexual assault and domestic violence; being able to move freely; having opportunities for sexual satisfaction and reproductive choice
4. Senses, imagination and thought: being able to think and reason in a way informed by education; being able to use thought in connection with material of one's own choice; being able to use one's mind freely and to have freedom of expression and choice
5. Emotions: being able to have attachments to people, to have feelings, and to love; freedom from impediments to emotional growth
6. Practical reason: being able to form one's own conception of the good and to critically reflect on one's own life plan; freedom of conscience and religion
7. Affiliation: being able to live with and interact with others, and to imagine another's situation (empathic development); freedom of assembly, freedom of speech; being able to enjoy social bases of self-respect through being seen as equal to others (freedom from discrimination on grounds of race, sex, sexual orientation, ethnicity, caste, religion, nationality)
8. Other species: being able to live with concern for the natural world
9. Play: being able to laugh, play, enjoy leisure and recreation
10. Control over one's environment: being able to participate in political choices, to possess property rights, and to seek employment on an equal basis with others

Without a minimum amount of certain goods, an individual child is unable to develop a cascade of other attributes, particularly cognitive and emotional skills. These then flow down into compromised development of other core capabilities. Some instances of a lack of a key capability will be particularly disadvantageous, creating what some have termed 'corrosive disadvantage' (Wolff and de-Shalit 2007), which produces a cascade of disadvantage by compromising or destroying other of the core capabilities. Here, Nussbaum urges focused investment of scarce resources. In addition, affiliation and practical reason are seen as being especially important capabilities that promote, and are necessary for, the attainment and use of others.

Nussbaum comments that 'capability-destruction in children is a particularly grave matter and as such should be off-limits' (Nussbaum 2011, p. 27), meaning those charged with the care of children must not be permitted to destroy their capabilities. As well, while accepting that parents have some degree of freedom to make decisions regarding their children, there are some types of activity which should not remain guarded by this private sphere: 'Some issues are, or should be, easy: we should all agree that domestic violence and child sexual abuse should be aggressively policed by the state' (Nussbaum 2011, p. 148). Nussbaum recognises that while the Capabilities Approach is concerned with the situation of all individuals in a society, as befits a theory flowing from political liberalism, it is 'concerned with entrenched social injustice and inequality, especially capability failures that are the result of discrimination or marginalization' (Nussbaum 2011, p. 19) and charges government and public policy with the task of improving the quality of all people's lives.

Child Development, Vulnerability, and Special Priority for Children's Rights For Dixon and Nussbaum (2012), the starting point for the Capabilities Approach is the simple fact that human beings are born into the world with multiple inchoate capacities that must be developed. The Capabilities Approach argues that these nascent abilities exert a moral claim, requiring support to be developed to the point at which they reach the threshold level of each capability specified on the capabilities list. Without this development, the individual's life potential is fundamentally compromised; she or he is rendered merely "a shadow of what they might be".

Dixon and Nussbaum (2012) consider the Capabilities Approach to be a species of a human rights approach, because it sees all human beings as having certain fundamental entitlements that cannot be undermined without causing injustice. It is relevant to both theory and law because it is concerned with "the formulation of basic political principles as a template for a nation's fundamental constitutional and legislative entitlements—as well as for norms in international law" (Dixon and Nussbaum 2012, p. 559). As articulated by Dixon and Nussbaum (2012), the Capabilities Approach gives a better theoretical justification for children's rights and the recognition of them as human rights, based on recognition of children's entitlement to respect for full human dignity. Animating this understanding is a more fully developed recognition of the centrality of early childhood and human development within this phase of life to the realization of a range of human capabilities. Their conclusion (Dixon and Nussbaum 2012, p. 559) is that the Capabilities Approach:

> provides a clear account not only for why children should be recognized as rights bearers, but also for why CROC and various national constitutions recognize various rights for children with sensitivity to both agency and welfare needs. The idea of agency has a central role to play in the CA: the CA sees people as striving agents, and in contrast to approaches that aim only at the satisfaction of preferences, it aims at supporting the growth of agency and practical reason. This emphasis on agency, under a Capabilities Approach, further means that children should be afforded the maximum scope for decisional freedom consistent with their actual—or potential—capacity for rational and reasoned forms of choice, or judgment.

Special Priority For Dixon and Nussbaum (2012), a special priority for children's rights can be justified on a Capabilities Approach theory for two reasons. First, children are especially vulnerable because of their legal and economic dependence on adults and because of their inherent physical or emotional vulnerability. In many cases, children are clearly different from adults because of the nascent development of their capabilities, and because of the support and protection they require from the state so that they can develop these capabilities and gain the benefit from them. Second, there is also a cost effectiveness principle, such that the cost of protecting children's rights is sufficiently low that failure to do so offends their dignity, or where it is more cost effective to protect that right than to protect the adult's right. They note that there can be tensions between adopting a Capabilities Approach to children's rights and principles in the UNCRC and national laws protecting children's rights on the one hand, and an adult's interests. However, tension arises most problematically only when the child's interest would violate the rights and or capabilities of the other. In any event, "the basic idea behind such a principle is clear: one person loses any legitimate claim to exercise their capabilities in a certain way when such action undermines the central, or fundamental, capabilities of others" (Dixon and Nussbaum 2012, pp. 565–566).

Children have a unique and special vulnerability from birth through late adolescence. This is produced by the child's innate and unavoidable dependence on adults, their multiple physical, cognitive and emotional developmental requirements, and the significant consequences of decisions and actions taken in these phases of life by adults who are legally and morally responsible for their care. In this respect, and especially in situations of tensions between competing interests (e.g., child marriage, female genital cutting), or simply of invidious social or economic circumstances (e.g., child sale), Dixon and Nussbaum (2012), state that the Capabilities Approach "recognizes human frailty and vulnerability as central parts of the human condition for adults as well as for children. Thus, a Capabilities Approach recognizes that parents themselves will often face tragic choices under the Capabilities Approach: if they cannot provide for themselves, as well as their children, they will have to make a tragic choice among competing capabilities. [However] A decent society will find ways to remove the need for parents to make such choices" (p. 584).

Implications for Child Sexual Abuse

A central dimension of the State's responsibility in a liberal democracy, and arguably any just society, is the protection of individuals' central rights and freedoms, and the creation of the minimum conditions under which each individual has an opportunity to lead a life of sufficient equality, dignity and value. A special subset of this responsibility is to protect those who are unable to protect themselves from harm. While its settings and characteristics take various forms, child sexual abuse involves violation of the child's body and breaches her or his individual rights to bodily integrity, protection and safety. Child sexual abuse occurs in situations of power asymmetry characterised by some or all dimensions of physical, psychological, emotional, cognitive, social and economic inequality. Children in general have unique developmental vulnerabilities, and are not generally able to protect themselves from this abuse. The individual's positive rights require the state to provide and protect fundamental individual rights and interests. This enlivens both the State's responsibility to protect the child, and the debate about how that responsibility can and should be discharged.

While this discussion has focused on rights within political theory, it is important to note that rights do not simply exist in the abstract. Rights derived from a theoretical standpoint must also made tangible. This is clear from the work of Kant, Locke, Mill, Rawls, Rorty and Nussbaum. As Hunt says (Hunt 2007, p. 21), human rights "only become meaningful when they gain political content". Freeman (2007) observes that children's rights are essential because one who possesses rights can exercise agency and participate meaningfully in their lives, demand that their rights be protected, and advocate for necessary responses. Similarly, Arneil (2002) recognises two important sets of rights, comprising welfare and agency rights, both of which aim to secure fundamental human entitlements, especially for the most vulnerable, and are logically accommodated by a conventional understanding of liberal theory and a fulsome application of it in practice. Welfare rights include the right to provision (which embraces fundamental human needs such as nutrition, shelter, care and education), and the right to protection, which includes protection from abuse, neglect, exploitation and danger. These kinds of rights require supervision and sometimes intervention by the state.

As applied to child sexual abuse, and especially to its clearer instances, these rights to welfare and protection find their natural place in a just society's legal and health systems. Whether being "aggressively policed" on Nussbaum's view (e.g., through criminal law for appropriate cases, and through child protection law in other appropriate cases), or as a basis for the provision of health rehabilitation and or compensation (e.g., through civil law), many instances of child sexual abuse can be the subject of legal and policy responses that are appropriately justified. Such responses do not exist in a vacuum, and contextual and systemic characteristics exert an influence on whether implementation of law and policy is effective. As well, the panoply of different circumstances of child sexual abuse will call for responses sensitive to the context and the facts of any particular situation. Yet, these systems are sufficiently flexible and comprehensive to facilitate such sensitivity and prudence. The core implications of this theoretical approach is that legal and social systems must recognise and uphold the rights of the child to bodily inviolability, must recognise the nature and context of sexual abuse, and must not exclude children and the phenomenon of sexual abuse from their circle of concern.

Another set of rights also exist, which Arneil defines as autonomy rights, and elsewhere are called agency rights (Brighouse 2002). Autonomy rights pose more complex theoretical and practical challenges because of the nature of childhood and the different cognitive capacities of children at different ages and stages of development, and because of the interaction of these kinds of rights with the role and duties of parents and the state. Yet, consideration of these rights is essential to any broader theory of children's rights. It is also relevant when examining matters of the individual's autonomy and choice, which can arise in particularly contentious areas of child sexual abuse. For example, some may consider female genital cutting and even child marriage to be capable of being seen as manifestations of child sexual abuse, depending on the circumstances (Mathews and Collin-Vézina 2017). These contexts concern matters of the child's autonomy (and related rights) as well as rights to protection and bodily inviolability.[2] Theoretical and practical approaches to issues involving agency rights or autonomy rights may appear to be more complex, especially where societies have different cultural values and customs. However, on their face, such an approach would carry the implication that female genital cutting clearly offends principles of bodily inviolability, choice, affiliation and autonomy, and compromises children's capabilities. Similarly, depending on the circumstances, child marriage may severely encroach upon a genuine commitment to individual autonomy, and may either directly breach or create an unacceptable risk in relation to the rights to safety, bodily integrity and protection from sexual abuse. This connects also with the Capabilities Approach's focus on ensuring that children should be afforded the maximum scope for decisional freedom.

In Chap. 4, I will detail some of the ways in which international instruments have accepted and promote children's rights, and the ways in which domestic legal systems entrench particular children's rights in civil and criminal law, and in child protection law. Before that discussion, we can also consider another body of theory. Public health theory provides further support for the rights of individuals, and indicates ways to promote Nussbaum's Capabilities Approach and promote a "decent society" even in situations of ethical tension and tragic choice. In common with liberalism's proper concern with individual freedom, flourishing and rights, public health is concerned with ideals of social justice, the responsibility of the state, and concrete measures promoting the health of the public, and of vulnerable subpopulations.

[2]Others have posited that a fourth dimension of children's rights is possible beyond autonomy, encompassing rights of political participation, although it is possible that these may be understood as a form of agency right. Arneil also highlighted an apparent conflict between a general rights-based approach, driven by an ethic of justice, and a different approach driven by an ethic of care. An ethic of care would have as its first priority to support parents rather than "enforce" rights. The State's scope and function would be more directed towards "a proactive integrated set of services available to parents and their children, even before the need arises" to provide the child with the necessary care (and promote their rights); families and society would be seen as communities working together, and would support relationships between individuals and institutions, rather than relying on an adversarial system. I do not seek to resolve all aspects of this conflict here, but would suggest that in responding to many challenges concerning rights to protection – and perhaps even in relation to child sexual abuse – a harmonious blend of both approaches may best be pursued, and often is pursued. In some settings, and depending on the circumstances, affording priority to one or another approach may be more justified and necessary; and in others, an approach combining both may be possible.

Public Health Theory

The Origins of Public Health

From its first manifestations, the idea of "public health" and the measures adopted to promote it have always been concerned with improving the health of the population and eliminating or reducing specific risks to health. As is well-established, some of the first such measures developed from the mid-nineteeth century to respond to clearly identifiable and even isolated sources of risk, especially infectious diseases. In Chicago, for example, a Board of Health was established in 1835 to respond to a cholera epidemic; health commissioners were empowered to inspect premises, visit those who were infected, and board ships (Turnock 2009). Vaccination programs were established soon after to respond to smallpox. Other measures followed to promote safe food and water: Chicago, for example, required all milk to be pasteurised from 1909, and water sterilisation measures followed.

Similarly, in England, the National Vaccination Board was established in 1837 and the General Board of Health was established in 1848. Edwin Chadwick's 1842 *Report on the Sanitary Condition of the Labouring Population of Great Britain* influenced the enactment of the first Public Health Act in 1848. This legislation established the first General Board of Health, which in turn created local health boards to regulate sewerage and water supply. In London, in 1854, an outbreak of cholera killed over 600 people. The public health pioneer John Snow famously traced the source to a single contaminated water pump in Broad Street; the simple act of disabling the pump halted the spread of the disease (Gostin 2008; Turnock 2009). Snow also determined locations which were, and were not, the source of other cholera outbreaks (Turnock 2009). In these decades of the second half of the nineteenth century, in both the USA and England, sewerage systems were created, and measures were established to ensure the safety of food, especially meat and milk.

By the late 1800s and early 1900s, the idea of "public health" had become more broadly recognised as a formal concept. In the USA, for example, the American Public Health Association was formed in 1872, the *American Journal of Public Hygiene* commenced publication under various names from 1873, and the *American Journal of Public Health* was launched in 1911 (Brown and Fee 2011). Scientific analysis was growing, and measurement of outcomes was informing government and the public of gains in health and living standards. In the USA, Charles Winslow (1926) observed an increase in life expectancy of almost 50% among New Yorkers between the years 1880 and 1920, moving from 36 years to 53 years. In 1920, in "The untilled field of public health" published in *Science*, Winslow had defined public health as (Winslow 1920, p. 30):

> The science and the art of preventing disease, prolonging life, and promoting physical health and efficiency through organized community efforts for the sanitation of the environment, the control of communicable infections, the education of the individual in principles of personal hygiene, the organization of medical and nursing service for the early diagnosis and preventive treatment of disease, and the development of the social machinery

> which will ensure to every individual in the community a standard of living adequate for the maintenance of health ... to enable every citizen to realize his birthright of health and longevity.

Importantly, these early phases of public health witnessed the emergence of an ideological dispute, epitomising the significance of different theories of public health. Some, including Chadwick, attributed much disease to the immorality of the poor; in contrast, others such as William Farr viewed poverty as both a direct cause of disease (e.g., via malnutrition and its conditions) and a social determinant of other adverse health and behavioural conditions (e.g., alcohol abuse and violence) (Hamlin 1995; Krieger and Birn 1998).

Waves of Public Health Many scholars have identified several temporal waves of public health measures from the 1800s to date, which have responded to different kinds of social and health concerns (e.g., Davies et al. 2014; Hanlon et al. 2011; Turnock 2009). While there are subtle differences between these understandings and time periods, the general interpretation of these parameters are similar, and these waves are a useful short-hand model for understanding the development and expanding contours of public health. The measures discussed above about the origins of public health in responding to infectious disease and sanitation exemplified the first two waves of public health. Wave 1 is generally understood as occurring from around 1830–1900, being focused on structural measures for public sanitation and disease control (e.g., sewerage, drainage, and clean water supply). Wave 2, viewed as occurring from roughly 1890–1950, was marked by the biomedical response, exemplified by the implementation of vaccination programs and antibiotic treatments, and the growth of hospitals. Wave 3, occurring from around 1950–1980, was characterised by attention to social and economic determinants, which were increasingly understood as contributing to health. Housing, education, employment and other social welfare measures aimed to remediate adversity in specific populations, as well as safeguarding the health of the population as a whole. Wave 4, from about 1960–2000, witnessed growing clinical responses to disease, and especially to disease related to lifestyle (e.g., disease related to consumption of tobacco and alcohol, and obesity). Some are now urging the next wave in public health to respond to persistent health inequalities, changes in the burden of disease, and the new conditions of modern society (Hanlon et al. 2011). For example, Davies et al. (2014, p. 1891) argue for a new culture of health, supported by institutional, social and physical environments, urging "the active participation of the community as a whole; and to renew focus on working together towards health as a common good".

Contemporary Nature of the Concept of Public Health In 1988, the Institute of Medicine's Committee for the Study of the Future of Public Health defined public health as "what we, as a society, do collectively to assure the conditions in which people can be healthy". Especially at the population-wide level, public health approaches seek to remedy the underlying causes of health adversity, therefore moulding societal conditions to reduce disease (Gostin 2008). Public health systems can be considered to comprise the collective of "people and actions, including laws, policies, practices, and activities, that have the primary purpose of protecting and improving the health of the public" (Childress et al. 2002, p. 170). Public health has prevention as a major focus; it seeks to create interventions to avoid the onset of disease and injury – e.g., through ensuring clean water supply – as well as to ameliorate disease and injury, such as through providing free health services for the poor. A core goal of public health is therefore to "identify risks and prevent or ameliorate harms or other undesirable consequences to humans and what they value" (Gostin 2008, p. 56). Risks may emanate from natural sources (e.g., chemicals and viruses), but also from human behaviour including interpersonal violence and the acts and omissions which cause it. Disease and injury may be caused accidentally (e.g., traffic accidents), naturally (e.g., an infectious disease), or intentionally (e.g., by human conduct such as violence). Risk assessment requires consideration of the nature of the risk, the duration of the risk, the likelihood that a disease, injury or event will cause harm, and the severity of the harm of the risk materialises (Gostin 2008).

Three Dimensions of Prevention, and Four Broad Strategies Public health approaches to problems have been founded on commitments to three dimensions of prevention and response (Turnock 2009). The general understanding is that the prevention and response to health problems require a prudent combination of all three dimensions. While not always expressed in the same way, the three dimensions of prevention are commonly understood as (Turnock 2009):

- Primary prevention: measures taken to prevent a condition occurring. These measures may be taken at the population-wide level or in a particular subset of the population known to be at particularly high risk of experiencing the condition (e.g., compulsory vaccination programs with newborns/infants). Primary prevention prioritises health promotion and protection from specific diseases.
- Secondary prevention: measures taken to identify a condition at an early stage where it has already occurred, and to quickly respond to interrupt the process of disease (e.g., screening tests, case identification policies, and periodic medical examinations). Secondary prevention prioritises early case finding and prompt, pre-emptive treatment to minimise symptoms and consequences.
- Tertiary prevention: measures taken to respond to the condition and limit its health impact when it has already been experienced (e.g., treatment of the individual by health services). This prioritises disability limitation and rehabilitation.

A **range of four public health strategies** are commonly understood as being required to prevent and respond to public health problems (Hammond et al. 2006; Mercy et al. 1993; McMahon and Puett 1999). These comprise:

1. surveillance (i.e., defining and measuring the prevalence of a condition and monitoring trends)
2. risk factor research (i.e., identifying what factors make individuals or subpopulations more or less likely to experience a condition)

3. program development and evaluation (evaluating the efficacy of existing programs, policies and strategies; and generating and testing new programs)
4. program implementation (creating the required agencies, mechanisms, policies, guidelines, infrastructure and education programs required to implement the program; monitoring and testing for effects; and refinement).

Public Health Theory

Public health theory is underpinned by the bedrock assumption that government has the primary responsibility for securing and promoting the health of its citizenry; the population has a reasonable expectation that one of the core roles of the government it has elected (or otherwise supports or enables to continue in power) is to protect and promote its health (Gostin 2008). This expectation arises because of the centrality of a certain level of human health to overall functioning on a daily basis, and the pursuit of a decent life through the lifespan. Public health is therefore concerned with the actions that governments and societies should and must take to protect people's health (Krieger and Birn 1998). Krieger and Birn (1998, p. 1605) observe that this understanding has always characterised the field: the concept of public health was originally used "to distinguish actions governments and societies–as opposed to private individuals–should take to preserve and protect the people's health."

As noted by Krieger and Birn (1998), the dispute from the 1840s exemplifies an ongoing challenge about a defensible theoretical understanding of the nature, role and implementation of public health and its measures. There may be general agreement about the broad nature of public health as a concept. However, depending on different preferred theoretical positions, there will be debates about its legitimate scope, priorities and purposes, the rightful arenas of individual choice and responsibility, the extent to which individual liberties may justifiably be infringed, and the appropriate tradeoffs between the benefits gained from public health interventions and the costs of their implementation. As Krieger and Birn (1998, p. 1604) observe, this dispute reflects "a set of debates, still ongoing, about what and who is responsible for inequality, disease, and suffering and what steps should be taken, by whom, to improve the public's health".

Any public health approach to a specific challenge must be driven by a theory that at its core is true to the original concept of public health and its fundamental concern to promote social justice. The concept of social justice contains notions of distributive and procedural justice, human rights, and the actions required of states and private and public institutions to "oppose or condone exploitation and to protect, promote, or violate human rights" (Krieger 2005, p. 466).

Accordingly, theoretical challenges that arise for a public health approach are driven by common questions. Which people in society are most vulnerable to a particular kind of disease, injury and or injustice? Given the State's responsibility to protect and promote the health of the populace, and especially of the vulnerable, how can and how should the State and other societal agencies best reduce the particular risk of disease and injury, and minimise the harm caused? How can, and how should, services and benefits be justly and efficiently created and distributed, without unduly infringing on individual rights and other societal interests? These questions become particularly vexed when there is scientific uncertainty; it is widely acknowledged that public health should not embed policy that is uninformed by rigorous science, but at the same time, if the risks to health are sufficiently great, then it may be unethical and practically disastrous to fail to take action simply if there is not complete scientific certainty about the costs and benefits of a proposed policy. Gostin (2008) has acknowledged that in some situations, the precautionary principle is proposed to manage such situations, which maintains an obligation to protect populations against reasonably foreseeable threats, even if the science is unclear: preventative action should be taken, bute ht. policy-maker has the burden of proof, alternatives must be explored, and the public should participate in decision-making. Gostin (2008) recommends as general principles for action in such situations that policy-makers make the reasons for their decisions transparent, and be flexible and agile in refining responses when warranted by new evidence. Yet, even in challenging situations, there may be theoretical principles that provide guidance.

Public Health as Social Justice The promotion of social justice is generally accepted as the central mission of public health (Beauchamp 1999; Gostin 2008; Krieger and Birn 1998; Powers and Faden 2006). The concept of social justice prioritises human rights, equality, and procedural justice, and demands action by states and private and public institutions to promote these aims. These goals include opposing the exploitation of individuals, especially those in vulnerable groups. Lawrence Gostin, the Director of the O'Neill Institute for National and Global Health Law at Georgetown University, states that social justice is "so central to the mission of public health that it has been described as the field's core value" (Gostin 2008, p. 21). For Gostin, the concept of social justice contains the two normative forces driving public health (Gostin 2008, p. 21–22):

> to advance human well-being by improving health, and to do so particularly by focusing on the needs of the most disadvantaged…An integral part of that aim is the task of identifying and ameliorating patterns of systemic disadvantage that profoundly and pervasively undermine the prospects for well-being of oppressed and subordinated groups – people whose prospects for good health are so limited that their life choices are not even remotely like those of others…Seen through the lens of social justice, the central mission of the public health system is to engage in systematic action to ensure the conditions for improved health for all members of the population, and to redress persistent patterns of systemic disadvantage.

In developing her ecosocial perspective on public health, and demanding a focus on public health as social justice, Krieger (2011) firmly places political and social forces, especially race and class, at the centre of population health and health inequities. Significantly, Krieger (2011) notes that "socially inflicted trauma" includes sexual assault.

Public Health, Social Justice, and Human Rights In the dedication to the foundational text, *Health and Human Rights: A Reader*, the influential physician, scholar and health administrator Jonathan Mann was described as the catalyst for the modern public health and human rights movement (Mann et al. 1999). Mann (1997) had earlier observed that the violation of human rights has significant adverse consequences on people's physical, mental and social well-being. Further, he insisted that the promotion of human rights was not only consistent with, but essential for, the promotion of public health, because the two were inextricably entwined as a matter of lived experience, as well as conceptually. For Mann, this was because the concept of human rights provided "a societal-level framework for identifying and responding to the underlying – societal – determinants of health. It is important to emphasize that human rights are respected not only for their instrumental value in contributing to public health goals, but for themselves as societal goods of preeminent importance." (Mann 1997, p. 10).

Mann drew attention to the fact that while public health policy can sometimes be a legitimate reason to limit the rights of some, in many important situations there is an "underlying complementarity" between public health and human rights. He preferred to employ the principles and language of human rights to indicate appropriate understandings and policy responses by governments and societies (including public health measures), and to use the principles and terminology of ethics to circumscribe the bounds of individual behaviour. There are substantively similar core values driving liberal democracies' fundamental ethical interests (autonomy, beneficence, non-maleficence, and justice) and human rights interests (e.g., rights to bodily inviolability, rights to equality). Mann (1997) urged that public health can be improved by adopting a human rights framework to analyse and respond to the social determinants of health. This could also prepare the ground for the emergence of an ethic of public health, promoting the same core ethical values as are upheld by the liberal democratic project.

The Concept of Dignity

In another important but less noted passage, Mann emphasised the centrality of dignity to the human rights movement, noting its priority in international instruments like the Universal Declaration of Human Rights (Mann 1997). As others do (Rosen 2012), Mann noted the elusiveness of dignity as a concept, although some have sought to crystallise the meaning of dignity, such as Charles Foster, whose work is further discussed below. As well as its elusiveness, there are ongoing debates about its utility as a concept; some dismiss the concept as redundant by arguing it is simply a reframing of autonomy (Macklin 2003), others understand it differently and employ it for broader and narrower purposes (Ashcroft 2005; Beyleveld and Brownsword 2001; Kass 2002). Nussbaum, for example, views dignity as an important concept in a group of concepts about capabilities, functionings, and social interactions (Nussbaum 2011); although her interpretation of dignity has been viewed as essentially consisting of respect for persons and or their autonomy (Foster 2014a; Nussbaum 2009).

Mann placed great store in the centrality of dignity to the human experience. His interpretation was more aligned with the school of thought that takes dignity very seriously, and sees its significance as a metaphysical property characteristic of all humans, which guides a deeper appreciation of moral reasoning and human rights. Mann (1997) was convinced that insults to one's dignity are powerful and likely cause adverse effects on health, especially if chronic. He noted that exploring the meaning of dignity and acknowledging how it can be violated, and the impacts of its violation, "may help uncover a new universe of human suffering … the power of naming, describing, and then measuring is truly enormous – child abuse did not exist in meaningful societal terms until it was named and then measured; nor did domestic violence" (Mann 1997, p. 12).

Dignity may indeed be a uniquely useful concept in bioethics, and in public health analyses. Dignity is an ineffable concept; it is not readily reducible to articulation in language, or discursive exposition. Accordingly, it is best captured by exemplification, by providing ostensive definitions.[3]

One of the foremost proponents of the indispensability of dignity for analytical purposes is Charles Foster, who adopts this approach in his use of multiple examples, most prominently with his example of the human ear ashtray.[4] The foundation of Foster's theory (Foster 2015) is that "sometimes nothing but dignity will do" to explain why something is wrong, or why something is harmful. Significantly, this approach can accommodate situations involving those who are deceased, who are unconscious, who are cognitively impaired, and who are asleep, since, on Foster's approach, the concept of dignity is an attribute inherent to human *being*, not to human *doing* (Foster 2014a). Dignity can provide first-order explanations of the wrongness of an experience, where other ethical concepts including autonomy and respect for persons cannot.

For Foster, the substantive meaning of dignity can be derived from empirical observation of what makes human beings thrive: "My definition of dignity expressly relates to human thriving, the essential conditions of which I suggest can be objectively determined." Foster maintains (Foster 2014b, pp. 421–422): "dignity is about being human well. A dignity-enhancing measure is a humanizing measure. There are things that are objectively humanizing and things that are not … there is, at least in theory, an ascertainable answer to the question, for any particular activity proposed by any particular person: "Will that help her thrive/humanize? … Dignity, then, is objective human flourishing." In this sense, it is substantially different from

[3] Such definitions have a "similarity rider", acknowledging that the example provided is non-exhaustive; it says that "this [example] and other similar examples exemplify the concept": thanks to Dr. Andrew McGee for explanation of these concepts.

[4] "Medical students steal an ear from the cadaver they are dissecting. They varnish it and use it as an ashtray. The cadaver was donated for the purposes of medical education. Liberal though he was, the donor did not regard use of an ear as an ashtray as one of those purposes."

autonomy; one can exercise one's autonomy in ways which contravene one's own thriving, and which undermine the broader interests and thriving of others and of society as a whole.

Importantly, in employing this understanding of dignity in analytical exercises, this approach examines the effect of an experience on the dignity (thriving, or flourishing) of multiple relevant parties, and not only on the subject person. Relevant is the dignity of not only the subject person, but also of the other actors (e.g., those exploiting or acting in relation to the subject person), and society as a whole. The analysis then takes a "transactional approach", calculating the "net change in the amount of dignity in the world that would be involved in the transaction. The outcome of the audit determines the ethical outcome" (Foster 2014b). In relation to the effect on the exploiting person and on society generally, Foster's approach maintains that "societies composed of, or endorsing, callous exploiters, are less happy, cohesive and generally functional, and that individuals within them are correspondingly less happy, cohesive and functional."

In the analysis of the ear example, then, Foster (2014a) concludes that a dignity-based approach results in a conclusion that this is wrong, because it does not promote human thriving. This analysis captures the instinctive feeling that most people would have about the wrongness of the medical student's behaviour, by pinning down the source of that discomfort, which is otherwise difficult to isolate and which does not otherwise breach principles of rights or the other bioethical principles of autonomy, beneficence, non-maleficence and justice that are normally relied on to assess human behaviour. Hence, Foster's dignity-driven transactional analysis of the experience recognises several impacts on the thriving or flourishing of the relevant actors, with only two relating to the subject; the analysis produces the outcome that the action of the medical students is wrong (Foster 2014a, p. 47):

1. Part of the ear-owner's being survives death. She lives on in the minds of others, and for that part of her to continue to flourish, her remains need to be treated with respect.
2. Her wishes (another part of her being), survive death. It's reasonable to presume that one does not want one's body parts abused.
3. The possibility of our body parts being so abused after our death interferes with our peace of mind and, hence, with our flourishing. Thus to prohibit such abuse, by way of law or ethical code, is to promote our present and future flourishing.
4. The abusers of the ear are doing something that diminishes their own flourishing: it dehumanises them.
5. Expressivism: a set of rules prohibiting this sort of abuse will exhibit and entrench flourishing-enhancing respect.

This kind of analysis can illuminate perceptions about why some kinds of sexual activity may rightly be regarded as wrong on the basis that they infringe human dignity. This approach to the concept of dignity also raises the intriguing prospect of whether a right to sexual dignity may provide insights or direction which can better protect children and promote their interests, including their thriving or flourishing. This could apply to children who experience sexual abuse of different kinds and in different situations – e.g., those abuse while infants without knowing the nature of the acts; those abused while drugged; those abused while asleep; those abused by use of their image in electronic means. It could also be applied to analysis of appropriate responses to children who themselves inflict sexual abuse: does a certain kind of response, such as through a legal system, infringe their dignity? It could also be applied to difficult questions about the permissibility of what might otherwise be seen as self-regarding conduct, such as the use of robots representing children for sexual purposes.

Public Health Theory and Child Sexual Abuse

Child sexual abuse is now generally understood as being a public health concern, although it has taken a long time for this relationship to crystallise. In the early 1990s, interpersonal violence was recognised as a public health issue, including violence affecting children at the population level (Mercy et al. 1993). In the mid-1990s, the Centers for Disease Control (Foege et al. 1995) and the World Health Assembly (1996) made public declarations of interpersonal violence being a public health priority.

This recognition of the broadening scope of public health extended more specifically to child sexual abuse in the late 1980s and early 1990s (Djeddah et al. 2000; Koop 1989; Krugman 1998; McMahon and Puett 1999; Mercy 2016; Zimmerman and Mercy 2010). In 1995, the American Medical Association found sexual assault to be "a silent violent epidemic" and released guidelines to medical practitioners on how to engage with patients who disclosed their abusive experiences (Washington Post 1995). The Centers for Disease Control (1997) commented on child sexual abuse as a public health problem. In 2000, Koplan and Fleming identified ten public health priorities for the coming century, three of which are relevant here: "focus on children's emotional and intellectual development … recognize and address the contributions of mental health to overall health and well-being … reduce the toll of violence in society".

This extension was given stronger impetus in the late 1990s, when a series of articles urged that child sexual abuse be viewed not only as a matter of criminal justice, violence, or individual medical need. A special edition of the journal *Sexual Abuse*: A Journal of Research and Treatment was published in 1999, which included papers on: the need for comprehensive collaborations for prevention (Wurtele 1999); an evaluation from Vermont of the first adult-focused prevention effort (Chasan-Taber and Tabachnick 1999); and a theoretical approach to prevention focused on offenders and alcohol abuse (Becker and Reilly 1999). Two other articles in this edition were particularly notable. First, James Mercy (2016) argued why a new understanding of child sexual abuse as a public health issue is appropriate. Mercy identified the substantial prevalence of child sexual abuse, its significant consequences on health and behaviour, its sometime replication, and its conceptual nature as a form of interpersonal violence not dissimilar to other types that are viewed as public health issues, such as youth violence and intimate partner violence. He urged treatment programs for victims and their families, as well as for offenders. However, he particularly urged primary prevention, including changing social norms and values about sexuality that may influence the likelihood of individuals sexually abusing children as well as others being unwilling to recognise it and intervene. This required asking "difficult questions" about the social norms and values supporting child sexual abuse, their expression and reinforcement, and the social institutions connected with these forces – noting families, media, churches and schools as examples – which could therefore be most influential in reform.

Second, McMahon and Puett (1999) reported on the recommendations made by members of an expert panel, convened for 2 days in 1997 by the Centers for Disease Control and Prevention to advise them about the raising of awareness about child sexual abuse as a public health problem. The CDC's objective was to develop an informed national agenda to prevent child sexual abuse, guided by insights from a range of experts from the worlds of government, service and advocacy organisations, hospitals and health services, researchers, clinicians, survivors and offenders. A comprehensive list of recommendations were formulated in three domains: research, surveillance and evaluation; public education and awareness; and public policy, as follows (McMahon and Puett (1999):

On research, surveillance and evaluation:

- Develop a surveillance system which will capture both reported and unreported cases
- Identify risk factors for perpetration of CSA
- Conduct research on normative sexual behaviors and fantasies at various developmental stages
- Develop techniques that allow for early identification and treatment for victims and abusers
- Encourage universities to offer courses on child abuse and neglect
- Increase funding for public health research on childhood sexual abuse

On public education and awareness:

- Quickly disseminate existing research to the public and to policy makers
- Create a public health infrastructure for dealing with CSA
- Develop powerful messages about CSA
- Create a new framework for the media to address CSA
- Develop consensus among experts to delineate how to prevent and intervene in cases of CSA
- Target educational efforts toward medical and mental health professionals, the public, and those employed in various media efforts

On public policy:

- Elevate the position of CSA on the public health agenda
- Encourage the federal Interagency Working Group on Child Abuse and Neglect and the Federal Forum to focus on CSA

- Encourage legislation to fund a study by the National Academy of Sciences focusing on CSA
- Encourage collaboration among agencies in their activities regarding CSA
- Encourage foundations to support prevention and research related to CSA
- Involve practitioner groups in urging the reauthorization of the Child Abuse Prevention and Treatment Act (CAPTA) and inclusion of a mandate for CSA prevention
- Increase federal funding for childhood sexual abuse
- Develop career development incentives in CSA
- Use various strategies to educate about CSA
- Develop CDC leadership in CSA prevention
- Develop a strategy to increase political activism among adult survivors and their families.

The inclusion of personal violence, and especially in this context, of child sexual abuse, as matters of public health concern, are interesting developments. In a sense, their inclusion is congruent with the third wave of public health and its recognition of the influence of social determinants on health. However, to the extent that this is so, the underlying rationale is more a recognition of the vulnerability of children as a social group to sexual victimization. In this sense, the acceptance of children's vulnerability is a closer fit with the kind of ecosocial approach adopted by Krieger, who focuses on the impact of race and class. Some dimensions of child sexual abuse, perhaps especially the significant portion involving teenagers who inflict sexual abuse, may also be understood as relevant to new fifth wave of public health as culture, as proposed by Davies et al. (2014).

Mercy's insights in 1999 remain as relevant today. Indeed, Daro (2016, p. 421), in the context of child maltreatment generally, stated that "Developing and fully implementing a public health approach to preventing child maltreatment is more complex than crafting new prevention strategies and improving the context in which parents raise their children, It will require changes in some of our traditions and deeply held values, our notions of risk and vulnerability, how we build service delivery infrastructure, and how we balance our political priorities." Similarly, Letourneau et al. (2014)) urged a comprehensive public health approach to preventing child sexual abuse.

Significance of Public Health for Child Sexual Abuse

Applied to this context, public health theory is concerned with the optimal ways to design, implement, and evaluate programs to prevent risk of sexual abuse of children (Mercy and Saul 2009), at the population level and to groups of children at higher risk, and the promotion of good governance to enhance health (Gostin 2008). Consistent with political theory discussed above, public health theory not only encourages but obliges action by states and private and public institutions to promote social justice, prevent child exploitation and protect children's human rights (Krieger, 2005, 2011). In this context, whether in cases of non-institutional or institutional child sexual abuse, a public health approach must appropriately accommodate the ecosocial dimensions relating to the child, the offender (as relevant), the institution (if one is involved), and the known factors which enable child sexual abuse to be inflicted, concealed, and in many cases repeated.

As already acknowledged, most child sexual abuse is hidden and is unlikely to be disclosed by the child or by the person who inflicted it. Much child sexual abuse causes substantial personal and economic harm to both individual and community, and infringes fundamental individual rights and freedoms. However, not every case is the same. Different settings of offending, and different types of offending, must also be acknowledged. For example, challenges posed by child sexual abuse within families may differ from those presented by abuse within child and youth-serving organisations. Prolific, dangerous recidivist offenders, including those who are protected by organisations, may pose different or additional challenges to the kind of offending constituted by isolated, less serious opportunistic acts by same-aged peers. Sexual abuse within a dating relationship may pose further different or additional challenges. Sensitivity to context, and to difference, is essential, and multi-pronged approaches are likely to be essential, customised to respond in nuanced ways to the needs of different situations.

Important questions arise for a public health response to child sexual abuse, which must consider the overall context of child sexual abuse, as well as specific subtypes regarding which we have sufficient scientific understanding:

1. How can and how should these different situations of child sexual abuse be prevented from occurring?
2. How can and should society identify these different situations so that the abuse can be interrupted, and the child's needs for safety and health be met?
3. How can and should society respond to these different situations after the event?

Adopting a public health approach to child sexual abuse requires a multidisciplinary approach to the four traditional tools required of any public health response (Hammond et al. 2006; Mercy et al. 1993). We must take appropriate steps in relation to:

- surveillance (i.e., defining and measuring the prevalence of child sexual abuse, and monitoring trends in its prevalence)
- identifying risk factors (i.e., identifying what factors make individuals or subpopulations more or less likely to experience child sexual abuse)
- program development and evaluation (evaluating the efficacy of existing child sexual abuse programs, policies and strategies; and generate and test new programs)
- program implementation (creating the required agencies, mechanisms, policies, guidelines, infrastructure and education programs required to implement the programs; monitoring and testing programs for effects; and refinement).

A public health response to child sexual abuse must also employ strategies for all three dimensions of prevention. As applied to child sexual abuse, these can be expressed as follows:

- Primary prevention: what measures can and should be taken to prevent child sexual abuse from occurring? These measures may be taken at the population-wide level, or in particular subsets of the population and or settings that are known to be at higher risk.
- Secondary prevention: what measures can and should be taken to identify child sexual abuse at an early stage where it has already occurred, and to quickly respond to interrupt the abuse, applied to both the child population as a whole, and particular subsets of the population and or settings that are known to be at higher risk.[5]
- Tertiary prevention: what measures can and should be taken to respond to child sexual abuse and limit its health impact when it has been experienced?

A public health response also means innovative measures should be considered, and multi-pronged approaches may be necessary (Hammond et al. 2006). Multi-pronged approaches enable policy measures to be sensitive to context and to different challenges posed by different kinds of child sexual abuse. Innovative public health measures tailored to specific contexts include specialized courts for specific kinds of injury, such as exposure to lead, dust diseases, and drug offenses (Campbell et al. 2013). Researchers have urged the creation of networks of private and public organizational capacity, including community-based organizations, to respond proactively to child sexual abuse (Zimmerman and Mercy 2010), to construct a new public health architecture to address the problem (Zimmerman and Mercy 2010).

A systematic public health approach cannot succeed without genuine commitment to prevention, early intervention, responding to root causes of violence, monitoring the efficacy of initiatives and refining them on an ongoing basis, and coordinated implementation of responses by agencies and communities (Mercy et al. 1993). Communities play a central role, and their full participation in violence prevention is essential to create ownership of the problem and its solutions (Hammond et al. 2006). Daro (2016) declared that "a new public health framework will create a social contract that requires accountability from all responsible parties – including parents themselves. Shared responsibility is an essential component of the public health approach."

[5] For example, through screening tests, case identification policies, and periodic medical examinations.

Conclusion

Public health and political theory as discussed in this chapter have much in common, sharing similar concerns with individual rights and social justice, and promoting similar goals. The Capabilities Approach, for example, is focused on protecting certain of the child's core capabilities in an immediate sense (eg life, bodily health and bodily integrity), and on creating the conditions under which other of the child's core capabilities can be nurtured and sustained in future (senses, emotion, practical reason, and affiliation). It is fundamentally faithful to the core principles of liberal society, children's rights as citizens, and recognises children's vulnerability as a basis for special priority in the protection and promotion of their fundamental human rights and capabilities. This approach extends traditional liberal theory, and complements and is consistent with a public health approach to child sexual abuse. Both urge action by the state, including through legislative and policy measures, to protect children's most fundamental rights, interests, capabilities and potential for future flourishing. Together with a sound understanding of the nature and consequences of child sexual abuse, these theoretical insights are instructive when considering what strategies can justifiably be adopted by social systems, health systems and legal systems, in preventing, identifying and responding to child sexual abuse.

Nussbaum is unapologetic in seeing child sexual abuse as a paradigm case of such clear injustice that it can and should be "aggressively policed" on an application of her Capabilities Approach. However, while most would agree with this sentiment and theoretical application in many kinds of case – including, for example, the worst kinds of cases – we can acknowledge a spectrum of cases which may not be quite so clear. Moreover, beyond that, there are hard cases such as female genital cutting and child marriage, which rightly should occupy the minds of legislators, policy-makers and the public. In these hard cases, many have an unshakeable sense that there is something seriously wrong with such practices, that we feel in some way they do constitute a species of sexual abuse, or, however we define them, that they are wrong and should be abolished. However, in such cases it can be difficult to articulate the reasons for this feeling, especially where an appeal to the child's rights, freedoms and even capabilities does not satisfactorily resolve the situation, or where the child herself may claim to want to participate, or where we confront opposing normative arguments or social customs that defend the practice.

Perhaps these are the kinds of cases in which a dignity-based approach provides a more satisfactory analysis. Female genital cutting is prohibited and no longer endorsed in many societies and communities; in these situations, it is difficult to mount any persuasive argument in its favour, assuming there is not even an interest in conforming with social custom, remaining accepted by one's social group, and being considered a suitable marriage partner. In other situations, where it is practiced and socially endorsed, female genital cutting – for argumentative purposes here, assuming its most minor form – may be seen as a practical requirement for marriageability and the individual's broader acceptance within society and relevant family and peer groups, and on this basis being related to the individual's chance to flourish in their society. Yet, adopting the approach of Foster, it appears plausible to suggest that even in such instances, female genital cutting in all its forms, and even in its "milder" forms, offends the dignity of the child; offends the dignity of those who inflict the cutting, and ultimately undermines the flourishing of the entire society. An analysis using Foster's concept of dignity here seems to pin down the basis for what is otherwise an elusive feeling that this practice "is just not right", even in its "milder" form, even when conducted for an apparently more innocuous purpose, and even if other rights do not appear infringed; for example, if practiced on an older child who ostensibly consented. The international human rights instruments honour dignity even before mentioning rights, and, in concert with theories of rights and public health, this useful operational application of the concept of dignity may offer insights into defensible rationales for further progress in child sexual abuse, both generally and in contentious cases.

In addition, it is notable that key public health theorists like James Mercy (2016) and Deborah Daro (2016) have observed that complex and apparently intractable problems like child sexual abuse may require substantial shifts in understanding and response, including development in social norms and values that influence its infliction and concealment. This insight becomes particularly relevant when considering existing and potential responses through legal systems, especially through a public health law approach.

References

Archard, D. (1993). *Children: Rights and childhood*. London: Routledge.

Archard, D. (2004). *Children: Rights and childhood* (2nd ed.). London: Routledge.

Arneil, B. (2002). Becoming versus being: A critical analysis of the child in liberal theory. In D. Archard & C. Macleod (Eds.), *The moral and political status of children* (pp. 79–94). Oxford: Oxford University Press.

Ashcroft, R. (2005). Making sense of dignity. *Journal of Medical Ethics, 31*, 679–682.

Bearinger, L., Sieving, R., Ferguson, J., & Sharma, V. (2007). Global perspectives on the sexual and reproductive health of adolescents: Patterns, prevention, and potential. *Lancet, 369*, 1220–1231.

Beauchamp, D. (1999). Public health as social justice. In D. Beauchamp & B. Steinbock (Eds.), *New ethics for the Public's health* (pp. 105–114). New York: Oxford University Press.

Becker, J., & Reilly, D. (1999). Preventing sexual abuse and assault. *Sexual Abuse: A Journal of Research and Treatment, 11*, 267–278.

Beyleveld, D., & Brownsword, R. (2001). *Human dignity in bioethics and biolaw*. Oxford: Oxford University Press.

Brighouse, H. (2002). What rights (if any) do children have? In D. Archard & C. Macleod (Eds.), *The moral and political status of children* (pp. 32–52). Oxford: Oxford University Press.

Brown, T., & Fee, E. (2011). Birth of the *American Journal of Public Health. American Journal of Public Health, 100*(1), 66–67.

Campbell, C., Grazely, E., Pan, S., Cummings, C., Palermo, P., & Gould, G. (2013). Public health and law collaboration: The Philadelphia lead court study. *American Journal of Public Health, 103*(7), 1271–1277.

Centers for Disease Control. (1997). Perceptions of child sexual abuse as a public health problem. *Morbidity and Mortality Weekly Report, 46*, 801–803.

Chasan-Taber, L., & Tabachnick, J. (1999). Evaluation of a child sexual abuse prevention program. *Sexual Abuse: A Journal of Research and Treatment, 11*, 279–292.

Childress, J., Faden, R., Gaare, R., Gostin, L., Kahn, J., Bonnie, R., Kass, N., Mastroianni, A., Moreno, J., & Nieburg, P. (2002). Public health ethics: Mapping the terrain. *Journal of Law, Medicine & Ethics, 30*, 170–178.

Committee for the Study of the Future of Public Health, Division of Health Care Services, Institute of Medicine. (1988). *The future of public health*. Washington, DC: National Academy Press.

Daro, D. (2016). A public health approach to prevention: What will it take? *Trauma, Violence, & Abuse, 17*(4), 420–421.

Davies, S. C., Winpenny, E., Ball, S., Fowler, T., Rubin, J., & Nolte, E. (2014). For debate: A new wave in public health improvement. *The Lancet, 384*(9957), 1889–1895.

Dixon, R., & Nussbaum, M. (2012). Children's rights and a capabilities approach: The question of special priority. *Cornell Law Review, 97*, 549–594.

Djeddah, C., Facchin, P., Ranzato, C., & Romer, C. (2000). Child abuse: Current problems and key public health challenges. *Social Science & Medicine, 51*(6), 905–915.

Dworkin, R. (1977). *Taking rights seriously*. London: Duckworth.

Eekelaar, J. (1986). The emergence of children's rights. *Oxford Journal of Legal Studies, 6*, 161–182.

Eekelaar, J. (1992). The importance of thinking that children have rights. *International Journal of Law, Policy and the Family, 6*, 221–235.

Foege, W., Rosenberg, M., & Mercy, J. (1995). Public health and violence prevention. *Current Issues in Public Health, 1*, 2–9.

Foster, C. (2014a). Dignity and the use of body parts. *Journal of Medical Ethics, 40*, 44–47.

Foster, C. (2014b). Dignity and the ownership and use of body parts. *Cambridge Quarterly of Healthcare Ethics, 23*, 417–430.

Foster, C. (2015). Human dignity in bioethics and law. *Journal of Medical Ethics, 41*, 935.

Freeman, M. (1980). The rights of children in the international year of the child. *Current Legal Problems, 33*, 1–31.

Freeman, M. (1983). *The rights and wrongs of children*. London: Frances Pinter.

Freeman, M. (2007). Why it remains important to take children's rights seriously. *International Journal of Children's Rights, 15*, 5–23.

Gostin, L. (2008). A theory and definition of public health law. In*Public health law power, duty, restraint: Revised & expanded second edition* (pp. 1–41). Washington, DC: Georgetown University Law Center.

Hamlin, C. (1995). Could you starve to death in England in 1839? The Chadwick-Farr controversy and the loss of the "social" in public health. *American Journal of Public Health, 85*, 856–866.

Hammond, W. R., Whitaker, D. J., Lutzker, J. R., Mercy, J., & Chin, P. M. (2006). Setting a violence prevention agenda at the centers for disease control and prevention. *Aggression and Violent Behavior, 11*(2), 112–119.

Hanlon, P., Carlisle, S., Hannah, M., Reilly, D., & Lyon, A. (2011). Making the case for a 'fifth wave' in public health. *Public Health, 125*, 30–36.

Hunt, L. (2007). *Inventing human rights*. New York: Norton.

Kass, L. (2002). *Life, liberty and the defence of dignity*. San Francisco: Encounter Books.

Kempe, H. (1977). A vindication of the rights of children. In G. Meade (Ed.), *Frontiers of medicine* (pp. 33–50). New York: Springer.

Koop, E. C. (1989). The challenge of definition. *Hastings Center Report, 19*(Special Supplement), 2–3.

Koplan, J., & Fleming, D. (2000). Current and future public health challenges. *JAMA Pediatrics, 284*, 1696–1698.

Krieger, N. (2005). Researching critical questions on social justice and public health: An ecosocial perspective. In B. Levy & V. Sidel (Eds.), *Social injustice and public health* (pp. 460–479). New York: Oxford University Press.

Krieger, N. (2011). *Epidemiology and the people's health: Theory and context*. New York: Oxford University Press.

Krieger, N., & Birn, A. E. (1998). A vision of social justice as the foundation of public health: Commemorating 150 years of the spirit of 1848. *American Journal of Public Health, 88*, 1603–1606.
Krugman, R. (1998). It's time to broaden the agenda. *Child Abuse & Neglect, 22*, 475–479.
Letourneau, E., Eaton, W., Bass, J., Berlin, F., & Moore, S. (2014). The need for a comprehensive public health approach to preventing child sexual abuse. *Public Health Reports, 129*(May–June), 222–228.
Locke, J. (1995). *Some thoughts concerning education*. Bristol: Thoemmes Press.
Locke, J. (2003). Two treatises of government. In I. Shapiro (Ed.), *Two treatises of government and a letter concerning toleration* (pp. 1–209). New Haven: Yale.
Macklin, R. (2003). Dignity is a useless concept. *British Medical Journal, 327*, 1419–1420.
Magnusson, R. (2007). Mapping the scope and opportunities for public health law in liberal democracies. *Global Health Law, Ethics, and Policy, 35*, 571–587.
Mann, J. (1997). Medicine and public health, ethics and human rights. *The Hastings Center Report, 27*, 6–13.
Mann, J., Gruskin, S., Grodin, M., & Annas, G. (1999). *Health and human rights: A reader*. New York: Routledge.
Mathews, B., & Collin-Vézina, D. (2017). Sexual abuse: Towards a conceptual model and definition. *Trauma, Violence, & Abuse, 21*, 1–18.
McMahon, P. M., & Puett, R. C. (1999). Child sexual abuse as a public health issue: Recommendations of an expert panel. *Sexual Abuse: A Journal of Research and Treatment, 11*(2), 257–266.
Mello, M. M., Wood, J., Burris, S., Wagenaar, A. C., Ibrahim, J. K., & Swanson, J. W. (2013). Critical opportunities for public health law: A call for action. *American Journal of Public Health, 103*(11), 1979–1988.
Mercy, J. A. (2016). Having new eyes: Viewing child sexual abuse as a public health problem. *Sexual Abuse: A Journal of Research and Treatment, 11*(4), 317–321.
Mercy, J. A., & Saul, J. (2009). Creating a healthier future through early interventions for children. *The Journal of the American Medical Association, 301*(21), 2262–2264.
Mercy, J. A., Rosenberg, M. L., Powell, K. E., Broome, C. V., & Roper, W. L. (1993). Public health policy for preventing violence. *Health Affairs, 12*(4), 7–29.
Mill, J. (1998). On liberty. In J. Gray (Ed.), *John Stuart mill on liberty and other essays* (pp. 5–128). Oxford: Oxford University Press.
Moyn, S. (2011). *The last utopia: Human rights in history*. Cambridge, MA: Harvard University Press.
Nussbaum, M. (2009). Human dignity and political entitlements. In E. Pellegrino, A. Schulman, & T. Merrill (Eds.), *Human dignity and bioethics* (pp. 351–380). Notre Dame: University of Notre Dame Press.
Nussbaum, M. (2011). *Creating capabilities*. Cambridge, MA: Harvard University Press.
Okin, S. M. (1989). *Gender, the public and the private*. Toronto: University of Toronto Press.
Okin, S. M. (2004). *Women in Western political thought*. Princeton: Princeton University Press.
Powers, M., & Faden, R. (2006). *Social justice: The moral foundations of public health and health policy*. New York: Oxford University Press.
Rawls, J. (1971). *A theory of justice*. Cambridge, MA: Harvard University Press.
Rawls, J. (1999). The idea of public reason revisited. In J. Rawls (Ed.), *The law of peoples* (pp. 129–180). Cambridge MA: Harvard University Press.
Rorty, R. (1999). *Philosophy and social hope*. London: Penguin.
Rosen, M. (2012). *Dignity: Its history and meaning*. Cambridge, MA: Harvard University Press.
Stacy, H. (2009). *Human rights for the 21st century*. Stanford: Stanford University Press.
Turnock, B. J. (2009). *Public health: What it is and how it works* (4th ed.). Sudbury: Jones and Bartlett Publishers.
Washington Post. (1995, November 7). Sexual assault called silent violent epidemic.
Winslow, C. (1920). The untilled fields of public health. *Science, 51*(1306), 23–33.

Winslow, C. (1926). Public health at the crossroads. *American Journal of Public Health, 16*, 1075–1085.

Wolff, J., & de-Shalit. (2007). *Disadvantage*. New York: Oxford University Press.

World Health Assembly. (1996). *Prevention of violence: Public health priority* (Resolution no. WHA 49, 25). Geneva: World Health Organization.

Wurtele, S. (1999). Comprehensiveness and collaboration: Key ingredients of an effective public health approach to preventing child sexual abuse. *Sexual Abuse: A Journal of Research and Treatment, 11*, 323–325.

Zimmerman, F., & Mercy, J. A. (2010). A better start: Child maltreatment prevention as a public health priority. *Zero to Three, 30*, 4–10.

Chapter 4
Law's Role in Preventing, Detecting and Responding to Child Sexual Abuse

Abstract This chapter discusses law's role in preventing, detecting and responding to child sexual abuse. It first notes the historical absence of children's legal rights and protections, and comments on the gradual social and legal change that has occurred. It identifies how political theory and public health theory translate into social norms, legal entitlements and protections, noting the recognition of children's rights by international law. Then, it focuses on the nature of national legal systems, conceiving domestic law as a social system required to protect individuals' personal security, and within this, performing the key role of recognising children's rights. It identifies law's role in the prevention, detection and response to child sexual abuse, and places this role in the context of the major sources of law: legislation, common law and international law. It then highlights key general principles from criminal law, civil law, and child protection law relevant to the context of child sexual abuse. It explores public health law and its range of mechanisms that are capable of preventing, detecting and responding to sexual abuse. Finally, it covers regulatory theory, an important consideration in any regulatory effort, and provides insights into institutional regulation; this is particularly relevant for institutional sexual abuse prevention and response. The key message of this chapter is that every society's legal system has a broad range of tools to create rights, obligations and remedies, and to set social norms, regarding child sexual abuse. Moreover, consistent with political theory and public health theory, every legitimate society has a responsibility to use these tools to protect its vulnerable citizens, including children, and to take reasonable actions to prevent, identify and respond to child sexual abuse.

Keywords Child sexual abuse · The role of laws in preventing, detecting and responding to child sexual abuse · The recognition of children's rights and their influence on law · Recognition in political theory and international law · Domestic law · Civil law and child sexual abuse · Civil compensation · Civil legal duties of individuals and organisations · Vicarious liability · 'Reform to statutes of limitation · Criminal law and child sexual abuse · Criminal offences · Criminal liability · Sentencing · Criminal law obligations to report known cases of child sexual abuse · The duties of the state to use laws to protect children from sexual abuse

B. Mathews, *New International Frontiers in Child Sexual Abuse*,
Child Maltreatment 7, https://doi.org/10.1007/978-3-319-99043-9_4

In a just society, including any liberal democracy, law is a tool for regulating conduct to promote and secure social justice, equality, dignity, and fundamental human rights, and for creating human capabilities. Landmark liberal theories have at their core a focus on the rights and needs of the individual – including the child as an individual – to dignity, equality, freedom, security, and ultimately, a minimal opportunity in life.

American jurist Benjamin Cardozo (1929) insisted that a law's justification was its furtherance of social welfare. The philosopher Richard Rorty (1999) said that the most worthy human endeavour is 'to work together so as to improve the future' by 'devising ways of diminishing human suffering and increasing human equality, increasing the ability of all human children to start life with an equal chance of happiness.' Law is a system fundamental to civil society to protect individuals and their most central human interests; moreover, it is a dynamic system capable of rapid change to respond to newly recognized problems and to make refinements to existing measures and responses.

However, legal systems have historically failed to promote and protect children's rights, and even today, there are gaps in legal systems and the social systems they regulate, which mean that prevention, identification and responses to child sexual abuse may be compromised.

It is instructive to consider some historical background to appreciate how far we have come in recognising and promoting children's rights, the use of legal and social systems to do so, and to more fully inform a consideration of the capacity of these systems to further develop and change to respond to the various challenges of child sexual abuse. This includes the legal recognition of rights to certain things, and against certain acts, and to create systemic responses, hence embedding rights in an instrumental way.

Historical Absence of Children's Legal Rights and Protections: Gradual Social and Legal Change

During the Dark Ages (approx. 476–1100 AD) and Middle Ages (1100–1500 AD), the time of life we now perceive as 'childhood' was, for many children, characterised by brutality and exploitation. Usually, children were seen as units of economic labour, or as saleable chattels. Abuse and neglect was commonplace. Children's almost complete lack of legal rights was embodied in the concept of patria potestas, which gave a father dominion over his children, and his wife. This power was so wide that in early Roman law the father had the right to abandon his infant child to the elements, and to punish his children, which could include death (Borkowski 1986; Gardner 1986). From at least the seventh century a father had the right to sell his child aged under seven (Thane 1981).

At least until the 1700s, law treated children over seven as adults; there are numerous records of children of seven and older being sentenced to death for trivial criminal offences (Blackstone 1982; Pinchbeck and Hewitt 1973). Children attained adult-like social standing from an early age, usually after attaining speech, and certainly from around seven. Rather than being seen as having different characteristics and needs from adults, the child became part of adult society, speaking, dressing and working as adults. The public conduct of life (and the lack of private space) meant the very young were exposed to adult behaviour and were treated similarly for nearly all purposes (Postman 1994).

A crucial reason for this social mixture of young and old was the absence of education. Postman (1994) viewed childhood in these times as barely distinguishable from adulthood, in large part because society's information availability determined its social structure. Most people were illiterate; life was conducted by oral sources. There was no demarcation of knowledge available to adults and barred to children. A limited concept of childhood existed because there was no literacy, education or shame; no secrecy about matters that could be quarantined to knowing adults. A different view of childhood began to develop in the late 1500s, influenced by Gutenberg's printing press and the possibility of literacy and education for wider sectors of the population. Economic and intellectual changes from the 1500s to the 1800s catalysed changing conceptions of childhood, and its demarcated from adulthood (Thane 1981). More adults had the opportunity to become literate, which took patience and the development of reason, reflection and conceptual thought. Childhood was understood to be characterized by those of a low age without the fully developed capacity to read (Postman 1994). Significantly, this new concept of childhood required schools to teach children to read and to develop the skills needed to become 'adult'.

Children thus came to be seen as qualitatively different from adults. John Locke (1632–1704), whose book *Some Thoughts Concerning Education* was published in 1693, influenced the evolving conception of childhood. Locke perceived a newborn child as a tabula rasa, a blank tablet on which an intellect needed to be imprinted. Education was required to develop rationality, self-control and autonomy. This imposed obligations on parents, educational institutions and the State. Around this time, other changes occurred, demonstrating growing recognition of children's qualitative differences from adults. Children were more likely to dress differently, had books written for them, and became owners of distinct names (in the Middle Ages siblings commonly shared the same name). By the 1600s, there were different ages of capacity for different legal abilities, indicating perceived standards of adulthood for different purposes including criminal responsibility (Hale 1971; Holdsworth 1936).

Yet, children's education in the 1600s and 1700s depended largely on their class, with formal education growing first within the middle class, and then in the lower classes (Postman 1994). Most lower class children were put to work as soon as possible without education. By the late 1700s, therefore, despite evolving conceptions of childhood and educational developments for some, it is likely that many children's lived experience did not differ markedly from that of their counterparts in previous centuries. While Blackstone (1982) recognized that legitimate children[1] at

---

[1] Legitimate children were those born in lawful wedlock or within a competent time of wedlock. A non-legitimate child was worse off; he or she was deemed 'the son [or daughter] of nobody' and had virtually no immediate rights.

this time were owed duties by their parents (at least nominally), children were subject to parental powers and owed duties to reciprocate their parents' procreative effort: 'to those, who gave us existence, we naturally owe subjection and obedience during our minority, and honour and reverence ever after' (p. 453). The duties owed to children were maintenance, protection and education. Parents had a duty to support and preserve (maintain) the child's life. Notably, Blackstone deemed the duty of education the most important, and condemned English law's failure to embed this in law.

Through the 1800s, then, a child remained completely within his or her father's power. A father's powers included correction, receipt of labour, receipt of profits, and consent to marriage, and these powers terminated only when the child attained majority at 21 (Blackstone 1982). This extent of the father's power was still evident as late as 1883, with courts recognizing a father had 'control over the person, education and conduct of his children ... [The court could not interfere with the] natural order and course of family life, the very basis of which is the authority of the father, except it be in those special cases in which the state is called upon, for reasons of urgency, to set aside the parental authority and to intervene for itself...to interfere further would be to ignore the one principle which is the most fundamental of all in the history of mankind.'[2] Children were at the mercy of the class and gender to which they were born, and of their parents' conduct. Pinchbeck and Hewitt (1973) note that many children were starving and indigent; children of the poor were still often forced to beg, steal or prostitute themselves; and it remained common for the poor to abandon children. Many children did not attend school and were forced to work, often in hazardous industries. In 1861, a third of boys aged 5–9 and over half of boys aged 10–14 were in employment; over a third of 5–9 year old girls and about half of 10–14 year old girls also worked for a living (Rose 1991). About half of all boys and girls aged 5–9 attended school, but this proportion decreased for the 10–14 year old age group. One seventh of the child population at that time was upper or middle class and were not employed.

John Stuart Mill and Children's Rights In 1859, the philosopher John Stuart Mill noted the potential for injustice contained in the father's power (Mill 1963). In an early statement identifying the necessity of some form of children's rights, Mill wrote that 'The fact itself, of causing the existence of a human being, is one of the most responsible actions in the range of human life. To undertake this responsibility...unless the being on whom it is to be bestowed will have at least the ordinary chances of a desired existence, is a crime against that being.'

Education Mill in 1859 had urged a minimum standard of education for all children, if not provided for by the child's parents, then by the State at the parents' expense. Mill despaired that 'It still remains unrecognised, that to bring a child into existence without a fair prospect of being able, not only to provide food for its body,

[2] *Agar Ellis* [1883], 337 (Bowen LJ).

but instruction and training for its mind, is a moral crime, both against the unfortunate offspring and against society.' (1963, p. 230). This formulation of a child's right to education was realised in 1880 through legislation requiring children to attend school. Generalized change solidified by about 1920 (Rose 1991). This development in England informed similar progress in compulsory education for children in English colonies.

Maltreatment At the time of the enactment of the education statutes, cruelty to children was still so accepted that there were no avenues of legal redress for acts short of murder. Indeed, the first statute to afford nominal protection for children from maltreatment arose in 1889 with the passing of the *Prevention of Cruelty to Children Act*. The Act made it possible for anyone to sue an adult having custody of a boy under 14 or a girl under 16, who maltreated, neglected or abandoned them in a way likely to cause unnecessary suffering or injury to health. However, children's rights remained nominal in practice, as children were still perceived overwhelmingly as chattels possessed by their parents (Rose 1991).[3]

Translation of Political Theory and Public Health Theory into Social Norms, Legal Entitlements and Protections: The Recognition of Children's Rights by International Law

As applied to children, the fundamental human rights expressed in political philosophy, including the individual child's right to protection, have been translated into several core human rights instruments. International human rights bodies first explicitly recognised children's rights in 1924 in the League of Nations' Declaration of the Rights of the Child. Subsequent developments were influenced by the creation of the United Nations, its founding UN Charter (1945) and the Universal Declaration of Human Rights 1948, which recognised that motherhood and childhood are special states of being entitled to special care and assistance (art 25), and which recognised a right to education (art 26), but did not further consider in detail the rights children require. These human rights instruments were motivated by the international community's responses to World War 2. Their influence on the development of children's rights was driven by their central idea that there are some

[3] Previously, the *Poor Law Act 1834* had imposed a requirement of parental support to children – though not from a recognition of children's rights but from a desire to reduce the number of individuals dependent on the State. The *Poor Law Act 1868* developed this position by making parents liable for willful neglect of a child under 14 that caused or threatened serious injury to health. Further legislative advances culminated in the *Children's Act 1908*, which established juvenile courts and extended the concept of neglect to include failure to provide sufficient food, clothing, medical aid or lodging, or, if the parents were unable to do this independently, to provide this through the laws for relief of the poor. This made poverty no longer an excuse for parental neglect.

rights so fundamental to individuals' chances of leading a fulfilling life, and to the development of a good society, that governments should respect them and the international community should protect them.

Important human rights instruments such as the International Convention on Civil and Political Rights 1966 promoted civil and political rights, such as freedom of assembly and freedom of expression, and the right to a fair trial. Others like the International Convention on Economic, Social and Cultural Rights 1966 promoted social and economic rights including rights to social welfare, education, health and housing. Solidarity rights, held by members of historically oppressed groups, were then recognized, such as the Convention on the Elimination of All Forms of Discrimination Against Women.

International rights instruments in the 1950s and 1960s had partially recognised the needs and rights of children as a group. In 1959, the Declaration of the Rights of the Child explicitly justified the need for children's rights: 'the child, by reason of his [or her] physical and mental immaturity, needs special safeguards and care, including appropriate legal protection' (Principle 2). Principle 7 promoted the idea that children are entitled to a free and compulsory elementary education. Other treaties in the 1960s incorporated isolated provisions concerning children, and education in particular.[4]

However, it was in the 1970s that reports of injustices afflicting children including high infant mortality, malnutrition, child abuse, recruitment as child soldiers and deficient education influenced a growing feeling that a dedicated charter of children's rights was required. In 1979, the International Year of the Child, Poland submitted a draft Convention on the Rights of the Child. Over the next decade, the draft was revised, and on 20 November 1989 the United Nations Convention on the Rights of the Child was adopted and opened for signature, ratification and accession. It entered into force on 2 September 1990 and soon became the most widely ratified human rights Convention.

The UNCRC purports to protect and promote a broad range of children's rights. These include the rights to life, identity, freedom of thought, privacy, a minimum standard of health, education, due process, to express views in decisions concerning them, and the right to have their best interests promoted in actions affecting them. There are also numerous rights to protection against harm, including protections from economic exploitation; all forms of sexual exploitation and abuse; sexual abuse while in the care of parents, guardians or any other person having the care of the child; sale, trafficking and abduction; torture and cruel and inhuman punishment; capital punishment; and unlawful deprivation of liberty.

[4] *Declaration on Social Progress and Development 1969*, arts 10, 11, 13; *International Covenant on Economic, Social and Cultural Rights 1966* art 13.

Recognition of Children's Rights and Interests in International Instruments

The **United Nations Convention on the Rights of the Child** (UNCRC) contains several articles relevant to this context. Most significant in this context are articles 19, 34 and 37. Article 19 obliges States Parties to take all appropriate measures to protect the child from all forms of violence, injury or abuse, including sexual abuse, while in the care of parent(s), legal guardian(s) or any other person who has the care of the child. These protective measures should include effective procedures for the establishment of social programmes to provide necessary support for the child and for those who have the care of the child, as well as for other forms of prevention and for identification, reporting, referral, investigation, treatment and follow-up of instances of child maltreatment.

Article 34 requires States Parties to undertake to protect the child from all forms of sexual exploitation and sexual abuse, and in particular to take all appropriate national measures to prevent (a) the inducement or coercion of a child to engage in any unlawful sexual activity; (b) the exploitative use of children in prostitution or other unlawful sexual practices; (c) the exploitative use of children in pornographic performances and materials. Article 39: States Parties shall take all appropriate measures to promote physical and psychological recovery and social reintegration of a child victim of any form of neglect, exploitation or abuse. These rights will be further discussed shortly; at this stage it is important simply to note the connection and theoretical basis for the actualisation of these rights.

Key articles are as follows:

Article 3(1): In all actions concerning children, including by public or private social welfare institutions and administrative authorities, the best interests of the child shall be a primary consideration

Article 3(2): States Parties shall take all appropriate legislative and administrative measures to ensure the child such protection and care as is necessary for his or her well-being, taking into account the rights and duties of his or her parents

Article 12: States Parties shall assure to the child who is capable of forming his or her own views the right to express those views freely in all matters affecting the child, the view of the child being given due weight in accordance with the age and maturity of the child

Article 19(1): States Parties shall take all appropriate measures to protect the child from all forms of violence, injury or abuse, including sexual abuse, while in the care of parent(s), legal guardian(s) or any other person who has the care of the child.

Article 19(2): Such protective measure should include effective procedures for the establishment of social programmes to provide necessary support for the child and for those who have the care of the child, as well as for other forms of prevention and for identification, reporting, referral, investigation, treatment and follow-up of instances of child maltreatment.

Article 24: States Parties recognize the right of the child to the enjoyment of the highest attainable standard of health and to facilities for the treatment of illness and rehabilitation of health.

Article 34: States Parties undertake to protect the child from all forms of sexual exploitation and sexual abuse. For these purposes, States Parties shall in particular take all appropriate national measures to prevent (a) the inducement or coercion of a child to engage in any unlawful sexual activity; (b) the exploitative use of children in prostitution or other unlawful sexual practices; (c) the exploitative use of children in pornographic performances and materials.

Article 39: States Parties shall take all appropriate measures to promote physical and psychological recovery and social reintegration of a child victim of any form of neglect, exploitation or abuse.

Parental rights are recognised by the UNCRC in several contexts, albeit limited by the evolving capacities of the child and by the requirement that such parental rights be exercised in a way consistent with the child's rights and capacities. The UNCRC article 5 also recognises the right of the parent "to provide, in a manner consistent with the evolving capacities of the child, appropriate direction and guidance in the exercise by the child of the rights recognized in the present Convention"; article 14(2) also says States Parties shall respect the rights of parents to provide such direction to the child when exercising her or his right to freedom of thought "in a manner consistent with the evolving capacities of the child".

The Committee on the Rights of the Child has reinforced these Convention rights and has made declarations which provide more substantive insights into the nature of the abstract rights. In 2011, the Committee elaborated on the meaning of "sexual abuse" for the purpose of interpreting and applying article 19 (the right to freedom from violence), stating (p. 10):

> Sexual abuse and exploitation. Sexual abuse and exploitation includes:
>
> (a) The inducement or coercion of a child to engage in any unlawful or psychologically harmful sexual activity;
> (b) The use of children in commercial sexual exploitation; and
> (c) The use of children in audio or visual images of child sexual abuse;
> (d) Child prostitution, sexual slavery, sexual exploitation in travel and tourism, trafficking (within and between countries) and sale of children for sexual purposes and forced marriage. Many children experience sexual victimization which is not accompanied by physical force or restraint but which is nonetheless psychologically intrusive, exploitive and traumatic.
>
> Sexual abuse comprises any sexual activities imposed by an adult on a child, against which the child is entitled to protection by criminal law. Sexual activities are also considered as abuse when committed against a child by another child, if the child offender is significantly older than the child victim or uses power, threat or other means of pressure. Sexual activities between children are not considered as sexual abuse if the children are older than the age limit defined by the State party for consensual sexual activities.

On the reporting of this abuse, the Committee stated (pp. 19–20):

> The Committee strongly recommends that all States parties develop safe, well-publicized, confidential and accessible support mechanisms for children, their representatives and

> others to report violence against children, including through the use of 24-h toll-free hotlines and other ICTs. The establishment of reporting mechanisms includes: (a) providing appropriate information to facilitate the making of complaints; (b) participation in investigations and court proceedings; (c) developing protocols which are appropriate for different circumstances and made widely known to children and the general public; (d) establishing related support services for children and families; and (e) training and providing ongoing support for personnel to receive and advance the information received through reporting systems. Reporting mechanisms must be coupled with, and should present themselves as help-oriented services offering public health and social support, rather than as triggering responses which are primarily punitive. Children's right to be heard and to have their views taken seriously must be respected. In every country, the reporting of instances, suspicion or risk of violence should, at a minimum, be required by professionals working directly with children. When reports are made in good faith, processes must be in place to ensure the protection of the professional making the report.

Statements and commitments in major reports support these principles. In 2006, in the Report of the independent expert for the United Nations study on violence against children, Paulo Sergio Pinheiro recommended (p. 27): "States should establish safe, well-publicized, confidential and accessible mechanisms for children, their representatives and others to report violence against children." At p. 26, Pinheiro recommended:

> The capacity of all those who work with and for children to contribute to eliminate all violence against them must be developed. Initial and in-service training which imparts knowledge and respect for children's rights should be provided. States should invest in systematic education and training programmes both for professionals and non-professionals who work with or for children and families to prevent, detect and respond to violence against children. Codes of conduct and clear standards for practice, incorporating the prohibition and rejection of all forms of violence, should be formulated and implemented.

In 2013, in its report entitled *Toward a World Free From Violence: Global Survey on Violence Against Children*, two of the key recommendations made by the Office of the Special Representative of the Secretary-General on Violence against Children were that:

- Explicit legal bans on violence against children should be enacted, accompanied by detailed measures for implementation and enforcement, including development of "well-resourced child protection services, well-trained professionals and a wide participatory process of public awareness and social mobilization" (Imperative recommendation 2: p xix, quote from p. 134); and
- Violence against children must be made a priority; the human dignity of children and their right to protection from violence must be at the heart of this global effort and national strategies (Imperative recommendation 8: p xix).

National Legal Systems: Law As a Social System Required to Protect Individuals' Personal Security

An individual nation's legal system provides mechanisms for promoting and securing the kinds of rights and interests discussed in the previous chapter. Political theory promotes the most fundamental rights and interests required of a decent human existence. Public health theory promotes social justice and individual human rights as applied to health-related dimensions of existence. This is consistent with rule of law theory, which set out core features of liberal democratic societies, and which require the legal protection of fundamental human rights (Bingham 2007; Tamanaha 2004).

These formal rights and interests would be of little use if not connected to a system that is capable of recognising them in substance, promoting their achievement, and providing tangible and accessible ways to obtain remedies when the interests have been breached and have caused injury. Here, the use of the term 'right' is used to mean that a person has a legal right to something, or from something. These are rights that are recognised by and can be enforced through the legal system. Legal rights accrue in civil and criminal law. In the civil system, a child has the right to bring an action seeking compensation for personal injuries. As a child cannot generally make a contract with a legal representative, and because a litigant needs to be able to instruct lawyers about the case, an action is usually brought for a child by a 'litigation guardian' or 'next friend'.[5] In the criminal context, a child can make a complaint concerning criminal acts committed against him or her, and the State can prosecute the accused wrongdoer. A child's possession of legal rights provides certain legal protections and remedies. These need to be enforceable against all responsible individuals, whether individuals or institutions, since it is a fundamental tenet of the rule of law that the law applies to all.

A jurisdiction's legal system is a social system required to protect individuals' personal security and provide appropriate redress. While different countries have different legal systems, most legal systems have common purposes and major elements. For our purposes here, we can understand a jurisdiction's legal system – whether national, provincial, or both – as comprising a system of rules created by two major sources of law.

First, there are laws made by Parliament (the legislature, as the representative of the people; this is legislation made in Parliament (Acts, or statutes) and any accompanying regulations (subordinate legislation, often made by the executive). Second, there is the body of law made by courts (the judiciary); this is case law (often called common law). Courts usually simply interpret and apply legislation in disputes brought before them. However, courts sometimes resolve uncertainty or ambiguity in disputes involving legislation, engaging in a more active role in law-making; similarly, where a novel case arises not covered by legislation, courts engage in

---

[5] Different legal systems achieve this in different ways. In some systems, this may be enshrined in legislation: see, e.g., *Uniform Civil Procedure Rules 1999* (Qld) r 93(1).

active law-making. Further, sometimes courts engage in a far more comprehensive law-making exercise, where the entire area of law is not governed by legislation, and instead is an area ruled by "common law".

There is a third source of law, which has greater or lesser force depending on other legal principles in the jurisdiction. This is international law, comprising international instruments such as Conventions (such as the Convention on the Rights of the Child), and customary law. The domestic force of international law depends on the jurisdiction's associated legal rules about this. In its simplest summation, some jurisdictions have an approach where if the nation's executive has ratified a treaty or convention, then the articles of that instrument automatically become law in the jurisdiction; that is, they are self-executing. This is the situation in the USA, for example. In other countries, such as Australia, an international instrument like the Convention on the Rights of the Child, even if ratified, does not automatically become "hard law" in the country; it does not become enforceable, unless further legislation is enacted to incorporate it within the domestic legal system. In this situation, however, ratification of some kinds of instruments can give other forms of legal entitlement, such as a legitimate expectation that the nation will make administrative decisions congruent with the articles of the Convention, and a right of procedural fairness to make a case against an intended decision which is contrary to those principles.

Dynamic Law: Legislative Change A crucial characteristic of both major sources of law, and especially of legislation, is their dynamism. Legislation in particular is a frequently changing organism, with developments influenced by social policy objectives and preferences. Legislative rules about a particular topic can therefore change dramatically, and change can occur frequently, to embed new policy principles and objectives. Legal reform creates rules where none existed before. Reforms create entitlements, and impose obligations, where previously they did not exist. Where existing legal rules are found to be not achieving their purpose, or to be causing unintended adverse consequences, reforms can be made to better promote their purpose, and reduce or eliminate unintended outcomes. In setting rules of individual behaviour and organisational conduct, or in failing to set such rules, law also sets social norms of every aspect of everyday life.

As will be discussed in detail in Chap. 5, clear examples of this have arisen recently in Australia, best exemplified by the state of Victoria. These developments have been informed by the findings of public inquiries and evidence of systematic concealment of child sexual abuse, especially in child and youth-serving organisations, and in particular by the managers of these organisations, and a new understanding that existing offences were also inadequate to prevent sexual abuse where a child was clearly being groomed for it.

Laws can also be created to deal with long-cherished customs, and in a generation can transform the legal landscape. As shown in Chap. 6, efforts to eliminate female genital mutilation or cutting (FGM/C) include criminal law prohibitions, which now exist in 26 countries in Africa and the Middle East, and in 33 other countries with migrant populations from countries that have traditionally practiced

FGM/C (World Health Organization 2018). These are very recent developments when one considers FGM/C has been practiced for thousands of years. Similarly, laws prohibiting child marriage can also rapidly undergo change, once sufficient momentum has developed to catalyse public policy reform.

Law is therefore the primary social system that regulates the lives of citizens and organisations and all juridical entities. Legislation and common law generally can be further understood as creating systems of enforceable rules in two broad bodies of law: criminal law, and civil law.

Criminal Law

General Principles from Criminal Law

Criminal law is generally understood as having several purposes. Certain acts and omissions are sufficiently harmful to individuals and or the community that they warrant formal prohibition and prosecution by the state. This also is a mechanism for creation of social norms. Offenders should be subject to appropriate and proportionate punishment. Where offenders are dangerous, incapacitation through imprisonment may be necessary to protect the public. Offenders may also require rehabilitation, which can in theory be facilitated through the criminal justice system. Criminal laws may also have a deterrent function. Criminal legal systems can also create special courts and procedures for certain categories of case, being sensitive to their qualitative differences. Drug courts and restorative justice processes are examples of this.

For Ashworth (2015), despite normative disputes about the theory and function of criminal law, and inevitable implementation challenges, there is a "principled core of criminal law" comprising four principles (pp. 28–29):

1. Criminal law should be used, and only used, to censure persons for substantial wrongdoing – noting that criminal law on its own is not an effective preventative policy, and appropriately targeted social, educational and housing policies may also have substantial preventative effects
2. Criminal laws should be enforced with respect for equal treatment and proportionality – authorities and policy related to enforcement must be cognisant of individual culpability and the seriousness of the wrongdoing
3. Persons accused of substantial wrongdoing ought to be given appropriate protections in criminal procedure
4. Maximum sentences and effective sentence levels should be proportionate to the seriousness of the wrongdoing.

Rules Prohibiting Specified Conduct In criminal law, rules are set down about what kinds of conduct are prohibited, or permitted, or required. Criminal law is normally set down in legislation, often in vast Criminal Codes, divided into different chapters which have a range of different offences relating to distinct kinds of context or behaviour (e.g., assaults and other offences involving violence against the person; sexual offences; property offences; fraud; homicide; offences related to corruption and abuse of office; drug offences; offences against morality). Each of these conceptual divisions of criminal law then contain numerous specific kinds of offence. Most such offences relate to conduct in relation to others. However, it is well established that the function of the criminal law also extends to regulating conduct concerning society as a whole, conduct purely in relation to oneself (e.g., drug-related behaviour) and conduct in relation to non-human objects (e.g., animals and machines), for the purpose of establishing and promoting public policy and social norms.

Breach of a criminal law – such as any one of dozens of laws about child sexual abuse – enables a person to make a complaint to police; police to investigate and arrest a suspect; and the suspected offender to be prosecuted by the State, and punished if pleading guilty or found guilty at trial. Here, the legal proceeding is brought by the State against the accused wrongdoer. The outcomes of a criminal prosecution are primarily aimed at punishing the offender, not at compensating the individual who has been wronged, although there are exceptions to this, such as in criminal compensation schemes.

A Range of Criminal Law Offences Relevant to Child Sexual Abuse Where a jurisdiction sets out a broad range of offences related to child sexual abuse, covering different specific acts, by different categories of offender, against children with different characteristics (e.g., children of different ages; children with impairments, and children with whom the offender is in a relationship of trust), the state has far greater potential to prosecute specific acts in a way that is more nuanced and sensitive to the situation. This is also more theoretically sound, in that it more closely reflects understandings of child sexual abuse from a theoretical standpoint. In contrast, where a jurisdiction has fewer behaviourally specific offences, and or where specific offences are framed more narrowly – for example, confining rape only to penetration by a penis, and excluding the use of body parts or objects – then the state has a more limited practical capacity to detect and prosecute crime, and protect children and the community.

Jurisdictions have naturally added new offences over time, as knowledge has accumulated, and as social circumstances have changed. In the Australian states of New South Wales and Victoria, for example, the legislation contains multiple extensive divisions of kinds of sexual offences, and lists of offences within those divisions, to ensure the reach of the criminal law is sufficiently broad to capture prohibited acts and to ensure culpability is extended to all those involved in their perpetration.[6] Depending on the approach taken in a particular jurisdiction, criminal sexual offences against children may include offences on a spectrum of perceived

[6] For example, the Crimes Act 1900 (NSW) Part 3 has entire Divisions covering sub-categories of offences: Division 10 covers Offences in the nature of rape, and offences relating to other acts of sexual assault'; Division 10A: sexual servitude; Division 15 Child prostitution; Division 15A Child abuse material; Division 15B Voyeurism and related offences; Division 15C Recording and distributing intimate images.

seriousness. At the less serious end of the spectrum, these offences may include those related to indecent exposure, and voyeurism. At the more serious end of the spectrum, these offences include indecent dealing with a child, unlawful carnal knowledge of a child, female genital mutilation, incest, maintaining a sexual relationship with a child, rape, sexual trafficking, torture, and maintaining a sexual relationship with a child. Detailed definitions set out the meaning of key concepts including "sexual assault", "sexual intercourse", 'child', "rape", what is required to constitute "consent", and all other relevant terms.

As shown further in Chap. 6, criminal law can and must evolve to deal with new technologies and social phenomena. Federal laws need to be created to punish offences committed outside the normal bounds of the jurisdiction to respond to child sex tourism. As well, new categories of criminal offence have been created in many jurisdictions to deal with offences related to the online creation, distribution and possession of child pornography, often referred to as 'child exploitation material'. New criminal offences are required to deal with the use of technology to access children for sexual activity, and to attempt to groom them for such activity. New criminal offences and exceptions need to be created to deal with a range of behaviours related to the creation, possession and distribution of sexual images.

Penalties and Sentencing Where criminal laws make it an offence to engage in specified conduct, each offence will specify the maximum term of imprisonment applicable. In addition, general legislative principles about sentencing will often exist, and these must be followed by the court. As well, previous sentences in similar cases often serve as a guideline for deciding on the appropriate sentence. A particularly significant policy decision confronting every jurisdiction is whether sentences for multiple convictions should be served concurrently (at the same time), or cumulatively (in succession). In some jurisdictions, sentencing principles include a long list of considerations, requiring the court to consider the seriousness of the offence, its circumstances, the presence of violence, the harm done to the victim, the presence of remorse, whether the accused assisted law enforcement agencies.[7] Where offences are committed against a child, additional considerations may be specified, including the effect on the child, the age of the child, the nature of the offence, the need to protect the child and other children, the need to deter others from committing the offence, and the offender's prospects of rehabilitation.

There may be further, separate principles about sentencing of offenders who are minors; for example, in Queensland, the Youth Justice Act 1992 s 150 sets out special principles for regarding child offenders, which prioritise rehabilitation, reintegration into the community, and detention as a last resort. This is an important dimension of this context, which should be closely considered when dealing with adolescent offenders, in conjunction with considering the nature of the offence, and the adolescent's background and rehabilitation prospects. Many jurisdictions have created special courts to deal only with children and youth offenders, recognising their qualitative differences to adults. In addition, criminal legislation may provide police and prosecutors with a range of powers and available responses for young

[7] See for example Queensland's Penalties and Sentences Act 1992 s 9.

offenders. Especially as applied to children and teenagers who may have committed a sexual offence against a child, it is important that these be applied prudently. Some jurisdictions enshrine legislative principles requiring this. In addition, most jurisdictions have special criminal responsibility provisions specifying that a child under a designated age cannot be considered criminally liable due to their lack of cognitive capacity. These laws are an important concession to child development, recognising still-developing cognitive capacity, and arguably even more importantly – even if not expressly imported into the law – the child's developing psychosocial capacity (Cauffman and Steinberg 2000; Mathews 2003). However, children who may not be considered as fully culpable moral agents because of these legal principles should still be held accountable for their acts, and must know what they have done is wrong and the effects their actions had on others. The balance lays in ensuring a child who sexually offends is made aware that what he or she has done is unacceptable, and providing supports to the child to reduce the likelihood of re-offending, while not unjustifiably punishing the child. A further interesting dimension of criminal justice responses is the use of conferencing. As a means of attempting to avoid some of the deficiencies of conventional criminal prosecutions and procedures, conferencing may offer a useful alternative means for resolution in some instances, but it is a complex intervention and in this context is applied to a complex scenario. This topic would require a comprehensive investigation all of its own, but useful guidance can be gained from the work of Kathleen Daly (see, e.g., Cossins 2008; Daly 2008; Daly and Wade 2012; Daly and Wade 2014).

Court decisions about sentencing of specific kinds of acts can also supplement legislative principles. So, for example, legislation may not provide specific direction about how a particular kind of act should be treated, or the extent to which a particular circumstance should attract more severe punishment. There are many examples of judicial principles filling these interstices in law, and this is an inevitable part of the judicial process in dealing with an endless variety of factual circumstances within which criminal offending takes place. As just a few examples, courts in Australia have determined that:

- The Victorian Court of Appeal has rejected the contention that digital rape is to be treated as less severe than penile rape[8];
- In sentencing offenders for sexual assault, threats to kill or inflict serious bodily harm are treated as aggravating factors[9];
- The offence of sexual assault is aggravated where the offence is repeated and there is infliction of indignities in addition to those implicit in the offence[10];
- In sentencing offenders for sexual assault, use of weapons constitutes an aggravating circumstance[11];

---

[8] *R v Brown* (2002) 5 VR 463.

[9] *R v Nichols* (1991) 57 A Crim R 391 (NSWCCA) (threat to kill victim's young son); *R v Keating* (1993) 65 A Crim R 315 (WACCA) (threat to kill); *R v Daniel* [1998] 1 Qd R 499.

[10] *Director of Public Prosecutions v Avci* 2008) 21 VR 310; *Leddin v The Queen* [2008] NSWCCA 242.

[11] *R v M* (2013) 116 SASR 219.

- The infliction of physical harm will aggravate the offence[12];
- In sentencing offenders for sexual assault, courts regard the psychological harm suffered by the victim as relevant.[13]

Obligations Imposed by Criminal Law to Assist Police and Notify Authorities The majority of criminal law is concerned with acts of commission. Criminal law offences generally state that it is unlawful to commit specified acts. However, there is a second dimension of criminal law, which is concerned with acts of omission.

Ashworth (2015) notes the duties that may legitimately be imposed by criminal law, and how these relate to the criminalisation of omissions. The conceptual normative argument for criminalising some kinds of omission has three strands (Ashworth 2015). First, there is the principle of urgency. The law may impose criminal liability when there are individual or social circumstances of sufficient urgency or emergency involving an interest of fundamental human or social value. Second, there is the principle of the priority of life. This recognises that each human individual and their right to life and survival is pre-eminent. There are situations where it is reasonable to require an individual to act to preserve this priority, such that omissions are legitimately criminalised. The strongest argument for application of this principle is to the priority of life and survival itself, although Ashworth notes that this argument may also extend to other fundamental human rights, such as the right not to be subjected to degrading treatment, and the right to liberty and security of the person. Third, there is the principle of opportunity and capacity. Where the first two principles already apply, it is legitimate to impose a duty in criminal law on a person who has the opportunity (for example, through physical presence or other sufficient connection with the circumstances) and the capacity to give assistance. In sum, the argument for creating criminal liability for omissions is at its highest when the interest in play is a person's life or other fundamental human interest; where protecting these interests is urgent; and where the individual has opportunity and capacity to assist in protecting those interests. In addition, there is a strong argument for omissions liability when an individual has a related obligation because of the nature of their personal role (such as their role as a parent or caregiver), or their professional role (such as their role as a medical practitioner or teacher).

Criminal law can therefore legitimately impose a range of civic obligations to promote both the social good, and the protection of individuals. These obligations can extend to assist in law enforcement and crime prevention, to notify police about known serious offences, and to notify authorities about serious offences against vulnerable persons. A range of these criminal law reporting duties exist in Australia, including some new duties created after recommendations made by the Royal Commission Into Institutional Responses to Child Sexual Abuse, and these will be discussed in Chap. 5.

[12] *R v Basic* [2000] QCA 155; *R v Daniel* [1998] 1 Qd R 499.

[13] *R v EK* [2013] QCA 278; *ZZ v The Queen* [2013] NSWCCA 83; *TB v New South Wales* [2012] NSWSC 143; *DC v New South Wales* [2012] NSWSC 142.

Civil Law

General Principles from Civil Law

As with all criminal offences, the criminal offences noted above primarily recognise that these duties are owed not only to the child victim, but are duties owed to the State. This remains so even with modern victims of crime compensation schemes. Yet, alongside the criminal offences, the law clearly recognises the rights possessed by the child victim as having their equivalent in civil law, with this branch of law giving the child victim the right to a personal remedy to gain access to compensation for harm, injury, pain and suffering and other loss (such as lost opportunity and economic loss), and to facilitate health rehabilitation. For both physical and sexual assaults, the relevant causes of action lie in tort law, in trespass to the person (common law assault and battery), and negligence. For neglect, the cause of action would lie in the tort of negligence.

These rights and remedies in civil law rest on foundational concepts resonating with the individual rights and liberties recognised by liberal theory. The basic right underpinning all these is the general legal right to bodily inviolability, or bodily integrity, clearly recognised for at least three centuries. The philosophical concept underpinning this legal principle is autonomy (self-rule); that is, an individual has a right to choose what happens regarding his or her own body, and this entails a right to bodily integrity. The principle of autonomy heavily informs the common law in general. Autonomy is an interest held not only by parents, but by children. The very basis of tort law is that one individual has interfered with the 'autonomy' of another person's body or private interests, either by an intentional act, a negligent manner of acting which has caused damage, or a failure to act when under a legal duty to do so.

Branches of Civil Law Providing Remedies for Breaches of Prohibited Conduct and Duties Owed to Others Civil law also sets down rules about what kinds of conduct are prohibited, or permitted, or required. Whereas criminal law is a discrete body of law, civil law has multiple branches. Civil law often comprises a mixture of legislation and common law. Familiar branches of civil law include contract law, constitutional law, corporations law, family law, environmental law, and administrative law. Other aspects of civil law are less discrete, and instead regulate specific domains of activity: for example, school systems may be regulated by multiple civil statutes.

A range of civil or regulatory processes are also regulated by civil law, via statutory enactments. These are all relevant in the child sexual abuse context, including measures implemented to better prevent, identify and respond to CSA in both institutional and non-institutional settings. For example, where a jurisdiction creates a redress scheme to compensate survivors of institutional child sexual abuse, the vehicle for this will be a legislative scheme which sets out its nature, objectives, parameters and mechanisms. Similarly, where a jurisdiction creates a "reportable conduct scheme", requiring managers of child and youth-serving organisations to report suspected cases of staff sexual abuse of children to an external independent government entity so that the reis objective oversight of how the organisation deals with the matter, the vehicle for this scheme will be a legislative scheme which sets out the nature, objectives, parameters and mechanisms of the scheme. Similarly, where legislative mandatory reporting duties are created, these will be implemented in statutory form, normally in child protection legislation. Similarly, where a jurisdiction decides that organisations serving children and youth need to adopt certain practices to minimise the likelihood of sexual abuse occurring within the organisation, or of inappropriate response to it, these policy objectives may be embedded in a legislative scheme requiring these kinds of child-safe standards to be adopted. Other civil legislation will set time limits – or will specify that there are no time limits – in which an individual who experiences child sexual abuse should bring a civil claim for compensation; these are civil statutes of limitation, and other statutes which set out procedural requirements for the brining of civil legal claims.

Of the vast body of civil law, the branch of tort law is particularly relevant to child sexual abuse (Hoyano and Keenan 2007).[14] Tort law itself has sub-branches, which include:

- the law of negligence (which includes laws about the nature and scope of the duty of care owed by an individual or institution to another person, and the circumstances under which this duty will be breached; these actions require the plaintiff to show that the defendant owed her or him a duty of care; that this duty was breached; and that the breach caused damage);
- the law of trespass to the person (laws about assault and battery; these actions are usually actionable *per se*, meaning without proof of damage);
- the law of vicarious liability (legal principles about when an employer will be held liable for the acts of its employees, including intentional criminal acts); and
- the law of damages (legal principles about what different kinds of financial compensation can be awarded for injury, and how the amount of financial compensation is calculated; for example, compensation for pain and suffering, for lost economic opportunity, for medical costs, and "exemplary damages", which can be awarded in situations of particularly egregious misconduct).

Where an individual's rights under civil law are infringed – for example, if a child is sexually abused – then depending on the factual circumstances, a range of entitlements under civil law may be activated and remedies may be available for the breach of these rights. Here, the legal proceeding is brought by the individual who has suffered injury or damage or breach of their rights, against the individual or institution (or both) who is responsible for the injury. Where a case involves an institution, then depending on the circumstances, it could involve a school authority (e.g., sexual abuse of a child attending a private school), a sporting organisation

[14] The extraordinary work by Hoyano & Keenan deserves special mention. It is not limited to sexual abuse, and covers issues, principles and remedies from family law, civil law, human rights law, and criminal law, with a focus on the UK but including coverage of other Western jurisdictions.

(e.g., abuse of a child occurring within a sports setting by an instructor or team doctor), a church or its juridical entity (e.g., sexual abuse by clergy or non-clergy in a religious school), or a government (e.g., sexual abuse by a staff member in a government school).

The law of negligence is relatively straightforward in its application to individual defendants or tortfeasors, including those who inflict sexual abuse. In such instances, the existence of a duty of care is clear, the breach of the duty is clear, and the task is then to identify the damage caused by the acts, which can be challenging. It is well established in common law jurisdictions that the intentional acts of child sexual abuse constitute negligence, as well as battery (Mathews 2003).[15]

Legal principles can be more complex in their application to institutional defendants. In these instances, the cause of action in negligence generally proceeds on the basis that the institution (1) owed the plaintiff a duty of care; (2) breached that duty because it either knew or ought to have known about the individual employee's conduct, or did not take reasonably practical steps to prevent it, or did not take sufficient steps to ensure the employee was hired with sufficient screening. So, for example, in the USA, school districts and school officials are most often held liable for staff members' sexual abuse of children due to negligent hiring practices, negligent supervision, or failure to investigate alleged misconduct (Fields 2017; McKee 2017; Payne 2017). Cases of negligent supervision can involve situations where either negligently or intentionally, a school authority: (1) failed to listen and respond promptly to reports from victims or other students about the CSA; (2) failed to listen and respond promptly to reports or complaints from co-workers, parents or other adults about their observations of inappropriate staff behavior; and (3) failed to look for, recognize, and respond promptly to other signs of staff misconduct (McKee 2017).

A Note on Vicarious Liability and Exemplary Damages

However, an institution can be held legally liable even where it is not directly liable in negligence. Under the principle of vicarious liability, an employing institution – which, for example, could be an individual employing school, or the broader educational authority – may be found liable for the acts of its employee or agent despite the employer not being at fault, provided the employee's wrongful act is committed in the course of employment.

Distributive Justice, Fairness, and Creation of Risk The principle of vicarious liability essentially embodies a public policy of distributive justice (Fleming 1998). It is a technical legal measure with the purpose of ensuring that injuries caused to individuals by individual tortfeasors whose conduct is sufficiently closely connected

[15] See, e.g., *Mason v Mason* [1997] 1 VR 325.

with the authority and opportunity provided to them by their employer can be compensated adequately, by the entity that created the risk and which has the funds to meet a judgment debt. The principle reflects a belief that one who employs others to advance one's own economic interest should be placed under a corresponding liability for losses incurred in the course of the enterprise.

Courts have considered the nature of the concept at length, since the appropriate understanding and application of the concept have significant consequences for both plaintiffs and defendants. For example, in *Viasystems (Tyneside) Ltd v Thermal Transfer Ltd and others*, Rix LJ stated (paragraphs 55, 79)[16]:

> The concept of vicarious liability does not depend on the employer's fault but on his role. Liability is imposed by a policy of the law upon an employer, even though he is not personally at fault, on the basis, generally speaking, that those who set in motion and profit from the activities of their employees should compensate those who are injured by such activities even when performed negligently. Liability is extended to the employer on the practical assumption that, inter alia because he can spread the risk through pricing and insurance, he is better organised and able to bear that risk than the employee, even if the latter himself of course remains responsible; and at the same time the employer is encouraged to control that risk ....
>
> What has to be recalled is that the vicarious liability in question is one which involves no fault on the part of the employer. It is a doctrine designed for the sake of the claimant imposing a liability incurred without fault because the employer is treated by the law as picking up the burden of an organisational or business relationship which he has undertaken for his own benefit.

Vicarious Liability of Employers for Child Sexual Abuse In countries including the UK,[17] Canada,[18] and New Zealand,[19] the courts have recognised the justifiability of

[16] [2006] QB 510.

[17] *Lister and Ors v Hesley Hall Ltd* [2001] UKHL 22. The "fair and just" consideration imports a value judgment, and has been criticised as being insufficiently grounded in principle: see Prince Alfred College v ADC, below. In the UK, other developments in the law of vicarious liability have clearly established that it is possible for an unincorporated association to be vicariously liable for the tortious acts of one or more of its members (*Heaton's Transport (St Helens) Ltd v Transport and General Workers' Union* [1973] AC 15, 99; *Dubai Aluminium Co Ltd v Salaam* [2002] UKHL 48); that an employer may be liable for its employee's tortious act even though it breaches the employee's duty to the employer, and even if it is a criminal offence (*Morris v CW Martin & Sons Ltd* [1966] 1 QB 716; *Dubai Aluminium; Brink's Global Services v Igrox* [2010] EWCA Civ 1207); that this extends to a criminal act of sexual assault (*Lister v Hesley Hall* [2001] UKHL 22); and that multiple defendants can each be vicariously liable for the single tortious act of an employee (*Viasystems (Tyneside) Ltd v Thermal Transfer (Northern) Ltd and others* [2006] QB 510).

[18] *Bazley v Currie* [1999] 2 SCR 534. The Court unanimously found the employer vicatiously liable. Here, the abuse was inflicted by an employee of a children's foundation which conducted residential care facilities for the treatment of emotionally troubled children. His role in relation to the children amounted to that of a substitute parent. There was little doubt about the authority, power and control he exerted over the children (which created vicarious liability due to the enterprise risk caused: contrast the related case of *Jacobi v Griffiths* [1999] 2 SCR 570, where vicarious liability was not found, although by a majority of 4:3). In *Bazley*, the Supreme Court of Canada considered that it is appropriate to impose liability where there is "a significant connection between the creation or enhancement of a risk and the wrong that accrues therefrom".

[19] *S v Attorney-General* [2003] 3 NZLR 450.

making the institution vicariously liable for the intentional acts of their employees or agents. The courts in these cases have considered that it is just, fair or reasonable to hold the employer or authority liable for intentional wrongful conduct of the employee or agent, in situations where the risk of child sexual absue occurring is sufficiently closely connected to the enterprise in which the employer or authority is engaged.

The case law from the UK is particularly instructive, including in its treatment of the Catholic Church. In the UK, for example, in *Lister and Ors v Hesley Hall Ltd* [2001] UKHL 22, the abuser was a warden of a boarding house where pupils of the school resided; the school was conducted by the warden's employer. The boarding house was intended to be the boys' home and the warden's role was one of complete supervision. It was found that his conduct in that role enabled him to establish control over the boys that he abused. The House of Lords determined vicarious liability on the basis that the employer undertook to care for the boys through the service of a warden, indicating a "very close connection between the torts of the warden and his employment". The means by which the requisite "closeness" of the connection was to be assessed was "whether the warden's torts were so closely connected with his employment that it would be fair and just to hold the employers vicariously liable"; the court found the sexual abuse was "inextricably interwoven" with the warden's performance of his duties. The connection is clearly not that the abuse was part of his duties; but that the duties performed by the warden created the circumstances of intimacy and opportunity that created the risk.

In *JGE v The Trustees of the Portsmouth Roman Catholic Diocesan Trust & Anor* [2012] 1 All ER 723, the Catholic Church resisted findings that it was vicariously liable for sexual abuse committed by a priest. This case was concerned first with the preliminary issue of whether the Diocesan Trust could be vicariously liable for acts of sexual abuse committed by a parish priest in the diocese: the majority of the court held that the Trust could be so liable. At first instance,[20] MacDuff J adopted the "close connection" test for vicarious liabilty, which comprised two stages. First, it was found that there was a sufficiently close connection, "akin to employment" between the tortfeasor and the defendant – even if not technically one of formal employment – for there to be a relationship that gave rise to vicarious liability. The second stage was to consider whether the tort was closely connected to the tortfeasor's employment. MacDuff J found the priest was appointed by the church to do work for its benefit. The Church had trained and ordained the priest for this purpose. The Church gave him the authority to act, a place to preach, a place to live and clerical robes to wear. The Church gave him "immense power" and appointed him to the position of trust he used to inflict the sexual abused.

The Church appealed, but the appeal was dismissed. A 2:1 majority of the Court of Appeal held that the relationship between a bishop and priest can be regarded as sufficiently akin to employment, so that the Church may be vicariously liable for

---

[20] *JGE v The English Province of Our Lady of Charity and The Trustees of the Portsmouth Roman Catholic Diocesan Trust* [2011] EWHC 2871.

abuse by a priest. The Court found the relationship between a bishop and priest has all the characteristics of an employment relationship, and that it was just and fair to impose vicarious liability. This judgment was significant in confirming the possiility of vicarious liability even in relationships akin to employment where there was no conventional formal employment contract. The Court of Appeal stated that such a relationship may exist where there was a sufficient degree of control by one party over the other, and where the wrongdoer was carrying out the purposes of the other, and if it was "fair, just and reasonable" to impute vicarious liability. All these factors were found to exist in the relationship between a bishop and priest.[21]

This outcome was highly significant, especially for the Catholic Church and its potential liability. The question of the scope of vicarious liability arose again shortly after, and was considered by the Supreme Court in *The Catholic Child Welfare Society and others (Appellants) v Various Claimants (FC) and The Institute of the Brothers of the Christian Schools and others (Respondents)*.[22] Here, the Supreme Court confirmed the existing two stage approach to whether vicarious liability is established. The first stage is to consider the relationship of the individual employee and the employer to see whether it is one that is capable of giving rise to vicarious liability. The second stage is to consider the connection that links *the relationship between* the individual employee and the employer, and the act or omission of the individual employee. In this case, both stages were in issue; namely, there was an issue as to whether the relationship between the Institute and the brothers teaching at St William's was one that was capable of giving rise to vicarious liability. There was also an issue as to whether the acts, or alleged acts, of sexual abuse were connected to that relationship in such a way as to give rise to vicarious liability.

The Court held both stages were satisfied. Regarding Stage 1, the Court held (paragraphs 56–58):

---

[21] In the Court of Appeal, Ward and Davis LJJ found it possible to describe the relationship between the bishop and the priest as being "akin to employment". Ward LJ achieved this by treating the ministry of the Roman Catholic Church as a business carried on by the bishop, by finding that the priest carried on that business under a degree of control by the bishop and by finding that the priest was part and parcel of the organisation of the business and integrated into it.

[22] [2012] UKSC 56. In this case, the issue was who, if anyone, was liable for a large number of alleged acts of sexual abuse of children at a residential care institution for boys which were originally operated by the Brothers of the Christian Schools. Civil claims had been brought against two groups of defendants by 170 men regarding abuse between 1958 and 1992. The first group (the Middlesborough defendants) had taken over the management of the school in 1973 and inherited, under statute, the liabilities of the school before that date. The second group (the De La Salle defendants) represented an institute known as the Brothers of the Christian Schools (lay brothers of the Catholic Church). In the Court of Appeal, the De La Salle defendants had been found not vicariously liable for acts of abuse committed by members of the institute. The Middlesborough defendants (who had used a brother as headmaster of the institute and contracted four brothers as employee teachers) were held vicariously liable for acts of abuse by the teachers. This was not challenged; what was in issue was whether the De La Salle defendants were also vicariously liable. The Supreme Court was required to determine whether the relationship between the De La Salle defendants and the brothers teaching at the residential care institution was capable of giving rise to vicarious liability.

> In the context of vicarious liability the relationship between the teaching brothers and the Institute had many of the elements, and all the essential elements, of the relationship between employer and employees:
>
> (i) The institute was subdivided into a hierarchical structure and conducted its activities as if it were a corporate body.
> (ii) The teaching activity of the brothers was undertaken because the Provincial directed the brothers to undertake it. True it is that the brothers entered into contracts of employment with the Middlesbrough Defendants, but they did so because the Provincial required them to do so.
> (iii) The teaching activity undertaken by the brothers was in furtherance of the objective, or mission, of the Institute.
> (iv) The manner in which the brother teachers were obliged to conduct themselves as teachers was dictated by the Institute's rules.
>
> The relationship between the teacher brothers and the Institute differed from that of the relationship between employer and employee in that:
>
> (i) The brothers were bound to the Institute not by contract, but by their vows.
> (ii) Far from the Institute paying the brothers, the brothers entered into deeds under which they were obliged to transfer all their earnings to the Institute. The Institute catered for their needs from these funds.
>
> Neither of these differences is material. Indeed they rendered the relationship between the brothers and the Institute closer than that of an employer and its employees.

Accordingly, the Supreme Court held that the relationship between the teaching brothers and the institute was sufficiently akin to that of employer and employees to satisfy stage one of the test for vicarious liability. Regarding Stage 2 – the connection between the brothers' acts of abuse and the relationship between the brothers and the Institute – the Court noted that vicarious liability attaches to acts done "in the course of the employment" of the employee (and in other relationships akin to employment), that this covers situations where the employee does something that he is employed to do in a manner that is negligent, and that in such cases the necessary connection between his relationship with his employer and his tortious act will be clearly established.

The Court noted the fact that child sexual abuse can never be a negligent way of performing such a requirement, and considered the circumstances under which such acts can give rise to vicarious liability. The Court identified the core aspect of the employer creating or significantly enhancing the risk of abuse due to the carrying on of its business. It held that[23]:

> The precise criteria for imposing vicarious liability for sexual abuse are still in the course of refinement by judicial decision. ...[This case] is concerned with the liability of bodies that have, in pursuance of their own interests, caused their employees or persons in a relationship similar to that of employees, to have access to children in circumstances where abuse has been facilitated.
>
> Starting with the Canadian authorities a common theme can be traced through most of the cases ... Vicarious liability is imposed where a defendant, whose relationship with the abuser put it in a position to use the abuser to carry on its business or to further its own interests, has done so in a manner which has created or significantly enhanced the risk that

[23] Paragraphs [85]–[87].

> the victim or victims would suffer the relevant abuse. The essential closeness of connection between the relationship between the defendant and the tortfeasor and the acts of abuse thus involves a strong causative link.
>
> These are the criteria that establish the necessary "close connection" between relationship and abuse. I do not think that it is right to say that creation of risk is simply a policy consideration and not one of the criteria. Creation of risk is not enough, of itself, to give rise to vicarious liability for abuse but it is always likely to be an important element in the facts that give rise to such liability.

The Court then considered the qualitative characteristics of the relationship between the employer and the individuals concerned, and of the acts of abuse.[24] The Court concluded that both the necessary relationship between the brothers and the Institute and the close connection between that relationship and the abuse committed at the school were proved. The Court found this was.

"not a borderline case. It is one where it is fair, just and reasonable, by reason of the satisfaction of the relevant criteria, for the Institute to share with the

---

[24] In the judgment of Lord Phillips, with whom Lady Hale, Lord Kerr, Lord Wilson and Lord Carnwath agreed, the Court stated at [89–91, my emphasis]: "The Institute was subdivided into a hierarchical structure and conducted its activities as if it were a corporate body. The brothers were subject to the directions as to their employment and the general supervision of the Provincial, their superior within that hierarchical structure. But the relationship was not simply one akin to that of employer and employee. The business and mission of the Institute was the common business and mission of every brother who was a member of it. ... That business was the provision of a Christian education to boys. It was to achieve that mission that the brothers joined and remained members of the Institute. ... *The relationship between the Institute and the brothers enabled the Institute to place the brothers in teaching positions and, in particular, in the position of headmaster at St William's. The standing that the brothers enjoyed as members of the Institute led the managers of that school to comply with the decisions of the Institute as to who should fill that key position. It is particularly significant that the Institute provided the headmasters, for the running of the school was largely carried out by the headmasters. The brother headmaster was almost always the Director of the Institute's community, living on the school premises. There was thus a very close connection between the relationship between the brothers and the Institute and the employment of the brothers as teachers in the school.*"

At [92–92, my emphasis], the Court considered the connection between the abuse, and the relationship between the brothers and the Institute: "Living cloistered on the school premises were vulnerable boys. They were triply vulnerable. They were vulnerable because they were children in a school; they were vulnerable because they were virtually prisoners in the school; and they were vulnerable because their personal histories made it even less likely that if they attempted to disclose what was happening to them they would be believed. *The brother teachers were placed in the school to care for the educational and religious needs of these pupils. Abusing the boys in their care was diametrically opposed to those objectives but, paradoxically, that very fact was one of the factors that provided the necessary close connection between the abuse and the relationship between the brothers and the Institute that gives rise to vicarious liability on the part of the latter.* ... There was a very close connection between the brother teachers' employment in the school and the sexual abuse that they committed, or must for present purposes be assumed to have committed ... the risk of sexual abuse was recognised, as demonstrated by the prohibition on touching the children in the chapter in the Rule dealing with chastity. No doubt the status of a brother was treated by the managers as an assurance that children could safely be entrusted to his care. *The placement of brother teachers in St William's, a residential school in the precincts of which they also resided, greatly enhanced the risk of abuse by them if they had a propensity for such misconduct.*"

Middlesbrough Defendants vicarious liability for the abuse committed by the brothers."

Australia Australian jurisprudence on vicarious liability, especially as applied to child sexual abuse in institutional settings, has been uncertain in recent years.[25] However, it is now more settled after the judgment of the High Court of Australia in *Prince Alfred College Inc v ADC*.[26] In this case, the High Court first clarified that an intentional criminal act may still give rise to vicarious liability, provided it is still sufficiently closely connected with the employment. The employment must do more than simply provide an opportunity to commit the act; it must also provide "the occasion" for the act.[27] Further, the Court then held that[28]:

> The role given to the employee, and the nature of their responsibilities, may justify a conclusion that the employment provided an opportunity for the wrongful act and was the occasion for the commission of the act ... [for example] it may be sufficient to hold an employer vicariously liable for a criminal act committed by an employee where, in the commission of that act, the employee used or took advantage of the position in which the employment placed the employee vis-à-vis the victim. ...
>
> Consequently, in cases of this kind, the relevant approach is to consider any special role that the employer has assigned to the employee and the position in which the employee is thereby placed vis-à-vis the victim. In determining whether the apparent performance of such a role may be said to give the "occasion" for the wrongful act, particular features may be taken into account. They include authority, power, trust, control and the ability to achieve intimacy with the victim. The latter feature may be especially important. Where, in such circumstances, the employee takes advantage of his or her position with respect to the victim, that may suffice to determine that the wrongful act should be regarded as committed in the course or scope of employment and as such render the employer vicariously liable ... In the present case, the appropriate inquiry is whether Bain's role as housemaster placed him in a position of power and intimacy vis-à-vis the respondent, such that Bain's apparent performance of his role as housemaster gave the occasion for the wrongful acts, and that because he misused or took advantage of his position, the wrongful acts could be regarded as having been committed in the course or scope of his employment.

Exemplary Damages Exemplary damages may also be awarded in some cases. These are a special category of damages, having the purposes of punishment, denun-

---

[25] *New South Wales v Lepore* (2003) 212 CLR 511, where members of the High Court approached vicarious liability on substantially different grounds.

[26] (2016) 90 ALJR 1085.

[27] The court explained that "the fact that employment affords an opportunity for the commission of a wrongful act is not of itself a sufficient reason to attract vicarious liability. ... depending on the circumstances, a wrongful act for which employment provides an opportunity may yet be entirely unconnected with the employment ... [but] The role given to the employee and the nature of the employee's responsibilities may justify the conclusion that the employment not only provided an opportunity but also was the occasion for the commission of the wrongful act. ... By way of example, it may be sufficient to hold an employer vicariously liable for a criminal act committed by an employee where, in the commission of that act, the employee used or took advantage of the position in which the employment placed the employee vis-à-vis the victim." (1099).

[28] At pp. 1098–1099 (French CJ, Kiefel, Bell, Keane, Nettle JJ; with whom Gageler and Gordon JJ agreed).

ciation and deterrence. They are directed towards cases of particularly wrongful intentional acts, constituting "conscious wrongdoing in contumelious disregard of another's rights". Exemplary damages have been awarded in cases of child sexual abuse in the USA, Canada and Ireland, but not in the UK. In Australia, they have also been awarded, including in the Toowoomba Preparatory School case, where $400,000 were awarded in addition to the award of damages on other grounds of over $400,000.[29] More recently, In *Erlich v Leifer & Anor* [2015] VSC 499, there was institutional cover-up of sexual abuse by the headmistress of an Ultra Orthodox Jewish school. Exemplary damages were awarded against both the staff member ($150,000) and the school ($100,000). Even in jurisdictions that have tightened legal principles for claiming compensation and the amounts of compensation available, such as many in Australia, exemplary damages may still be claimed for acts of intentional wrongdoing. New South Wales, Queensland, and Victoria provide clear examples of this public policy measure.[30] In some jurisdictions, if the defendant is already considered to have been sufficiently punished, exemplary damages may not be awarded.[31]

[29] *S v Corporation of the Synod of the Diocese of Brisbane* [2001] QSC 473 (Wilson J, 6 December 2001, unreported, BC200108976).

[30] Section 52(1) of the *Civil Liability Act 2003* (Qld) generally prohibits exemplary damages for personal injury, however this ban does not apply to a claim for personal injury damages in relation to an unlawful intentional act done with the intent to cause personal injury (s 52(2)(a)) or unlawful sexual assault or unlawful sexual misconduct (s 52(2)(b)). Section 21 of the *Civil Liability Act 2002* (NSW) prohibits exemplary damages for personal injury in the case of negligence. This means that exemplary damages may still be ordered in the case of an intentional action. An exception to this can be found in s 26X, which prohibits the court from awarding exemplary damages in a case in which a protected defendant is vicariously liable for the tortious actions (whether or not negligence) of the person whose actions caused the personal injury. A 'protected defendant' under 26A of the Act essentially means the Crown, Government departments, and public servants. As an example, this means that the Crown will not have to pay exemplary damages where it is found to be vicariously liable for the actions of its employee– whether or not the employee's action was negligent or intentional. Section 24AP(d) of the *Wrongs Act 1958* (Vic) states that a court is not prevented from awarding exemplary or punitive damages against a defendant in a proceeding.

[31] See, e.g., *B v Reineker* [2015] NSWSC 949, where the plaintiff was regularly abused by the defendant, who was the plaintiff's teacher and swim coach. The defendant pleaded guilty to two counts of aggravated indecent assault of the plaintiff and four counts of unlawful sexual intercourse with plaintiff and was sentenced to a term of imprisonment. The defendant was serving his sentence at the time of the hearing. Adamson J found that despite the defendant's conduct meeting the description required for an award of exemplary damages of "conscious wrongdoing in contumelious disregard of another's rights" it was not appropriate to award exemplary damages against the defendant. This was because exemplary damages extend beyond compensation and are intended to fulfil the purposes of punishment, denunciation and deterrence; and in this case, the defendant had been imprisoned for the crimes on which the plaintiff's claim was founded. This amounted to substantial punishment, which operated as a bar to an award of exemplary damages.

Statutes of Limitation: Civil Claims for Compensation Brought by Individuals

Statutes of limitation give plaintiffs in civil actions a designated time period in which the action should be commenced. Normally, they provide the plaintiff with a relatively short time – often 3 years – to commence a civil claim after the events which caused the injury. Usually, if the plaintiff is a child, the time period is suspended until the plaintiff becomes an adult, and so in most jurisdictions where sexual abuse is the basis of the cause of action, the general position is that the plaintiff has until age 21 to commence proceedings.

These time limitation periods are animated by two broad policy considerations. These policy reasons have been articulated by the Supreme Court of the United States in *Order of Railroad Telegraphers v Railway Express Agency*,[32] the Supreme Court of Canada in *M(H) v M(K)*,[33] and by the High Court of Australia in *Brisbane South Regional Health Authority v Taylor*.[34] The primary justification is to secure a fair trial for the defendant by ensuring as far as possible that defendants can draw on sufficiently fresh and available evidence. The second consideration is the public interest in the prompt settlement of disputes, which is connected with the need to administer an efficient court system, and the general principles that defendants' lives should not be encumbered by the threat of claims about long-past events, and that plaintiffs should not slumber on their rights.

These policy reasons are generally sound, but they do not apply to all categories of injury. Moreover, these legal provisions are adaptable rules of procedure, and do not confer substantive rights on defendants. Expiry of a limitation period does not automatically terminate an entitlement to bring a claim. A defendant must consciously choose to elect to rely on the expiry of time to block the plaintiff's claim from proceeding. This was established by the High Court of Australia in *Commonwealth v Verwayen*,[35] where it was also held that time limits are simply procedural rules which do not automatically bar actions. Similarly, in *Chase Securities Corporation v Donaldson*, the Supreme Court of the United States has held that limitation laws are an adaptable policy statement rather than an intractable bright line barrier to litigation.[36] Moreover, the Supreme Court has confirmed the constitutionality of retroactive legislation to revive previously time-barred claims. *Chase Securities* held that limitation provisions are simply rules of procedure, not substantive rights. For this reason, and because the entitlement to rely on a limitation provision was not a fundamental right to life or property embraced by the due

[32] 321 US 342 (1944).

[33] [1992] 3 SCR 6.

[34] (1996) 186 CLR 541.

[35] (1990) 170 CLR 394.

[36] 325 US 304 (1945). Mr. Justice Jackson declared that statutes of limitation "are by definition arbitrary…[and] represent a public policy about the privilege to litigate. Their shelter has never been regarded as [a] 'fundamental' right" (p. 314).

process clause of the Fourteenth amendment, retroactive limitation provisions are constitutional. This was confirmed in *Landgraf v USI Film Products*,[37] which further held that retroactive legislation is valid if the statute expressly indicates this intended application.

These principles are significant because in the context of child sexual abuse, defendants, and particularly institutional defendants, have frequently relied on the expiry of the "time limit" to discourage or prevent a plaintiff accessing the civil courts to seek compensation. The denial of access to civil courts is an extremely serious issue, because it undermines an essential dimension of the rule of law, compounds the initial abuse, enables culpable defendants to evade justice, and prevents the justice system having a deterrent effect. Especially in the USA and Australia, in recent years a major public policy question has arisen about whether reform of statutes of limitation is necessary and justifiable to prevent these tactics and to recognise the qualitative differences in child sexual abuse claims compared to ordinary personal injuries claims. Major legislative reforms have occurred, and these are discussed in Chap. 5.

Statutes of Limitation: Criminal Prosecutions by the State

Many jurisdictions have no limitation period for criminal prosecutions, at least for offences beyond misdemeanours, regulatory offences, simple offences, or other offences designated by the legal system as a more minor form of offence. Accordingly, for serious offences, or indictable offences, or in some other way specified by the jurisdiction, the state will not be subject to a time limit in commencing a criminal prosecution against an alleged criminal offender. This is the general position in Australia, for example, although there are some exceptions to this which the Royal Commission recommended be reformed.

The rationale for this general principle, which differs from the starting point for civil claims brought by individuals, is that the state brings criminal prosecutions and has such a strong interest in being able to do so that it should not be fettered by the lapse of time. It is expressed in the maxim *nullum tempus occurrit regi* — time does not run against the Crown. As held by the High Court of Australia, individuals who are accused of committing criminal acts do not have a right to a speedy trial, or even to trial within a reasonable time.[38] There are still protections for an accused: so, for example, a court can stay proceedings if the effect of the delay makes the trial of the accused unfair or oppressive. To decide this, the following factors are considered: the length of the delay, reasons for the delay, the accused's responsibility for the delay and past attitude to it, prejudice to the accused, and the public interest in trying charges of serious offences and the conviction of guilty parties. In cases of child sexual abuse where the report has been delayed, applications for a stay of proceedings

[37] 511 US 244 (1994).

[38] *Jago v District Court of New South Wales* (1989) 168 CLR 23.

have been denied, even where the delay has been extremely long.[39] On a practical level, the reasons for this are that it is still logistically possible to prosecute the accused since the most relevant testimonial evidence will still exist, and no unfairness or oppression is caused. The accused must prove that specific prejudice would result to such an extent that the trial would be unfair, and that this prejudice could not be nullified by judicial action.

In some other jurisdictions, there are time limits for criminal prosecutions, even for serious offences. On grounds of public policy, these limits should be reassessed, as they are clearly capable of preventing appropriate prosecutions for serious cases of criminal conduct. It is essential for the justice system to protect the rights of the accused, but there are numerous measures built in to the system to do this – including the court's inherent power to stay proceedings if they should amount to an abuse of process – and the burden of proof (being on the Crown) and the higher standard of proof (beyond reasonable doubt) are also powerful measures. It can clearly be seen that a time limitation for criminal prosecutions can work to unfairly protect offenders in cases of historic abuse, especially for the most serious prolific offenders.

Public Health Law

Scholars have long recognized the immense benefits to public health and broader social wellbeing of legal regulation in multiple areas, including food safety, sanitation, immunization, and others (Gostin 2008; Mello et al. 2013). Gostin states that "law can be an essential tool for creating conditions to enable people to lead healthier and safer lives" (2008, p. 4). Gostin (2008) notes that, at least in the United States, the major breakthroughs in public health throughout the twentieth century were typically enacted through, or assisted by, legal measures. As listed by the Centers for Disease Control and Prevention (1999), these were: vaccination programs; infectious disease control; food safety; workplace safety; motor vehicle safety; tobacco control; water fluoridation; family planning; health programs for mothers and infants; and responses to heart disease and strokes.

Public health law urges a more complete and scientific understanding of the role of laws and policies in the prevention of and response to social and health problems (Gostin 2008). The concept of "public health law" is central to any discussion of a public health approach, yet is often ignored or glossed over, misunderstood, or misinterpreted. It is useful to set out a definition. For Gostin, public health law is (2008, p. 4):

---

[39] See *R v Birdsall* (NSW CCA, 3 March 1997, unreported, BC9701099), involving acts allegedly committed between 1961 and 1967, with the report occurring in 1995; *R v Dodds and Harris* (Qld CA, 18 October 1996, unreported), involving acts allegedly committed between 1984 and 1986, with proceedings instituted in 1994.

> The study of the legal powers and duties of the state, in collaboration with its partners (e.g., health care, business, the community, the media, and academe), to ensure the conditions for people to be healthy, to identify, prevent, and meliorate risks to health in the population, and of the limitations on the power of the state to constrain for the common good the autonomy, privacy, liberty, proprietary and other legally protected interests of individuals. The prime objective of public health law is to pursue the highest possible level of physical and mental health in the population, consistent with the values of social justice.

Public health law scholars explore the nature of effective legal techniques to regulate individual and institutional behaviour, provide remedies, and overcome political inertia and industry opposition (Mello et al. 2013). The legal tools to advance public health are diverse and powerful, and enable coercive interventions and the conferral of powers and benefits in a constant balancing act between respecting individuals' rights, and securing the health of the population and particular high-risk groups within the population (Gostin 2008). As conceptualised by Gostin (2008), these powers include:

1. The power to tax and spend (which also includes the power to provide tax benefits and provide funding to services and stakeholders)
2. The power to alter the informational environment (to provide information and education to the public, both generally, and in specific settings, such as in schools to children, and in organisations that would serve children and youth)
3. The power to alter the built environment (here, related to situational crime prevention in organisations)
4. The power to alter the socio-economic environment (especially to alleviate poverty)
5. The power to directly regulate persons, professionals and businesses (here, for example, laws regulating persons and professionals through mandatory reporting laws; and laws regulating organisations through licensing conditions, and reportable conduct schemes)
6. Indirect regulation through the tort system (for example, enacting law reform to enable responsible organisations to be sued in civil compensation claims; laws to create liability for directors of companies and organisations; laws creating higher claimable damages and civil penalties)
7. Deregulation by removing legal barriers (e.g., approaches to harm reduction through exempting those who are deemed not fully responsible for their acts, such as young children who commit sexual abuse; or providing alternative pathways for non-dangerous persons).

Public health law scholars are agreed that in some contexts the use of law may be not only necessary, but optimal. Some have commented that if anything, law is under-used: Mello et al. (2013, p. 1979) view law as "an underutilized resource in public health". They consider that promising legal interventions are often hindered by opposition from industry, and simply by failure to convince legislators of the need to act. They suggest that priority areas for public health law exist where there is a significant public health problem, where the mechanism underlying the problem is understood well enough to conclude legal responses are part of the solution, and where a specific legal intervention could be useful. Similarly, others have identified the avenues and opportunities by which law can create the conditions for improved public health, both amongst the population as a whole, and in specific high-risk groups (Attaran et al. 2012; Magnusson 2007).

While unintended consequences must be cautioned against, law may achieve outcomes that cannot otherwise be provided. For example, a legislative scheme can: provide mechanisms, services and funds;

- prescribe duties, obligations and penalties;
- establish organisations and confer powers;
- require accountability;
- embed mechanisms for monitoring and refinement.

In Chap. 5, examples of all of these mechanisms will be provided in societies' attempts to better prevent, identify, and respond to child sexual abuse, in both institutional and non-institutional settings.

Regulatory Theory and Insights into Legal Responses to CYSOs

Because of the prevalence of child sexual abuse in CYSOs, the diverse range of these settings, and the challenges faced by legal systems in designing methods of response which will attract compliance, some observations are warranted about regulatory theory and its relevance to this context. These issues were considered at length by Australia's Royal Commission in working out the kinds of measures which should be required to be applied in institutional settings, and how those measures should be legally created and enforced. The Child Safe Standards legislation, and the reportable conduct schemes, are two prime examples of this.

In the context of CYSOs, efforts to prevent, identify and respond appropriately to CSA involve multiple challenges including vulnerable children, high risk, and multiple sectors or industries serving children and youth which are fragmented and geographically widespread, and which have diverse workforces and varying levels of knowledge of and cultural commitment to CSA prevention (Mathews 2017). Two core concerns of regulatory theory are: (1) what kind of approach to the setting and enforcement of rules is both appropriate to the context and likely to be successful; and (2) how can society and industry best secure compliance with rules and overcome resistance at the individual, organizational and cultural levels, created by factors including ignorance, resource scarcity, and fear of exposure (Baldwin et al. 2012). Applied to the context of optimal approaches to prevention, identification and responses to CSA in CYSOs, regulatory theory offers insights into key questions including: (1) does the context of CSA require stronger government oversight of CYSOs and other centralized supportive measures in designing and implementing CSA prevention policies and programs?; (2) is the optimal factor motivating policy compliance in CYSOs the development of genuine moral commitment to norms of behavior (Parker 2006), and if so, how might this be developed in the context of CSA and CYSOs?; (3) do other major factors such as fear of sanctions, and fear of damage to reputation, influence individual and institutional CYSO practice and compliance, and what does this imply for optimal regulatory methods?

Different regulatory models exist and are thought to be suited to different environments (Cave and Baldwin 1999). Generally, direct government regulation is required for situations of high risk, high complexity, and uncertain industry or sector commitment to robust policy. Direct government regulation, where a formal directive such as through legislation is supported by the deterrent threat of a punitive sanction, is deemed preferable where the subject is inherently of high risk and significance, such as a major public health or safety issue, and where the government desires certainty about the nature of the policy, seeks universal application across an industry or sector, and existing regulatory bodies such as those internal to organizations may not have the capacity or commitment to respond to the particular problem. In contrast, self-regulation is suitable for settings where the subject matter is low risk, does not involve a strong public interest or health and safety concern, and can be effectively governed by the market. It will likely be effective where the industry or sector is cohesive, with individuals sharing a commitment to core goals. Co-regulation (industry-developed arrangements, supported by legislation to enable enforcement) and quasi-regulation (where the government imposes pressure to behave in a certain way but without legislative backing) are appropriate where the subject matter involves some kind of public interest, but less formal approaches are judged adequate to deal with the regulatory challenge, the regulation may only involve one branch of an industry, and it is appropriate for the industry to have ownership of the nature of the scheme.

The theory of responsive regulation prioritizes the nurturing of voluntary compliance through self-regulation and persuasive, informal enforcement escalating to coercion only if other methods fail, and has influenced a variety of fields including occupational health and safety law, environmental law, and public health regulation of food and alcohol (Baldwin and Black 2010; Parker 2013). This assumes regulated parties will comply due to intrinsic motivations and desire for social legitimacy, ideally eventually inculcating internalization of regulatory norms and trust between the regulators and the regulated (Parker 2000).

However, it can be difficult for policy to attract intrinsic commitment (Parker 2006). The central factor motivating policy compliance is thought to be the development of genuine moral commitment to a norm of behavior (Parker 2006), which represents a cultural and ethical stance held by the institution, its leaders, and its staff. More significantly, it has been proposed that robust approaches with strong government regulation and oversight are required for contexts of high risk, major public health issues, and multiple industries or sectors which are fragmented and geographically widespread (Hutter 2011; Mathews 2017). Hutter (2011) warns that compliance is influenced by a complex nexus of legal, economic, social and political forces, which create multiple sites of tension and risk. A single large or fragmented organization can possess wide variance in culture, risk management, and compliance expectations. Organizational fragmentation, exacerbated by geographical diffusion, the presence of multiple professional groups, different levels of knowledge of regulatory obligations, and cultural differences, present additional challenges for compliance. In addition, regulation and compliance should be seen not as a short-term goal, but as a long-term strategy involving entire diversified organizations.

A fundamental challenge faced by any regulatory regime is the question of what strategy will produce optimal compliance. Theoretical understandings of compliance suggest three motivational factors influence compliance by organizations and individuals with regulatory requirements: fear of detection of non-compliance and associated sanctions; adverse reputational consequences upon exposure; and a desire to conform to an internal norm about what is the right thing to do (Yeung 2004). In a study of regulatory approaches in a child protection context, it has been theorized that ten factors are required to optimize regulatory performance (Dorbeck-Jung et al. 2010): (1) Regulatees' ability and willingness to obey the rules; (2) Sufficient overlap between private and public interests within self-regulation; (3) A small number of actors in an organized and homogenous sector; (4) A high level of social responsibility in the regulated sector; (5) A high level of oversight of employees; (6) A high level of enforcement or pressure to respond to non-compliance; (7) Standards covering all essential matters; (8) Consistent regulatory strategies; (9) A high level of oversight of system performance; and (10) Corrective responses to counterproductive system performance.

The insights from regulatory theory are of great significance for an understanding of optimal forms of regulation in CYSOs to prevent, identify and respond to CSA. Insights from regulatory theory, combined with knowledge gained from the lived experience of CSA in CYSOs and the factors shown to have contributed to it, indicate major impediments to a regulatory strategy of organizational self-regulation or co-regulation. Even where the organization wished to do so, it is inherently challenging and often simply unviable for an organization by itself to develop a robust, scientifically and operationally sound policy infrastructure with effective implementation and oversight. Other organizations, whether through unconscious inadvertence or conscious opposition, will not be motivated or able to do so. The organizational, attitudinal and economic factors identified by Hutter (2011), and the features required for compliance posited by Dorbeck-Jung et al. (2010), will frequently be absent. In many cases, the development of sound and comprehensive policy, of cultural and individual commitment to it, and effective organizational oversight and enforcement, are fundamentally compromised. This may not be intentional or sinister; it may simply be a product of the nature of the organization and its lack of resources, knowledge and capacity. In some organizations, including those with higher risk of CSA, there may be an intrinsic absence of the qualities required for effective self-regulation of prevention, identification and response. The features of the Catholic Church enumerated earlier in this article present an embodiment of one such organization, both generally, and especially in the context of offending by ordained priests and non-ordained religious.

Multiple obstacles must be overcome to create and successfully implement CSA prevention and response strategies in all CYSOs. Challenges are presented by individual factors (personal fears; lack of knowledge; unhelpful attitudes; lack of time), and organizational factors (including lack of financial resources, time and expertise; size and diffusion of the organization's work; staff turnover; and problematic culture) (Saul and Audage 2007; Wurtele 2012). These may be viewed as factors of inadvertence (ignorance, incompetence, denial) or intentional wrongdoing (cover-ups, reputational control, financial protection, complicity) (Lanning and Dietz 2014). Accordingly, some CYSOs may not have cultural problems, and may possess intrinsic commitment, but implementation problems will still be posed by lack of scientific expertise, lack of financial resources, lack of time, high staff turnover, and the presence of volunteers (Wurtele 2012).

However, even more problematically, other CYSOs may possess cultural problems and a lack of intrinsic commitment to the problem of CSA, such that they intentionally cover up CSA, have a priority of protecting the institution's reputation, and may have senior staff who are complicit in CSA (Boyle 2014; Lanning and Dietz 2014). These circumstances may present an insuperable obstacle to self-driven change and sound practice. Such organizations are unlikely of their own volition, and without any external oversight, to embed the kinds of measures required, and to educate staff appropriately, to protect staff who make reports, to have leadership take credible responsibility, to create robust codes of conduct, to properly report alleged cases, to appropriately deal with suspected and known offenders, to have transparent decision-making, to resist protective measures to protect the institution's reputation, to instill a culture of ethical behaviour, and to voluntarily allow external oversight of their processes and outcomes.

The problem of poor organizational culture is particularly powerful and challenging for reform efforts. Smith and Freyd (2014) have concluded that organizations having certain cultural characteristics are more likely to provide an environment within which CSA can both occur, and be the subject of inadequate responses. These cultural characteristics include the organization possessing: (1) strict membership requirements (with a high level of institutional or societal value being placed on membership); (2) the institution (and or its leaders) having a prestigious position in society; (3) the institution valuing its prestige, reputation and public image more than the welfare of the children it provides for; (4) strict hierarchies without viable reporting pathways; (5) relationships of power imbalance; (6) relationships of trust and dependency; (7) prestige or high value to the abused child in remaining in the organization, despite the experience; (8) Prestige or high value to the abused child in remaining connected to the abuser, despite the experience; (9) fear of the consequences that can be visited upon it; and (10) operational lack of an organizational strategy to deal with CSA (including lack of a lexicon around the issue; ignorance of the issue; outright denial of the issue; all characterized by absence of adequate screening; absence of adequate reporting mechanisms and recording systems; absence of staff training/education; absence of policy; overt cover-ups; use of rhetoric and euphemisms to describe allegations; reprisals and adverse consequences for victims and whistle-blowers). The range of measures that can be adopted to create healthier organizational culture has been explored in depth by Palmer (2016, 2017). Knowledgeable and ethical leadership in every CYSO is a precondition for effective and morally defensible responses. The culture established and exercised in both policy and daily demonstration by an institution's leadership is critical in shaping events, attitudes and behavior of individuals in the group.

All these challenges inherent to the context of CSA prevention in CYSOs have major consequences for not only the need for regulatory responses to prevent and respond to institutional CSA, but for decisions about what are the more appropriate regulatory methods. This applies to different kinds of organizations, of different size, geographical diffusion, employee/volunteer composition, child clientele, and both the type of activity in which the organization is engaged. Responses must be tailored to the context, and be practicable. A major challenge is in determining the method of moving from public health strategy to public health implementation: how should, or how must, a particular strategy be implemented to give it its best likelihood of being adopted, of having its intended results, and minimizing unintended adverse results? How can a public health strategy best achieve coordinated implementation in different agencies and communities, and how can the full participation of communities be achieved? For example, even if there is broad consensus about the practices CYSOs should adopt, does this context present features suggesting CYSOs themselves should be entrusted with these tasks, without external oversight? Or, is a stronger independent oversight needed, to enhance compliance?

A public health approach should accommodate a confluence of several ecosocial dimensions. With respect to the child, we should consider children's high physical, emotional and sexual vulnerability due to their age, development, and dependence on institutional authority figures, their inability to represent themselves individually and collectively; their sex, since girls are more often victimized generally, and boys are more often abused in religious contexts. In relation to the offender, factors include spiritual authority, and professional power over the child's status and advancement. In relation to the institution, we should respond to organizational hierarchical features exacerbating children's vulnerability and embedding the power of individual offenders and their protective institutions, such as in settings of religious authority, private education, and elite sports. Even when without gross culpability, several other factors require attention: institutions may lack the desire or capacity to independently develop and implement required best practices to prevent and respond to institutional CSA; others may both wish and have capacity to do so, but may be hindered in such efforts due to lack of skill, diffusion of the institution's activity across multiple locations and settings, and logistical and financial limitations.

Conclusion

Overall, then, a jurisdiction's legal system is an essential mechanism to protect fundamental human rights and liberties, and promote individual and public health. A legal system is the dominant social system that can provide publicly-sanctioned formal means for criminal punishment. It is also the method by which a society chooses, or does not choose, to confer remedies on individuals who have suffered breaches of their rights and liberties, and damage to their health. A legal system embodies a society's systemic approach to the obligations and duties imposed on individuals and organisations, as set out in both civil law and criminal law. It also confers formal individual entitlements in both civil law and criminal law, and remedies for breach of these entitlements, and systems of independent oversight. It establishes penalties for individuals and obligations for individuals and institutions who breach their obligations, again set out in both civil law and criminal law, which have multiple purposes ranging from punishment, to ensuring compensation of those harmed, to deterrence. It can establish mechanisms to prevent, identify, and respond to child sexual abuse, applying in different settings of individual and institutional conduct. The principles in a society's legal system embody the recognised individual rights and preferred principles of individual life and social organisation. In forming a system of expected behaviour, duties and entitlements, legal systems create a set of social norms.

As will now be shown in Chaps. 5 and 6, this dynamic nature of legal systems endows society with a capacity to rapidly create substantial change in how that society responds to prevent, identify and respond to child sexual abuse. The choice to create this change sometimes takes generations to develop and must overcome entrenched social and legal norms of discrimination and violence against children generally or girls in particular. In other cases, however, these choices can quickly crystallise in response to shifts in social attitudes and a demand to end clear injustice, especially when supported by courageous lobbyists and survivors, politically powerful individuals or groups, public inquiries, women's voices, and the media. Such change can overturn centuries of injustice, as we will now see.

References

Ashworth, A. (2015). *Positive obligations in criminal law*. Oxford: Bloomsbury.

Attaran, A., Pang, T., Whitworth, J., Oxman, A., & McKee, M. (2012). Healthy by law: The missed opportunity to use laws for public health. *Lancet, 379*, 283–285.

Baldwin, R., & Black, J. (2010). Really responsive regulation. *Modern Law Review, 71*, 59–94.

Baldwin, R., Cave, M., & Lodge, M. (2012). *Understanding regulation: Theory, strategy and practice*. Oxford: Oxford University Press.

Bingham, T. (2007). The rule of law. *Cambridge Law Journal, 66*, 67–85.

Blackstone, W. (1982). Commentaries on the laws of England 4. In E. Christian (Ed.), *15th Edition, 23*. Abingdon: Professional Books.

Borkowski, A. (1986). *Textbook on Roman law*. London: Blackstone Press.

Boyle, P. (2014). How youth-serving organizations enable acquaintance molesters. *Journal of Interpersonal Violence, 29*(15), 2839–2848.

Cardozo, B. (1929). *The nature of the judicial process*. New Haven: Yale University Press.

Cave, M., & Baldwin, R. (1999). *Understanding regulation*. Oxford: Oxford University Press.

Cauffman, E., & Steinberg, L. (2000). (Im)maturity of judgment in adolescence: Why adolescents may be less culpable than adults. *Behavioral Sciences & the Law, 18*, 741–760.

Cossins, A. (2008). Restorative justice and child sex offences: The theory and the practice. *British Journal of Criminology, 48*(3), 359–378.

Daly, K. (2008). Setting the record straight and a call for radical change: A reply to Annie Cossins on 'restorative justice and child sex offences'. *British Journal of Criminology, 48*(4), 557–566.

Daly, K., & Wade, D. (2012). *SAJJ-CJ South Australia juvenile justice and criminal justice research on conferencing and sentencing: Technical report no. 5 - in-depth study of sexual assault and family violence cases part II*. Brisbane: Griffith University.

Daly, K., & Wade, D. (2014). Sibling sexual abuse: Offending patterns and dynamics in youth justice conferences. In A. Hayden, L. Gelsthorpe, V. Kingi, & A. Morris (Eds.), *A restorative justice approach to family violence: Changing tack* (pp. 185–195). Farnham: Ashgate.

Dorbeck-Jung, B., Vrielink, M., Gosselt, J., van Hoof, J., & de Jong, M. (2010). Contested hybridization of regulation: Failure of the Dutch regulatory system to protect minors from harmful media. *Regulation & Governance, 4*, 154–174.

Fields, S. A. (2017). Legal issues involving educator sexual misconduct: Understanding the risks and assessing the consequences. In C. Schwilk, R. Stevenson, & D. Bateman (Eds.), *Sexual misconduct in the education and human services sector* (pp. 91–101). Hershey: IGI Global.

Fleming, J. (1998). *The law of torts* (9th ed.). Sydney: Law Book Company.

Gardner, J. (1986). *Women in Roman law and society*. London: Routledge.

Gostin, L. (2008). *Public health law: Power, duty, restraint*. Berkeley: University of California Press.

Hale, M. (1971). *Pleas of the crown: Volume I*. London: Professional Books.

Holdsworth, W. (1936). *A history of English law: Volume II*. London: Sweet & Maxwell.

Hoyano, L., & Keenan, C. (2007). *Child abuse: Law and policy across boundaries*. Oxford: Oxford University Press.

Hutter, B. (2011). Negotiating social, economic and political environments: Compliance with regulation within and beyond the state. In V. Nielsen & C. Parker (Eds.), *Explaining compliance* (pp. 305–321). Cheltenham: Edward Elgar.

Lanning, K. V., & Dietz, P. E. (2014). Acquaintance molestation and youth-serving organizations. *Journal of Interpersonal Violence, 29*(15), 2815–2838.

Magnusson, R. (2007). Mapping the scope and opportunities for public health law in liberal democracies. *The Journal of Law, Medicine & Ethics, 35*(4), 571–587.

Mathews, B. (2003). Limitation periods and child sexual abuse cases: Law, psychology, time and justice. *Torts Law Journal, 11*(3), 218–243.

Mathews, B. (2017). Optimising implementation of reforms to better prevent and respond to child sexual abuse in institutions: Insights from public health, regulatory theory, and Australia's Royal Commission. *Child Abuse and Neglect, 74*, 86–98.

McKee, D. (2017). Liability of School Districts Under Common Law Tort Theories for the Sexual Molestation of a Student by a Teacher. 31 American Jur. Proof of Facts 3d 261.

Mello, M. M., Wood, J., Burris, S., Wagenaar, A. C., Ibrahim, J. K., & Swanson, J. W. (2013). Critical opportunities for public health law: A call for action. *American Journal of Public Health, 103*(11), 1979–1988.

Mill, J. (1963). On liberty. In *The six great humanistic essays of John Stuart mill*. New York: Washington Square Press.

Parker, C. (2000). Reinventing regulation within the corporation: Compliance-oriented regulatory innovation. *Administration & Society, 32*, 529–565.

Parker, C. (2006). The compliance trap: The moral message in responsive regulatory enforcement. *Law and Society Review, 40*, 591–622.

Parker, C. (2013). Twenty years of responsive regulation: An appreciation and appraisal. *Regulation & Governance, 7*(1), 2–13.

Payne, A. (2017). Proof of Public School District Liability for Injuries or Damages to Student Resulting from Harassment of Student by Teacher or Other District Staff Member. 108 Am. Jur. Proof of Facts 3d 87.

Pinchbeck, I., & Hewitt, M. (1973). *Children in English society, volume II: From the eighteenth century to the children act of 1948*. Toronto: University of Toronto Press.

Postman, N. (1994). *The disappearance of childhood*. New York: Vintage.
Rorty, R. (1999). *Philosophy and social hope*. London: Penguin.
Rose, L. (1991). *The Erosion of childhood*. London: Routledge.
Saul, J., & Audage, N. C. (2007). *Preventing child sexual abuse within youth-serving organisations: Getting started on policies and procedures*. Atlanta: Centers for Disease Control and Prevention, National Centre for Injury Prevention and Control.
Smith, C., & Freyd, J. (2014). Institutional betrayal. *American Psychologist, 69*, 575–587.
Tamanaha, B. Z. (2004). *On the rule of law: History, politics, theory*. New York: Cambridge University Press.
Thane, P. (1981). Childhood in history. In M. King (Ed.), *Childhood, welfare & justice, 12*. London: Batsford.
United Nations. (1945). *The charter of the United Nations*. San Francisco: United Nations Conference on International Organization.
United Nations General Assembly. (1948). *Universal declaration of human rights*. Paris: United Nations.
United Nations General Assembly. (1966). *International covenant on economic, social and cultural rights*. New York: United Nations.
United Nations General Assembly. (1989). *Convention on the rights of the child*. New York: United Nations.
World Health Organization. (2018). *Female genital mutilation: Fact sheet*. Geneva: World Health Organization.
Wurtele, S. (2012). Preventing the sexual exploitation of minors in youth-serving organizations. *Children and Youth Services Review, 34*, 2442–2453.
Yeung, K. (2004). *Securing compliance*. Oxford: Hart.

Part III
Problems and Progress: Contemporary Challenges and Responses

Chapter 5
Child Sexual Abuse in Institutional and Non-institutional Contexts

Abstract This chapter first focuses on major challenges confronting child and youth-serving organisations and high-risk settings. It then discusses the nature, key findings and major recommendations of Australia's Royal Commission Into Institutional Responses to Child Sexual Abuse, a landmark public inquiry into institutional sexual abuse, including a special focus on the Roman Catholic Church. The chapter then focuses on several recent examples of progress in responses to major problems presented by child sexual abuse in institutional and non-institutional settings. Developments from Australia in particular, but also from other countries, will show how new public health law responses, including through civil law, and with various emphases on primary prevention and secondary prevention, can create frameworks for enhanced prevention, identification, and response to cases of child sexual abuse. Some of these responses, such as redress schemes, reportable conduct schemes and child safe standards legislation, have specific application to institutional settings. Other responses, such as the abolition of statutes of limitation for civil claims for injuries caused by sexual abuse, and other kinds of legislative reporting duties, have broader application across society, as they apply to sexual abuse in all settings, whether within institutions, families, private settings, or other community settings. These responses are of broad application regarding prevention of child sexual abuse, early identification of child sexual offending, and ensuring appropriate responses once it is known or suspected. They are particularly relevant when dealing with high risk institutional settings and prolific individual offenders, both of which present especially urgent examples of the need for an appropriate societal approach to child sexual abuse informed by public health and social justice.

Keywords Child sexual abuse generally, and in institutions and organisations · Schools · Churches · Sports, cultural, arts and recreation settings · Prevention approaches · Australia's Royal Commission Into Institutional Responses to Child Sexual Abuse · Key case studies · Catholic Church · Major findings and reform recommendations in 2017 · Key recent progress in reforms to enhance prevention, identification and responses to child sexual Abuse · Legal reforms · Public health reforms · Institutional reforms · Child safe standards for organisations · Education and codes of conduct · Reporting schemes · Redress schemes · Abolition of civil statutes of limitation

B. Mathews, *New International Frontiers in Child Sexual Abuse*,
Child Maltreatment 7, https://doi.org/10.1007/978-3-319-99043-9_5

Sexual Abuse in Child and Youth-Serving Organisations

Child and youth-serving organisations (CYSOs) rely on staff and volunteers (both adult and adolescent) to design, supervise and engage in activities and interactions with participating children and youth. The supportive relationships formed between CYSO staff and the children and youth they serve is a key component of their success. However, under the wrong conditions these relationships can place youth at risk of maltreatment, including sexual abuse. Organisations have long recognised the risk of sexual abuse posed by people who are either preferentially attracted to prepubescent or pubescent children (i.e., pedophiles and hebophiles, respectively), or who may offend opportunistically. In addition, other children at the CYSO may inflict sexual abuse on their peers.

Comprehensive data do not exist about prevalence in child and youth-serving organisations (CYSOs), although there is evidence that such victimisation is common. Throughout childhood, approximately 9.6% of children have been found to experience sexual abuse in educational settings (Shakeshaft 2004), 10.0% in sport (Leahy et al. 2002), and an annual incidence of 9.5% has been found in juvenile detention settings (Beck et al. 2010). Accumulated data over extensive time periods have shown conservative estimates of the proportion of Catholic priests who have sexually abused children of 5% in the U.S.A. (Terry et al. 2011) and 7% in Australia (Australian Government Royal Commission Into Institutional Responses to Child Sexual Abuse 2017a).

Features of Youth-Serving Institutions that Create Opportunities for Child Sexual Abuse

In the context of CYSOs, CSA is a challenging context involving vulnerable children, high risk, and multiple industries which are fragmented and geographically widespread, and which have diverse workforces, and varying levels of knowledge of and cultural commitment to CSA prevention (Mathews 2017). Several features of the context of CYSOs create opportunities for CSA, both by adults who work or volunteer of the organisation, and by other children and youths who attend. There are features at the level of the child, the offender, and the organisation.

The child As recognised by Wurtele (2012), one feature is related to the natural vulnerability of children. Adolescent children often have an inherent vulnerability, due to their natural sexual curiosity, needs for intimacy and romantic connections, and still-developing skills of impulse control and self-regulation. In a related sense, pre-pubertal children are generally vulnerable to predation for slightly different reasons. However, these reasons are also related to their emotional needs and vulnerability, their early cognitive development, physical vulnerability, and other components of their personality that contribute to a profound imbalance of power between the child and the adult offender or the older or more powerful child offender. Some children have heightened vulnerability, particularly those with a history of victimisation, low self-esteem, loneliness, those from single parent homes and or those with low parental supervision, those with disabilities, and those with minority sexuality.

The Offender A second feature is related to the offender. Some individual offenders purposely seek employment in environments where there are vulnerable children to execute a premeditated plan of action, while other adult offenders exploit advantages and opportunities to offend based on environmental characteristics and personal attributes. In both cases, and especially in some types of organisations where the adult occupies a position of substantial power, the offender's status magnifies the opportunity to exploit the relationship of power imbalance. Especially where the offender is a particularly trusted adult, because of the nature of institutional abuse, the trauma is often magnified beyond the level that would have been reached were the abuse inflicted in another context.

The Organisation Third, there are features related to the organisation. Some of these features concern the physical environment, aspects of which can help to facilitate or reduce the perpetration of sexual abuse. These features include structural materials and design: do offices and other rooms have closed doors, windows, and sightlines; are there any surveillance cameras; is there sufficient privacy in bathroom facilities while also providing security. Other aspects relate to the specific organisational context and activities, embracing matters such as:

- the type, size and geographical location of the organisations
- the employee/volunteer composition
- the child clientele
- the general type of activity in which the organisation is engaged and the ways in which this activity is conducted (e.g. whether there are trips away from home; the level and type of supervision provided)
- the degree of control over the child exercised by the adult, for example whether it extends to training, diet, medical treatment, social activity; physical touch; whether there are ongoing relationships; presence of alcohol; rewards systems.

Sporting Organisations For example, sporting organisations may possess several features which create particular kinds of risks. The nature of sports presents multiple factors creating a substantial enterprise risk of CSA. Training often requires direct physical instruction, such as in athletics, swimming, martial arts, gymnastics and ball sports. Travel to competitive events can create further opportunities for offending. Many sports require physical treatment such as massage, and others require specialised attire which may be brief, such as in swimming and gymnastics. Many sports require changing and bathing facilities. Sporting organisations typically are characterised by highly competitive hierarchies in which children compete for status, representative selection, awards and career progression, and this can increase the closeness and dependency which often normally accompanies the relationship of coach and pupil. Other related aspects further create an atmosphere in which a relationship of dependence and trust and confidence can solidify between child and coach: the intensely competitive nature of sports can produce emotional highs and shared celebrations, while also producing emotional lows and crises.

Cultural, Arts, Recreational and Religious Organisations Other groups – cultural, arts and recreational – may share some of these features. In addition, the literature on CSA in religious contexts suggests that some key themes about CSA in that context may have parallels in some sporting, cultural, arts and recreational groups. Terry and Ackerman (2008) and Smallbone and Wortley (2001) found that substantial proportions of offending are committed in the offender's residence (41% of religious offenders in the Terry and Ackerman study; and 68.9% in the Smallbone and Wortley study of non-religious offenders). Terry and Ackerman (2008) found that a further 17.8% of offending was committed during travel, and similarly, Smallbone and Wortley (2001) found 20% of abuse was committed on an overnight trip.

Organisational Culture However, even more problematically, other CYSOs may possess cultural problems and a lack of intrinsic commitment to the problem of CSA, such that they intentionally cover up CSA, have a priority of protecting the institution's reputation, and may have senior staff who are complicit in CSA (Boyle 2014; Lanning and Dietz 2014). These circumstances may present an insuperable obstacle to self-driven change and sound practice. Such organisations are highly unlikely of their own volition, and without any external oversight, to embed the kinds of measures required, and to educate staff appropriately, to protect staff who make reports, to have leadership take credible responsibility, to create robust codes of conduct, to properly report alleged cases, to appropriately deal with suspected and known offenders, to have transparent decision-making, to resist protective measures to protect the institution's reputation, to instill a culture of ethical behaviour, and to voluntarily allow external oversight of their processes and outcomes.

The problem of poor organisational culture is particularly powerful and challenging for reform efforts. In the context of the Catholic Church, Sipe (2011, p.125) has concluded that "culture trumps reason every time". Smith and Freyd (2014) have concluded that organisations having certain cultural characteristics are more likely to provide an environment within which CSA can both occur, and be inadequately treated. These include the organisation possessing:

(1) strict membership requirements (with a high level of institutional or societal value being placed on membership);
(2) the institution (and or its leaders) having a prestigious position in society;
(3) the institution valuing its prestige, reputation and public image more than the welfare of the children it provides for;
(4) strict hierarchies without viable reporting pathways;
(5) relationships of power imbalance;

(6) relationships of trust and dependency;
(7) prestige or high value to the abused child in remaining in the organisation, despite the experience;
(8) Prestige or high value to the abused child in remaining connected to the abuser, despite the experience;
(9) fear of the consequences that can be visited upon it;
(10) operational lack of an organisational strategy to deal with CSA (including lack of a lexicon around the issue; ignorance of the issue; outright denial of the issue; all characterised by absence of adequate screening; absence of adequate reporting mechanisms and recording systems; absence of staff training/education; absence of policy; overt cover-ups; use of rhetoric and euphemisms to describe allegations; reprisals and adverse consequences for victims and whistle-blowers).

Lanning and Dietz (2014) and Wurtele (2012) also identified many of these organisational features. In addition, Wurtele noted the following:

- Centralised power in strict hierarchies;
- Lack of transparent and shared responsibility for decision-making (leaders make decisions secretly and internally with an emphasis on protection of institutional reputation rather than acting in the child's best interests);
- A sexualised work environment (characterised, for example, by language, dress, behaviour and other sexualised material);
- Lack of a culture of zero tolerance.

Multiple obstacles must be overcome to create and successfully implement CSA prevention and response strategies in all CYSOs. Challenges are presented by individual factors (personal fears; lack of knowledge; unhelpful attitudes; lack of time), and organisational factors (lack of financial resources, time and expertise; size and diffusion; staff turnover; culture (Saul and Audage 2007; Wurtele 2012). These may be viewed as factors of inadvertence (ignorance, incompetence, denial) or intentional wrongdoing (cover-ups, reputational control, financial protection, complicity) (Lanning and Dietz 2014). Accordingly, some CYSOs may not have cultural problems, and may possess intrinsic commitment, but implementation problems will still be posed by lack of scientific expertise, lack of financial resources, lack of time, high staff turnover, volunteers (Wurtele 2012). These organisations may still be reticent to discuss CSA (Wurtele 2012).

The range of measures that can be adopted to create healthier organisational culture has been explored in depth by Palmer (2016). Knowledgeable and ethical leadership in every CYSO is a precondition for effective and morally defensible responses (Mathews 2017). The culture established and exercised in both policy and daily demonstration by an institution's leadership is critical in shaping events, attitudes and behaviour of individuals in the group.

Hallmarks of Child-Safe Organisations

Conceptual advances have been made concerning what kinds of measures may assist in reducing CSA in CYSOs and in identifying and responding to it more appropriately. There is now quite a strong degree of agreement about what kinds of measures should be adopted by CYSOs to minimize risk and ensure appropriate responses. This is evident in approaches and organisational tools proposed by the Centers for Disease Control (Saul and Audage 2007) and by other leading scholars (Wurtele 2012, 2014), which are substantially supported in other approaches and analyses (Parent and Demers 2011; Walsh et al. 2013). These models have subtle differences but all have a common fundamental basis, which emphasise the necessity for seven key prevention dimensions like those articulated in extensive detail by Wurtele (2012, 2014) and further discussed elsewhere (Mathews 2017). These can be briefly detailed here, before examining them in more detail in Parts 1.4.1 and 1.4.2.

First, the CYSO must have a detailed *organisational policy* (including fundamental principles, definitions, objectives, a zero tolerance approach, endorsement by management, and designated contacts). Second, there must be *safe screening and hiring practices*. Third, there must be a robust and detailed *Code of Conduct* (specifying prohibited conduct across a range of situations, and acceptable conduct). Fourth, there must be measures for *implementation and monitoring* (including formal staff supervision, and external auditing). Fifth, actions must be taken to create *safe environments* (at a lower level, requiring further embedding and dissemination of policy and code of conduct, such as by prominent placement in workplaces, websites, and contractual appointments; at a higher level, requiring safe approaches to environmental structures). Sixth, there must be measures embedded to ensure staff appropriately r*eport and respond to suspected cases, disclosures and allegations* (including processes for making, recording and dealing with such reports, and for ensuring the child's safety). Seventh, there must be sufficiently detailed and sophisticated education and training of personnel about the nature and consequences of CSA, organisational policy, reporting duties, and legal and ethical obligations. Such education is viewed by Wurtele (2012) as the cornerstone of prevention.

It should be noted that involving children in relevant components of the strategy is necessary and desirable (Wurtele 2012). There should be provision of clear, direct instruction to children and youth in the organisation that specific kinds of sexual acts are not only not accepted in the organisation, but are illegal, expose the offender to legal sanctions, and can cause devastating consequences (Wurtele 2012; Lanning and Dietz 2014).

Wurtele's Model Informed by an ecological perspective, Sandy Wurtele has systematically described a detailed multi-layered approach to prevention of child sexual abuse in CYSOs. Wurtele's model and the *CSA Prevention Evaluation Tool for Organizations: Child Protection Policy & Procedures* sets out a matrix of seven key prevention dimensions, with each having multiple subcomponents. Wurtele's model is consistent with others in this field, but appears the most detailed. This approach includes responses at both the macro level, through national law and policy to implement measures such as: creating specific criminal offences for CSA in institutional contexts; creating common approaches to employee criminal history screening; compulsory employee education about CSA; establishing a national centre which sets standards for institutions, collects and publishes data, and provides leadership and resources to assist in educational and prevention efforts. Her approach also includes responses at the micro level. Components of this approach, such as screening, and the development of a code of conduct, are supported by other experts in this field. This includes insights into offenders (Erooga 2012a; Erooga et al. 2012; Plummer 2013; Smallbone et al. 2013), and insights about effective and ineffective organisations (Erooga 2012b). Both will be discussed further below.

At the organisational level, Wurtele suggests a variety of measures to improve situational contexts and ameliorate risk factors:

- *Securing situational factors* such as features of the physical environment can be addressed to reduce the opportunity for CSA in private spaces;
- *Healthy agency culture* can be developed to ensure a promotion of children's safety through key dimensions of:
  - decision-making processes;
  - organisational openness;
  - healthy relationships between staff members and between staff and students;
  - appropriate language and attire;
  - recruitment processes; and
  - zero tolerance of any form of abuse of children;
- *Risk-management strategies* can include:
  - employee screening (which must include more than simply criminal record checks, extending to properly informed personal interview strategies);
  - child protection policies (which, for example, can include limits on one-on-one interactions between children and adults especially in high-risk environments such as private accommodation, showering and sleeping arrangements on trips);
  - adequate supervisory policies in relation to staff, including regular professional supervision sessions;
  - robust approaches to interaction between staff and students using electronic communications and social media;
  - a code of conduct clearly establishing acceptable and unacceptable behaviour;
  - education about CSA for staff, children's parents, and children;
  - ongoing staff training while in-service, including about sexual boundary violations (physical, emotional, and via diverse kinds of communication).

Wurtele's model is a comprehensive strategic approach to the prevention of institutional child sexual abuse. It is a practical model which is informed by the literature and an ecological framework, and offers concrete operational guidance on multiple dimensions of law, policy, education and organisational practice.

Wurtele's CSA Prevention Evaluation Tool for Organizations These elements are embodied in Wurtele's *CSA Prevention Evaluation Tool for Organizations: Child Protection Policy & Procedures* sets out a systematic matrix of seven key prevention dimensions (comprising an organisational policy, and six standards), with multiple subcomponents clearly set out for each:

- *The organisational policy* (14 subcomponents),
- Standard 1: *Safe screening and hiring practices* (18 subcomponents),
- Standard 2: *Code of Conduct* (21 subcomponents),
- Standard 3: *Implementation and monitoring* (10 subcomponents),
- Standard 4: *Ensuring Safe Environments* (10 subcomponents),
- Standard 5: *Reporting and responding to concerns, disclosures and allegations* (21 subcomponents),
- Standard 6: *Training and education* (14 subcomponents).

The Organisational Policy Standards (14 Subcomponents) Every sound policy in this context must possess several key components. Some of these, such as definitions of key terms, and the principles which underpin the policy, are universal. The 14 subcomponents of the Organisational Policy Standards are: it contains definitions of key terms; is publicised, displayed, promoted and distributed to all in the organisation; states purpose to protect children from harm in the organisation; states principles underlying the standards e.g. children's right to safety and freedom from abuse; describes zero tolerance for sexual misconduct; policy approved and endorsed by the relevant management or oversight body; policy specifies to whom standards apply; policy developed with relevant stakeholders; policy encourages parents and staff to work together to keep children safe; is reviewed on a regular basis; has process to consult children and parents in the review; identifies personnel with roles and responsibilities in relation to child protection; provides information and contact details about where to seek help, and a designated contact person.

Situations known to present the highest level of risk may be made subject to universal policy approaches. For example, Wurtele has observed that some organizations such as the Boy Scouts of America have a policy requiring separate sleeping and showering accommodations for youth and adults, and limits one-on-one interactions between youth and adults through a "two-deep leadership" policy requiring that at least two adults supervise all scouting activities. Another high-risk situation is when staff members have contact with youth outside the context of the program. A universal policy could limit contact between staff and youth to organization-sanctioned activities and programs (Kenny and Wurtele 2012). Sports coaches could be prohibited from going on trips alone with athletes, and from staying together in hotel rooms. Wurtele also observed that all organisations should develop and implement an appropriate electronic communication policy which sets out acceptable and unacceptable uses of electronic communications with youth, including via social networking sites. Contextually relevant aspects of policy and implementation may require material specific to the organisation and activity.

Standard 1: Safe Screening and Hiring Practices Working with children checks are often subject to legislative schemes. They are a useful tool and serve the clear function of helping to prevent individuals with a relevant criminal history from gaining employment-related access to children with the intention of offending. However, all such screening schemes have limitations, the most obvious one being that most individuals who have inflicted child sexual abuse and who continue to pose a risk will not have a criminal record, because so few cases are disclosed, and then prosecuted, and then result in a conviction. In addition, such schemes need to be adequately framed and implemented so that agencies within and across jurisdictions have immediate and accurate access to shared data systems.

Standard 2: Code of Conduct Similar to the organisational policy, many aspects of an organisation's Code of Conduct must possess several key components. As recommended by Wurtele, every CYSO should *possess* a Code of Conduct (on Wurtele's model, the CC should have 21 components). Its purpose is to "describe how adults should always maintain professional relationships with youth, both in and outside the agency. It is a straight-forward guide of do's and don'ts to assist staff and volunteers to conduct their work professionally and effectively. It lets everyone know what behaviors are acceptable and unacceptable." The "do's and don'ts" encompass multiple aspects (enumerated as many of the 21 sub-components), including discipline practices, internet use, photography, electronic communications with children, other communication and language, transport, and alcohol and drugs.

Standard 3: Implementation and Monitoring There are several elements in the 10 enumerated subcomponents which clearly relate to internal CYSO implementation and monitoring. Some of these, such as therapeutic supervision and formal supervision, are complex and present substantial challenges (such as professional supervision and mentoring). Modified versions of this may be possible if specific organisations have dedicated child protection leaders, and supervision could be conducted using innovative methods beyond traditional face-to-face debriefings. The other focus of this standard is the task of auditing organisations.

Standard 4: Ensuring Safe Environments There is some overlap with this standard and the Code of Conduct, since many of its 10 enumerated subcomponents relate to the same kinds of "do's and don'ts" which are the subject of that Code. However, this standard is directed towards ensuring these principles are observed in practice, as well as further elaborating on them in the manner of situational crime prevention. These principles draw on situational crime prevention theory, explored below, and accordingly some of them have resource implications (such as the use of windows in doors). However, others require only that established policy measures as detailed in the policy and the Code of Conduct are further embedded, disseminated and made known throughout the organisation (such as openly displaying and making available the policy and code of conduct to all staff, parents and children).

Standard 5: Reporting and Responding to Concerns, Disclosures and Allegations.[1] In Wurtele's model, there are 21 subcomponents in this dimension. Some of these overlap with aspects of the Code of Conduct dimension, and some overlap with the education and training dimension (e.g., staff being trained about recognising indicators of CSA, and staff, parents and youth being educated about how to report suspected cases). However, a considerable number of these subcomponents relate directly to the development and implementation of processes for receiving, recording and dealing with complaints and allegations. A key question arising here is whether it is preferable, and possible, to develop a single approach to the treatment of such concerns or allegations, detailing what an organisation must do (although in consideration of the different nature of organisations, there could be variations in details, such as which staff member is designated as responsible for doing specific acts such as recording details; and passing on the information to child welfare authorities and or law enforcement; communicating with the staff, parents and children during and following the events; supporting the child; dealing with media; post-resolution processes).

Standard 6: Training and Education Wurtele (2012, p. 2448) has observed that "Education is the cornerstone of preventing CSA and sexual boundary violations by YSO staff members." This dimension has 14 subcomponents, as follows:

- the CYSO has developed and implemented education specifically designed for youth, parents and professionals, staff and volunteers who have significant contact with children;
- all groups are educated about child abuse with in-depth coverage of CSA;
- includes material on professional boundaries (multiple further subcomponents relate to this);
- includes material on ethical conflicts;
- includes material on self-regulation;
- includes material on cognitive distortions and rationalisations;
- includes material on how to recognise and respond to a colleague's inappropriate actions;
- includes material on information about duties to report;
- inclusion of a means of confirming an individual's completion of training;
- training provided before commencement of interaction with children; and
- that education and training be repeated periodically.

Importantly, education and training needs to be implemented comprehensively and appropriately, primarily for staff, but also for children and parents. Wurtele

[1] There are 21 subcomponents of the Reporting and responding dimension: copy on file with author.

urges that children be provided with information about CSA, including material about appropriate and inappropriate interactions online and offline with adults. For further staff development generally, including on sexual boundary education, Wurtele recommended that:

> once selected for positions in YSOs, it is critical that in-service training programs be offered to inform all employees and volunteers about institutional CSA. These trainings can give all adults a heightened awareness of an organization's commitment to youth safety and intolerance of sexual misconduct. Training objectives should include understanding the complex dynamics of child sexual abuse and how youth are harmed by sexual exploitation, recognizing signs that a youth is being sexually abused, responding sensitively to a victim's disclosure, understanding the agency's zero-tolerance policies and consequences, and knowing the agency's reporting policies and state laws. Everyone working with children must be aware of their ethical and legal duty to report any reasonable suspicions of CSA to a designated state agency or to law enforcement.

As noted by Mathews and Collin-Vézina (2016), there are many required elements of staff and volunteer training in relation to child sexual abuse that are universal, such as: the definition of child sexual abuse; its prevalence; its criminality; its serious consequences; who experiences it, and at what ages; who inflicts it; the tendency towards nondisclosure and delayed disclosure; children's truthfulness in disclosure (even if they recant); the indicators of CSA (typical emotional, social and behavioural responses after victimization, including how they may indicate their experience without clear disclosure); and legal and ethical duties to report, and processes for reporting.

Situational Crime Prevention The literature on situational crime prevention, and especially as applied to child sexual abuse in CYSOs, is also instructive. Situational crime prevention does not aim to reduce offending through measures related directly to the offender or the victim. Rather, it is a criminological model concerned with actions taken about the "situation" or environment within which crime occurs to reduce the likelihood of offending. As explained by Smallbone et al. (2013), the questions ask: what is the nature of the crime; where does it occur; when it occur; who is involved; and how does it occur? Preventative approaches from the perspective of situational crime prevention aim to alter the environment in which crime occurs to reduce the likelihood of offending, informed by the nature, location, timing and method of the crime (Boyle 2014; Kaufman et al. 2012; Leclerc et al. 2011; Smallbone et al. 2013; Terry and Freilich 2012; Terry 2015; Wurtele 2012).

Smallbone et al. (2013, pp. 166–171) emphasise that regardless of the strength of the offender's motivation, child sexual offending requires a "conducive immediate environment". They propose methods of situational prevention for different contexts, including the institutional context. Key proposals, grouped under conceptualised strategic methods, include:

- "Increasing effort": effective strategies to screen personnel; inclusion of material in formal job descriptions about expected and prohibited behaviour towards children; presence of a specialised risk management position dedicated to prevention

of harm to children; presence of a formal action plan to reduce risk of harm; staff awareness of the plan; regular review of the plan;
- "Increasing risks to offenders": reducing opportunities for adults to be alone with children; physical redesign of the environment through, for example, glass panels; requiring staff to make reports of abuse; enhancing opportunities for disclosure by the child; a requirement of inspections and reviews by an independent authority;
- "Removing excuses/reducing permissibility": ensuring the institution is not a "pathological institution" in which a culture of abuse distorts individual moral judgments, enabling rationalisation of illegal and otherwise prohibited acts, through the use of formal protocols about conduct between staff and children to set clear rules which unequivocally establish acceptable and unacceptable conduct. These should establish acceptable and unacceptable conduct to ensure children are safe, and opportunities for CSA and grooming are minimised (e.g. regarding being alone with children, travel, overnight stays, bathing, communication, and grooming behaviors, and prohibition on taking children to the staff member's home). Punishment of breaches is also essential.

Similarly, Leclerc et al. (2015) proposed a series of key measures, informed by a study of sexual offenders and their insights into effective situational prevention. They recommended:

- In *screening at intake of new recruits*: verifying criminal records; and including questions about the person's motivations for working with children; ensure the interview process includes clear discussion of the organisation's commitment to child protection and expectations of staff conduct, and require signed commitments from the individual to this;
- In *developing policies and regulations about staff conduct to prevent offending*: never leaving a child alone with an adult; prohibiting staff from taking children to the staff member's home; prohibiting adults from showering with children and from showering at the same time; prohibit mobile phone communication between staff member and child; prohibit gift-giving between staff and children; limit contact outside institutional hours; where abuse becomes known, a requirement that the organisation report it immediately to authorities;
- In *environmental design of the institution*: eliminating hidden areas and rooms; using windows to overlook corridors; installing closed circuit cameras at entrances and exits.

Consensus on Measures to Prevent, Identify and Respond to CSA Other insights from the general literature are consistent with Wurtele's model (Kaufman et al. 1998, 2012; Saul and Audage 2007). This is also evident in approaches and organizational tools proposed by the Centers for Disease Control (Saul and Audage 2007) and by other leading scholars (Wurtele 2012, 2014), which are substantially supported in other approaches and analyses (Parent and Demers 2011; Valentine et al. 2016; Walsh et al. 2013). In addition, literature on situational crime prevention of CSA in religious contexts indicates key themes that may have application there and in other CYSO contexts (Terry and Freilich 2012; Terry and Ackerman 2008). Terry (2015) integrated sociocultural, psychological, situational, and organizational perspectives, and concluded that prevention approaches should focus on situational prevention, as well as education, and oversight and accountability. These models have subtle differences but all have a common fundamental basis, which emphasize the necessity for the key prevention dimensions like those articulated in extensive detail by Wurtele (2012, 2014) as further discussed elsewhere (Mathews 2017).

For convenience, these can be summarised as follows. First, the CYSO must have a detailed organizational policy (including fundamental principles, definitions, objectives, a zero tolerance approach, endorsement by management, and designated contacts). Second, there must be safe screening and hiring practices. Third, there must be a robust and detailed Code of Conduct (specifying prohibited conduct across a range of situations, and acceptable conduct). Fourth, there must be measures for implementation and monitoring (including formal staff supervision, and external auditing). Fifth, actions must be taken to create safe environments (at a lower level, requiring further embedding and dissemination of policy and code of conduct, such as by prominent placement in workplaces, websites, and contractual appointments; at a higher level, requiring safe approaches to environmental structures). Sixth, there must be measures embedded to ensure staff appropriately report and respond to suspected cases, disclosures and allegations (including processes for making, recording and dealing with such reports, and for ensuring the child's safety). Seventh, there must be sufficiently detailed and sophisticated education and training of personnel about the nature and consequences of CSA, organizational policy, reporting duties, and legal and ethical obligations.

Implementation Challenges The challenges are then to achieve coordinated implementation of such responses by CYSOs, government agencies and communities, for responses to be practicable and tailored to the context, and to foster the participation of communities. Lived experience, public health and regulatory theory, and the nature of CSA in CYSOs, all indicate that organizational self-regulation is unviable to meet the social justice imperative in this context. It has been argued elsewhere (Mathews 2017) that a model of direct legislative regulation is required, driven by a posture of responsive regulation, tailored to the context, and with CYSOs being nurtured towards voluntary compliance and informal enforcement but with stronger coercive measures available if necessary to compel compliance and penalize breaches (Dorbeck-Jung et al. 2010; Hutter 2011).

In advancing any centralized program based on direct regulation, it is important to promote the public health tenet that community participation and ownership is vital, and to accept that modifications are permissible where appropriate. Accordingly, this approach should not be simply a "top-down" approach relying only on direct regulation. Rather, guided by public health principles and insights, it requires fostering productive, collaborative partnerships with CYSOs, and strategies involving organizational leadership and individual staff members (Palmer 2016), to help develop intrinsic organizational and individual attitudes to heighten the likelihood of compliance and sustained cultural change. The benefits of the preferred approach to CYSOs should be emphasized, including savings to CYSOs of money, time, expertise and personnel, and, more importantly, providing assistance in improving organizational capacity to protect the children and youth they serve, professionalizing staff and management, and minimization of organizational liability. As well, it is important to note that, in the spirit of public health as originally conceived and with regulatory theory as applied to high risk environments with diverse industrial participation and varied intrinsic commitment, government has not only a role to play, but an obligation to do so.

In general, then, based on an analysis of public health theory and regulatory theory (Mathews,2017), the features of the context of CSA and CYSOs indicate direct government regulation is required for situations of high risk, high complexity, and uncertain industry or sector commitment to robust policy. The optimal approach to implementing many of the required dimensions of regulation is a unified, centralized approach implemented by a central authority having the power and capacity to develop, communicate, administer and enforce the desired measures. This offers the greatest likelihood of promoting quality of design and best practice, avoiding fragmentation of policy and practice, using resources efficiently, and enhancing child protection. Achieving this requires direct regulation, involving a small number of organizational actors in an organized, centralized and homogenous environment, which can: enable cooperative and coordinated support between major government and nongovernment actors; create consistent, sound, simple procedural structures; and aim to develop genuine organizational and individual commitment to the policy measures and practices through the development of attitudinal factors which underpin an internalized normative duty.

This would generally require a legislative scheme, endorsement by government and major nongovernment organizations, and financial support from the state, all of which are consistent with public health law and public health theory. It would need to be supported and enforceable by an external framework of recognition and enforcement. A single, centralized national regulatory body should have responsibility for as many of the seven key dimensions discussed above as possible. This body could be supported financially and logistically by governments at national and or provincial levels. It should have considerable strength in its regulatory actions, being supported by a legislative scheme, or could at least have power to compel certain acts through organizational accreditation or registration requirements, or made a condition of receiving state financial support. In developing harmonized, common approaches to as many of the relevant aspects of the regulated subject matter as possible, this body could consult with peak organizations while retaining ultimate decision-making power. Mechanisms for providing aspects of the prevention approach could be simple, streamlined, and cost-efficient, such as using online methods for education. Quality assurance and review could be conducted at practicable intervals, conducted by one body or a small number of auditing bodies, themselves overseen by the central agency. At all stages of this approach, provision of support by the government regulator to CYSOs should aim to foster dispositions conducive to a child-centred approach.

As will be seen below in this chapter, the significance of his emerging body of knowledge is that it can be used to inform developments in legislative requirements and policy guidance applied to CYSOs, responding to key dimensions of how best to prevent, identify and respond appropriately to CSA.

Australia's Royal Commission into Institutional Responses to Child Sexual Abuse: Its Nature, Key Findings and Major Recommendations – The Roman Catholic Church

The Australian Royal Commission Into Institutional Responses to Child Sexual Abuse delivered its Final Report in December 2017. While other countries have conducted similar inquiries, due to the nature and scope of Australia's Royal Commission, it can reasonably be judged to be the single most extensive Inquiry of its type ever undertaken. It made 400 recommendations, targeting the most significant problems and shortcomings presented by social and legal systems, and institutional practice and malpractice, related to the prevention, identification, and response of child sexual abuse. The recommendations were made generally to cover all CYSOs, but with further recommendations specific to some CYSOs, including the Roman Catholic Church, which was the institution most frequently involved in cases of CSA brought to its attention. The recommendations encompass direct recommendations for specific legislative reform, policy reform, and practical reform. Separate reports published during its tenure provided recommendations about criminal justice systems, civil justice systems and redress schemes, and criminal history screening. For any society wishing to take steps to improve the prevention and appropriate responses to child sexual abuse in CYSOs, the work of Australia's Royal Commission constitutes an invaluable resource.

Background to Australia's Royal Commission

Australia's Royal Commission Into Institutional Responses to Child Sexual Abuse (the Royal Commission) was initiated on 12 November 2012 by the then Prime Minister of Australia, Julia Gillard, due to growing concern about the prevalence of child sexual abuse within public and private institutional contexts, the inadequacy of preventative and responsive measures undertaken by institutions, and active concealment of such abuse by institutions including most notably the Catholic Church (Australian Government 2013; Australian Government Royal Commission Into Institutional Responses to Child Sexual Abuse 2014). This concern existed despite numerous prior inquiries into institutional CSA, which had less extensive powers, narrower scope, and lacked the support of state and territory governments.

The Letters Patent gave the Royal Commission a broad remit, including to "inquire into institutional responses to allegations and incidents of child sexual abuse and…what institutions and governments should do to better protect children against child sexual abuse and related matters in institutional contexts in the future… [and] to achieve best practice in encouraging the reporting of, and responding to reports or information about, allegations, incidents or risks of child sexual abuse" (Australian Government 2013).

The Royal Commission initially received $285 million in funding for 4 years, and this tenure was extended until December 2017 with further funding of $104 million (Australian Government Royal Commission Into Institutional Responses to Child Sexual Abuse 2014). Six Commissioners were appointed with collective experience across multiple fields, and the Commission employed approximately 250 fulltime staff by April 2014 (Australian Government Royal Commission Into Institutional Responses to Child Sexual Abuse 2014).

Broadly, the Royal Commission engaged in three major fields of work. First, it convened private sessions to listen to survivors, bear witness to their experience, validate their experience, and learn from their accounts. Here, it conducted 8013 private sessions, and referred 2562 matters to police). Second, it conducted 57 public hearings to formally conduct investigations and obtain detailed evidence about institutions and cases of particular interest. This function was supported by extensive powers, including the ability to call witnesses and compel testimony and the production of documents. Some of these lasted for weeks. Third, the Commission engaged in a detailed research and policy program, involving both work conducted by its own staff, and 59 externally commissioned research projects conducted by Australian and international researchers, most of which were published on the Commission's website. This program of research was organized around eight themes (causes; prevention; identification; institutional responses; government responses; treatment and support needs; institutions of interest; ensuring a positive impact).

In addition, the Royal Commission engaged in a comprehensive program of public engagement, to create community awareness of its work and to build trust and confidence in its activity. This included engagement with the broader community including through media and numerous formal speeches, as well as with specific groups such as children, people with disabilities, people in correctional institutions, people experiencing homelessness, and people from culturally and linguistically diverse groups. The Commission developed a comprehensive website which made materials available for public consumption, streamed public hearings live to the public, and archived transcripts of evidence from hearings. Special measures were devised to give survivors facilities to share their experiences and views about desired reforms.

Its major final report was released in December 2017, comprising 17 Volumes, and this will be returned to shortly. Here, it can also be noted that the Commission completed and released an Interim Report (Australian Government Royal Commission Into Institutional Responses to Child Sexual Abuse 2014) and major reports including on Civil Litigation and Redress (Australian Government Royal

Commission Into Institutional Responses to Child Sexual Abuse 2015a) to enable immediate reforms to law, policy and practice.

Key Findings on Demographics

Before proceeding, it is useful to note some key findings about the demographics and reported experiences of those who appeared in private sessions with the Commission (Royal Commission 2017 – Final Report). While not strictly able to be considered a representative sample because of self-selection, this sample is nevertheless a very large sample of self-selected individuals, gathered over several years, who reported experiencing sexual abuse while a child in an organisation providing services to children (broadly defined to include religion, education, sport, culture, arts, recreation, welfare, out-of-home care, foster care, and juvenile detention).

- Average age when first abused: 10.4 years (males 10.8 years; females 9.7 years).
- Sex: 63.6% male; 36.1% female.
- Offender's age: 85.2% reported being abused by an adult perpetrator.
- Offender type: 31.8% reported being abused by a person in religious ministry; 20.4% by a teacher; 13.5% by a residential care worker; 11.3% by a foster carer.
- Frequency: 85.4% said they were abused multiple times.
- Severity/nature: 55.7% reported experiencing penetrative abuse; 71.4% other contact abuse.
- Organisation type: 58.1% reported the CSA occurred in a religious organisation[2]; 32.5% in a government-run institution, and 10.5% in a non-government, non-religious institution.
- Denomination of religious organisation: Of those abused in a religious organisation, 61.4% were in a Catholic institution; 14.8% Anglican.
- Catholic CYSOs: As a proportion of all survivors, 35.7% said they experienced CSA in a Catholic institution.

Case Study Investigations An important part of the Royal Commission's activity was to conduct investigations into specific institutions. These aimed to understand systemic issues, identify ways to learn from institutional errors, and inform recommendations for reform. The case studies had a strong focus on religious institutions, with the Catholic Church prominent, being the subject of 15 case studies including the Church as a whole (Case Study 50) and in specific dioceses including Melbourne (Case Studies 16, 28, 35), Ballarat (Case Study 28), Toowoomba (Case Study 6), Wollongong (Case Study 14), and Maitland-Newcastle (Case Study 43), and Marist Brothers schools (Case Study 13). Other religious institutions were also investigated,

---

[2] In May 2017, reporting the most recent data, the Chair of the Royal Commission, the Honourable Peter McClellan, stated that Of those who reported abuse in a religious institution, over half (51%) stated the abuser was a person in religious ministry, and almost one quarter (22%) reported the abuser was a teacher (McClellan 2017).

including the Anglican Church (Case Study 42), Jehovah's Witnesses (Case Studies 29, 54), and Yeshiva Colleges (Case Study 22). Educational institutions were prominent, including private boys' schools in Brisbane (Case Study 34), Geelong (Case Study 32), and Sydney (Case Study 23). Numerous other educational and out-of-home care institutions were investigated, as were organizations including scouts (Case Studies 1, 48), sporting clubs (Case Study 39), swimming groups (Case Study 15), YMCA (Case Studies 2, 47), and performing arts (Case Study 37).

Features Contributing to CSA in CYSOs Identified in Hearings and Case Studies A major result of the public hearings undertaken as part of the case studies was that they revealed the features and actions of institutions where CSA occurred, and was concealed and facilitated. These findings are instructive generally, and reveal similar themes to other national inquiries, especially in Ireland (Ryan 2009; Wright 2017). Conceptually, they may be grouped under themes of:

- an organizational culture of concealment, corruption and protection of individual and institutional reputations;
- managers' and staff members' ignorance and inadvertence;
- absence of child protection policy, or lack of compliance with policy;
- lack of staff and student education about CSA;
- lack of effective reporting mechanisms internally and to external agencies;
- allowing known offenders to have continued access to children, enabling further abuse;
- allowing unsupervised private access to children;
- failure to prioritize children's welfare; and
- lack of external oversight.

These findings helped to inform many of the Royal Commission's recommendations for reform.

In the Yeshiva hearing, for example, the Commission identified many of these problems (Australian Government Royal Commission Into Institutional Responses to Child Sexual Abuse 2016). Regarding responses to allegations against three staff at Yeshiva Melbourne, it was found, for example, that within this extremely insular group there was a consistent pattern of total inaction despite repeated allegations by parents and children of CSA by several staff; ignorance amongst Rabbis about what constitutes CSA and the nature of grooming; rhetorical minimization of CSA; punishment and isolation of anyone who spoke out; absence of support for survivors; a lack of adequate policies, processes and practices for responding to complaints for over 20 years; and confusion about whether Jewish law allowed reporting of abuse to police leading to cover-ups.

Similar findings were made in the hearing into the Marist Brothers, which focused on the prolific offending by two known offenders against multiple children periods in multiple locations over extended periods of time (Australian Government Royal Commission Into Institutional Responses to Child Sexual Abuse 2015b). One of these offenders was promoted to Principal even after it was known he had sexually abused children; he then continued to offend and was transferred to another school, again as Principal, despite the school authority's knowledge of his further offending.

Similar findings have been made in other secular and non-secular educational settings. In Case Study 34, which concerned abuse at two private schools, several similar themes emerged (Australian Government Royal Commission Into Institutional Responses to Child Sexual Abuse 2017b). In relation to the first school (Brisbane Grammar School), it was found that the school counsellor had a locked private room where he sexually abused boys who were seeing him for counselling. He abused multiple students for years at this first school, and then left the school in 1988 and joined the second school investigated in this case study. At the first school, the principal was told in 1981 by a student's father that his son had been abused by the school counsellor. The Commission found that the principal failed to investigate the allegations, failed to report the matter to the police or the school board of trustees, and that during this principal's tenure there was a culture where boys who made allegations of CSA were not believed and their claims were not acted upon (pp. 9, 73); and that there was a culture which did not encourage or facilitate the reporting by students to staff of CSA. It was found that during the period this counsellor was employed (1973–1988), the school had no systems, policies or procedures to deal with allegations of CSA (p. 12), and there was no adequate system of record-keeping of the sessions or of the boys' absences from class, and this precluded prevention of further abuse.

In relation to the second school (St Paul's School), where the counsellor worked from 1989–1997, again with a system of a locked room, it was found that in 1996 the principal dismissed two boys' allegations of CSA by the counsellor, told them they were lying, and threatened to punish them if they continued making the allegations (p. 10). In January 1997, the counsellor was charged by police with offences regarding abuse of another student over a period of 2 years, and the counsellor committed suicide the next day (p. 10). Subsequently, this same principal at the second school was promoted to an executive director position with responsibility to create and implement child protection education policy throughout Brisbane; this appointment was by a Diocesan committee including two members who knew of the principal's prior failure to act, with one of these being the Archbishop of Brisbane (pp. 11, 57–58). The Commission found the principal's inaction meant he failed his most fundamental obligation of keeping the students safe, and that there were no systems, policies or procedures to deal with allegations of CSA.

Frequency of Offending in the Anglican Church and the Catholic Church

The Commission also undertook analyses of claims made with respect to CSA in Catholic Church institutions and Anglican Church institutions respectively (Australian Government Royal Commission Into Institutional Responses to Child

Sexual Abuse 2017c, d). For the Anglican Church, the Commission found there were 1119 complaints of CSA made to all 23 Anglican Church dioceses between 1980 and 2015, involving 1085 individual complainants, with 75% being male and the average age at the time of the first alleged incident being 11.8 years of age; these allegations involved 569 alleged offenders of whom 43% were ordained clergy and 94% were male (Australian Government Royal Commission Into Institutional Responses to Child Sexual Abuse 2017d). These data were limited because not all complaints made to Anglican institutions such as schools were received and recorded by the diocese, and the data did not enable estimates of prevalence of offending by Anglican clergy and non-clergy. Even taking into account the different time periods studied, these data appear to show a higher frequency of complaints than those from an earlier study. This Anglican Church study used data from church files from 20 dioceses between 1990 and 2008, and found there were 191 allegations made by 180 individuals against 135 Anglican clergy and non-clergy, with 58% involving clergy, 76% of complainants being male, and large proportions of alleged abuse occurring in the alleged offender's home, especially those involving clergy (Parkinson et al. 2012). While this study could not calculate the proportion of Anglican clergy to be subject to allegations, the authors estimated it as fewer than 1%. Caveats on this finding would include the general tendency for nondisclosure of CSA in all circumstances (Alaggia, 2005; Collin-Vézina, De La Sablonniere-Griffin, Palmer, & Milne, 2015), and, for CSA in Church contexts, for nondisclosure to the Church in particular.

The Roman Catholic Church: Frequency of Offending Findings ion the frequency of offending in Catholic institutions were particularly notable. The Commission obtained data from 201 Catholic Church authorities to identify the number and features of claims of alleged CSA made to these authorities between January 1, 1980 and February 28, 2015, regarding abuse from 1950–2010 (Australian Government Royal Commission Into Institutional Responses to Child Sexual Abuse 2017c). "Claims" were limited to those subject to a formal application for redress through judicial or non-judicial processes, and those made where redress was not sought but which were substantiated after investigation by the Church or another body, or were otherwise accepted by the Church) (Australian Government Royal Commission Into Institutional Responses to Child Sexual Abuse 2017c). The survey also captured data on the number of clergy and non-clergy employed from 1950 to 2010 to enable estimation of the proportion of offenders.

It was found that: 4445 claimants alleged incidents of CSA, involving 1880 identified offenders and 530 other unspecified offenders; 78% of claimants were male; the average age of claimants at the first alleged incident was 11.4 years (11.6 for males; 10.5 for females); 90% of alleged offenders were male; 37% of alleged offenders were non-ordained religious, 30% priests, and 29% lay people. Allegations involved 1049 institutions. Of all Catholic authorities with priest members, 7.0% of priests were alleged offenders, and some authorities had much higher rates. Of all non-ordained religious who were alleged offenders, some institutes also had substantial proportions of offenders: 22% of non-ordained Christian Brothers were alleged offenders (n = 483). Given that many incidents of CSA are not disclosed at all, or are not disclosed to authorities (including the offending institution), it is clear that the estimates generated are conservative. These data represent only the fraction of cases that were disclosed, and were made the subject of a formal complaint, and accepted as proven. The results are broadly comparable to those in the United States. The John Jay College of Criminal Justice (2004) estimated 4% of Catholic priests and deacons from 1950 to 2002 were subject to allegations, and subsequent data placed this figure at 5%, involving 15,000 children (Terry et al. 2011; Terry 2015).

The Roman Catholic Church: Cultural Problems, Corruption, and Concealment The issues raised by the unique organization that is the Roman Catholic Church would require an entirely separate treatment, and it is beyond the scope of this book to thoroughly examine its nature, history, canon law, governance, and culture. However, it is essential to identify important characteristics of the Catholic Church that are relevant to this context. This institution was the locus of the majority of institutional CSA revealed to the Commission, and has been the subject of multiple industrial scale cover-ups and major inquiries in the USA, Canada, Ireland, Belgium, Germany and the Netherlands (Böhm et al. 2014; Murphy 2009, 2011; Ryan 2009; Terry 2015). After the release of the Cloyne Report (Murphy 2011), the Prime Minister of Ireland, Enda Kenny, famously eviscerated the Roman Catholic Church in an unprecedented attack, declaring that it had brought to light "the dysfunction, disconnection, elitism [and] narcissism that dominate the culture of the Vatican to this day. The rape and torture of children were downplayed or "managed" to uphold, instead, the primacy of the institution, its power, standing and "reputation"...[the Vatican has responded] with the gimlet eye of a canon lawyer. This calculated, withering position being the polar opposite of the radicalism, humility and compassion upon which the Roman Church was founded" (Kenny 2011). Kenny was particularly incensed because the Cloyne Inquiry exposed "an attempt by the Holy See, to frustrate an Inquiry in a sovereign, democratic republic...as little as three years ago".[3]

One cannot ignore this particular institution because it qualitatively different from others, and because its uniquely high risk of child sexual abuse and its concealment make it a special case requiring special attention. In addition, it is the

[3] Kenny was also endorsing the Irish Government's new efforts to protect children, including through its Children First bill. He stated (my emphasis): "Cardinal Josef Ratzinger said: 'Standards of conduct appropriate to civil society or the workings of a democracy cannot be purely and simply applied to the Church.' As the Holy See prepares its considered response to the Cloyne Report, as Taoiseach, I am making it absolutely clear, that when it comes to the protection of the children of this State, *the standards of conduct which the Church deems appropriate to itself, cannot and will not, be applied to the workings of democracy and civil society in this republic*. Not purely, or simply or otherwise. Children...First" ... through our legislation, through our Government"s action to put Children First., those who have been abused can take some small comfort in knowing that they belong to a nation, to a democracy where humanity, power, rights, responsibility are enshrined and enacted, always....always.... for their good. Where the law - their law - as citizens of this country, will always supercede canon laws that have neither legitimacy nor place in the affairs of this country."

largest Christian church globally with over 3000 dioceses and archdioceses in scores of countries, and accordingly presents both the highest risk and the risk of greatest magnitude. This extends to nations where the population may be at even greater risk, due to poverty, and less stringent adherence to the rule of law. Brazil, Mexico and the Philippines, for example, have a combined population of 400 million Catholics. The populations in Ireland and Australia (around four million and five million respectively) pale by comparison.

Many scholars have sought to understand the factors contributing to CSA within it, and have criticized the separate and combined devastating effects of a range of its specific features (e.g., Doyle et al. 2006; Frawley-O'Dea 2004; Keenan 2012; Lothstein 2004; Parkinson 2016; Robertson 2010; Robinson 2007; Sipe 2011; Tapsell 2014). These may be understood as a group of five conceptually distinct features which are related to and reinforce one another:

- Culture (an exceptionally strong hierarchical power structure requires complete obedience to Church rules to protect one's personal standing, job security and career prospects, and, for some, vaulting ambition[4]; strong obligations are owed by clerics to superiors and to the Pope; total conformity with organizational attitudes and beliefs is required; dissent is silenced; objectors are marginalized);
- Dominance of internal organizational rules (where canon law and Church doctrine take priority over civil law and criminal law; the authority of national civil and criminal law is not recognized; the organization considers itself not only separate from but superior to civil society, and administers its own discipline even for matters which otherwise would attract sanctions by civil and criminal legal systems; there is internalized fusion of organizational and state-like power);
- Protection of the institution's existence and reputation at all costs (complete secrecy of any impropriety is required at the cost of personal expulsion from the group; the top priority is the avoidance of "scandal", i.e., anything that can damage the reputation of the Church or its priests; protection is provided to individual sexual offenders; whistleblowers are punished and even excommunicated; secret internal administrative and governance mechanisms are used to deal with known and alleged offenders);
- Governance that is authoritarian, and both centralized and fragmented (where authority and rule-making are both entirely at the behest of one individual, yet are also otherwise fragmented and where each bishop is endowed with almost unlimited authority over the management and administration of his diocese, subject to canon law and Papal direction); and
- Sexual distortion and dysfunction (distorted masculinity, psychosexual development and personal sexual functioning is embedded by culture, conditions and rules including celibacy and rationalization of sex with males or boys as not

[4] The analyses of the career of Cardinal George Pell, who at the time of writing has been committed to stand trial in Melbourne, Victoria, for a range of child sexual offences, may provide insights into this and other aspects of Church culture: see Marr (2014) and Milligan (2017). The Royal Commission's case studies also detailed the testimony of Cardinal Pell, which included some admissions about his conduct in responding to complaints.

violating celibacy; a limited homogenous ideal of personhood exists; illicit sex is treated institutionally as sin rather than crime).

Royal Commission Findings on the Catholic Church

All these features were noted by the Royal Commission in 15 case studies into Catholic institutions. These case studies were exceptionally thorough analyses of what happened, and why it happened, in dioceses, archdioceses, and particular settings. Reports of the case studies included findings about what happened (or, if the institution claimed otherwise, was more likely to have happened), which then informed recommendations for reform. The thoroughness of these studies can be appreciated immediately by noting the length of the reports. The Report of *Case Study 28: Catholic Church authorities in Ballarat* alone is 536 pages.[5] It is instructive to note some key findings from this specific case study example of Ballarat, and then to summarise the Commission's findings from all 15 case studies as applied generally to this institution.

A Specific Case Study Example of Catastrophic Failure and Appalling Malfeasance: Case Study 28 (Ballarat) Ballarat has frequently been described as the epicentre of child sexual abuse in Australia. It is known as the location of Church parishes (including St Alipius) and schools where some of the most widespread clergy child sexual abuse occurred over decade. It is known as the location where 140 people had made a claim of child sexual abuse against priests and religious staff during the time period of the Royal Commission's data analysis. It is known as the location where some of the worst prolific offenders – including Gerald Ridsdale (who held 16 appointments over 29 years as a priest), Robert Best, and Edward Dowlan – perpetrated child sexual offending on an industrial scale. It is known as the location where Church leaders for decades harboured known groups of offenders, and individual offenders; and it is known as the location of some of the individual bishops

[5] In Case Study 28 the Royal Commission inquired into "the response of the Congregation of Chris an Brothers in the St Patrick's Province of Ballarat and the Catholic Diocese of Ballarat (the Diocese) to complaints and allegations of child sexual abuse by Chris an Brothers, clergy and religious." The Christian Brothers operated or provided staff for six primary and secondary schools in Ballarat and Warrnambool. St Alipius Boys' School, a primary school in Ballarat East, and St Patrick's College, a secondary school in Ballarat, were primarily staffed by Christian Brothers and were the principal focus of this study. Part One of the public hearing examined the response of relevant Catholic Church authorities to the impact of child sexual abuse on survivors, their families and the community of Ballarat. It also examined their responses to survivors, their families and the community of Ballarat following the conviction of clergy and religious for acts of child sexual abuse committed at institutions associated with Catholic Church authorities in Ballarat. Part Two examined the knowledge of Catholic Church authorities in and around Ballarat to allegations of child sexual abuse and their response to those allegations. It also examined the response of Victoria Police. Part Three examined the knowledge of and response to allegations of child sexual abuse by Christian Brothers in St Patrick's Province, specifically in institutions within the Diocese: See Case Study 28, Executive Summary, p. 21.

most heavily criticised for its concealment and continued facilitation, including Ronald Mulkearns (Marr 2014; Milligan 2017). It should be taken as a model of what an organisation must not allow itself to do. It must be taken as a model of what a society must not allow an organisation to do.

In Case Study 28, the Commissioners drew conclusions about the nature and adequacy of responses of the Christian Brothers (pp. 192–3), and of the Catholic Diocese of Ballarat (pp. 403–420), to allegations and complaints of child sexual abuse. Regarding the Christian Brothers, for example, it was found that (pp. 192–3):

> The response of those in positions of authority within the Christian Brothers in St Patrick's Province ... was grossly inadequate... On some occasions, the response to allegations or reports of Christian Brothers conducting themselves in a sexually inappropriate manner with children was dismissive. Questions were not asked and details not sought, when they should have been. Few investigations were undertaken. For example, in relation to Dowlan, we are satisfied that there was no effective response to any of the many reports or complaints in order to manage the risk to children that Dowlan posed. ... Often, the Christian Brother in question was allowed to remain in the position he held where the allegations arose, with continuing access to children. On many occasions, the Brother was moved to a new location after a complaint or allegation was made about his conduct. In some cases, the reason given for the move was to conceal the true reason for it and to protect the reputation of the Christian Brothers and avoid scandal and embarrassment. Whether the Brother remained in place or was moved, few effective restrictions were placed on his movements. The Christian Brothers did not share information about allegations or complaints of child sexual abuse against Christian Brothers when that information should have been shared. It is clear that the systems and procedures in place which permitted each of these to occur were inadequate and unacceptable. We are satisfied that the Christian Brothers, similar to other Catholic orders, have a structure in which ultimate power and responsibility rests with one person: the provincial. A system without checks and balances has the obvious potential for mismanagement or abuse of that power and neglect of that responsibility.

Regarding the Catholic Diocese of Ballarat, it was found that (pp. 403–4):

> This case study exposed a catastrophic failure in the leadership of the Diocese and ultimately in the structure and culture of the Church over decades to effectively respond to the sexual abuse of children by its priests. That failure led to the suffering and often irreparable harm to children, their families and the wider community. That harm could have been avoided if the Church had acted in the interests of children rather than in its own interests.
>
> The response of the Diocese to complaints and concerns about four of its priests was remarkably and disturbingly similar. It is apparent that the avoidance of scandal, the maintenance of the reputation of the Church and loyalty to priests alone determined the response. It was only when there was a possibility that the sexual abuse of children by a priest would become widely known that any ac on was taken. Invariably, that ac on was to remove the priest from the community for a short period and then place him in another, more distant parish. Restrictions were not placed on priests and supervision was not given.
>
> Untrue or misleading reasons for the priest's departure were given to the old parish, and no warning was given to the new parish ...
>
> Euphemistic and elliptical language was often used in correspondence and minutes to mask the true nature of the conduct discussed. There was repeated reference to 'pressures', 'strains' and unspecified 'problems'. On occasions, records were deliberately not made or kept or were destroyed. Bishop Mulkearns and other clergy were dismissive of complaints

and complainants. The response to reports was characterised by the encouragement of secrecy, assurances that the matter would be dealt with and a failure to follow up, ask questions or investigate reports. Reports were never made to the police and victims were not supported. This pattern was repeated. The structure of the Diocese was flawed and lacked any accountability. The bishop was autonomous. He alone was the decision-maker about his priests. The structure was hierarchical and did not encourage priests to challenge or otherwise influence the actions that the bishop took. Even if the structure had done so, other priests in the Diocese, including consultors and vicars general, were part of the same culture as the bishop. They too sought to avoid scandal and negative publicity and protect the Church and fellow priests. Such a hierarchical structure of Church authority has the obvious potential for mismanagement and abuse of power.

At p. 404 (my emphasis):

We have found that on many occasions the most likely explanation for the conduct of Bishop Mulkearns and other senior clergy in the Diocese was that they were trying to minimise the risk of scandal and protect the reputation of the Catholic Church. The grave consequence was that the safety and welfare of children were not given the highest priority. *The Church parties acknowledged that the evidence repeatedly exposed a tendency or instinct on the part of those in positions of authority, once they learned of the occurrences or of an accusation of child sexual abuse, to seek to keep the spread of knowledge of such matters to a minimum, with a view to ensuring that the reputation and good name of the Church were not harmed.* They conceded that such an approach is plain in the ways in which Bishop Mulkearns responded to his receipt of information of various kinds about Ridsdale [and others].

At p. 405:

We accept ... that only the bishop had the power and authority to take action in respect of a priest against whom an allegation had been made. It was the bishop who had exclusive authority to appoint, remove or transfer a priest in his diocese. Such a hierarchical structure of Church authority has the obvious potential for mismanagement and abuse of power. ... However [we have also found that] Bishop Mulkearns discussed allegations about priests with his consultors. ... The evidence revealed that the true reason that a priest was being removed from a parish was not disclosed outside the bishop's close advisors. In some cases, parishes were lied to about the reason their priest was being or had been transferred following allegations or complaints of child sexual abuse by that priest. In no case were parishes told the true reason. The Church parties accepted this.

At p. 420:

The evidence in this case study revealed an extraordinary failure within the Diocese to respond adequately to allegations and complaints about the sexual abuse of children by clergy over the course of at least three decades. The response primarily revealed a desire to prevent or minimise the risk of scandal and to protect the reputation of the Catholic Church. It also revealed a tendency by Bishop Mulkearns and other clergy to treat complaints or allegations dismissively and in favour of the priest the subject of the allegation. The response to reports was characterised by the encouragement of secrecy, assurances that the matter would be dealt with and failure to follow up, ask questions or investigate reports.

The offending priest was often removed from the parish where the allegations had arisen and moved to a new location where the allegations were unknown. Untrue or misleading reasons for the priest's departure were given to the old parish, and no warning was given to the new parish. ... Either restrictions or conditions were not imposed on the priest in his new parish or there was no effective supervision of his conduct. Often, more allegations against the priest emerged in the new parish.

> The result of these inexcusable failures was that more children were sexually abused by Catholic clergy in the Diocese. There was a catastrophic institutional failure which resulted in many children being sexually abused. We heard about the devastating, often lifelong, consequences in the lives of those children. The welfare of children was not the primary concern of Bishop Mulkearns and other senior members of the Diocese when responding to complaints and allegations of child sexual abuse against their priests. There is no doubt it should have been.

Just one particular example from loved experience of this catastrophic failure was described as follows, regarding Ridsdale and one of his scores of victims, Paul Levey. The Commissioners accepted that "at various times, Bishop Mulkearns, the Bishop of Ballarat, knew or strongly suspected that these priests [including Ridsdale] had sexually abused children in the diocese" and they were satisfied that "by late 1975 Ridsdale had admitted to Bishop Mulkearns that he had offended against children and that Bishop Mulkearns knew that Ridsdale's conduct was known to the police in Bendigo". The Commissioners found that "His concern was overwhelmingly about protecting the reputation of the church and avoiding scandal. There was little evidence that he was concerned to protect children from these priests."

When aged 14, after the breakdown of his parents' marriage, but despite his mother's misgivings, Paul Levey had been invited to live with Ridsdale in the presbytery, and did so for about 6 months. He had previously been sexually abused by Ridsdale, some 2 years earlier, on a camping trip. The Commission accepted his testimony that while living at the presbytery, Paul was sexually abused "all the time, just about every day".

The Commissioners concluded that (p. 66):

> We are satisfied that, by about April 1982, Bishop Mulkearns knew that Mr Levey was living with Ridsdale in the presbytery at Mortlake. He knew that the boy's mother was concerned about the situation and sought his assistance, but he ignored her. By this time, Bishop Mulkearns knew of Ridsdale's admission of offending against boys. It is inconceivable that it would not have occurred to him that Ridsdale should not have had a boy living with him and that the boy was, at least, at risk of sexual abuse by Ridsdale. Bishop Mulkearns' response to Mr Levey living with Ridsdale in the Mortlake presbytery demonstrated a total absence of concern for the welfare of that boy. Bishop Mulkearns deliberately left Mr Levey in danger. The Church parties properly conceded the possibility that Ridsdale was abusing Mr Levey should have occurred to Bishop Mulkearns and, given the knowledge he already had about Ridsdale by this me, he should have insisted that the boy be removed from the presbytery immediately. This was an extraordinary and inexcusable failure by Bishop Mulkearns, and his failure to act subjected Mr Levey to ongoing sexual abuse by Ridsdale. Bishop Mulkearns' conduct was appalling.

Major Findings Applying Generally from the Case Studies into Catholic Church Institutions

Major findings about the problems in Catholic Church institutions can be distilled from the collection of these 15 case studies. These findings are made across the 15 case studies, and were synthesised by the Royal Commission in its *Final*

Report – Preface and Executive Summary (2017a). They cover aspects of: the nature of the Catholic Church's decentralised structure and governance; lack of accountability of bishops and other senior clergy; the exclusion of lay people and women from leadership positions; the nature of Church doctrine and procedures; unswerving obedience to these doctrine and procedures by individuals and leaders; clericalism[6]; abuse of religious and spiritual power and authority; the nature of activities undertaken and unsupervised access to children; inadequate training and formation practices; inadequate training in professional responsibility, ethics, and boundaries; the practice of confession being conducted in private; celibacy not being a direct cause, but being a contributing cause to child sexual abuse, especially when combined with other risk factors.

In sum, key themes recognised as facilitating the systematic infliction, continuance and concealment of child sexual abuse, and systematic failure to respond appropriately, can be grouped conceptually as follows:

- Overarching abuse of enormous power held through religious status and clericalism, both by the abuser, and by leaders in the institution who were knowingly acted inadequately before and after the events
- The theme of inadequate leadership was ever-present. The Royal Commission concluded that "In its response to child sexual abuse, the leadership of the Catholic Church has failed the people of the Catholic Church in Australia, in particular its children. The results of that failure have been catastrophic." (*Final Report – Preface and Executive Summary* 2017a, p. 70).
- Leaders failing to take any effective disciplinary action in relation to the offender, despite knowing the abuse had happened and who had inflicted it
- Leaders transferring offenders, including serial and dangerous offenders, to other parishes, with no penalty, supervision or oversight, and often still allowing the offender to have access to children
- Leaders' actions all being directed towards preserving secrecy and the reputation of the Church
- Leaders failing to take any appropriate action to support the child
- Leaders minimising the sexual conduct and claiming it was not criminal
- Leaders and others failing to report cases of child sexual abuse to police or other domestic authorities, and instead complying with Church doctrine to maintain secrecy
- Leaders treating child sexual abuse as a remediable and forgiveable sin to be dealt with as an internal Church matter, rather than as a crime to be dealt with by domestic legal authorities
- Leaders silencing those who knew about the abuse from disclosing it to authorities
- Abusers grooming not only the child but the child's family, capitalizing on their clericalism and status as representatives of God, gaining unfettered access to

[6] Kenny declared: "Clericalism has rendered some of Ireland"s brightest, most privileged and powerful men, either unwilling or unable to address the horrors cited in the Ryan and Murphy Reports".

children, and manipulating the religious belief held by the child through threats (including of being sent to hell) if they disclosed

- Abusers exploiting the devoutness of children's parents, who would frequently not believe their children, and the religious community itself, which often either disbelieved the child or ostracized the child who disclosed
- Abusers telling the child who disclosed that they did not believe them (whether they did or not), and often punishing the child for disclosing
- Cruel responses to claims made by children or adult survivors for redress through internal Church schemes (including the Melbourne Response, established by George Pell), often exacerbating the initial trauma, and failing all tests of transparency, fairness and humane treatment
- Other exploitation of technical legal loopholes to evade civil liability for the acts of its clergy and non-clergy offenders, even when there was no doubt as to liability (relying on statutes of limitation, and on the church's status as an unincorporated association without normal juridical status, and its reliance on property trusts, meaning there was no juridical entity that could be sued).[7]

[7] Most notoriously regarding this, see Ellis v Pell [2006] NSWSC 109, where Cardinal George Pell was heavily involved in the proceedings and litigation strategy: see the comprehensive account provided in Marr (2014), and Royal Commission transcripts in Case Study 8: Mr. John Ellis, Towards Healing and civil litigation. Here, the plaintiff was John Ellis, who it was accepted experienced sexual abuse between 1974 and 1979 while he was an altar server, by Father Duggan, who was the third defendant. The first defendant was "His Eminence Cardinal George Pell Archbishop of Sydney for and on behalf of the Roman Catholic Church in the Archdiocese of Sydney"; and the second defendant was The Trustees of the Roman Catholic Church for the Archdiocese of Sydney. At this first hearing, Patten AJ granted an extension of time in which to commence civil legal proceedings, also finding that while there would be some prejudice to the defendants' fair trial rights, this did not preclude there being a fair trial. Patten AJ further held that, while it did not need to be determined finally, there was at least "an arguable case that the Trustees, at all relevant times, constituted the entity which the Roman Catholic Church in the Archdiocese of Sydney adopted and put forward as the permanent corporate entity or interface between the spiritual and temporal sides of the Church legally responsible for the Acts and omissions of the Archbishop and his subordinates", meaning that there was an entity that could be sued.

However, this second finding was overturned on appeal by the Church in The Trustees of the Roman Catholic Church v Ellis [2007] NSWCA 117. While the court accepted that statute may modify the situation, the Court accepted the Church's argument that the Trustees could not be liable. The key finding [47] was that the Church was an unincorporated association, and "An unincorporated association that is not a partnership is a group of individuals associated together for some lawful purpose other than profit that may or may not have a rigid constitution or a fixed and finite membership. Procedurally, it cannot (at common law) sue or be sued in its own name because, among other reasons, it does not exist as a juridical entity."

Individuals within an unincorporated association can assume an active or managerial role, and if the activity in which they exercise control creates a contractual or tortious claim, they can be held liable individually as principals; however, this liability remains *personal* and not representative in nature, and liability remains with the members who formed the committee or other controlling body who were in office *at the relevant time* of the tort. The relationship between individual office holders and the "members of the Church as a whole" was not sufficiently strong to establish liability of the broader organisation either in contract, or through vicarious liability in tort (negligence). Further, there was insufficient evidence of a relationship of employment of Father Duggan by Pell or by the Trustees; it was not suggested in evidence that the priest was "engaged or employed by

In Volume 16 of its Final Report, entitled *Religious institutions*, the Royal Commission made a large number of specific recommendations for reform in the Catholic Church (Recommendations 16.6–16.26), which supplement other recommendations applying to CYSOS generally including the Catholic Church. Some of these will be detailed below. In addition, I will also elaborate on some of the difficulties facing the Catholic Church, and will make some specific recommendations to respond to its unique governance arrangements. These recommendations may have particular resonance for the Catholic Church, but they have been conceived to apply generally to provide a more suitable response to heinous cover-ups and malfeasance, and to other particularly high risk situations.

While all these features of the Catholic Church are not shared by all CYSOs which have experienced problems in appropriate prevention and response to CSA, some are clearly present in cases of particularly inadequate institutional practice and coverups. In particular, these include individuals' perceived need to comply with an organizational culture of silence, and not make reports of wrongdoing due to the cost of reprisals; the institution's protection of its reputation at all costs; and authoritarian governance. Such features are instructive when considering what is required, and legitimately necessary, to overcome these forces and become embedded in domestic legal frameworks to better prevent child sexual abuse within high-risk CYSO settings. In their study of the Catholic Church, Terry et al. (2011) recognized that overall culture change was essential, and that such culture change must be led from the highest levels of management. Terry et al. (2011) concluded that mechanisms of transparency and accountability must be installed, and must become ordinary practice in every diocese. However, the problems in achieving this were not specified; and moreover, the specifics of what is involved in "accountability" and "oversight" were not articulated. Who is to be accountable, for what, to whom, and under what circumstances? Who or what bodies, internal or external, are to have oversight of these accountability mechanisms and cultural practices, and how is such oversight to be implemented?

As discussed previously in this chapter, the challenges then become not only to work out the content of such education, code of conduct, appropriate responses to

---

either named defendant, let alone by all of the members of the Church in the Archdiocese during the relevant years... the evidence showed the trustees "played no role in the appointment or oversight of priests in the Archdiocese in the 1970s". Regarding Archbishop Pell's liability, the Court observed that "liability in tort (even vicarious liability) is personal". Most actions in tort die with the wrongdoer. In this case, Archbishop Pell was not in office during the period of abuse. Argument was made, however, that the Archbishop is a corporation sole, with obligations to settle claims. The Court rejected this, finding there was "no statute or Crown grant constituting the Roman Catholic Archbishop of Sydney a corporation sole".

In New South Wales each diocese has established such a legal entity under the Roman Catholic Church Trust Property Act of 1936. For the Archdiocese of Sydney, its body corporate is The Trustees of the Roman Catholic Church for the Archdiocese of Sydney, who hold legal title to the real property owned by the Archdiocese of Sydney and by all the parishes within the Archdiocese. This land is held for the Church or for the use or benefit or for any purpose of the Church, unless subject to a specific trust. The Trustees of the Roman Catholic Church for the Archdiocese of Sydney is the legal entity used in all matters relating to contracts as required by the norms of canon law.

allegations, situational prevention, and the other strategies noted above. There need to be mechanisms to ensure that the recognised components of a holistic system of prevention, identification and appropriate response are installed, and that the elements of transparency accountability and independent external oversight are built in to the system. In the section of this chapter on progress and responses, methods of pursuing these aims are detailed. We can now consider some of the major recommendations of the Australian Royal Commission Into Institutional Responses to Child Sexual Abuse, which have as their object the development and enforcement of such systems, and which are already catalysing reform of law, policy and practice.

Major Recommendations by the Royal Commission for Reform of Law, Policy and Practice

The Australian Royal Commission Into Institutional Responses to Child Sexual Abuse (the Royal Commission) delivered its Final Report in December 2017 (Royal Commission Into Institutional Responses to Child Sexual Abuse 2017a). This is the single most extensive Inquiry of its type ever undertaken, and its work contributes a historic, international legacy. It made 400 recommendations for legal, policy and practical reforms. Many of these are already beginning to be translated into civil law, criminal law, and policy and practice.

The Final Report in 17 Volumes The Final Report comprised 17 Volumes, devoted to specific issues, and specific contexts. Selected major recommendations include (Recommendation numbers in parentheses)[8]:

Volume 6 (Making institutions child safe): A national strategy to prevent child sexual abuse should be developed, overseen by a federal government office (6.1); that all CYSOs should implement the Child Safe Standards identified by the Royal Commission (6.4), as outlined in 6.5–6.14, requiring child and youth-serving organisations to take measures to improve prevention and response mechanisms; and that education ministers should establish a nationally consistent curriculum for online safety education in schools (6.19);

Volume 7 (Improving institutional responding and reporting):

Improve reporting by:

- Government-issued written guides for mandatory reporters (7.1)
- Provide mandated reporters with access to experts who can provide advice (7.2)

[8] Other Volumes with findings and recommendations not covered here are: Vol 8: Record-keeping and information sharing; Vol 9: advocacy, support and therapeutic treatment services; Vol 10: Children with harmful sexual behaviours; Vol 12: Contemporary out-of-home care; Vol 15: Contemporary detention environments; Vol 17: Beyond the Royal Commission.

- Amend mandatory reporting laws so there is national consistency in reporter groups, and add to existing laws the following groups: out-of-home care workers, youth justice workers, early childhood workers, psychologists and school counsellors, and people in religious ministry (7.3)
- Religious ministers should not be exempted from reporting where knowledge or suspicion is gained in confession (7.4)
- Mandatory reporting legislation should provide comprehensive protection for reporters, including from liability and reprisals (7.5)
- Amend legislation to protect those who make complaints or reports in good faith to any institution about CSA in the institution, or its responses to it (7.6)

Improve responding by:

- Under Child safe standard 6, having clear processes for responding to complaints that are child-centred (7.7)
- Under Child safe standard 1, having a clear Code of Conduct to embed in institutional leadership, governance and culture, clear expectations about acceptable and unacceptable behaviour, reporting requirements, and protections for reporters (7.8).

Improve oversight of institutions' handling of responses by:

- The enactment of nationally consistent "reportable conduct schemes", based on the New South Wales scheme, obliging heads of institutions to notify an external oversight body of any reportable allegation, conduct or conviction involving any of the institution's employees (7.9–7.12)

Volume 13 (Schools) should implement the Child Safe Standards (13.1), with a particular focus on boarding schools (13.3). Similarly, in Volume 14 (Sport, recreation, arts, culture, community and hobby groups), it was stated that these groups should implement the Child Safe Standards (14.1), and that independent State and territory oversight bodies implementing Child Safe Standards should establish free, efficient communications to provide resources to the sports and recreation groups (14.4)

Volume 16 (Religious institutions) applied extensive recommendations to all religious institutions, requiring that they:

- Implement the Child Safe Standards (16.31–16.42)
- Implement comprehensive education and training for candidates for religious ministry, including on policies and codes of conduct (16.43, 16.47), and for all other ministers, leaders and employees (16.50)
- Implement oversight and supervision (16.44–16.45)
- Screen, train and monitor those employed from overseas (16.46)
- Ensure any rite of confession be conducted in an open space within clear line of sight of another adult (16.48)

- Ensure any plausible complaint of child sexual abuse against a person in religious ministry should result in standing down of the person while the complaint is investigated (16.52)
- Ensure permanent removal from ministry of any person found to have inflicted sexual abuse on the balance of probabilities, or convicted of an offence (16.55)
- Ensure dismissal, deposition, or effective removal from ministry of any person convicted of an offence relating to child sexual abuse (16.56)

Special recommendations applied to the Catholic Church, as follows:

- Bishops of each diocese were to ensure parish priests are not the employers of principals and teachers in Catholic schools (16.6)
- The Australian Catholic Bishops Conference should conduct a national review of governance and management structures of dioceses and parishes to improve transparency, accountability, consultation, and participation of lay men and women (16.7)
- Multiple recommendations regarding celibacy changes and management, and screening of candidates (16.18–16.25)
- Request the Holy See to reform numerous aspects of the 1983 Code of Canon Law to (16.9–16.14):
  - Create a new series of canons so that all acts of child sexual abuse are designated as canonical crimes, and not as moral failings or breaches of celibacy
  - That this applies to any person holding a "dignity, office or responsibility" in the Church, whether ordained or not
  - Pornographic image crimes should refer to children aged under 18, not under 14
  - Ensure the "pontifical secret" does not apply to any aspect of allegations or canonical disciplinary processes relating to child sexual abuse (16.10)
  - Remove the "pastoral approach" as a precondition to action in sexual abuse cases
  - Retrospectively remove the time limit for commencement of canonical actions relating to child sexual abuse
  - Remove the "imputability test" so that a diagnosis of paedophilia is not relevant to prosecution and sentencing for child sexual abuse offences
  - Give effect to recommendatons 16.55 and 16.56

Redress, Civil Justice and Criminal Justice In other separate accompanying Reports, the Royal Commission had also made major reform recommendations. These included a range of recommendations in relation to Redress and Civil Litigation about (Recommendation numbers in parentheses):

- Implementing a national redress scheme (1–84)
- Removing the statute of limitations for civil claims for child sexual abuse, with retrospective and prospective effect, meaning that survivors can commence a civil lawsuit at any time after the event (85–88)

- Passing legislation to impose a non-delegable duty on selected institutions even where the act is a deliberate criminal act (89–90)
- Passing legislation to make all institutions legally liable unless it is proven they took reasonable steps to prevent the abuse (reverse onus legislation) (91–93)
- Passing legislation to ensure the Catholic church cannot evade liability due to its lack of juridical status and ensuring its property trust is a proper defendant to sue (94)
- Ensuring that institutions adopt model litigant guidelines when dealing with child sexual abuse claims (96–99)
- Passing special laws to prevent the Catholic Church exploiting a technical legal loophole and evading liability for the acts of its clergy and non-clergy offenders.[9]

Criminal Justice On criminal justice, the Royal Commission also made extensive recommendations on police responses (2–13); prosecution responses (37–43); evidence laws and procedures (44–63); judicial directions and jury management (64–71); sentencing reform (74–78); enhancing appeals capacity and performance (79–82). It also recommended abolition of any remaining statutes of limitations within states on criminal offences involving sexual abuse of children (30–31). It recommended the creation of new offences, including maintaining a sexual relationship (21–24), grooming (25–26), position of authority offences (27–29), failure to report (where an owner, manager, staff member or volunteer of an institution fails to report to police in circumstances where they know, suspect, or should have suspected that an adult associated with the institution was sexually abusing or had sexually abused a child) (33) with no exemption for religious confession (35); failure to protect a child (where an adult knows there is a substantial risk another "adult associated with the institution" will commit a sexual offence against a child under 16, or a child aged 16 or 17 if the "adult associated with the institution" is in a position of authority over the child, and the person has the power or responsibility to reduce or remove the risk and the person negligently fails to reduce or remove the risk (36).[10]

Summary The Royal Commission identified a range of problems in institutional settings, including insufficient education of personnel, inadequate institutional governance and external oversight, failure to report known and suspected cases. Some of the measures proposed to respond to these problems have application to both institutional and non-institutional settings. As the next part of this chapter will show, while many problems have been uncovered by the Royal Commission, its wide-ranging recommendations for reform have already begun to have considerable effect through legislative and policy change.

[9] See for example Western Australia's Civil Liability Legislation Amendment (Child Sexual Abuse Actions) Act 2018; see also Victoria's Legal Identity of Defendants (Organisational Child Abuse) Bill 2018.

[10] Modelled on Victoria's s 49C.

Progress and Responses

Redress Schemes to Compensate Those Abused in Institutions

Redress Schemes Generally As seen later in this chapter, for multiple reasons including but not limited to the reliance by defendants on statutes of limitation, it can be impossible or extremely difficult for individuals who have experienced child sexual abuse in institutional settings to obtain compensation for their injuries through the civil legal system. Many jurisdictions that have accepted the widespread infliction of child sexual abuse in state and private institutional settings have adopted redress schemes to provide a survivor-centred alternative pathway to justice. Kathleen Daly, one of the world's leading redress scholars, reported recently that by January 2016, 15 jurisdictions had established redress schemes: Australia, Austria, Belgium, Canada, Germany, Iceland, Ireland, the Netherlands, New Zealand, Norway, Scotland, the States of Jersey, Sweden, Switzerland, and the US (Daly 2017). Within nations, redress schemes have frequently been established at state or provincial level, so that by January 2016, there were at least 35 schemes across a range of jurisdictions (Daly 2017). The legislative enactment of a redress scheme was a key recommendation of the Australian Royal Commission Into Institutional Responses to Child Sexual Abuse.

These schemes have been designed with different parameters in the various jurisdictions that have employed them, with significant differences involving claimant eligibility, the process of providing evidence of one's experience and injury, the amount of redress available as a whole, the amount of redress available to each individual claimant depending on their experiences and injuries, and the method of calculation of individuals' redress. However, all these schemes share similar rationales and purposes.

Redress Schemes aim to recognise and respond to the child sexual abuse of each individual in an entire class of individuals across a state or province, or indeed an entire nation, in one holistic scheme. They differ from conventional civil legal proceedings in that they are a less formal administrative process with different rules of procedure and evidence. They are more flexible and speedy, with less formality and cost, and less trauma and confrontation than conventional legal proceedings. Being an administrative process, redress schemes are concerned with establishing participant eligibility, and this does involve an element of demonstrating the experience of abuse in a relevant institution, and usually some evidence of the injuries caused; however, the process involves an informal procedure for establishing such eligibility and a significantly lower evidentiary standard than civil litigation. Especially when designed as a result of the findings of inquiries into historical abuse, a redress scheme may provide the only realistic option for justice when very substantial amounts of time have elapsed since the events, when witnesses and defendants have died, and when institutions may even have ceased to exist. Not all survivors will apply to the scheme, as many survivors do not wish to engage any further with any institution responsible for their abuse, or with any process that reminds them of their experience. In addition, many survivors have no financial motivation. However, it is clear from the experience of survivors' involvement in these schemes that the level of participation far exceeds what otherwise occurs through the formal legal system.

Redress Schemes have additional features beyond those available in civil legal claims that aim to provide further meaningful amelioration of the impact of institutional child sexual abuse and related non-sexual abuse, and provide justice for survivors. Usually, they include the availability of formal group and individualised apologies, commitments to take steps to prevent re-occurrence of child sexual abuse within their institutions, rehabilitative services including counselling, and public memorials and commemorative activities (Daly 2014; Mathews 2004a). Such additional non-pecuniary features are widely considered essential therapeutic gestures, which are an essential part of a healing response.

A significant difference between redress schemes and civil legal claims is that redress schemes involve payments of "redress" rather than "compensation". This means that financial payments, while recognising the fact of abuse and the injuries and losses caused, and while recognising liability in fact, are not intended to replicate the amount of compensation payable under a formal civil compensation claim through calculation of the full quantum of damages taking into account all available legal heads of damage. As a result, payments of redress are far lower than payments of compensation through the courts. Accordingly, institutions that act ethically in taking responsibility for their acts and omissions, and that contribute financially to such schemes, ultimately benefit financially through a substantially lower pecuniary commitment than would be required through settlement or litigation of formal civil compensation claims. Also significant is that normally, the terms of acceptance of a redress payment require claimants to waive other rights to bring civil proceedings.

Nationally Established Independently Administered Schemes Compared with In-House Schemes In some instances, such as the Irish Scheme, and the anticipated Australian Scheme, Redress Schemes are established through national legislation and administered by a centralised secular authority that is independent from the institutions responsible from the abuse. Such schemes contain clear checks on abuses of power, prevent the likelihood of pressure and coercion, and preclude the provision of inappropriate advice about whether or not to accept the offer, and why. Often, other measures are built in to ensure transparency, accountability, reporting to an oversight body, and review of the scheme.

This is clearly far more appropriate than other in-house administrative schemes that have been established privately, without adequate design, without adequate and consistent measures regarding process and decision-making, without proper external oversight, and implemented by non-independent actors. There is clear evidence that these schemes have facilitated further egregious abuse of power, coerced acceptance of desultory amounts of redress, pressured waiver of rights to sue, forced confidentiality agreements, and other breaches of administrative justice that have compounded the initial abuse.[11]

The Australian National Redress Scheme

The Australian Parliament has introduced legislation to create a national redress scheme in the wake of the findings and recommendations of the Royal Commission Into Institutional Responses to Child Sexual Abuse. At the time of writing, the Redress Scheme for Institutional Child Sexual Abuse Bill 2017 remains before Parliament, and is yet to receive the commitment of all States, Territories, and relevant organisations. The Royal Commission Into Institutional Responses to Child Sexual Abuse recommended that a national redress scheme be enacted and operational by 1 July 2017.[12] It recommended that the Scheme should have an upper cap of $200,000, with an average redress payment of $65,000. Under the bill, the Scheme's cap is $150,000, substantially below the recommendation, and even further below the average payment in Ireland of over €60,000, where the highest payment exceeded €300,000.[13] The Royal Commission recommended extensive measures for transparency and accountability (Rec 69) and counselling support (Recs 66–68).

As envisaged by the Royal Commission, the Australian scheme contains three elements. First, a monetary payment as tangible recognition of the wrong suffered by a survivor; second, access to counselling and psychological services (estimated at an average of A$5500 per person); and third, if requested, a direct personal response from the responsible institution(s), such as an apology. It is estimated tat the scheme may be open to an estimated 60,000 eligible claimants, with an overall maximum cost of approximately 4 billion.[14] Taking population difference into

[11] See for example Marr (2014) and the discussion of the Melbourne Response, established by Cardinal Pell in the Catholic Archdiocese of Melbourne, with an initial cap of $50,000. This was later slightly increased (first to $55,000, then to $75,000), but this process has been estimated to have saved the Catholic Church hundreds of millions of dollars. Pell's scheme was expedited at a time when the Australian Catholic Bishops' Conference was seeking to create a national scheme, named Towards Healing; this scheme did not cap the redress payment. See also the discussion of this in: Royal Commission Into Institutional Responses to Child Sexual Abuse (2015). Report of Case Study 16: The Melbourne Response; and Royal Commission Into Institutional Responses to Child Sexual Abuse (2015). Redress and Civil Litigation Report, including Part 11.6.

[12] Royal Commission Into Institutional Responses to Child Sexual Abuse (2015). Redress and Civil Litigation Report, Chapters 1–12, especially Chapters 10 and 11.

[13] Residential Institutions Redress Board. (2011). Annual Report of The Residential Institutions Redress Board 2011.

[14] The Royal Commission identified more than 4000 institutions where sexual abuse took place. The Commission estimated that almost 40,000 survivors were sexually abused in institutions run by non-government bodies such as those run by churches and charities, and 20,000 survivors were sexually abused in state and territory government institutions.

account, this is broadly comparable although somewhat less than the Irish scheme outlined below.

Other key aspects of the proposed Australian Scheme are:

- People are eligible to apply to the Scheme if they experienced sexual abuse in an institution while they were a child, before 1 July 2018.
- A lower evidentiary threshold applies, meaning that eligibility for a redress payment is assessed on whether there was "a reasonable likelihood" the person suffered institutional sexual abuse as a child (reflecting Rec 56, Redress and Civil Litigation Report).
- Applicants who have received redress under another scheme or compensation through a settlement or court judgment are still eligible, but prior payments by the institution will be deducted from the amount of redress.
- Only one application can be made per person; if abused in more than one institution, the decision-maker can determine the appropriate share of each institution.
- Applicants can access legal assistance to help determine whether to accept an offer (reflecting Rec 64, Redress and Civil Litigation Report).
- A person who accepts an offer of redress must sign a deed of release, meaning the institution(s) responsible for the abuse will not be subject to other civil liability (Rec 63); but without confidentiality obligations (reflecting Rec 65, Redress and Civil Litigation Report).
- No income tax is levied on payments.
- Reviews of decisions are limited to internal review, and not to merits review or judicial review.
- Criminal liability of offenders is not affected.
- The Scheme is intended to open on 1 July 2018 and operate for 10 years; applications need to be made at least 12 months before the closing date of 30 June 2028.

By the end of May 2018, seven of Australia's eight state and territory governments had formally committed to the scheme.[15] The remaining government (Western Australia) and institutions must opt in and commit resources to discharge their duty. In March 2018, 3 months after the Final Report, former Commissioner Robert Fitzgerald condemned the Catholic Church for still failing to fully accept its responsibility for the abuse, and for inadequate responses to abuse survivors. Part of this criticism related to the Church's failure to commit to participate in the Australian federal government's redress scheme (Schneiders et al. 2018). In addition, the Church had actively misled the Royal Commission by grossly undervaluing its property portfolio; a media investigation found the Church held more than $30 billion in property and assets in Australia (Millar et al. 2018). After continued delays, the Prime Minister of Australia, Malcolm Turnbull, wrote personally to the Catholic Church, and other churches, to urge their immediate commitment to the scheme

[15] On 22 May 2018, the Tasmanian Government committed to join the Scheme. On 28 May 2018, the South Australian and Northern Territory governments also announced they would join the Scheme. Victoria, New South Wales, the Australian Capital Territory and Queensland had previously committed.

(Koziol 2018). The Catholic Church finally committed to the scheme on 30 May 2018. On Thursday 31 May 2018, the Anglican Church, Salvation Army, Scouts Australia and YMCA made a joint announcement committing to join the Scheme. To ensure the scheme does not fail, the Australian Government and state and territory governments should be the funder of last resort in all cases where the institution is unable to reimburse the Commonwealth.

The Irish Scheme The Irish Redress Scheme is arguably the most extensive yet implemented at a national level. It was established under the Residential Institutions Redress Act 2002. Section 5 of the Act sets out the functions of the Residential Institutions Redress Board. The first function was that of public information and transparency: to make all reasonable efforts, through public advertisement, direct correspondence and otherwise, to ensure that persons who were residents of an institution listed in the Act were made aware of the existence of the Board, so they could consider making an application for redress.

The Board's second function in each application is to determine whether the applicant is entitled to an award, and, if so, to make an award in accordance with the Act which is fair and reasonable having regard to the unique circumstances of the applicant.

The procedure followed by the Board for processing applications is prescribed by the Residential Institutions Redress Act 2002, as amended by subsesquent legislation.[16] All Regulations and the legislation were freely available to potential applicants from the Board's office and website. Applications for redress were submitted on a standard application form. The Board issued several accompanying documents to assist applicants and their advisors.[17] These publications provided information to applicants and their legal advisers so they knew what was involved in making an application. They informed the applicants what was involved in the process and what options weere available to them. They explaidn the difference between settlements and hearings and informed applicants what to expect when they arrived at the Board's offices. These were thorough, sensitive approaches to the individuals who wereeligible to make applications. Along with the Board's newsletters they also provided plain English information on costs and expenses, and on procedure at a hearing, and what the applicant could do after receiving an offer. In addition, the Board established a free, confidential and independent financial management service available to all award recipients. In addition, to further inform applicants, advisors and the public of the Board's activities and outcomes, the Board published regular newsletters and statements, and annual reports.

[16] Part 4 of the Commission to Inquire into Child Abuse (Amendment) Act, 2005, The Residential Institutions Redress (Amendment) Act 2011, The Residential Institutions Statutory Fund Act 2012 and by Regulations made by the Minister for Education and Skills in accordance with the Act.

[17] These were: A Guide to the Redress Scheme under the Residential Institutions Redress Act 2002; A Short Guide to the Redress Scheme under the Residential Institutions Redress Act 2002; The Residential Institutions Redress Board Guide to Hearing Procedures.

Number and Amounts of Awards The scheme adopted a method of calculating the amount of redress payable based on the severity of the abuse and injury suffered. The Board commenced making awards in May 2003. Where applications were refused, the reason was generally that the application was outside the Board's terms of reference as laid down in the 2002 Act due to the nature of the institution. Where applications were refused, the reason was generally that the application was outside the Board's terms of reference as laid down in the 2002 Act due to the nature of the institution.

By 31 December 2011, the Board had completed the process in 14,856 cases. This had resulted in 10,873 offers/awards made following settlement talks; 2613 awards made following hearings (12 awards were rejected by the applicant); 430 awards following Review; and 940 applications being withdrawn, refused or resulting in no award. The total awards made to 31st December 2011 amounted to €875.25million. The average value of awards was approximately €62,895, the largest award being €300,500.

A final 1 year extension to 31 December 2012 resulted in the Board having completed the process in 15,396 cases, with 11,197 offers following settlement talks; 2725 awards following hearings; 456 awards following Review; 16 applicants rejecting their awards; and 1018 applications being withdrawn, refused or resulting in no award. Overall, the average value of awards was €62,860, with the largest award being €300,500. Almost half the awards were in the range of €50,000 – €100,000. Table 5.1 provides a breakdown of the redress payments.

Child Safe Standards Legislation for CYSOs

In 2015, the Australian state of Victoria created a legislative scheme to implement a set of Child Safe Standards in a range of CYSOs. This scheme was embedded in the Child Wellbeing and Safety Act 2005, and established by Ministerial declaration on 31 December 2015 (Victoria Government Gazette G52). The standards were created as part of the state's response to the *Betrayal of Trust Inquiry* (Victorian Family and Community Development Committee, 2013), and are directed to all types of child

Table 5.1 Awards of redress under Ireland's Redress Scheme, 2003–2012

Redress Bands	Total Weightings for Severity of Abuse and Injury/Effects of Abuse	Award Payable by way of Redress	Number	Percentage (%)
V	70 or more	€200,000 – €300,000	43	0.30
IV	55–69	€150,000 – €200,000	261	1.82
III	40–54	€100,000 – €150,000	1954	13.59
II	25–39	€50,000 – €100,000	7018	48.81
I	Less than 25	Up to €50,000	5102	35.48
Total			**14,378**	**100.00**

maltreatment within CYSOs, going beyond CSA. The seven standards require CYSOs to: embed an organizational culture of child safety; create a child safe policy; create a code of conduct; screen, supervise and train staff; have processes for reporting and responding; have strategies to identify and reduce risk; and promote child participation.

The Child Safe Standards promoted by the Royal Commission (Rec. 6.4–6.11) are substantially embedded in legislation in several states, requiring organisations to adopt comprehensive measures to prevent, identify, and respond appropriately to child sexual abuse. The purposes are to:

- promote the safety of all children in these institutional settings;
- prevent child abuse; and
- ensure allegations of abuse are properly responded to.

In Victoria, for example, the Child Wellbeing and Safety Act Part 6, s 17 and the Ministerial Order, sets the following standards, which apply to CYSOs (education, early childhood education and care, out of home care, health, religious, cultural, sporting and recreation services, other welfare services)

- Standard 1: Strategies to embed an organisational culture of child safety, including through effective leadership arrangements
- Standard 2: A child safe policy or statement of commitment to child safety
- Standard 3: A code of conduct that establishes clear expectations for appropriate behaviour with children
- Standard 4: Screening, supervision, training and other HR practices that reduce the risk of child abuse by new and existing personnel
- Standard 5: Processes for responding to and reporting suspected child abuse
- Standard 6: Strategies to identify and reduce or remove risks of child abuse
- Standard 7: Strategies to promote the participation and empowerment of children.

The Child Wellbeing and Safety Act 2005 Part 6 makes oversight and enforcement of the Victorian child safe standards the responsibility of the Commission for Children and Young People. The Commission can take action to investigate whether an entity is complying with the standards – for example, by inspecting an institution or requesting information. The Commission can then take the necessary steps to achieve compliance, such as by issuing a notice to comply or by seeking court orders. Funding authorities as well as sector regulators have a role in oversight and compliance, and the Commission has functions to educate and advise other regulators and funders about the child safe standards. The Commission's annual report should include information about compliance with the child safe standards.

These standards came into effect for the first phase of institutions in 2016, with full implementation from 2017. The standards are mandatory for a broad range of institutions working with children. The Commission for Children and Young People helps institutions comply with the standards. In some sectors, existing regulatory arrangements have been expanded to include monitoring of and compliance with the standards. For example, in Victorian schools, the standards have been incorporated into school registration requirements.

The Commission for Children and Young People has an essential role in this field and much depends on how well it discharges its role. The Commission must:

- educate and provide advice to CYSO authorities to promote compliance within CYSOs
- educate and advise CYSOs
- oversee and enforce compliance by CYSOs (e.g., inspections, audits, notices to comply, penalties for non-compliance)
- promote continuous improvement in CYSOs.

Victoria's legislative scheme therefore includes enforcement and oversight measures, but remains a model of co-regulation model rather than direct regulation. This is because, while other materials provide further abstract detail about what the standards should achieve and how they could be implemented, the scheme requires CYSOs to create their own substantive approaches to each requirement, rather than having all or some of the requirements centrally prescribed and administered. As a result, the scheme may face challenges in ensuring consistent quality of design, fragmentation within and across CYSOs, duplication of cost, and difficulties in implementation.

Several other jurisdictions in Australia have since made changes in this area, but these have taken different forms. For example, at the time of writing, in New South Wales, in September 2017, the Children's Guardian published non-prescriptive "Principles for Child-Safe Organisations" which were informed by the findings of the Royal Commission into Institutional Responses to Child Sexual Abuse. In Western Australia, the Commission for Children and Young People developed the "Child Safe Organisations WA: Guidelines" in April 2016, informed by the Interim Report (2014) of the Royal Commission into Institutional Responses to Child Sexual Abuse. South Australia had a weaker legislative scheme.

As discussed in Mathews (2017), different models of regulation and implementation of complex systemic responses in diverse CYSO settings all present challenges. Models of pure organisational self-regulation with no direct or indirect influence by the state have been shown by the weight of history to be unsustainable. Co-regulation, as exemplified by the current Victorian model, offers some benefits, but also contains risks. Direct regulation, where there is greater direction by the state about not only what standards exist, but what their precise nature must be, may offer superior quality, cost-efficiency, and efficacy, but faces challenges of responding to situational differences and attracting CYSO commitment and buy-in.

Yet, some dimensions of the Child Safe Standards may perhaps more readily be the subject of direct regulation, with others more suited to co-regulation (Mathews 2017). For example, legislative reporting duties apply state-wide, meaning CYSO policies about reporting could readily be designed robustly, with expert input, and made applicable state-wide to virtually all CYSOs. Similarly, the core elements of a code of conduct could be promulgated to ensure prohibitions on high-risk contexts are clear and universal, and situations of the highest risk are avoided, while allowing for modifications to suit the nature of the CYSO's activities and the local context. Common approaches to these matters could arguably be developed through a process of consultation and consensus-building with community partners. A centralized approach to some important components would enable enormous savings of cost and time, ensure higher scientific quality, and would relieve organizations of the requirement to generate their own approaches to matters that can be designed by a central, specialized authority. Finally, education programs in CSA involve common principles (definition of CSA; its prevalence; its criminality; its serious consequences; who experiences it, and at what ages; who inflicts it; the tendency towards nondisclosure; children's truthfulness in disclosure; the indicators of CSA: boundary violations; children's typical emotional, social and behavioural responses after victimization). A high quality training program could be designed through a robust process of expert development, and delivered economically online. CSA education programs directed towards professionals serving children and youth have shown positive effects on knowledge, attitudinal dispositions, preventative behavior and reporting (Letourneau et al. 2016; Rheingold et al. 2015). In their best form, some aspects of education are arguably connected with cultural development through genuine change to individuals' empathic concern, especially amongst CYSO leaders, and these aspects of education may be the most challenging to achieve given their complexity (Mathews and Collin-Vézina 2016). However, such efforts are required if society and its key institutions are to meet the social justice concern of public health, and to garner effective participation from relevant communities and their leaders.

As with any policy response, whether a jurisdiction adopts a model of direct regulation, co-regulation, or self-regulation by CYSOs in the prevention and response to CSA, limitations may become apparent, and a robust public health approach should identify these by monitoring outcomes, with refinements made through a commitment to ongoing review and improvement (Mercy et al. 1993). With any direct regulation or co-regulation, challenges include the attraction of genuine commitment to change and oversight, especially amongst organizational leaders. Reassuring stakeholders about the precise nature, extent and practicability of any new policy measure, and of how it strengthens their organization, is an important part of recruiting and retaining participation by CYSOs and the development of authentic commitment. A multi-dimensional model of child safety in CYSOs, especially within those presenting higher risk to children because of the nature of their activities, can be generated as a cooperative and supportive exercise to reduce the likelihood of CSA in CYSOs, enhance its identification, and end active concealment of known cases. Ultimately, such an approach may help to develop and embed new social norms and cultural shifts which promote the fundamental aim of reducing suffering and enhancing social justice.

These kinds of organisational approaches can be one part of a broader social response to child sexual abuse. Other dimensions of legal systems are aimed at ensuring appropriate reports are made of known and suspected allegations, both within and beyond organisational settings. This focus on reporting overlaps with one of the elements of the Child Safe Standards outlined above, but as we will now see, a jurisdiction's legal duties to report known and suspected cases of child sexual abuse can take different forms. Common to all these reporting duties is the objective of interrupting cases of child sexual abuse at an early stage, which can have other potential benefits; this responds to the child's most urgent need, which is for the abuse to stop. However, further significance lies in how these different reporting duties apply to different settings, both individual and organisational, in the consequences for individuals and their employers when the duties are breached, and in how these duties could perhaps be better implemented and or modified to encourage better outcomes, especially in cases of the most egregious malfeasance.

Duties to Report Child Sexual Abuse: A Common Law Duty; Occupational Policy-Based Duties; Reporting Duties in Criminal Law; Legislative Reportable Conduct Schemes; Legislative Mandatory Reporting Laws

Legal systems have created different kinds of duties to report known cases of child sexual abuse, and suspected cases of child sexual abuse. These duties have several common rationales. Especially when they are in criminal law, these duties are imposed to recognise that citizens have a duty to assist police and the state in the detection of serious crimes, and a similar duty not to engage in acts or omissions to impede detection of the offender. As well, they overcome the human tendency towards official corruption, especially in instances of child sexual abuse within organisations. When imposed in civil laws, such as in mandatory reporting legislation, and reportable conduct schemes, they are imposed primarily to avoid the phenomenon of gaze aversion, the strong tendency for people to look the other way and avoid acting even when confronted with clear evidence of serious wrongdoing. In both cases, when applied to child sexual abuse offences, these duties to report also recognise that the phenomenon occurs in secret, is likely to remain hidden, and the child is unable or unlikely to seek assistance. In all these cases, the essence of the duty to report is based on ethical principles requiring the taking of action to prevent harm to a vulnerable child who cannot protect herself or himself.

Impediments to disclosure by the child are well-known in all contexts of sexual abuse, including organisational contexts, and have been discussed earlier in this book. Some of these impediments are derived from the child's attributes (e.g., not knowing that what is being done to them is wrong); others relate to the offender (e.g., where threats are made to the child). However, there may be particularly powerful barriers to disclosure that are presented by the organisational context. Connected to this, in toxic organisational environments there may be powerful cultural factors which also discourage reporting by employees or volunteers who suspect or even know of child sexual abuse. These situations have been uncovered in multiple jurisdictions and in numerous organisational contexts. Because reporting of unethical conduct by employees require strong ethical leadership and trust in the organisation's leaders, as well as a culture of ethical behaviour at the employee level, efforts to prevent and neutralise such cultural postures likely require systematic multi-stage interventions, sustained over time.

For these reasons, numerous public inquiries have repeatedly endorsed the use of mandatory reporting laws for child sexual abuse (Mathews 2013). Recently, for example, the Protecting Victoria's Vulnerable Children Inquiry investigated systemic problems in Victoria's child protection and services system (Cummins et al. 2012) recommended the expansion of mandatory reporting duties to further professional groups (p. 349) and amendment of the Crimes Act 1958 to require the reporting by any religious minister, office-holder, employee, member or volunteer of a religious or spiritual organisation providing services to children of a reasonable suspicion of physical or sexual abuse of a child committed by an individual in a religious or spiritual organisation (p. 355). In addition, Australia's Royal Commission (2017) recommended the harmonisation of all Australian state and territory mandatory reporting laws so that a common minimum range of professional groups are designated as mandated reporters across the country (Rec. 7.3).

It is instructive to provide some further detail about these formal legislative reporting duties. Before doing do, we can briefly note other legal and policy-based reporting duties that may coexist with these legal duties, but take different forms and are accompanied by different systemic structures and enforcement measures.

Duties Based in the Common Law In many common law jurisdictions, there will be a duty to take action based in the common law of negligence (Mathews et al. 2009b). Here, depending on the circumstances, an individual (and especially one who has a professionally-based duty to take care of the child, such as a teacher) will have a duty to take reasonable steps to prevent further harm to a child where the person knows or ought to have known, or even has a reasonable suspicion, that a child in their care has been sexually abused. If this duty to act – which can be practicably fulfilled by reporting the suspicion to the relevant department of child protection – is breached by not taking any action, and if the child then suffers further harm through further abuse for example, then the teacher will be deemed to have breached their duty of care to the child. Through the principle of vicarious liability, the teacher's employer would be liable for the teacher's negligence, as occurred, for example, in AB v Victoria (Unreported, Supreme Court of Victoria, Gillard J, 15 June 2000), and as has occurred in medical settings in Canada in Brown v University of Alberta Hospital (1997) 145 DLR 4th 63, and in the USA in Landeros v Flood (1976) 551 P 2d 389.

This common law duty can co-exist with other legislative reporting duties in a jurisdiction which has legislative reporting duties, providing multiple different causes of action, having different ultimate purposes. However, its presence also means that in a common law jurisdiction that does not have a legislative reporting duty (in criminal law, mandatory reporting laws, or both), there can still be a similar substantive legal duty to report. This was discussed by Mathews et al. (2009b) in further detail in the context of medical practitioners in the UK. In the UK, there is no legislative mandatory reporting duty to report child sexual abuse, nor is there such a duty sourced in criminal law. However, in JD v East Berkshire Community Health NHS Trust & Ors [2005] UKHL 23, the House of Lords held that where a paediatrician suspects child abuse:

1. the paediatrician owes a legal duty of care to the child;
2. there is no competing duty owed to the child's parents, so if a report of suspected abuse is unproven the parents cannot sue for negligence;
3. the proper protection for a parent is that the paediatrician's investigations be conducted in good faith.

This meant that doctors had a common law duty of care towards the child, which took priority over any duty owed to the child's parent. In cases where a doctor suspects child sexual abuse, that duty should be discharged by taking appropriate steps to protect the child from further abuse, which could involve making a report to the relevant government child protect agency. Similar common law principles have been set down in Australia by the High Court in Sullivan v Moody (2001) 207 CLR 562. In 2007, confusion over the situation in England led the Department for Children, Schools and Families and the Department of Health to jointly release a statement of advice supporting paediatricians in England and Wales and clarifying the legal position if parents were to complain. An accompanying letter recognised concerns about parents' complaints but urged that this "should not deter anyone from reporting suspected cases of child abuse provided they have acted in good faith".

Duties Based in Occupational Policy Similarly, a distinct policy-based reporting duty may exist for individuals in a particular occupation. Teachers, doctors, nurses and police, for example, will commonly have professional duties and protocols set out, which will include duties in relation to known and suspected cases of child sexual abuse they encounter in the course of their work. A failure to comply with these occupational policy duties may create liability under industrial policy, such as professional disciplinary measures, as well as other forms of legal liability (Mathews et al. 2008a).

The relevance of both these kinds of duties is that they may exist even in jurisdictions where the more formal reporting duties outlined below are entirely absent, or are not as extensive. Accordingly, for example, even if a jurisdiction has no legislative mandatory reporting law, and no criminal law duty to report child sexual abuse, there may be other duties that require the same kind of action to be taken.

Reporting Duties in Criminal Law

Reporting duties in criminal law can have a unique impact due to their special character and consequences. Legislation can impose a special kind of reporting duty in criminal law, effectively requiring all adults who have knowledge or belief that child sexual abuse has been committed to report this to the police. In Australia, these duties exist in New South Wales (implicitly through the Crimes Act 1900 s 316), and Victoria, expressly through the Crimes Act 1958 s 327.

Victoria By way of example, in Victoria the Crimes Act 1958 s 327 expressly makes it an offence to fail to disclose a sexual offence committed against a child under the age of 16 years. Section 327(2) requires an adult "who has information that leads the person to form a reasonable belief that a sexual offence has been committed in Victoria against a child under the age of 16 years by another person of or over the age of 18 years" to disclose the information to a police officer as soon as it is practicable to do so, unless they have a reasonable excuse. The provision contains several exceptions, and provides protections from liability for those who make disclosures. The maximum penalty is 3 years imprisonment. This provision was inserted in 2014, in response to the Betrayal of Trust Inquiry's recommendation.[18]

New Additional Reporting Duties: Failure by a Person in Authority to Protect a Child from a Sexual Offence Victoria also has enacted a new additional reporting duty applied specifically to those in management roles in organizations, requiring them to report to police a known risk to a child of sexual abuse by someone in the organization (Crimes Act 1958 (Vic) s 49O).[19] The new duty in s 49O is extremely significant and aims to prevent and punish gross malfeasance in failing to respond appropriately to protect a child in cases of known risk.

A paraphrasing of key parts of s 49O shows its intent and effect (my italics):

> Failure by a person in authority to protect a child from a sexual offence
> (1) A person (A) commits an offence if—
> (a) A occupies a position within, or in relation to, a relevant organisation; and (b) there is a substantial risk that a relevant child will become the victim of a sexual offence committed by another person who is—(i) 18 years of age or more; and (ii) a person associated with the relevant organisation; and
> (c) A knows that the risk exists; and
> (d) A, by reason of A's position, has the power or responsibility to reduce or remove that risk; and.
> (e) A negligently fails to reduce or remove that risk. …
> (3) a person negligently fails to reduce or remove a risk if that failure involves *a great falling short of the standard of care that a reasonable person would exercise in the circumstances*. …
> (4) For the avoidance of doubt, in a prosecution for an offence against subsection (1), it is not necessary to prove that a sexual offence has been committed.

A Grooming Offence At the same time as this provision was enacted, Victoria also created a new criminal offence of grooming, making it unlawful for an adult to communicate with a child aged under 16 with the intention that the communication

[18] Inserted by the Crimes Amendment (Protection of Children) Act 2014.

[19] In s 49O(7), a *relevant organisation* means— (a) an organisation that exercises care, supervision or authority over children, whether as its primary function or otherwise, and includes but is not limited to— (i) a church; and (ii) a religious body; and (iii) a school; and 11 other types of child and youth serving organisations.

facilitate the child engaging or being involved in the commission of a sexual offence (Crimes Act 1958 s 49M). Victoria's reforms to these criminal law reporting duties were a response to recommendations of its Betrayal of Trust Inquiry (Victorian Family and Community Development Committee, 2013), which found religious organisations had made grossly inadequate responses to cases of child sexual abuse.

New South Wales The current New South Wales benchmark provision (s 316) makes it an offence to conceal a serious indictable offence. Section 316 requires a person who "knows or believes" a serious indictable offence has been committed and "has information which might be of material assistance" in securing the apprehension, prosecution or conviction of the offender must "bring that information to the attention of a member of the Police Force or other appropriate authority". The maximum penalty is 2 years imprisonment. This does not expressly apply to sexual offences against children under 16, but has this consequential effect through the operation of associated definitions and provisions.

New Additional Reporting Duties New South Wales is now in the process of enacting new additional reporting duties similar to those in Victoria, regarding failure by a person in authority to protect a child from a sexual offence, failure by any adult to report a sexual offence involving a child aged under 16, and a grooming offence.[20] These new duties respond to recommendations made by the Royal Commission, as outlined above. The New South Wales Government announced in 2018 that it is making extensive reforms to implement more than 50 recommendations of the Royal Commission, including the these new offences.[21]

Prosecutions The benchmark provisions in New South Wales (s 316) and Victoria (s 327) can be used to prosecute cases where the failure to comply with the duty happened long ago, because in Australia there is no statute of limitations on criminal prosecutions for offences of this nature (Mathews 2003). It is apposite to note that because of the high standard of proof in criminal prosecutions, the difficulties of proving states of mind, and the reluctance of many to bring criminal complaints in such cases, it is rare for a prosecution to be commenced. Nevertheless, especially in cases where clear evidence is present, and egregious misconduct through omissions is apparent these provisions are an important acknowledgment of citizens' duties in society in circumstances of known serious criminal offending. A finding of guilt is possible, provided there is sufficient evidence to meet the normal criminal standard

[20] New South Wales Government, Press Release, 3 April 2018, Holding child sex abusers to account.

[21] Other developments include: legislating a maximum life sentence for a strengthened offence of persistent child sexual abuse; requiring courts sentencing historic child sexual assault offences to apply current sentencing standards and the present understanding about the lifelong effects of sexual abuse on children; requiring courts not to take into account an offender's good character when sentencing for historic offences where their reputation facilitated the offending; and introducing a new offence of grooming an adult to access a child and strengthening the grooming offence to include providing a child with gifts or money.

of proof that that the offence is proven beyond reasonable doubt. Because of this precise kind of criminal law duty and offence, the New South Wales provision was able to be used in a ground-breaking case in 2018 to convict the most senior Catholic clergy member worldwide ever prosecuted for this offence.

The Prosecution of Archbishop Wilson In May 2018, Philip Wilson, the archbishop of Adelaide, was found guilty of concealing his knowledge of child sexual abuse committed by a priest named James Fletcher against two altar boys in the 1970s (Khan 2018). Fletcher had earlier been found guilty of nine counts of child sexual abuse and died in prison in 2006. Wilson now awaits sentence. Wilson claimed he could not remember either boy telling him they were abused, and his counsel argued there was no evidence to prove the archbishop was told about the abuse, believed it was true, or remembered being told about it. However, the Court believed the testimony of Peter Creigh, one of the altar boys. Mr. Creigh testified that he had trusted that Wilson, who at the time was an assistant priest, would take appropriate action after he told him that Fletcher had abused him repeatedly in 1971 when he was 10. He testified that Wilson had a "look of horror" on his face when he heard this, but took no action and did not tell police. The other former altar boy said he went to confession in 1976 when he was aged 11, and told Wilson that Fletcher had abused him. He testified that Wilson refused to believe him because Fletcher "was a good bloke", and ordered the boy out of the confessional with a demand to say 10 Hail Mary prayers as an act of contrition.

Archbishop Wilson exhausted every legal avenue before the case came to trial. He made several attempts to have the case dismissed on technical grounds, and all failed. On 12 February 2015, in the Local Court, Stone LCM refused an application to quash or permanently stay a court attendance notice, in which it was alleged that in 2004–2006 the Archbishop committed an offence under s 316(1) of the Crimes Act 1900 (NSW) (concealing a serious indictable offence) in connection with a sexual assault of a 10 year old boy by another priest in 1971. Then, in Wilson v Department of Public Prosecutions (NSW) [2016] NSWSC 1458, Archbishop Wilson sought leave to appeal this decision by Stone LCM. Schmidt J granted leave to appeal the decision, but dismissed the appeal. This decision by Schmidt J was also then appealed, to the New South Wales Court of Appeal (Wilson v Director of Public Prosecutions (NSW) [2017] NSWCA 128). The issue before the Court was whether at the time Wilson was alleged to have withheld information relevant to Father Fletcher's alleged offence, s 81 (indecent assault on male) was a "serious indictable offence" within the meaning of the Crimes Act s 4. The Court of Appeal dismissed the appeal.

Finally on this point, two other related kinds of criminal law offences can be noted. First, in Queensland, it is an offence to "compound" an indictable offence committed by another person. The Criminal Code s 133 states that a person commits an offence if he "asks for, receives, or obtains, or agrees or attempts to receive or obtain, any property or benefit of any kind for himself, herself or any other person, upon any agreement or understanding that the person will compound or conceal an indictable offence, or will abstain from, discontinue, or delay, a prosecution for an indictable offence, or will withhold any evidence thereof." This offence has a broad scope, due to its references to simply "receiving" any "benefit of any kind" on any "understanding" that he will conceal an offence or withhold evidence about it.

Second, a standard group of criminal offences in common law jurisdictions provide for accessorial liability. These offences create liability in three categories beyond those who actually commit the relevant act. First, any person who aids the principal offender will also be deemed liable for the offence (e.g., Criminal Code (Qld) s 7(1)(c)). Notably, while aiding is usually constituted by positive acts, it can also be constituted in some jurisdictions by a mere calculated presence which is meant to encourage the principal offender (R v Beck [1990] Qd R 30). Second, those who solicit or procure the offence, but who themselves do not actually commit it, will also be deemed liable for it (e.g., Criminal Code (Qld) s 7(1)(d)). Third, those who are "accessories after the fact" in assisting the primary offender to evade liability, will also be deemed liable (e.g., Criminal Code (Qld) s 10). All these categories of liability extend the reach of the criminal law to ensure those who bear sufficient responsibility and culpability for criminal offending are not permitted to evade liability.

Significance in Organisations Including the Catholic Church The significance of these kinds of criminal offences are particularly notable in the context of any organisation that issues a policy directive to its employees or members not to report known cases and suspected cases to the police. This is even more clearly egregious in cases of known abuse; and it is even more heinous in cases of severe, prolific offending. Plainly, the Roman Catholic Church is the most prominent organisation that issues such a directive. As explained by Robertson (2010) and Tapsell (2014), the Catholic Church's official policy in this regard is sourced in its "canon law" provisions and associated procedural rules prescribed in the 1962 *Crimen Sollicitationis*. Canon law is, to say the least, confusing, and was described by the eminent human rights jurist Geoffrey Robertson (2010, p. 44) as a "mish-mash of divine law (dogmatic moral truths); ecclesiastical law (internal church rules, for example about priestly celibacy) and civil law." However, the core principles of this organisation's policy in this context are sufficiently clear, and their strict observance by clergy is required and enforced by threat of discipline and expulsion, and more immediately and effectively, more subtle methods of career destruction. Most significantly, the relevant principles are that (Robertson 2010; Tapsell 2014):

- The first and paramount obligation is to maintain secrecy regarding any allegation, so as to avoid scandal in the community and damage to the reputation of the Church;
- This obligation of secrecy applies to the accuser, the accused, and all involved in the process, and is enforced by the severest of penalties including excommunication;
- Any proceeding in relation to an allegation must be kept secret;

- The overarching purpose of any proceeding that does occur under Crimen is to maintain secrecy around the entire process and its outcome
- Any proceeding is intended to be restricted to a private internal forum – conducted by priests and presided over by a bishop – therefore lacking impartiality and independence, and further using a mechanism lacking all due process;
- The decision process has the paramount priority of preservation of the clergy member's standing – and thereby that of the Church – and use of the least intrusive punishment possible;
- There is no or virtually no concern regarding the immediate child victim, other past or present child victims of the offender, or other future potential victims of the offender.

In addition, despite several misleading claims to the contrary in recent years, the Catholic Church has not changed its law or ordered its clergy to report cases to domestic authorities (Marr 2014; Robertson 2010). Informal statements, such as Pope Benedict's in 2010, saying "Civil law concerning reporting of crimes to the appropriate authorities should always be followed", have not superseded canon law or Crimen procedure, and were in any case misleading because so few jurisdictions actually have such a clear domestic reporting requirement, and those that do tend to be in countries with a relatively low Catholic population.

In sum, these principles in canon law do not in fact supersede domestic law, but are used by the Catholic Church to dictate what clergy must do to preserve their careers. The Catholic Church's extensive history of concealing even the most heinous prolific offenders, and the intentional concealment of their offending by transferring them between parishes and even countries, demonstrates the extreme level of compliance with these occupational requirements. The record of Church authorities knowingly permitting and facilitating the continued offending by compulsive, dangerous and violent sexual predators is extensive and egregious. It is difficult to conceive of more wrongful action than the conscious aiding of continued offending by those in senior positions in an organisation that holds itself out as a moral beacon. While many clergy have implored their local bishops to take proper action, and many others have resigned in disgust at such clearly unethical conduct, it is clear that there is a system of concealment throughout the structure of the organisation, perpetrated and facilitated and continued by those in extremely senior positions, and with silencing also permeating lower levels. The occupational rules, threat of career destruction, exile and even laicization, combines with self-interest to perpetuate this toxic cover-up.

Criminal Law Responses: The Need for Appropriate Criminal Responses for Leaders of Organisations; Sentencing of Dangerous Offenders Because of this, I recommend a special class of new criminal offences to properly recognise the depravity of this conduct, to provide more appropriate criminal punishment, to enable more meaningful criminal prosecution, and which may help to catalyse change. This approach has a legitimate conceptual basis in other branches of law; for example, breaches of important duties by company directors constitute more serious offences, with more severe punishments, to recognise their gravity, to acknowledge their effect or potential effect on a wider population, and to encourage compliance. The new offences could be framed as several related offences covering:

- Active concealment by an office-bearer in an organisation of a known child sexual offence by a member of the organisation.
- Transfer by an office-bearer in an organisation of a known child sexual offender to another organisational unit.
- Failure by an office-bearer in an organisation to report known child sexual offences committed by a member of the organisation.
- Offences, and their penalties, could have a sliding scale, to accommodate situations where the concealed offending or the transferred offender involved more egregious child sexual offending.

Multiple instances of offending could constitute a circumstance of aggravation warranting even stronger penalties. The penalties could include long terms of imprisonment, as well as large financial penalties to express the egregiousness of the offence and the damage done or risked by the offending. The offences could also apply to both the principal offender, and to those who aided in the offence. Appropriate definitions of key terms could be added as necessary. For example, the concept of "knowledge" could embrace actual knowledge, constructive knowledge, and reasonable suspicion. The definition of "office-bearer" could clearly and non-exhaustively list all those covered. The concept of "child sexual offence" could be extensively detailed. In addition, notes in the legislation could provide non-exhaustive examples of what conduct will be covered by the offence.

Reportable Conduct Schemes

In Australia, the essence of some of these concepts are reflected in new legislative "reportable conduct schemes", although they are not comprehensively embedded. These schemes aim to ensure that where child sexual abuse occurs in CYSOs, the organisation takes appropriate steps to investigate, and reports the matter to an independent external oversight agency. This agency has powers to initiate its own investigation of particular matters that are brought to its attention, and other powers of audit and oversight.

A reportable conduct scheme has existed in New South Wales since 1998. Influenced by findings of the Victorian Betrayal of Trust Inquiry, and the Royal Commission, schemes have recently been enacted in 2015 in Victoria in the Child Wellbeing and Safety Act 2005 Part 5A, and in 2016 in the Australian Capital Territory in its Ombudsman Act 1989. These schemes aim to overcome malfeasance and conflicts of interest where agencies investigate CSA allegations against their own staff, and instead seek to create a culture of integrity, transparency, and accountability to external independent oversight. Heads of specified agencies are compelled to notify an external independent agency of allegations involving their employees.[22]

This external independent agency, which, in Australia, depending on the jurisdiction, is the Ombudsman, or an oversight body such as a Commission for Children and Young People, is empowered to monitor investigations, and may in some circumstances conduct its own investigation. Movements towards transparency and accountability are evident in these schemes, but they require effective compliance by organisations, and robust oversight by the external agency. The task of encouraging compliance confronts many organisations and regulators in this and other contexts (Mathews 2017). The nature of organisations themselves can encourage or inhibit compliance (Palmer 2016; Yeung 2004). The task of monitoring and auditing CYSOs requires independence, expertise and resources, and must be supported by the availability and use of appropriate sanctions. Combined, the measures in this approach are consistent with insights from theory, and may in practice help to overcome many of the organizational, cultural, attitudinal and behavioural factors which have facilitated the infliction of CSA in CYSOs.

Other Australian jurisdictions are now in the process of implementing similar schemes, while some have expressed reservations. In 2016, at its 42nd meeting, the Council of Australian Governments (a committee of all eight state and territory governments) agreed, in-principle, to harmonise reportable conduct schemes in a form similar to the model in operation in New South Wales. At the time of writing, Queensland and Western Australia have taken steps to implement a reportable conduct scheme. The Northern Territory appears to have expressed in principle approval while expressing reservations about its cost. Tasmania appears to have expressed concern about the cost of implementation. South Australia has not indicated express support, and has indicated its current area of priority is in more fundamental reform of its overall child protection system.

[22] See for example the New South Wales scheme, set out in the Ombudsman Act 1974 Part 3A. Under s 25C, the head of a designated government or non-government agency is required to notify the Ombudsman of: (a) any reportable allegation, or reportable conviction, against an employee of the agency of which the head of the agency becomes aware; (b) whether or not the agency proposes to take any disciplinary or other action in relation to the employee and the reasons why it intends to take or not to take any such action; (c) any written submissions made to the head of the agency concerning any such allegation or conviction that the employee concerned wished to have considered in determining what (if any) disciplinary or other action should be taken in relation to the employee. Under s 25F, results of an investigation and the action taken or proposed to be taken must also be reported to the Ombudsman. The key investigative power possessed by the Ombudsman is in s 25G. This empowers the Ombudsman to conduct an investigation concerning any reportable allegation, or reportable conviction, against an employee of a designated government or non-government agency of which the Ombudsman has been notified under this Part or otherwise becomes aware. In addition, the Ombudsman may conduct an investigation concerning any inappropriate handling of or response to any such reportable allegation or reportable conviction, whether on the Ombudsman's own initiative or in response to a complaint.

Mandatory Reporting Laws

A separate category of reporting duty is present in what are commonly called "mandatory reporting laws". To avoid confusion, I will here refer to these as "legislative mandatory reporting laws" to reflect their origin, and to distinguish these duties from other common law duties, non-legislative occupational duties, criminal law reporting duties and other reporting duties discussed above, As shown by an extensive program of research (discussed below), these legislative reporting duties are theoretically warranted due to the hidden nature of child sexual abuse, are legally justifiable given their consistency with other legal duties, are ethically congruent with both bioethical principles and dignity and public health, are empirically successful given the findings of multiple studies about their outcomes, and are practically useful in assisting and protecting practitioners who bear the duty and in assisting the children they serve. However, because these duties are complex, differ in presence and nature across jurisdictions, and are situated and expressed in complex technical legislation, these duties are frequently misunderstood in theory and practice. This, and their significance in practice, means some discussion is warranted to explain their nature, their particular application in the context of sexual abuse, and their role within child protection systems.

Nature of Mandatory Reporting Laws

The prevalence and harmfulness of CSA, together with its hidden nature, presents a challenge for all societies from the perspectives of individual child safety, public health, social justice and crime prevention. One response adopted by many jurisdictions in an effort to identify cases that would otherwise remain hidden and liable to continue, has been to recruit as sentinels other adults who deal with children in their professional capacity and who are well-placed to detect signs of CSA or to receive disclosures. This strategy has been deployed most systematically through the use of legislative mandatory reporting laws, situated within child protection legislation, following the model of the original laws of this type which were created after identification of the Battered-child Syndrome by Kempe et al. (1962). Having this similar genesis, the laws are also intended to overcome the phenomenon of "gaze aversion", where those who know of or suspect serious child abuse choose to avert their attention and do nothing, leaving the child exposed and at risk, instead of reporting it to police, child protective services or other social welfare agencies.

These laws have been enacted in dozens of nations worldwide (Mathews 2014), including every single state, territory and province in the USA, Canada and Australia (Mathews and Kenny 2008; Mathews et al. 2009a). Most recently, they have been enacted in Ireland, with relevant provisions of the Children First Act (Part 3, ss 14–19) commencing on 11 December 2017. Within a country, the laws may differ across states and territories, so that depending on the jurisdiction, these reporting duties may or may not extend to individuals in particular occupations (Mathews and Kenny 2008). There may also be differences in penalties and procedures, and in other technical aspects of the law.

However, the laws have common elements. Typically, the laws require designated professionals who deal with children in the course of their work (such as teachers, police, doctors and nurses) to report known and suspected cases of CSA by any person to government child protection agencies, or sometimes to police. Those who make reports are given protections from liability (in civil courts, criminal courts, and in administrative proceedings) provided the report is made in good faith. As well, reporters' anonymity is protected from disclosure. These laws will also provide that those who are not designated by the law as a mandated reporter are still empowered by these laws to make a report, and will receive the same protections as those conferred on mandated reporters.

The department for child protection which receives the report will then determine if the report contains sufficient information to require that the agency commence an investigation, or whether the report does not contain such information and can be screened out, or added to an existing file. An investigation can involve as little as telephone inquiries, but can sometimes extend to consultation with the child, the child's parents, and other involved professional. The agency will often has such as the child's teacher. The agency will often have dedicated specialised multidisciplinary teams to discharge this role. The child protection agency will involve and work with the police department in appropriate cases to discharge their respective functions. The child protection agency's statutory role is to protect the child, especially from familial maltreatment, and to take action to protect the child, provide health and rehabilitation services, and assistance to the family as needed. The primary beneficiary is the child and the child's family. Police are concerned with the investigation of criminal offending and enforcing the law on behalf of the State, and do not provide health or other rehabilitative services to the child or the family. Due to its nature, reports of suspected CSA will often involve an unknown offender, but in some cases may involve a known familial offender, or a known extra-familial offender.[23]

[23] It is axiomatic that modern child protection investigation teams must use all possible measures to avoid unnecessary distress and intrusion both during and after investigations. There is not a body of compelling and representative evidence about whether and to what extent investigations cause unavoidable trauma for children, parents and others, including for different types of maltreatment. The quantitative study in Iowa by Fryer et al. (1990) of 176 families with parents reported for abuse or neglect found that 74% of respondents rated their overall experience of the quality and impact of CPS ser-vice as either excellent or good, with satisfaction levels the same for both substantiated and unsubstantiated outcomes. Detailed analyses by Finkelhor et al. (1990) and Drake and Jonson-Reid (2007) have concluded there is no compelling empirical evidence that investigating unsubstantiated reports causes undue distress. Drake and Jonson-Reid (2007) found that a range of studies yielded a proportion of two thirds to three quarters of CPS clients being satisfied with the investigation process and services received, and concluded that "From the client's perspective, the common and much-repeated assertion that CPS is viewed negatively and is harmful to most families is simply wrong" (p. 357). It is also arguable that the need to protect children from such fundamental violations outweighs mere distress and intrusion (Finkelhor et al. 1990).

These legal reporting duties are intended to be only one part of a systematic approach to child protection, involving the education of mandated reporters and the resourcing of child welfare and law enforcement agencies including their response teams, to increase the identification of cases of CSA which otherwise would remain hidden. The overarching goal is clearly not to prevent the initial CSA, as this could only be the task of systematic primary prevention; accordingly, eradication of CSA is not the measure of policy success. Rather, the goal of a mandatory reporting system is to increase identification of cases of CSA and the facilitation of provision to children in need of assistance, thereby preventing further abuse of the child and possibly of other children, enabling health and safety responses for the child, and criminal justice responses to detect perpetrators.

Reasonable Expectations The creation of a legislative mandatory duty to report, together with professional education about the duty and the context of child sexual abuse, can be expected to better enable reports of appropriate cases and overcome reluctance and lack of awareness that otherwise suppress reporting activity. However, child sexual abuse occurs in secret and is not readily identified even by mandated professionals, and unreasonable expectations should not be formed about the capacity of reporters to suspect a case of CSA. Many behavioural indicators of CSA are consistent with innocent explanations or other childhood adversities. Most CSA leaves no physical evidence (Anderst et al. 2009; Heger et al. 2002), so even doctors who can physically examine a child may legitimately not detect indicators. Therefore, even where reporting laws exist, expectations must be tempered about the degree to which reports will be made, and the extent to which reports will turn

---

Yet, small qualitative studies of the experience of mothers have identified both positive and negative experiences with CPS investigations and other systemic interactions, which indicate that at the very least, ongoing efforts are required to develop the required professional attributes and monitor investigators' practice. Plummer and Eastin (2007) conducted focus groups (n = 19) and a survey (n = 40) with mothers who themselves suspected their child had been sexually abused, and whose suspicions had been confirmed by a CPS process or other professional decision. While some mothers reported that CPS workers, police, therapists and attorneys were "very helpful", other responses indicated delays, unprofessional comments, and disrespectful treatment. In Norway, Softestad and Toverud (2012) interviewed 19 parents. Most welcomed professional involvement, but also reported problems with delay, variable professional competence, and in some cases severe emotional strain, especially in cases where the parent was suspected. There is a clear need for rigorous research, including mixed methods research going beyond small qualitative studies, into the experience of children, parents and families regarding investigation, to identify the nature and extent of adverse consequences, their causes, and how they can be ameliorated. This would be particularly useful for different kinds of maltreatment. The experiences and challenges of investigations for CSA may be less common as most investigated CSA reports will not focus on parental behaviour, whereas virtually all other maltreatment reports (neglect, physical abuse, psychological abuse) will relate to the parent's acts or omissions. Finally, some have argued that the cost of investigation and its impact on other areas of the child protection system is also an important consideration. Yet, Drake and Jonson-Reid (2007, 2015) have argued that the actual cost of investigating cases in the USA is an extremely small proportion of the child protection budget, "most likely below 10% of total costs, and possibly below 5%" (2015, p. 41). Others have concluded that in Australia mandatory reporting is not producing excessive rates of reports and investigations in relation to identified cases (Segal 2015).

out to involve CSA or other significant harm. Nevertheless, the laws do have as their primary goal the enhanced reporting of known and suspected cases where the abuse has already occurred.

Substantiation v Investigation of Child Sexual Abuse Reports A brief observation is warranted on official outcomes of cases reported to government agencies. Many cases that are reported to child protection systems do not result in a finding of being "substantiated", either because they are not investigated, or because they are investigated but cannot meet the agency requirements to meet substantiation (e.g., through lack of evidence of harm despite abuse, or through lack of evidence of abuse despite harm): (Cross and Casanueva 2009; Drake and Jonson-Reid 2007; Drake and Pandey 1996; Fallon et al. 2011; Kohl et al. 2009; Mathews 2012). However, a body of research in the USA into the outcomes of reports of all forms of abuse and neglect has consistently concluded that unsubstantiated reports do not differ markedly from substantiated reports in the child's behavioural and developmental outcomes and service need (Drake and Pandey 1996; Hussey et al. 2005; Kohl et al. 2009). Many reports of abuse and neglect that are investigated but unsubstantiated do involve abuse and provide opportunities for early intervention (Drake and Jonson-Reid 2007; Drake et al. 2003; Kohl et al. 2009). Numerically, more unsubstantiated reports result in provision of services than those that are substantiated (Drake and Jonson-Reid 2007). This research into reports of all forms of abuse and neglect taken as a whole, and their outcomes, has resulted in conclusions that the substantiation outcome is "a distinction without a difference" (Hussey et al. 2005), that it is "time to leave substantiation behind" (Kohl et al. 2009), and that "substantiation is a flawed measure of child maltreatment...policy and practice related to substantiation are due for a fresh appraisal" (Cross and Casanueva 2009).[24]

[24]These findings are likely related to the factors affecting agency capacity to substantiate a report, including: evidentiary thresholds for reaching a finding of substantiated; availability of evidence of harm even where there is sufficient evidence of abuse; availability of evidence of abuse even where there is sufficient evidence of harm. As well, reports may not be comprehensively investigated due to internal agency factors such as availability of personnel and resources, and multiple reports about the same child being recorded as one investigation. A limitation of this body of research is that, while some studies expressly include a proportion of CSA reports in their designs and others did not exclude CSA report outcomes from their findings (Cross and Casanueva 2009; Drake et al. 2003; Kohl et al. 2009), the strength of the application of these general findings to the subset of CSA reports is not entirely clear. It is plausible that these findings could apply to the subset of CSA reports, given that a report of suspected CSA is frequently based on the reporter observing the child's adverse health symptomatology, behaviour, and social context, with the child's symptomatology and hence health and welfare need as the basis of the report being unaltered even where the report is unsubstantiated. Nevertheless, further research into this question is necessary to clarify the situation. What seems clear is that there is not firm ground for concluding that when exploring trends in reporting and report outcomes, the sole measure of the "soundness" of a report of suspected CSA is whether it is substantiated. Outcomes such as actual service provision to the child, and perceived need for service provision even if this is unable to be provided, are among those that are also relevant.

Accordingly, it is not legitimate to solely rely on numbers and rates of "substantiated reports" as a proxy measure of a "valid" or worthwhile report of child sexual abuse.

A Program of Research on Legislative Mandatory Reporting Laws for Child Sexual Abuse

Researchers in Australia have conducted a program of research to consider trends in numbers of reports of child sexual abuse, the sources of these reports (stratifying by different mandated and non-mandated reporter group), and outcomes of those reports. These studies, both individually and taken as a whole, have shown the generally positive effects of these legislative mandatory reporting duties as applied to child sexual abuse.

1. A 10 year national study of trends in reports of child sexual abuse, comparing different states, and reporter groups (Mathews et al. 2015)
2. A 7 year study in the state of Western Australia comparing trends in numbers and outcomes of reports of child sexual abuse before and after the introduction of a mandatory reporting law (Mathews et al. 2016).
3. A 20 year study of reports of child sexual abuse in the state of Victoria, comparing trends in numbers and outcomes of reports for girls and boys (Mathews et al. 2017)
4. Comparison between similar jurisdictions, only one of which has a mandatory reporting law (Mathews 2014).

A 10 Year National Study of Trends in Reports of Child Sexual Abuse, Comparing Different States, and Reporter Groups Mathews et al. (2015) conducted a national study in Australia using government administrative data to examine reporting practices for all types of child abuse and neglect, by all mandated and non-mandated reporter groups, in each state and territory over a 10 year period. Most relevant to this book is the data on reporting of child sexual abuse. Analysis of these data examined: the total number and proportion of reports of CSA compared to other forms of maltreatment; the proportion of mandated reports of CSA to non-mandated reports of CSA; report outcomes; and variance over time.

It was found that:

- Across the nation, reports of CSA were approximately 10% of the total number of reports, by all reporter groups combined, of all types of child abuse and neglect (physical, sexual and emotional abuse, neglect, and exposure to domestic violence).
- Non-mandated reporters (e.g., family, neighbours, friends, non-professionals) make almost half of all CSA reports, and mandated reporters make slightly more than half.

- Mandated reports of CSA therefore accounted for approximately 5%–6% of all reports of all types of child abuse and neglect combined (physical, sexual and emotional abuse, neglect, and exposure to domestic violence).[25]
- In each state and territory, trends in numbers of reports of CSA varied across reporter groups. Police were the mandated group who make the most CSA reports (13%–29%), followed by teachers (13%–23%) and health personnel (doctors & nurses: 4%–15%).
- In each state and territory, trends in numbers of CSA reports varied slightly over time, but far less so than for other maltreatment types. Numbers of reports of CSA are relatively stable over time.
- Nationally, on the data provided,[26] there were 37,056 investigated reports[27] of CSA that resulted from reports from the four key mandated groups.
- Nationally, on the data provided, there were 40,698 substantiated reports of CSA over the decade (20,741 from the four major mandated groups, and 19,957 from other reporters; mandated reports therefore accounted for >50% of substantiated reports of CSA.
- When missing data was added, there was a national total for the decade of 64,717 substantiated reports of CSA from all sources, involving a slightly lower number of children; in total, this amounted to approximately one in 75 children, or 1.3% of children).

A 7 Year Study in the State of Western Australia Comparing Trends in Numbers and Outcomes of Reports of Child Sexual Abuse Before and After the Introduction of a Mandatory Reporting Law Another way to analyze the effect of a mandatory reporting law is to explore what happens to the number of CSA reports made, and their outcomes, after a jurisdiction introduces a mandatory reporting law for the first time. Mathews et al. (2016) reported the results of the first detailed exploration over a substantial period of time of the effect of introducing a mandatory reporting duty for CSA.

Western Australia did not have mandatory reporting laws for CSA or any other form of abuse or neglect until 1 January 2009, when the Children and Community Services Amendment (Reporting Sexual Abuse of Children) Act 2008 inserted new provisions into the Children and Community Services Act 2004. These new manda-

---

[25] For the purposes of the study, the researchers collated data on reports by the four major mandated reporter groups – police, teachers, doctors and nurses and grouped these as mandated reports. These four groups account for the overwhelming majority of all reports of CSA. The estimate is conservative in that for illustrative purposes, it counted as "mandated reports" reports by police even if the state legislation did not expressly designate police as mandated reporters (e.g., Queensland), or if the mandated reporting duty only commenced at some point in time during the ten year period (e.g., Western Australia, where the duty commenced on 1 January 2009).

[26] One small state provided data for 9 years; and one large state provided data for 3 years. Data on substantiated cases could be located for the 7 years in the large state from other sources, resulting in a further 24,019 CSA substantiations.

[27] Some jurisdictions have different approaches to counting reports and making decisions about whether or how to investigate, so that proportions of investigated reports varied.

tory reporting provisions applied only to child sexual abuse. Section 124B(1) set out the reporting duty, which required reports of a "belief on reasonable grounds" of past or presently occurring sexual abuse of a child aged under 18 years of age. The duty did not extend to belief about the likelihood of future CSA, such as grooming or other clear risk. The occupational groups required to report were doctors, nurses, midwives, police officers, and teachers. Such beliefs about the existence of CSA were required to be reported without any consideration of the extent or significance of the abuse or of the harm which may have been caused or which may be likely to be caused. Unusually, the term 'child sexual abuse' was defined, albeit non-exhaustively in s 5, as "sexual behaviour in circumstances where (a) the child is the subject of bribery, coercion, a threat, exploitation or violence; or (b) the child has less power than another person involved in the behaviour; or (c) there is a significant disparity in the developmental function or maturity of the child and another person involved in the behaviour". The term "sexual behaviour" was not defined. The penalty for failure to report was $6000 (s 124B(1)). Reports were required to be made to the Chief Executive Officer (CEO) of the Department, a person approved by the CEO, or a member of a class of persons approved by the CEO: s 124B(2), who then was required to give a copy of the report to the police: s 124D. In practice, reports are made to a Departmental telephone hotline and contact. Reports were required to contain specific details about the case: s 124C. The report could be written or oral but if oral, the reporter was required to make a written report as soon as practicable, with a penalty of $3000: s 124C. For all reports made in good faith, the reporter was given immunity from civil, criminal and administrative legal proceedings: s129. The reporter's identity was kept confidential (s 124F), with specified exemptions to permit the administration of justice.[28]

Three research questions were examined in this study (Mathews et al. 2016). First, we identified the change in numbers of reports of CSA after introduction of the mandatory reporting law for mandated reporters as a combined group, and for distinct groups of mandated reporters (and the rate of reports per 100,000 children). Second, we identified the change in numbers of investigated reports of CSA after introduction of the mandatory reporting law by mandated reporters as a combined group, and by distinct groups of mandated reporters (and the proportion of reports that were investigated). Third, we identified the change in numbers of substantiated reports of CSA after introduction of the mandatory reporting law by mandated

[28] The introduction of the duty did not constitute a single new factor in a pure social experiment. First, a policy-based reporting duty had existed for these professionals for many years, although there was evidence that it had been widely unrecognized (Mathews et al. 2009c). Second, a research study had been conducted with teachers in 2006–2008, which heightened awareness of CSA and spurred new teacher training efforts (Mathews et al. 2009c). Third, the issue of CSA had attracted media attention because of government inquiries into child abuse (Ford 2007) and debate over several years about the introduction of a reporting law (Mathews et al. 2009a). Fourth, some of the professions to be mandated had received further instruction about the duty prior to its commencement. Therefore, it could be expected that the public as a whole, and those in the mandated professions in particular, had a recent and heightened level of sensitization to CSA over the period before the introduction of the duty.

reporters as a combined group, and by distinct groups of mandated reporters (and the proportion of investigated reports that were substantiated).

We analyzed data about numbers and outcomes of reports by mandated reporters, for periods before the law (2006–2008) and after the law (2009–2012). Results indicate that the number of *reports* by mandated reporters of suspected child sexual abuse increased by a factor of 3.7, from an annual mean of 662 in the 3 year pre-law period to 2448 in the 4 year post-law period. The increase in the first two post-law years was contextually and statistically significant. Report numbers stabilized in 2010–2012, at one report per 210 children. The number of *investigated reports* increased threefold, from an annual mean of 451 in the pre-law period to 1363 in the post-law period. Significant decline in the proportion of mandated reports that were investigated in the first two post-law years suggested the new level of reporting and investigative need exceeded what was anticipated. However, a subsequent significant increase restored the pre-law proportion, suggesting systemic adaptive capacity. The number of *substantiated investigations* doubled, from an annual mean of 160 in the pre-law period to 327 in the post-law period, indicating that conservatively, twice as many sexually abused children were being identified.

These findings are consistent with other considerations of these trends by government inquiries. The Victorian Law Reform Commission (1988) found that doctors in Victoria (then without mandatory reporting) reported five to nine times fewer cases of CSA than their counterparts in jurisdictions having mandatory reporting. During debates in the Victorian Parliament (1993, p. 1384) it was observed that in a 12-month period, the State of Victoria (then without mandatory reporting) received almost five times fewer reports of CSA than the State of New South Wales, which had mandatory reporting. Even more starkly, one can note the position in Queensland, where in the 12 month period to 30 June 1981, only 13 complaints of 'incest' were reported and investigated; the year before that, there were eight reports, and the year before that, there were 14 (MacMillan and Jefferies 1981). Similar extremely low rates of reports of CSA have been noted in jurisdictions before the introduction of mandatory reporting laws (Mathews 2014).

A 20 Year Study of Reports of Child Sexual Abuse in the State of Victoria, Comparing Trends in Numbers and Outcomes of Reports for Girls and Boys Mathews et al. (2017) conducted a 20-year longitudinal time-trend analysis of government data to identify reporting trends and report outcomes for CSA in Victoria, Australia from 1993 to 2012. The study examined several key questions: trends in reports of suspected CSA, and their outcomes, for girls and boys over time; trends in reports and report outcomes stratified by different reporter group; and the effect of a mandatory reporting duty on reports of CSA over a 20 year period (Victoria introduced mandatory reporting in 1993).

The study made several significant findings:

- Results indicated a new sensitisation to CSA, especially for boys, although this trend was not stable over the 20 year period. A marked change occurred in the last 5 years, likely influenced by major social factors (including awareness raised through government inquiries), and political and agency-related factors (including investment).

- Comparison revealed that from 1993 to 2012, the rate/100,000 of reports of boys increased 2.6-fold, whereas rate/100,000 of reports of girls increased 1.5-fold.
- Comparing sexes, with regards to the rate of reporting, in 1993, the sex ratio of girls to boys was 2:1, while by 2012 this ratio changed to 1.14:1 (almost parity).
- Numerically, reflecting contextual significance, for boys, there were 1356 reports in 1993 (1127 from non-mandated reporters and 229 from mandated reporters), and 3942 in 2012 (1657 from non-mandated reporters and 2285 from mandated reporters).
- Numerically, reflecting contextual significance, for girls, there were 2620 reports in 1993 (2119 from non-mandated reporters and 501 from mandated reporters), and 4280 in 2012 (1864 from non-mandated reporters and 2416 from mandated reporters).
- Reports by police and other mandated reporters accounted for the majority of the increase in reports over the 20-year period.
- Positive report outcomes (i.e. substantiations, findings of harm, and referral to services) increased twelve-fold for boys, and nearly five-fold for girls, indicating the increased levels of reports were based on actual clinical need.
- There were four trends over the 20 year period: an initial increase for 2 years after introduction of mandatory reporting; a period of stability for around 12 years; a decline for around 2 years likely connected to a change in agency practice only; and a dramatic increase in the last 4–5 years, likely influenced by major social factors (including awareness raised through government inquiries), and political and agency-related factors including investment in the agency.

Comparison Between Similar Jurisdictions, Only One of Which Has a Mandatory Reporting Law Mathews (2014) compared the experience of the Australian state of Victoria, and Ireland, two jurisdictions which are demographically and culturally similar and which had a virtually identical child population. The significant difference between the two jurisdictions was that only Victoria had a mandatory reporting law for child sexual abuse.

Analysis examined government data on the number, source and outcomes of reports of child sexual abuse from a single year. It was found that, as compared with Ireland (having no mandatory reporting), Victoria, which had mandatory reporting:

- received two times the number of reports of CSA (with 53% of these made by mandated reporters);
- identified 4.73 times the number of sexually abused children; and
- confirmed cases of CSA identified as a result of reports by mandated reporters were 2.5 times the entire amount identified by all reporters in Ireland.

A Final Note on Legislative Mandatory Reporting Laws for Child Sexual Abuse

In sum, there is a strong body of evidence indicating legislative mandatory reporting laws for child sexual abuse are sound in theory, required in practice, and empirically successful in identifying substantially more cases of sexual abuse than would otherwise occur. These reporting laws have also been supported in scholarly literature, especially for sexual abuse (Drake and Jonson-Reid 2015; Finkelhor 2005; Mathews and Bross 2008; Mathews 2012, 2015). In Australia, government inquiries have supported mandatory reporting of CSA as a necessary component of social policy, even after scrutinizing the validity of child protection systems and attempting to control expenditure (Carmody 2013; Cummins et al. 2012; Layton 2003; Wood 2008). Quantitative studies have shown that a mandatory reporting duty has been supported in diverse nations and professions, including by physicians in countries ranging from New Zealand (Rodriguez 2016), Singapore (Fung and Chow 1998), Taiwan (Lee et al. 2007); nurses in Australia (Mathews et al. 2008b) and Taiwan (Feng and Levine (2005), and psychologists in Canada (Beck and Ogloff 1995). A large qualitative study in Nepal also found strong support by health practitioners for a mandatory reporting duty (UNICEF Nepal, 2006).

While some have opposed mandatory reporting laws in general as applied to all child maltreatment (Hansen and Ainsworth 2013; Melton 2005), these claims have been strongly challenged (Drake and Jonson-Reid 2007; Mathews and Bross 2008), and moreover, no opponent has explicitly made such a claim in relation to mandatory reporting of CSA. There are at least three reasons for this. First, CSA is qualitatively very different from other instances of other types of maltreatment (Mathews 2014). Second, the well-established gap between the real and disclosed incidence of CSA nullifies any claim that case-finding is not a challenge. Third, reports of CSA to government agencies account for a very small proportion of all reports of child maltreatment, repelling any claim that CSA reports intolerably overwhelm child protection systems or divert resources from other priorities. Mandated reports of CSA across Australia over a 10 year period accounted for just 6% of all reports of child maltreatment from all reporter groups (Mathews et al. 2015), and USA annual data are similar (U.S. Department of Health and Human Services, 2009). A cautionary note may be made about social context. So, for example, in some extreme socio-economic settings, such as a state that is war-torn, riven with social strife, or lacking in any semblance of a child protection system because of even more urgent priorities of subsistence, there may be no functional child protection agency to respond to reports; clearly, other kinds of response may be warranted. However, any society must be alert to the hidden phenomenon of child sexual abuse and is responsible for taking practicable steps to respond to it.

Other Civil Law Responses: Removing Unjust Barriers by Reforming Statutes of Limitation

Background: The Nature and Rationales for Statutes of Limitation

Statutes of limitation give plaintiffs in civil actions a designated time period in which the action should be commenced. These time limitation periods are animated by two broad policy considerations. As explained in Chap. 4, these policy reasons have been articulated by the highest courts in the USA, Canada and Australia. The primary justification is to secure a fair trial for the defendant by ensuring that defendants can draw on fresh and available evidence. The second consideration is the public interest in the prompt settlement of disputes, which is connected with the need to administer an efficient court system, and the general principles that defendants' lives should not be encumbered by the threat of claims about long-past events, and that plaintiffs should not slumber on their rights.

Adaptable Rules of Procedure, Not Conferring Substantive Rights on Defendants Expiry of a limitation period does not automatically terminate an entitlement to bring a claim. A defendant must consciously choose to elect to rely on the expiry of time to block the plaintiff's claim from proceeding. This was established by the High Court of Australia in *Commonwealth v Verwayen*,[29] where it was also held that time limits are simply procedural rules which do not automatically bar actions. Similarly, the Supreme Court of the United States has held that limitation laws are an adaptable policy statement rather than an intractable bright line barrier to litigation, and are simply rules of procedure, not substantive rights.[30]

Legislatures have further demonstrated that these laws are not an intractable bright line barrier to the bringing of a claim. For specified types of claims and injuries, some legislatures have removed limitation periods, based on an acknowledgment that these claims' special nature and context justifies different treatment allowing an action to be brought at any time. So, for example, time limits have been removed in Canada for multiple claims, including debt recovery,[31] and Australian state legislatures have removed time limits for claims for injuries from latent dust-related diseases.[32]

---

[29] (1990) 170 CLR 394.

[30] *Chase Securities Corporation v Donaldson* 325 US 304 (1945).

[31] See for example Limitations Act, 2002, SO 2002, c 24, s 16.

[32] See for example the Limitation of Actions Act 1974 (Qld) s 11(2), and the Dust Diseases Tribunal Act 1989 (NSW) s 12A.

A Summary of the Reforms Recommended by, and Enacted Since, the Australian Royal Commission

Are conventional statutes of limitation a theoretically, ethically and practically legitimate approach by a legal system to civil claims for child sexual abuse? In Chapter 14 of its 2015 Civil Litigation and Redress Report, the Royal Commission considered whether Australian civil statutes of limitation were appropriate for civil claims for personal injuries arising out of child sexual abuse. There were several main features of the legislative context and practical operative background at the time that were particularly relevant. First, for civil claims for damages arising out of child sexual abuse, most Australian states and territories provided a standard limitation period that applied to any personal injury claim; this translated to 3 years post-majority, which then equates to age 21. There were some exceptions to this in several states that had provided for longer time periods in cases where the abuser was a parent or a close associate of the child's parent (Mathews 2003, 2004b).

Second, while it was technically possible to seek an extension of time due to recent discovery of a decisive material fact – such as the nature or extent of the injury, or the connection of the injury with the abuse suffered – and while some plaintiffs had been granted such an extension,[33] this process was costly, lengthy, and frequently vigorously defended by powerful defendants, including Churches and governments.[34] In addition, Australian courts had often rejected such an application to extend time, based on alternative grounds of either failing to take reasonable steps to ascertain the relevant facts, or due to a residual discretion available to the court, and how that discretion had been applied (Mathews 2003, 2004b; Sarmas 2008).[35]

Further, in many claims, the defendant is a government or one of its agencies, such as a department of education. This is significant because when governments are involved in litigation as defendants, there is a public policy principle that they should conduct themselves as a "model litigant". The model litigant principle requires governments not to rely on legal technicalities to deny a plaintiff who has a sound claim supported by compelling evidence. The model litigant principle has

[33] See for example in Australia the cases of *GGG v YYY* [2011] VSC 429; *NF v State of Queensland* [2005] QCA 110; *State of Queensland v RAF* [2010] QCA 332.

[34] In Australia, examples include *A, DC v Prince Alfred College Inc* [2015] SASC 12; *Carter v Corporation of the Sisters of Mercy of the Diocese of Rockhampton* [2001] QCA 335; *Ellis v Pell* [2006] NSWSC 109; *Hopkins v State of Queensland*[2004] QDC 021 (Unreported, McGill J, 24 February 2004); *HWC v The Corporation of the Synod of the Diocese of Brisbane* [2009] QCA 168; *NF v State of Queensland* [2005] QCA 110; *Salvation Army v Rundle* [2008] NSWCA 347; *Tusyn v State of Tasmania* [2010] TASSC 55; *VMT v Corporation of the Synod of the Diocese of Brisbane* [2007] QSC 219. Scholars have criticised defendants' exploitation of the time bar in cases of clear liability, and the complexity of extension provisions and judicial interpretation of them, in the USA, Canada, Australia, the UK, and New Zealand.

[35] Reflecting the experience of other jurisdictions including the UK (Godden 2010), New Zealand (Manning 2000) and the USA (Hamilton 2012).

long been recognised in the USA,[36] Canada,[37] and Australia,[38] and is reflected in policy statements by governments (Royal Commission into Institutional Responses to Child Sexual Abuse 2015a). It requires the State and its agencies when acting as a defendant to act fairly, to settle legitimate claims without recourse to litigation, to resist reliance on superior financial resources and access to legal advice to defeat plaintiffs, and not to plead legal technicalities when liability is not in dispute. It does not technically apply to religious institutions, although based on their professed nature, it would be a reasonable assumption that such institutions should not behave in litigation in a way that offends the principle.

Radical Reform: A Seismic Shift The Commission determined that conventional approaches were clearly not justifiable in child sexual abuse claims. It recommended radical legislative reform to civil statutes of limitation, making four recommendations. It recommended (Ch 14, Recns 85–88):

- Legislative reform in every state and territory, to remove all time limitation periods for civil claims arising out of child sexual abuse in institutional settings
- Removal with both prospective and retrospective effect
- Retention of court powers to stay proceedings where there was such overwhelming prejudice to a defendant's right to a fair trial
- That these reforms occur immediately.

These were ground-breaking recommendations, and they have resulted in a seismic shift in the legal landscape in Australia. I will shortly set out the legal changes made since these recommendations. First, it is important to note that the Royal Commission accepted several rationales for these reforms. These rationales are underpinned by an appreciation of the nature and purpose of statutes of limitation, and an understanding of their possible exploitation. However, even more significantly, the rationales are animated by an ethical and scientific understanding of the nature of child sexual abuse and its characteristics. Once it is understood that there is a profound power imbalance in all cases of child sexual abuse, which is exacerbated in institutional claims, one can immediately begin to appreciate that there is a fundamental injustice in applying conventional time limitation periods meant for standard personal injury claims to this qualitatively different class of case. These differences arise from the nature of the plaintiff (being a child), the nature of the acts (being secret, hidden, and shameful), the power dynamic (often involving fear, and threats), and the nature of the injuries (frequently including PTSD, which by its very nature precludes revisiting the acts, disclosing the acts, and the activities necessary to bring a legal claim, and often, the difficulty in connecting injuries with the acts, this preventing the plaintiff from knowing the nature and extent and timing of their injuries. Significantly, the Royal Commission found that for those who did actually disclose their abuse in an institutional setting, the average time to disclosure was

[36] *Berger v United States* 295 US 78 (1935).

[37] *Skogman v The Queen* [1984] 2 SCR 93.

[38] *Melbourne Steamship Co Ltd v Moorehead* (1912) 15 CLR 333.

22 years (Australian Government Royal Commission into Institutional Responses to Child Sexual Abuse 2015a, p. 6). This clearly took many of these survivors well outside the standard period in Australia of 3 years post-majority. A brief summary of these bodies of knowledge is instructive.

Non-disclosure and Delayed Disclosure Delayed disclosure is crucial in this context, and must be considered when analysing the nature and justifiability of civil statutes of limitation. Some survivors of child sexual abuse are able to disclose, and can do so proximate to the events. However, due to its nature and context, many survivors will not ever disclose, or will only do so years or decades after the events (Smith et al. 2000). A review of studies found that 60–70% of adult survivors of child sexual abuse said they did not disclose their abuse during childhood (London et al. 2007). Non-disclosure and delayed disclosure is influenced by factors at individual, offender-related, and societal levels (Collin-Vézina et al. 2015; Fontes and Plummer 2010). Individually, the child may be pre-verbal, induced to believe the acts are normal, or have disclosure inhibited by threats, shame, internalised blame, and lack of a trusted confidante. Disclosure is further stifled by the offender's superior psychological, cognitive, age-based, emotional, social, and physical status as parent, caregiver, family member, trusted acquaintance, institutional authority, or older youth. Societal and cultural forces also impede disclosure through the taboo of sexuality, and stigma contaminating survivors (Fontes and Plummer 2010). As discussed earlier in this book, sexual abuse of children in institutional contexts can produce particularly powerful silencing effects due to the nature of individual and organisational authority, and abuse of spiritual authority.

Post–Traumatic Stress Disorder and Avoidance Alongside these behavioural and contextual factors influencing non-disclosure and hence neutralising the survivor's ability to being a legal claim, further significant factors preserving silence and disengagement from the legal system are the nature of the psychological injuries typically caused. As well as secrecy, shame and delayed disclosure, and the disinclination many survivors may feel to take formal legal proceedings against a known and powerful offender, the general avoidance symptom intrinsic to the commonly experienced injury of PTSD produces a second massive impediment to compliance with time limits.

PTSD is particularly relevant because it neutralises a person's ability to bring a civil lawsuit. As recognised by the *Diagnostic and Statistical Manual 5*, PTSD is a trauma- or stress-related disorder, triggered by exposure to actual or threatened death, serious injury or sexual violation (American Psychiatric Association 2013). PTSD impairs social interactions and the individual's functional capacity in myriad aspects of life. In particular, its avoidance symptom means the survivor will persistently avoid all stimuli related to their experience: thoughts, memories, conversations, activities, people and places. The negative cognitions and mood symptom induces self-blame, and the arousal symptom causes self-destructive behaviour. The symptoms of PTSD therefore inherently prevent engagement with the legal system. When compelled to avoid trauma-related stimuli, a survivor with PTSD will find it impossible or extremely difficult to engage cognitive functions and perform acts required to commence a civil suit. Many survivors will be unable to instruct counsel; revisit and talk about the events; obtain medical evidence of the nature and extent of psychological injury and its connection with the events; recall, see or interact with people, places and phenomena associated with the events; and testify in court and withstand cross-examination. The capacity of survivors with these injuries to engage legal systems is therefore compromised on multiple dimensions. These consequences of PTSD in the context of child sexual abuse survivors and their incapacity to bring a claim have been repeatedly seen in the reported cases in the USA, Canada, and Australia.[39]

It is clear that in the civil legal context, many survivors of child sexual abuse are unable to ever bring a lawsuit to claim financial compensation for injuries and economic loss, and to hold individual and institutional offenders accountable. Even for those who can bring such a claim at some stage in their lives, in most jurisdictions the civil statute of limitation gives only a short time after attaining legal adulthood to commence a claim, meaning many survivors are unable to begin proceedings in sufficient time to seek compensation. This confluence of acts, injuries, abuse of power, and legal technicality can often deny survivors of sexual abuse the capacity to access the justice system, which is a bedrock principle of societies upholding the rule of law.

A Summary of Australian Reforms

Significantly, while the recommendations made by the Royal Commission were of necessity limited to its statutory remit of institutional sexual abuse, broader legislative reforms since made by Australian states and territories indicate that the rationale for reform applies to all cases of child sexual abuse, regardless of setting.

While Victoria had already enacted reforms based on its state inquiry, the Royal Commission's recommendations were decisive in influencing other Australian jurisdictions to implement change.[40] New South Wales then enacted almost identical

---

[39] See for example the case authorities detailed below, in notes 10–11.

[40] Victoria was the first state to enact reform, with a bill introduced on 23 February 2015, which commenced on 1 July 2015. The bill had three components. First, it removed the limitation period for personal injury claims arising from child sexual abuse, physical abuse, and psychological abuse arising from those acts. Second, it applied this with both retroactive and prospective effect. Third, to protect defendants' fair trial rights and prevent abuse of process, it preserved courts' powers to stay proceedings. These reforms were influenced by a government inquiry into the mishandling of abuse allegations in religious and other non-government institutions. The *Betrayal of Trust - Inquiry into the Handling of Child Abuse by Religious and other Non-Government Organisations* (Victorian Government Family and Community Development Committee, 2013) exposed widespread child sexual abuse in these organisations, and unjustifiable reliance by defendants on the expiry of limitation periods to block survivors from accessing civil courts. The inquiry recommended abolition of the time limit for civil claims in child abuse cases, finding "There is no public policy justification for applying limitation periods to civil cases relating to criminal child abuse" (Volume 2, Finding 26.7, p. 542–3).

legislation through its Limitation Amendment (Child Abuse) Bill 2016, which commenced on 17 March 2016. In addition, the legislation expressly stated that prior causes of action may be brought even if a court had previously barred a claim because of lapsed time. This express provision constitutes a limited incursion into *res judicata* – that previously settled claims cannot be re-litigated – but otherwise preserves that doctrine so that previously finalised matters cannot be re-litigated.[41]

Other states and territories gradually enacted reforms, as shown in Table 5.2. Reforms apply to both institutional and non-institutional CSA, and generally also to physical abuse, and to psychological injury arising from sexual abuse or physical abuse. In all instances, legislative provisions expressly preserve courts' powers to protect defendant's rights to a fair trial (e.g., by staying proceedings in the event of insuperable prejudice).[42] The Australian Capital Territory and Queensland applied its reforms to child sexual abuse, but not to physical abuse. Only one State, South Australia, is yet to introduce a government bill, despite the introduction of two private members' bills.

Significantly, some states have taken further steps to secure justice for plaintiffs. Queensland enacted an additional unique provision favouring plaintiffs, enabling revival of actions previously settled by deed in cases where the court accepts "it is just and reasonable to do so". This special exception to *res judicata* recognises that claims in this context may have been settled in circumstances where the plaintiff was under duress and felt compelled to accept a small offer of recompense in return for the defendant not defeating the claim outright by relying on expiry of time. The Northern Territory and Western Australia have enacted similar provisions, applying to both previously barred causes of action, and to previously settled causes of action.[43] In addition, Western Australia has enacted special provisions in its new

[41] It is not expressly applied to matters that have been settled, although there is conflicting information about this. The second reading speech indicates not; but the definition of "judgment" in Sched 5 Pt 3 s 8(2) as "a judgment given extends to a judgment entered and also to an agreement entered into before and in connection with any such judgment" indicates it may.

[42] Court retains its power to summarily dismiss, or permanently stay proceedings, where lapse of time creates overwhelming burden to defendant's fair trial rights, through the court's inherent, implied, statutory or other common law jurisdiction, or under a rule of court, practice note or practice direction – see, e.g., NSW s 6A(6); Vic s 27R).

[43] In the Northern Territory, the provisions effectively allow the bringing of a new claim if a previous judgment was given on the basis of expiry of time. "Judgment" includes an agreement entered into, providing further protection and capacity for plaintiffs. Under s 54(5), if an action is brought, the court may, if it considers it is just and reasonable to do so: (a) set aside any [previous] judgment; (b) take into account any amounts paid or payable by way of damages under such a judgment'; and(c) take into account costs paid or payable in connection with any such judgment.

In Western Australia, the Civil Liability Legislation Amendment (Child Sexual Abuse Actions) Bill 2017 was introduced into Parliament 22 November 2017, and was passed on 19 April 2018; the provisions amending the Limitation Act 2005 have not yet been proclaimed. The key provisions are s 6A, and Part 7 (ss 89–92). Section 91(1) allows an action on a "previously barred cause of action" to be commenced where the action was statute barred; or an action had been commenced but discontinued or not finalized; or a judgment was given, or an action was dismissed, on the ground that the action was statute barred. Under s 91(3), the court may, if it is satisfied that it is just and reasonable to do so, set aside the previous judgment. Under s 91(4), if an action on a previously

Table 5.2 Australian statutes of limitation of civil claims for child sexual abuse

State / Territory – legislation – commencement of reforms	Effect: removal and retrospective effect	Types of abuse	Court powers preserved	Approach to previously barred / settled claims
Australian Capital Territory Limitation Act 1985 (ACT) ss 21C, 30 May 2017	No limitation period; applied retrospectively and prospectively.	SA only	S 21C(3)	n.a
New South Wales Limitation Act 1969 (NSW) s 6A, Sched 5 ss 8-10 17 March 2016	No limitation period; applied retrospectively and prospectively	SA, serious PA, and connected psychological abuse	S 6A(6)	Allows an action on a "previously barred cause of action" to be commenced where a judgment has been previously given on the ground that the action was statute barred (Sched 5).
Northern Territory Limitation Act 1981 (NT) ss 5A, 53-55 15 June 2017	No limitation period; applied retrospectively and prospectively.	SA, serious PA, and connected psychological abuse	S 5A(5)	Allows an action on a "pre-existing judgment" where given on the ground a limitation period had expired (s 54(1)). Under s 53(2) "Judgment" includes "an agreement entered into in relation to settlement of a matter of damages for personal injury".
Queensland Limitation of Actions Act 1974 (Qld) ss 11A, 48 1 March 2017	No limitation period; applied retrospectively and prospectively.	SA only	S 11A(5)	Section 48(2)-(5) allows an action on a previously barred right of action. Section 48(5A)-(5C) allows an action on a previously settled right of action
South Australia Limitation of Actions Act 1936 (SA) ss 36, 45	3 years from majority i.e. must commence by age 21	n.a	n.a	n.a
Tasmania Limitation Act 1974 (Tas) ss 5B, 38 Passed and assent 20 Dec 2017; commences when proclaimed	No limitation period; applied retrospectively and prospectively	SA, serious PA, and connected psychological abuse	S 5B(3)	Does not allow bringing of previously barred claims Does not allow bringing of previously settled claims

(continued)

Table 5.2 (continued)

State / Territory – legislation – commencement of reforms	Effect: removal and retrospective effect	Types of abuse	Court powers preserved	Approach to previously barred / settled claims
Victoria Limitation of Actions Act 1958 (Vic) ss 1, 4, 27O, 27P 1 July 2015	No limitation period; applied retrospectively and prospectively	SA, PA, and connected psychological abuse	S 27R	Does not explicitly allow bringing of a claim previously the subject of judgment Does not allow re-opening of previously settled claims or claims that have been subject to final judgment
Western Australia Limitation Act 2005 (WA) ss 6A(2), 89-92 am by *Civil Liability Legislation Amendment (Child Sexual Abuse Actions) Act 2018* Passed and assent 19 April 2018; commences on proclamation	No limitation period; applied retrospectively and prospectively	SA only S 6A(1) "child sexual abuse" means an act that is sexual abuse"	S 6A(5)	Section 91(1) allows an action on a "previously barred cause of action". Section 92 allows an action to be brought on a "previously settled cause of action".

Part 2A of the Civil Liability Act 2002 ss 15A-15 L,[44] to enable a plaintiff to identify a "proper defendant". These provisions are directed at ensuring organisations like the Catholic Church may effectively be held liable despite their nominal lack of juridical status.[45] The provisions create exceptions to normal corporations laws,

barred cause of action is commenced, the Court may, if it is satisfied that it is just and reasonable to do so, take into account any amount paid under a previous judgment.

Similar provisions apply to "previously settled" causes of action. Section 92 allows an action to be brought on a "previously settled cause of action". Under s 92(2) the plaintiff must apply for leave to commence the action. Under s 92(3), the Court may, if satisfied it is just and reasonable to do so, grant leave to commence the action, and set aside the settlement agreement and any judgment giving effect to the settlement. Under s 92(4), if the action is commenced, the agreement relating to the settlement is void to the extent to which it relates to the CSA the subject of the cause of action. Under s 92(6), the Court may, if satisfied it is just and reasonable to do so, take into account any amount paid under an agreement, to the extent to which it related to the child sexual abuse the subject of the cause of action.

[44] As amended by the Civil Liability Legislation Amendment (Child Sexual Abuse Actions) Act 2018 (WA), passed on 19 April 2018; the relevant provisions have not yet been proclaimed.

[45] Section 15B(1)–(3) effectively provides that if the office holder at the time of the CSA is no longer in office, an action can be brought against the current office holder of an unincorporated association, and the current office holder is liable for the former office holder's liability. Further, s 15C provides that the holder of the office may satisfy the liability out of assets held by or for the office of the institution, including assets of a trust, whether or not a charitable trust.

allowing an action to be brought against the current office holder of an unincorporated association, and authorising the office holder to use assets held by the institution (including trust assets) to satisfy a judgment debt. In Victoria, similar legislation was passed on 24 May 2018,[46] and New South Wales has also enacted this legislation.

Canada In Canada, eleven of the thirteen provinces and territories have also removed limitation periods for child sexual abuse civil claims (Table 5.3). All removals apply retroactively as well as prospectively, and enable suits to be brought against both individual and institutional tortfeasors. Quebec has not removed the

Table 5.3 Civil limitation periods for claims based on child sexual abuse: Canada

Province/territory	Legislative provisions	Effect
Alberta	Limitations Act, RSA 2000, c L-12, ss 3(1), 5.1(2)	No time limit
British Columbia	Limitation Act, SBC 2012, c 13, s 3(1)(i)	No time limit
Manitoba	The Limitation of Actions Act, CCSM c L 150, s 2.1(2)(a)	No time limit
New Brunswick	Limitation of Actions Act, SNB 2009, c L-8.5, s 14.1	No time limit
Newfoundland and Labrador	Limitations Act, SNL 1995, c L-16.1, s 8(2)	No time limit
Northwest Territories	Limitation of Actions Act, RSNWT 1988, c L-8, s 2.1(2)	No time limit
Nova Scotia	Limitation of Actions Act, RSNS 2014, c 35, section 11	No time limit
Nunavut	Limitation of Actions Act, RSNWT (Nu) 1988, c L-8, s 2.1(2)	No time limit
Ontario	Limitations Act, 2002, SO 2002, c 24, s 16(1)(h.1)	No time limit
Prince Edward Island	Statute of Limitations, RSPEI 1988, c S-7, ss 2(1)(d), 5	Must commence action within 2 years of majority
Quebec	Civil Code of Quebec, LRQ, c C-1991, s 2926.1	Must commence action within 30 years from the date the victim becomes aware the injury suffered is attributable to the sexual act
Saskatchewan	The Limitation Act, SS 2004, c L-16.1, s 16(1)(a)	No time limit

[46] Legal Identity of Defendants (Organisational Child Abuse) Bill 2018 (Vic).

limitation period entirely, but has created a special limitation period of 30 years after knowledge the injury was caused by the sexual assault. Only Prince Edward Island retains traditional time limits, generally requiring actions within 2 years of majority.

Canadian jurisdictions were the first to enact reforms, doing so in the 1990s led by British Columbia in 1992, hence predating the American and Australian movements (Roach 2001). This landmark shift in access to justice may have been seen as a natural consequence after the Supreme Court of Canada's insistence in *City of Kamloops v Nielson*[47] that reasonable discoverability had to be accommodated alongside the standard limitation period. As well, further judicial incursions into traditional limitation principles had promoted plaintiffs' rights to proceed in all types of civil claims. This was epitomised in *Novak v Bond*,[48] and in *M(K) v M(H)*,[49] where the plaintiff claimed compensation for injuries caused by incest. Reforms were driven by recognition of the qualitative differences in child sexual abuse cases, which were judged to invalidate traditional policy reasons for limitation periods (Roach 2001). Despite their breadth – with these reforms also applying to claims of adult sexual assault – the reforms in Canada do not appear to have created an intolerable burden for court systems, or gross injustice for defendants (British Columbia Ministry of Justice, 2013).[50]

---

[47] (1984) 10 DLR (4th) 641.

[48] (1999) 172 DLR (4th) 385.

[49] (1992) 3 SCR 6.

[50] The lack of such an impact can be explained by two main factors. First, while an initial increase in lawsuits is to be expected, especially where a revival window or retroactive removal of the time period is part of the reform, even those claims that are commenced are likely to be settled out of court without reaching the trial stage. Accordingly, the burden on the court system is diluted. Second, for a range of reasons, most survivors of child sexual abuse will not wish to institute legal proceedings. Many survivors will not experience personal injuries of an extent sufficient to warrant a legal claim. Even for those who do, a substantial proportion of potential claims will never be brought because civil suits are futile where the defendant is deceased, unable to be located, or impecunious. Many survivors will lack the agency and capacity to bring proceedings; many will be unable to pursue a claim due to existing trauma, fear of re-traumatisation, distrust of the legal system, inability to navigate the system, or lack of funds. As well, many survivors' primary desire is not financial compensation, but an assurance that steps be taken to diminish the likelihood of sexual abuse in future, especially in institutional contexts (Law Commission of Canada, 2000). Further, for cases of sexual abuse in institutional contexts, many jurisdictions have created informal methods of providing redress or ex gratia payments. These have proven to be accessible to survivors, and preclude pursuit of civil remedies (Australian Government Royal Commission into Institutional Responses to Child Sexual Abuse 2015a).

Note also that scholarly analysis has concluded that claims about "false memories" not supported by strong evidence (Bulkley and Horwitz 1994). Based on an analysis of the literature, including the review of 25 studies by Scheflin and Brown (1996), Freyd (1998, p. 103) concluded "there is no research to date documenting a "false memory syndrome"" and that "there is a large and growing body of evidence documenting the occurrence of essentially accurate recovered memories" (p. 107). Studies have indicated that, as a natural defence mechanism, individuals are more likely to forget details of abuse or to have periods of forgetting when they are abused by parents or caregivers (Freyd et al. 2001; Williams 1995). Freyd (1998) also concluded that in terms of persis-

USA No state in the USA has enacted reforms quite as extensive as those in Canada and Australia. However, some states have enacted substantial reforms short of prospective and retrospective abolition. Delaware and Minnesota have removed limitation periods prospectively (for events occurring after commencement of the amending law); and have created a revival window to provide a limited period of time in which previously lapsed claims can be brought, without any limit on the age of the plaintiff. Similarly, Connecticut has removed the limitation period prospectively for designated serious sexual assaults, and has enacted a revival window for plaintiffs aged under 48, giving a period of 30 years after turning 18 (i.e., age 48). In Massachusetts, reforms took effect on 26 June 2016, giving until age 53 for prospective suits against any defendant, with partial retroactive effect for individual offenders but not institutional wrongdoers (Coalition to Reform Sex Abuse Laws, 2016). Some states have enacted a longer than normal period of time for prospective claims but with no revival period for lapsed claims. Illinois, for example, gives 20 years after turning 18, and Oregon gives until age 40. Other states – Iowa, Maryland, New York, North Dakota, Pennsylvania, Texas, and Utah, and the District of Columbia – have bills pending which make similar amendments, indicating growing momentum for reform. In Illinois, pressure is building to remove the time bar entirely (Schaper 2016). Reform efforts have met substantial institutional opposition in many states including Massachusetts, New York, and Pennsylvania (De Jesus 2016; Hamilton 2012; Holpuch 2016). Advocates continue to lobby for reform, often supported by revelations of abuse in institutions or by powerful individuals who have evaded accountability through expiry of time. Despite these reforms, most states in the USA retain their traditional model and usually give no more than 6 years to bring a civil claim (National District Attorney Association, 2013).

Other Nations It is likely that other nations and jurisdictions will gradually follow the example set by Canada and Australia. In 2017, the Canadian province of Alberta enacted reforms, leaving only Quebec and Prince Edward Island yet to make reforms in that country. Also in 2017, Scotland removed its limitation periods for child sexual abuse cases, with the Limitation (Childhood Abuse) (Scotland) Act 2017 amending the Prescription and Limitation (Scotland) Act 1973. Interestingly, the Scottish reforms apply not only to sexual abuse, but to physical abuse, emotional abuse, and neglect (s 17A).

---

tence of memory – namely, whether a memory can be recalled at different points in time – recovered memories of CSA are neither more nor less likely to be inaccurate than continuously accessible memories of sexual abuse. Accordingly, delayed disclosure may sometimes be caused by lack of memory (whether through suppression or blocking), which is subsequently reliably retrieved. Further research into the neuroscience of suppression of memory has confirmed the normality and mechanism of "motivated forgetting" (Anderson and Green 2001; Anderson and Hanslmayr 2014; Benoit and Anderson 2012). Overall, the evidence indicates there is not compelling evidence of "false memories" to cast doubt on the viability of reforms to civil statutes of limitation.

Implications of Reforms to Time Limitation Periods in Civil Sexual Abuse Claims

Fairness for Defendants Fairness for defendants must remain embedded in the civil litigation system to protect its status as a hallmark of rule of law societies. Even where removal of the time limitation period is retroactive, there is a clear argument that this fairness is achieved through multiple measures. First, the doctrine of *res judicata*, a cornerstone of Western common law, means that previously finalised claims cannot be re-litigated (Currie 1978). Arguably, from a policy perspective this rule is not satisfied where a plaintiff's agreement to settle was induced by the defendant's threat to rely on expiry of time. Second, the judiciary possesses strong residual controls on civil lawsuits. Most notably, courts have inherent powers to dismiss or permanently stay civil proceedings where lapse of time creates clear insuperable prejudice to a defendant's fair trial rights. So, where a claim is based on events from so long ago there is no possibility of the defendant being able to defend their case, a plaintiff's claim will not be allowed to proceed. Third, courts retain their normal role and specialised power to determine whether sufficient evidence exists to support a claim. This applies regarding the factual basis of a claim, liability, causation, and quantum of damages. Accordingly, even with time periods removed, many potential plaintiffs will still face substantial challenges in compiling an evidentiary case – with compelling evidence beyond mere memory, including reliable medical evidence – sufficient to establish liability. This is one reason why even with removal of the time limitation, especially when retroactive, most potential claims will not be made through the civil justice system. Finally, reform to the statute of limitations does not guarantee a plaintiff of success; it merely provides an opportunity to have access to the justice system and commence proceedings. There is no substantial evidence to date that such reforms have caused undue prejudice to defendants' rights, either in this context, or in other contexts where limitation periods have been removed.

Fairness for Plaintiffs In a liberal democratic society governed by the rule of law, it is axiomatic that individuals must not be impeded from exercising legal rights (Bingham 2007). Access to courts should be unimpeded and protected as a basic right, adjudicative procedures should be fair, and the law must protect fundamental human rights (Bingham 2007). There is a general case supporting limitation periods for conventional personal injuries suits. In general, a civil claim should be brought in a relatively short period of time where the suit involves a plaintiff injured as an adult, with clear and immediate injuries clearly related to the event, with witnesses and where the gathering of evidence is uncomplicated and non-traumatic, where the plaintiff's capacity to proceed is not intrinsically compromised by injury, where disclosure is not compromised, where there is no power imbalance affecting capacity to commence proceedings, and where failure to proceed promptly may reflect culpable "sleeping on one's rights".

Yet, child sexual abuse cases are qualitatively different from generic civil disputes on all these grounds. The policy reasons for limitation periods are overcome in this different context, which was not publicly recognised or considered when standard limitation periods were devised. The distinction applies to cases involving child sexual abuse occurring in both institutional settings and non-institutional settings. It applies with greater strength when the person inflicting the abuse, and or the institution concealing it, occupies a position of psychological, emotional, economic or institutional power over the victim.

Challenges Remain for Plaintiffs These reforms in Canada and Australia are remarkable breakthroughs in jurisprudence, overturning historical impediments to access to justice. They provide those who wish to commence civil proceedings with much greater capacity to do so. However, major challenges remain. First, the patchwork quilt of legal approaches within a federated country is unsatisfactory. Individuals should all have the same level of access to justice regarding the same types of claims, and the highest level of access to justice. Accordingly, the clearly superior positions adopted by some Australian jurisdictions should serve as a model of reform for the other states and territories, and the laws should be harmonised.[51] The progressive approach to previously settled and barred claims should be adopted by all jurisdictions. The approach to identifying a proper defendant must also be adopted nationally; there is little point removing one barrier to justice if another remains, even if it applies to one particular kind of defendant. Further challenges also remain. There are reports that some powerful defendants are still using technicalities to deny, dispute and delay justice to survivors. This is simply unconscionable institutional conduct, knowingly causing further trauma, and the leaders of these institutions have an ethical responsibility to ensure that it ends.

Above all this, though, remains the fact that it is still extremely difficult for survivors of child sexual abuse to commence a civil claim, even with an appropriately reformed approach to statutes of limitation. The civil litigation system presents an inherent deterrent effect due to its adversarial nature, technical formalities, economic costs, length of time involved, and the traumatic consequences that can flow from involvement in formal proceedings. Many defendants have relatively low levels of agency, may seek relatively low awards of damages perceived as not worth the difficulty and cost of formal civil proceedings, and, especially in the case of individual non-institutional offenders many defendants who inflicted the abuse are

[51] Healing requires survivors to be able to articulate their suffering, be heard, and taken seriously (Herman 1997). Yet, the presence and use of the time limit silences the survivor once more. Judith Lewis Herman has noted the indifference of bystanders can be particularly traumatic, exceeding even the initial abuse (1997, p. 100–101). For survivors, legislatures which do not enact reform can make them a special class of bystander, exacerbating trauma. Rosanne Sliney, whose testimony influenced reform in Massachusetts, crystallised this when she said: "I felt like the state of Massachusetts was like my family…They all were ignoring the fact that I"m suffering. … No one protected me...and now my state wasn't protecting me." (De Jesus 2016). In contrast, a legislature enacting reform to allow claims recognises and validates the experience of CSA survivors, even for those who do not make a claim.

impecunious and cannot satisfy any judgment debt. These characteristics of the context raise the broader question of whether this qualitatively different class of case merits a specialised tribunal with modified rules and processes, and expert staff. Such tribunals have been created for other contexts in civil and criminal law, and this should be seriously considered if we are to make future progress in this domain.

References

Alaggia, R. (2005). Disclosing the trauma of child sexual abuse: A gender analysis. *Journal of Loss and Trauma, 10*(5), 453–470.

American Psychiatric Association. (2013). *Diagnostic and statistical manual of mental disorders – Fifth edition (DSM-V)*. Arlington: American Psychiatric Association.

Anderson, M., & Green, C. (2001). Suppressing unwanted memories by executive control. *Nature, 410*, 366–369.

Anderson, M., & Hanslmayr, S. (2014). Neural mechanisms of motivated forgetting. *Trends in Cognitive Sciences, 18*(6), 279–292.

Anderst, J., Kellogg, N., & Jung, I. (2009). Reports of repetitive penile-genital penetration often have no definitive evidence of penetration. *Pediatrics, 124*(3), 403–409.

Australian Government. (2013). Letters Patent for the Royal Commission into Institutional Responses to Child Sexual Abuse, S No 12 of 2013, 11 January 2013.

Australian Government Royal Commission Into Institutional Responses to Child Sexual Abuse. (2014). *Interim Report*. Sydney: Commonwealth of Australia.

Australian Government Royal Commission Into Institutional Responses to Child Sexual Abuse. (2015a). *Redress and civil litigation report*. Sydney: Commonwealth of Australia.

Australian Government Royal Commission Into Institutional Responses to Child Sexual Abuse. (2015b). *Report of case study 13: The response of the Marist Brothers to allegations of child sexual abuse against Brothers Kostka Chute and Gregory Sutton*. Sydney: Commonwealth of Australia.

Australian Government Royal Commission Into Institutional Responses to Child Sexual Abuse. (2016). *Report of case study 22: The response of Yeshiva Bondi and Yeshivah Melbourne to allegations of child sexual abuse made against people associated with those institutions*. Sydney: Commonwealth of Australia.

Australian Government Royal Commission Into Institutional Responses to Child Sexual Abuse. (2017a). *Final report: Preface and executive summary*. Sydney: Commonwealth of Australia.

Australian Government Royal Commission Into Institutional Responses to Child Sexual Abuse. (2017b). *Report of case study 34: The response of Brisbane Grammar School and St Paul's School to allegations of child sexual abuse*. Sydney: Commonwealth of Australia.

Australian Government Royal Commission Into Institutional Responses to Child Sexual Abuse. (2017c). *Analysis of claims of child sexual abuse made with respect to Catholic Church institutions in Australia*. Sydney: Commonwealth of Australia.

Australian Government Royal Commission Into Institutional Responses to Child Sexual Abuse. (2017d). *Analysis of complaints of child sexual abuse received by Anglican church dioceses in Australia*. Sydney: Commonwealth of Australia.

Beck, A.J., Harrison, P.M., & Guerino, P. (2010). *Sexual victimization in juvenile facilities reported by youth, 2008–2009*. Bureau of Justice Statistics.

Beck, K., & Ogloff, J. (1995). Child abuse reporting in British Columbia: Psychologists' knowledge of and compliance with the reporting law. *Professional Psychology: Research and Practice, 26*(3), 245–251.

Benoit, R., & Anderson, M. (2012). Opposing mechanisms support the voluntary forgetting of unwanted memories. *Neuron, 76*, 450–460.

Bingham, T. (2007). The rule of law. *Cambridge Law Journal, 66*, 67–85.

Böhm, B., Zollner, H., Fegert, J., & Liebhardt, H. (2014). Child sexual abuse in the context of the Roman Catholic Church: A review of literature from 1981–2013. *Journal of Child Sexual Abuse, 23*(6), 635–656.

Boyle, P. (2014). How youth-serving organizations enable acquaintance molesters. *Journal of Interpersonal Violence, 29*(15), 2839–2848.

Bulkley, J., & Horwitz, M. (1994). Adults sexually abused as children: Legal actions and issues. *Behavioral Sciences and the Law, 12*, 65–87.

Carmody, T. (2013). *Taking responsibility: A roadmap for Queensland child protection*. Brisbane: Queensland Child Protection Commission of Inquiry.

Collin-Vézina, D., De La Sablonniere-Griffin, M., Palmer, A., & Milne, L. (2015). A preliminary mapping of individual, relational and social factors that impede disclosure of childhood sexual abuse. *Child Abuse and Neglect, 43*, 123–134.

Cross, T., & Casanueva, C. (2009). Caseworker judgments and substantiation. *Child Maltreatment, 14*(1), 38–52.

Cummins, P., Scott, D., & Scales, B. (2012). *Report of the protecting Victoria's vulnerable children inquiry*. Melbourne: State of Victoria Department of Premier and Cabinet.

Currie, D. (1978). Res judicata: The neglected defense. *University of Chicago Law Review, 45*, 317–350.

Daly, K. (2014). *Redressing institutional abuse of children*. Basingstoke: Palgrave Macmillan.

Daly, K. (2017). Redress for historical institutional abuse of children. In A. Deckert & R. Sarre (Eds.), *Australian and New Zealand handbook of criminology, crime, and justice*. London: Palgrave Macmillan.

De Jesus, I. (2016). *'One woman's journey out of child sex abuse helps reform Massachusetts child sex crimes law'*. PENNLIVE.

Dorbeck-Jung, B., Vrielink, M., Gosselt, J., van Hoof, J., & de Jong, M. (2010). Contested hybridization of regulation: Failure of the Dutch regulatory system to protect minors from harmful media. *Regulation & Governance, 4*, 154–174.

Doyle, T. P., Sipe, A. W. R., & Wall, P. J. (2006). *Sex, priests, and secret codes: The Catholic Church's 2000-year paper trail of sexual abuse*. Los Angeles: Volt Press.

Drake, B., & Jonson-Reid, M. (2007). A response to Melton based on the best available data. *Child Abuse & Neglect, 31*, 343–360.

Drake, B., & Pandey, S. (1996). Understanding the relationship between neighborhood poverty and child maltreatment. *Child Abuse and Neglect, 20*, 1003–1018.

Drake, B., Jonson-Reid, M., Way, I., & Chung, S. (2003). Substantiation and recidivism. *Child Maltreatment, 8*, 248–260.

Drake, B., & Jonson-Reid, M. (2015). Competing values and evidence: How do we evaluate mandated reporting and CPS response? In B. Mathews & D. Bross (Eds.), *Mandatory reporting laws and the identification of severe child abuse and neglect* (pp. 33–60). Dordrecht: Springer.

Erooga, M. (2012a). *Creating safer organisations: Practical steps to prevent the abuse of children by those working with them*. Sussex: Wiley.

Erooga, M. (2012b). Understanding and responding to people who sexually abuse children whilst employed in positions of trust: An overview of the relevant literature – Part One: Offenders. In M. Erooga (Ed.), *Creating safer Organisations: Practical steps to prevent the abuse of children by those working with them* (pp. 7–43). Malden: Wiley.

Erooga, M., Allnock, D., & Telford, P. (2012). Sexual abuse of children by people in organisations: What offenders can teach us about protection. In M. Erooga (Ed.), *Creating safer 250 organisations: Practical steps to prevent the abuse of children by those working with them* (pp. 63–84). Malden: Wiley.

Fallon, B., Trocmé, N., & MacLaurin, B. (2011). Should child protection services respond differently to maltreatment, risk of maltreatment, and risk of harm? *Child Abuse & Neglect, 35*, 236–239.

Finkelhor, D. (2005). The main problem is underreporting child abuse and neglect. In D. Loseke, R. Gelles, & M. Cavanaugh (Eds.), *Current controversies on family violence* (2nd ed., pp. 299–310). Thousand Oaks, CA: Sage.

Finkelhor, D., Hotaling, G., Lewis, I., & Smith, C. (1990). Sexual abuse in a national survey of adult men and women: Prevalence, characteristics, and risk factors. *Child Abuse & Neglect, 14*, 19–28.

Fontes, L., & Plummer, C. (2010). Cultural issues in disclosures of child sexual abuse. *Journal of Child Sexual Abuse, 19*(5), 491–518.

Ford, P. (2007). *Review of the department for community development*. Perth: Department for Community Development.

Frawley-O'Dea, M. (2004). Psychosocial anatomy of the Catholic sexual abuse scandal. *Studies in Gender and Sexuality, 5*, 121–137.

Freyd, J. (1998). Science in the memory debate. *Ethics & Behavior, 8*, 101–113.

Freyd, J., DePrince, A., & Zurbriggen, E. (2001). Self-reported memory for abuse depends on victim-perpetrator relationship. *Journal of Trauma and Dissociation, 2*, 5–16.

Fryer, G., Bross, D., Krugman, R., Benson, D., & Baird, D. (1990). Good news for CPS workers. *Public Welfare, 48*(1), 38–41.

Fung, D. S., & Chow, M. H. (1998). Doctors' and lawyers' perspectives of child abuse and neglect in Singapore. *Singapore Medical Journal, 39*(4), 160–165.

Godden, N. (2010). Sexual abuse and claims in tort. *Feminist Legal Studies, 18*, 179–190.

Hamilton, M. (2012). Child sex abuse in institutional settings: What is next. *University of Detroit Mercy Law Review, 89*, 421–440.

Hansen, P., & Ainsworth, F. (2013). Australian child protection services: A game without end. *International Journal of Social Welfare, 22*, 104–110.

Heger, A., Ticson, L., Velasquez, O., & Bernier, R. (2002). Children referred for possible sexual abuse: Medical findings in 2384 children. *Child Abuse & Neglect, 26*, 645–659.

Herman, J. L. (1997). *Trauma and recovery*. New York: Basic Books.

Holpuch, A. (2016). *Windows closing for clergy sex abuse victims to sue Catholic Church*. The Guardian.

Hussey, J., Marshall, J. M., English, D., Knight, E., Lau, A. S., Dubowitz, H., & Kotch, J. B. (2005). Defining maltreatment according to substantiation: Distinction without a difference? *Child Abuse and Neglect, 29*, 279–292.

Hutter, B. (2011). Negotiating social, economic and political environments: Compliance with regulation within and beyond the state. In V. Nielsen & C. Parker (Eds.), *Explaining compliance* (pp. 305–321). Cheltenham: Edward Elgar.

Kaufman, K. L., Holmberg, J. K., Orts, K. A., & Hilliker, D. (1998). Factors influencing sexual offenders' modus operandi: An examination of victim-offender relatedness and age. *Child Maltreatment, 3*(4), 349–361.

Kaufman, K. L., Tews, H., Schuett, J. M., & Kaufman, B. R. (2012). Prevention is better than cure: The value of situational prevention in organisations. In M. Erooga (Ed.), *Creating safer Organisations: Practical steps to prevent the abuse of children by those working with them* (pp. 140–166). West Sussex: Wiley.

Keenan, M. (2012). *Child sexual abuse & the Catholic Church: Gender, power, and organizational culture*. Oxford: Oxford University Press.

Kempe, C. H., Silverman, F., Steele, B., Droegemueller, W., & Silver, H. (1962). The battered-child syndrome. *Journal of the American Medical Association, 181*, 17–24.

Kenny, E. (2011). Enda Kenny speech on Cloyne report. https://www.rte.ie/news/2011/0720/303965-cloyne1/

Kenny, M. C., & Wurtele, S. K. (2012). Preventing childhood sexual abuse: An ecological approach. *Journal of Child Sexual Abuse, 21*(4), 361–367.

Khan, S. (2018). *Australian archbishop becomes most senior Catholic clergyman to be convicted of covering up child sex abuse*. The Independent. 22 May.

Kohl, P., Jonson-Reid, M., & Drake, B. (2009). Time to leave substantiation behind: Findings from a national probability study. *Child Maltreatment, 14*(17), 26.

Koziol, M. (2018). *Malcolm Turnbull blasts 'indifference and resistance' by churches in child sex abuse letter*. Sydney Morning Herald. 28 March.

Lanning, K., & Dietz, P. (2014). Acquaintance molestation and youth-serving organizations. *Journal of Interpersonal Violence, 29*(15), 2815–2838.

Layton, R. (2003). *Our best investment: A state plan to protect and advance the interests of children (Review of Child Protection in South Australia).* Adelaide: Government of South Australia.

Leahy, T., Pretty, G., & Tenenbaum, G. (2002). Prevalence of sexual abuse in organised competitive sport in Australia. *Journal of Sexual Aggression, 8*(2), 16–36.

Leclerc, B., Wortley, R., & Smallbone, S. (2011). Getting into the script of adult child sex offenders and mapping out situational prevention measures. *Research in Crime and Delinquency, 48*(2), 209–237.

Leclerc, B., Feakes, J., & Cale, J. (2015). Child sexual abuse in youth-oriented organisations: Tapping into situational crime prevention from the offenders perspective. *Crime Science, 4*(1), 209–237.

Lee, P.-Y., Fraser, J., & Chou, F.-H. (2007). Nurse reporting of known and suspected child abuse and neglect cases in Taiwan. *The Kaohsiung Journal of Medical Sciences, 23*(3), 128–137.

Letourneau, E., Nietert, P., & Rheingold, A. (2016). Initial assessment of stewards of children program effects on child sexual abuse reporting rates in selected South Carolina counties. *Child Maltreatment, 21*, 74–79.

London, K., Bruck, M., Ceci, S., & Shuman, D. (2007). Disclosure of child sexual abuse: A review of the contemporary empirical literature. In M.-E. Pipe, M. Lamb, Y. Orbach, & A.-C. Cederborg (Eds.), *Child sexual abuse: Disclosure, delay, and denial* (pp. 11–39). New York: Routledge.

Lothstein, L. (2004). Men of the flesh: The evaluation and treatment of sexually abusing priests. *Studies in Gender and Sexuality, 5*, 167–195.

MacMillan, D., & Jefferies, D. (1981). Sexual abuse of children: A police overview. *Australian Crime Prevention Council Forum, 4*(6), 17–23.

Manning, J. (2000). The reasonable sexual abuse victim: "A grotesque invention of the law"? *Torts Law Journal, 8*, 1–9.

Marr, D. (2014). *The prince: Faith, Abuse & George Pell*. Melbourne: Black.

Mathews, B. (2003). Limitation periods and child sexual abuse cases: Law, psychology, time and justice. *Torts Law Journal, 11*(3), 218–243.

Mathews, B. (2004a). Queensland government actions to compensate survivors of institutional abuse: A critical and comparative evaluation. *Queensland University of Technology Law & Justice Journal, 4*(1), 23–45.

Mathews, B. (2004b). Post-Ipp special limitation periods for cases of injury to a child by a parent or close associate: New jurisdictional gulfs. *Torts Law Journal, 12*(3), 239–258.

Mathews, B. (2012). Exploring the contested role of mandatory reporting laws in the identification of severe child abuse and neglect. In M. Freeman (Ed.), *Current legal issues volume 14: Law and childhood studies* (pp. 302–338). Oxford: Oxford University Press.

Mathews, B. (2013). Legal cultural and practical developments in responding to female genital mutilation. In R. Maguire, B. Lewis, & C. Sampford (Eds.), *Shifting global powers and international law: Challenges and opportunities* (pp. 207–222). London/New York: Routledge.

Mathews, B. (2014). *Mandatory reporting Laws for child sexual abuse in Australia: A legislative history*. Sydney: Royal Commission into institutional Responses to Child Sexual Abuse.

Mathews, B. (2015). A theoretical framework for designing and evaluating strategies to identify cases of serious child abuse and neglect. In B. Mathews & D. Bross (Eds.), *Mandatory reporting Laws and the identification of severe child abuse and neglect* (pp. 127–156). Dordrecht: Springer.

Mathews, B. (2017). Optimising implementation of reforms to better prevent and respond to child sexual abuse in institutions: Insights from public health, regulatory theory, and Australia's Royal Commission. *Child Abuse and Neglect, 74*, 86–98.

Mathews, B., & Bross, D. (2008). Mandated reporting is still a policy with reason: Empirical evidence and philosophical grounds. *Child Abuse & Neglect, 32*(5), 511–516.

Mathews, B., & Collin-Vézina, D. (2016). Child sexual abuse: Raising awareness and empathy is essential to promote new public health responses. *Journal of Public Health Policy, 37*(3), 304–314.

Mathews, B., & Kenny, M. (2008). Mandatory reporting legislation in the USA, Canada and Australia: A cross-jurisdictional review of key features, differences and issues. *Child Maltreatment, 13*, 50–63.

Mathews, B., Cronan, J., Walsh, K., Butler, D., & Farrell, A. (2008a). Teachers' policy-based duties to report child sexual abuse: A comparative study. *Australia & New Zealand Journal of Law & Education, 13*(2), 23–37.

Mathews, B., Fraser, J., Walsh, K., Dunne, M., Kilby, S., & Chen, L. (2008b). Queensland nurses' attitudes towards and knowledge of the legislative duty to report child abuse and neglect: Results of a state-wide survey. *Journal of Law and Medicine, 16*, 288–304.

Mathews, B., Goddard, C., Lonne, B., Short, S., & Briggs, F. (2009a). Developments in Australian laws requiring the reporting of suspected child sexual abuse. *Children Australia, 34*(3), 18–23.

Mathews, B., Payne, H., Bonnet, C., & Chadwick, D. (2009b). A way to restore British paediatricians' engagement with child protection. *Archives of Disease in Childhood, 94*, 329–332.

Mathews, B., Walsh, K., Rassafiani, M., Butler, D., & Farrell, A. (2009c). Teachers reporting suspected child sexual abuse: Results of a three-state study. *University of New South Wales Law Journal, 32*(3), 772–813.

Mathews, B., Bromfield, L., Walsh, K., & Vimpani, G. (2015). *Child abuse and neglect: A socio-legal study of mandatory reporting in Australia –report for the Australian Government* (Vol. 1–9). Brisbane: QUT.

Mathews, B., Lee, X., & Norman, R. (2016). Impact of a new mandatory reporting law on reporting and identification of child sexual abuse: A seven-year time trend analysis. *Child Abuse & Neglect, 56*, 62–79.

Mathews, B., Bromfield, L., Walsh, K., Cheng, Q., & Norman, R. (2017). Reports of child sexual abuse of boys and girls: Longitudinal trends over a 20-year period in Victoria, Australia. *Child Abuse & Neglect, 66*, 9–22.

McClellan, P, The Honourable Justice. (2017). Address to the National Council of Churches.

Melton, G. (2005). Mandated reporting: A policy without reason. *Child Abuse & Neglect, 29*, 9–18.

Mercy, J., Rosenberg, M., Powell, K., Broome, C., & Roper, W. (1993). Public health policy for preventing violence. *Health Affairs, 12*(4), 7–29.

Millar, R., Schneiders, B., & Vedelago, C. (2018). *Catholic Inc. What the Church is really worth.* The Age. 12 February.

Milligan, L. (2017). *Cardinal: The rise and fall of George Pell.* Melbourne: Melbourne University Press.

Murphy Commission of Investigation. (2009). *Report into the Catholic archdiocese of Dublin.* Dublin: Department of Justice, Equality and Law Reform.

Murphy Commission of Investigation. (2011). *Report by Commission of Investigation into Catholic Diocese of Cloyne.* Archdiocese of Cloyne.

Palmer, D. (2016). *The role of organizational culture in child sexual abuse in institutional contexts.* Sydney: Commonwealth of Australia.

Parent, S., & Demers, G. (2011). Sexual abuse in sport: A model to prevent and protect athletes. *Child Abuse Review, 20*(2), 120–133.

Parkinson, P. (2016). Submission to the Royal Commission on institutional responses to child sexual abuse issues paper 11: The Catholic Church.

Parkinson, P., Oates, K., & Jayakody, A. (2012). Child sexual abuse in the Anglican Church of Australia. *Journal of Child Sexual Abuse, 21*(5), 553–570.

Plummer, C. (2013). *Using policies to promote child sexual abuse prevention: What is working?* Harrisburg: VAW net, a project of the National Resource Center on Domestic Violence.

Plummer, C., & Eastin, J. (2007). The effect of child sexual abuse allegations/investigations on the mother/child relationship. *Violence Against Women, 13*(10), 1053–1071.

Residential Institutions Redress Board. (2011). Annual Report of the Residential Institutions Redress Board 2011.

Rheingold, A., Zajac, K., Chapman, J., Patton, M., de Arellano, M., Saunders, B., et al. (2015). Child sexual abuse prevention training for childcare professionals: An independent multi-site randomized controlled trial of stewards of children. *Prevention Science, 16*(3), 374–385.

Roach, K. (2001). Reforming statutes of limitations. *University of New Brunswick Law Journal, 50*, 25–55.
Robertson, G. (2010). *The case of the pope: Vatican accountability for human rights abuse*. Camberwell: Penguin.
Robinson, G. (2007). *Confronting power and sex in the Catholic Church*. Mulgrave: John Garratt.
Rodriguez, C. (2016). Professionals' attitudes and accuracy on child abuse reporting decisions in New Zealand. *Journal of Interpersonal Violence, 17*(3), 320–342.
Ryan, P. (2009). *The commission to inquire into child abuse*. Dublin: Department of Justice.
Sarmas, L. (2008). Mixed messages on sexual assault and the statute of limitations. *Melbourne University Law Review, 32*, 609–638.
Saul, J., & Audage, N. (2007). *Preventing child sexual abuse within youth-serving organizations: Getting started on policies and procedures*. Atlanta: Centers for Disease Control and Prevention, National Center for Injury Prevention and Control.
Schaper, D. (2016). *In aftermath of Hastert case, states push to change reporting of child sex abuse*. NPR News.
Scheflin, A., & Brown, D. (1996). Repressed memory or dissociative amnesia: What the science says. *The Journal of Psychiatry & Law, 24*, 143–188.
Schneiders, B., Millar, R., & Vedelago, C. (2018). *Catholic Church fails to confront tragedy of 'epic proportions'*. The Age. 10 March.
Segal, L. (2015). Economic issues in the community response to child maltreatment. In B. Mathews & D. Bross (Eds.), *Mandatory reporting laws and the identification of severe child abuse and neglect* (pp. 193–218). Dordrecht: Springer.
Shakeshaft, C. (2004). *Educator sexual misconduct: A synthesis of existing literature*. Washington, DC: U.S. Department of Education.
Sipe, R. (2011). Scandal versus culture. In T. Plante & K. McChesney (Eds.), *Sexual abuse in the Catholic Church: A decade of Crisis, 2002–2012* (pp. 117–129). Santa Barbara: Praeger.
Smallbone, S. W., & Wortley, R. K. (2001). Child sexual abuse: Offender characteristics and modus operandi. *Australian Institute of Criminology, 193*, 1–6.
Smallbone, S., Marshall, W. L., & Wortley, R. (2013). *Preventing child sexual abuse: Evidence, policy and practice*. New York: Routledge.
Smith, C., & Freyd, J. (2014). Institutional betrayal. *American Psychologist, 69*, 575–587.
Smith, D., Letourneau, E., Saunders, B., Kilpatrick, D., Resnick, H., & Best, C. (2000). Delay in disclosure of childhood rape: Results from a national survey. *Child Abuse & Neglect, 24*(2), 273–287.
Softestad, S., & Toverud, R. (2012). Parenting conditions in the midst of suspicion of child sexual abuse. *Child and Family Social Work, 17*, 75–84.
Tapsell, K. (2014). *Potiphar's wife: The Vatican's secret and child sexual abuse*. Adelaide: ATF.
Terry, K. (2015). Child sexual abuse within the Catholic Church: A review of global perspectives. *International Journal of Comparative and Applied Criminal Justice, 39*(2), 139–154.
Terry, K. J., & Ackerman, A. (2008). Child sexual abuse in the Catholic Church: How situational crime prevention strategies can help create safe environments. *Criminal Justice and Behavior, 35*, 643–657.
Terry, K. J., & Freilich, J. D. (2012). Understanding child sexual abuse by Catholic priests from a situational perspective. *Journal of Child Sexual Abuse, 21*(4), 437–455.
Terry, K., Smith, M., Schuth, K., Kelly, J., Vollman, B., & Massey, C. (2011). *Causes and context of the sexual abuse crisis in the Catholic Church*. Washington, DC: United States Conference of Catholic Bishops.
Valentine, K., Katz, I., Smyth, C., Bent, C., Rinaldis, S., Wade, C., et al. (2016). *Key elements of child safe organizations*. Sydney: Commonwealth of Australia.
Walsh, K., Berthelsen, D., Nicholson, J. M., Brandon, L., Stevens, J., & Rachele, J. N. (2013). Child sexual abuse prevention education: A review of school policy and curriculum provision in Australia. *Oxford Review of Education, 39*(5), 649–680.
Williams, L. (1995). Recovered memories of abuse in women with documented child sexual victimization histories. *Journal of Traumatic Stress, 8*, 649–673.

Wood, J. (2008). *Report of the special committee of inquiry into child protection services in New South Wales*. Sydney: Government of the State of New South Wales.

Wright, K. (2017). Remaking collective knowledge: An analysis of the complex and multiple effects of inquiries into historical institutional child abuse. *Child Abuse & Neglect, 74*, 10–22.

Wurtele, S. (2012). Preventing the sexual exploitation of minors in youth-serving organizations. *Children and Youth Services Review, 34*, 2442–2453.

Wurtele, S. (2014). *Child sexual abuse prevention evaluation tool for organizations*. On file with author.

Yeung, K. (2004). *Securing compliance*. Oxford: Hart.

Chapter 6
Cultural and Technological Challenges

Abstract This chapter first discusses a range of contemporary cultural challenges regarding child sexual abuse, some of which have existed for thousands of years, and some of which are of more recent origin. It discusses child marriage, and female genital mutilation/cutting, covering their nature and consequences. It poses the question of whether they constitute species of child sexual abuse, and whether or not they do, refers to concepts of rights to explain why action can legitimately be taken to end these practices. Then, it considers the more recent phenomenon of child sex tourism. For these three cultural problems, it considers recent progress and responses, which have occurred through legal and regulatory responses, community involvement, the generation of new social norms, and multinational cooperation. The second part of this chapter considers recent and emerging technological challenges: online sexual abuse and child pornography; sexting and coercive online practices; and robotics. It considers recent progress and responses to these phenomena, noting new criminal prohibitions, and prevention considerations. It then considers the need to develop a new ethic of technology to respond to the new digital epoch, incorporating a consideration of the responsibilities of individuals, of social systems such as schools, and corporate responsibility and regulation. Key messages of this chapter are that some cultural challenges such as FGM/C have recently witnessed seismic reform, influenced by new conceptions of rights, legal protections, the involvement of women and communities, and scientific understanding. Others, however, such as child marriage, have not yet experienced significant change, and require ongoing multidimensional efforts responding to root causes. Technological challenges are substantial and growing, and legal regulation of individuals and corporations is necessary but not sufficient. There is a need for a public health approach to have a greater focus on prevention, requiring education from early childhood to enhance gender equality, skills and attitudes, and develop a new ethic of technology.

Keywords Child sexual abuse and cultural challenges · Child marriage · Female genital mutilation/cutting · Child sex tourism · Children's rights · Legal responses to prohibit and respond to these challenges · Social and community responses · Public health responses · New social norms · Child sexual abuse and technological challenges · Child pornography · Sexting and coercive online practices · Robotics · New legal protections · Remaining challenges · Education and children's capabilities · A new ethic of technology · Digital rights and responsibilities

B. Mathews, *New International Frontiers in Child Sexual Abuse*,
Child Maltreatment 7, https://doi.org/10.1007/978-3-319-99043-9_6

Cultural Challenges

Child Marriage

Child marriage is widespread, involving an estimated one in six girls aged 15–19 globally, and one in seven girls aged less than 15 in the developing world, and with higher prevalence in some nations and regions (UNICEF 2014). Jain and Kurz (2007) found that child marriage is associated with four factors, with the most prominent of these being lower education, as well as the presence of a greater age gap between girl and husband, poverty, and the particular region. Similarly, Rumble et al. (2018) found that in Indonesia, approximately 17% were married before age 18, and 6% were married before age 16. Most respondents indicated a preference to be married later in life (around 26 years), and significantly, only 5% approved of child marriage. Education, wealth and media exposure were protective factors for child marriage.[1]

As indicated by the Joint Statement of the Committee on the Elimination of Discrimination against Women and the Committee on the Rights of the Child (2014, paragraph 20), child marriage is considered to take place whenever one party is aged under 18, and child marriage is considered to be a form of forced marriage, "given that one and/or both parties have not expressed full, free and informed consent." Forced marriage occurs in diverse circumstances, with some of these inherently involving an even greater degree of coercion, violence and violation of dignity and autonomy. As reported by the Joint Statement (2014), forced marriage may occur when a rapist is permitted to escape criminal sanctions by marrying the victim; in the context of migration to ensure a girl marries within the family's community of origin, or to provide extended family members or others with documents to migrate to and/or live in a particular destination; when used by armed groups during conflict; or to escape post-conflict poverty. Also exacerbating the potential for violence is the associated practice of the payment of dowries and bride prices. The husband or his family members may engage in acts of serious physical or psychological violence to compel certain behaviour or to punish failure to meet perceived expectations. Families also sometimes arrange the temporary "marriage" of their daughter for financial gains, essentially constituting a form of trafficking.

A Violation of Human Rights, and a Barrier to the Realisation of Human Capabilities Amongst researchers, nongovernment organisations and policy bodies alike, child marriage is widely considered a human rights violation that deprives

[1] In Indonesia, the law appears unsettled and in need of clarification. As reported by UNICEF Indonesia (2016), the 2002 Law on Child Protection prohibits marriage under the age of 18 under any circumstances; however the 1974 Marriage Law states that females can legally marry at the age of 16 and males at 19, provided there is parental consent.

a girl of her childhood, jeopardises her health and development, disrupts or terminates her education, limits her broader opportunities for empowerment and social development, and increases her vulnerability to intimate partner violence (Chaudhuri 2015; Jain and Kurz 2007; Kidman 2017; Klugman et al. 2014; Parsons et al. 2015; Peterman et al. 2015; UNICEF 2014). Child marriage is a severe and enduring barrier to human development through its profound effects on the girl's education, economic capacity, personal safety, sexual autonomy, and freedom to choose whom she marries and how her married life is conducted. It is a paradigm case of a condition compromising multiple capabilities (Nussbaum 2011).

Child marriage causes severe detriment to economic educational attainment, employment opportunities, and economic welfare, and produces ongoing and intergenerational poverty (Mathur et al. 2003; Parsons et al. 2015). Major consequences include elevated risk of early childbirth due to pressure placed on the girl by the husband and broader family to immediately bear children, cultural expectations about gender roles, and social customs where childbirth is seen as the primary or even the sole role of a female of child-bearing age. Because of this, child-bearing before the girl's body is adequately prepared for it is widespread. This creates higher mortality and morbidity including obstructed labor, pregnancy-induced hypertension, and obstetric fistula (Jain and Kurz 2007). Complications of pregnancy and childbirth are the second leading causes of death among adolescent girls ages 15–19 globally, with nearly 70,000 dying each year (UNFPA 2013). The children of teenaged mothers are twice as likely to die in the first year of life as the child of a woman in her twenties. In addition, as shown by a study spanning 29 countries in Africa and Latin America, there is also elevated risk of HIV, since they are far more likely than unmarried adolescents to engage in frequent unprotected sex, have much older husbands (mean age difference 5–14 years), have little bargaining power in the relationship, little access to information about HIV, and diminished capacity to abstain, resist or insist on the use of condoms (Clark et al. 2006).

Higher Exposure to Intimate Partner Violence and Child Sexual Abuse Because of their lack of status and power, girls who marry young are more likely to experience domestic violence, sexual abuse, and isolation from family and community (Jain and Kurz 2007; Jenson and Thornton 2003; UNICEF 2005). In India, compared with girls who married at a later age, girls married before 18 were twice as likely to experience physical violence and three times as likely to experience sexual violence (International Center for Research on Women 2005). In Afghanistan, government data suggests 2400 women may commit self-immolation each year in the country, with early and forced marriage and sexual and domestic violence identified as key causes (Khanna et al. 2013).

As shown by Kidman (2017), the elevated risk of experiencing violence in general in child marriage extends to sexual abuse. Kidman (2017) analysed data from demographic and health surveys in 34 countries to identify the level of risk for young women aged 20–24 who had married as children to experiencing physical and/or sexual intimate partner violence, compared to their counterparts who married as adults. Kidman found that globally, 9% of respondents were married before age 15, and another 25% were married between age 15–17. The experience of past year physical and/or sexual IPV was higher among women who married as children (29%) compared with those who married as adults (20%). There was higher risk depending on the country of residence, and was most marked in sub-Saharan Africa: marriage before age 15 was associated with a combined measure of past year physical and/or sexual IPV in nine countries; women married between 15 and 17 were at increased risk of physical and/or sexual IPV in 19 countries.

Domestic Legal Prohibitions of Child Marriage Remain Inadequate Problematically as reported by the United Nations Human Rights Council. (2014), 147 countries at that time permitted marriage below the age of 18, either with parental, spousal or caregiver consent, with court permission, or in accordance with cultural practices or religious laws. Scolaro et al. (2015) analysed legal frameworks in 37 nations in the Asia-Pacific region and reported that only four countries had established the age of marriage as 18 without any exceptions such as parental consent or court consent (Bhutan, China, Mongolia, and Vietnam).

Progress appears slow, although in recognition of the nature of the practice and its often devastating effects, some jurisdictions are changing their laws to prohibit child marriage before the age of 18, or to tighten the exceptions based on parental consent. Other laws enabling or endorsing child marriage, or excusing sexual violence before or within it, are also experiencing change. Laws allowing a rapist to escape punishment if he marries his child victim, are being repealed in numerous countries (Sengupta 2017). In India, where the legal age of marriage is 18, the Supreme Court ruled that sexual intercourse with an unlawfully married child aged 15–18 constitutes rape (Aziz 2017).

An Entrenched Social Custom Even when it is prohibited by domestic laws, the practice of forced child marriage continues, demonstrating the durability of the social custom and proving much work remains to shift gender norms and eradicate the practice. In Sudan in May 2018, 19 year old Noura Hussein was sentenced to death (Beaumont 2018). Aged 16, she had been forcibly married against her will. Terrified, she had fled to live with her aunt in secret. Aged 19, her family tricked her into returning, and handed her over to her husband. Six days into this new arrangement, he recruited three others to assist him and he raped her. She then murdered him. Her husband's family rejected financial compensation and requested she be executed. An advocacy group, Equality Now, sought presidential clemency, arguing that her punishment was manifestly unjust, and that her rights under the Sudanese Constitution and international law had been violated. Specifically, they argued her rights had been violated under article 15 (that marriage can only occur with free and full consent), and article 14 (protection of children violated by mental and physical abuse). In addition, the Constitution provides that the state shall protect women from injustice and promote gender equality, and that all persons are equal before the law and are entitled without discrimination, to the equal protection of the law.

Informed by the evidence of its nature and consequences, the UN Committees have noted that child marriage is a particularly harmful practice, deeply embedded in social customs under which women and girls are regarded as inferior to men and boys because of limited stereotyped roles in society. The practice is inherently animated by a gendered ordering of society which endorses fundamental and enduring power imbalance, inequality and discrimination. These postures and practices then create a context where coercion and violence is facilitated and encouraged. For those engaging in child marriage without full and free consent, the harms caused are acknowledged as including immediate physical and psychological consequences, and extending beyond these to cause lasting impairment to the enjoyment of human rights and fundamental freedoms regarding bodily inviolability, social participation, health, education, employment and social status both individually and as a group. These are powerful reasons underpinning and justifying international prohibitions on child marriage.

International Legal Prohibitions and Statements by International Human Rights Bodies

While the UNCRC does not have an article specifically and expressly prohibiting child marriage, there are several articles which should implicitly protect the child against it. These include article 3(1) (the best interests of the child shall be a primary consideration in all actions concerning children, whether undertaken by public or private social welfare institutions, courts of law, administrative authorities or legislative bodies); article 15 (right to freedom of association); article 12 (the right to express views freely in all matters affecting the child and for those views to be given due weight); article 8 (the right to preserve identity, including name and family relations), and article 36 (the right to protection against all other forms of exploitation prejudicial to the child's welfare).

Despite this, a range of other international instruments and regional instruments prohibit child marriage, clearly recognising the gravity of the issue, especially for girls and women (Chaudhuri 2015). Three of the major international conventions that prohibit child marriage are as follows. First, the Universal Declaration of Human Rights 1948 art 16 states that:

1. Men and women of full age, without any limitation due to race, nationality or religion, have the right to marry and to found a family. They are entitled to equal rights as to marriage, during marriage and at its dissolution.
2. Marriage shall be entered into only with the free and full consent of the intending spouses.
3. The family is the natural and fundamental group unit of society and is entitled to protection by society and the State.

Second, the Convention on Consent to Marriage, Minimum Age for Marriage, and Registration of Marriages 1962 art 1 stated that "No marriage shall be legally entered into without the full and free consent of both parties…". Article 2 required States Parties shall take legislative action to specify a minimum age for marriage, but problematically did not specify what that age should be. Similarly, the UDHR art 16 used the expression "full age" but did not specify what that age should be. Both Conventions instead relied on the requirement that marriage only be entered with free and full consent.

More specific and more recent is the treatment of child marriage by The Convention on the Elimination of All Forms of Discrimination against Women (CEDAW). This Convention was adopted by the United Nations General Assembly on 18 December 1979, and entered into force on 3 September 1981. CEDAW is a cornerstone of gender equality in international law and social practice. As an indication of just how difficult it was for this development to materialise, one need only acknowledge that it took almost three decades for the treaty to be formed, and centuries of slow, painful progress since the original women's right theorists and activists began advocating for social change.

Article 16 is particularly relevant to child marriage. It declares (my emphasis):

1. *States Parties shall take all appropriate measures to eliminate discrimination against women in all matters relating to marriage and family relations* and in particular shall ensure, on a basis of equality of men and women:
   (a) *The same right to enter into marriage*;
   (b) *The same right freely to choose a spouse and to enter into marriage only with their free and full consent*;
   (c) The same rights and responsibilities during marriage and at its dissolution;
   (d) The same rights and responsibilities as parents, irrespective of their marital status, in matters relating to their children; in all cases the interests of the children shall be paramount;
   (e) *The same rights to decide freely and responsibly on the number and spacing of their children and to have access to the information, education and means to enable them to exercise these rights*;
   (f) The same rights and responsibilities with regard to guardianship, wardship, trusteeship and adoption of children, or similar institutions where these concepts exist in national legislation; in all cases the interests of the children shall be paramount;
   (g) The same personal rights as husband and wife, including the right to choose a family name, a profession and an occupation;
   (h) The same rights for both spouses in respect of the ownership, acquisition, management, administration, enjoyment and disposition of property, whether free of charge or for a valuable consideration.
2. *The betrothal and the marriage of a child shall have no legal effect, and all necessary action, including legislation, shall be taken to specify a minimum age for marriage and to make the registration of marriages in an official registry compulsory.*

These articles elaborate on those in the 1962 Convention and the UDHR art 16, but they too do not specify a minimum age of marriage, instead relying on the requirement that marriage only be entered with "full and free consent". While art 16(2) states the marriage of a "child" shall have no effect, a jurisdiction would technically be able to avoid this injunction by setting a low age of majority or entitlement to marry.

United Nations Committee Statements, Including a Declaration on the Minimum Age for Marriage The intent behind these prohibitions continue to be supported by United Nations Committees urging the development of domestic legal frameworks to prohibit child marriage, and for legal and policy frameworks to ensure these laws are observed. In 1994, this was made clear by the Committee on the Elimination of Discrimination against Women, which affirmed that the minimum age for marriage should be 18 years for both men and women.[2]

Twenty years later, in 2014, the Committee on the Elimination of Discrimination against Women and the Committee on the Rights of the Child made a *Joint general recommendation No. 31 of the Committee on the Elimination of Discrimination against Women/General comment No. 18 of the Committee on the Rights of the Child on harmful practices*.[3] This Joint Statement repeated a clear statement about the requisite age qualification for marriage. It declared that States parties adopt or amend legislation to effectively address and eliminate harmful practices, including by ensuring (para 55(f) and (g)):

(f) That a minimum legal age of marriage for girls and boys, with or without parental consent, is established at 18 years. When a marriage at an earlier age is allowed in exceptional circumstances, the absolute minimum age must not be below 16 years, the grounds for obtaining permission must be legitimate and strictly defined by law and the marriage must be permitted only by a court of law upon the full, free and informed consent of the child or both children, who must appear in person before the court;

(g) That a legal requirement of marriage registration is established and effective implementation is provided through awareness-raising, education and the existence of adequate infrastructure to make registration accessible to all persons within their jurisdiction;

Further, in 2016, in General Comment 20, statements reaffirmed the need to protect girls form harmful cultural practices, and reminded States parties of "the obligation to recognize that persons up to the age of 18 years are entitled to continuing protection from all forms of exploitation and abuse. It reaffirms that the minimum age limit should be 18 years for marriage".[4]

---

[2] CEDAW General Recommendation No. 21, UN Doc. A/39/48, (1994), para. 36.

[3] Committee on the Elimination of Discrimination against Women and Committee on the Rights of the Child. Joint general recommendation No. 31 of the Committee on the Elimination of Discrimination against Women/general comment No. 18 of the Committee on the Rights of the Child on harmful practices. (2014). CEDAW/C/GC/31-CRC/C/GC/18.

[4] General comment No. 20 (2016) on the implementation of the rights of the child during adolescence. CRC/C/GC/20. See paras 27–28: "During adolescence, gender inequalities become more significant. Manifestations of discrimination, inequality and stereotyping against girls often intensify, leading to more serious violations of their rights, including child and forced marriage, early pregnancy, female genital mutilation, gender-based physical, mental and sexual violence, abuse, exploitation and trafficking. Cultural norms ascribing lower status to girls can increase the likelihood of confinement to the home, lack of access to secondary and tertiary education, limited opportunities for leisure, sport, recreation and income generation, lack of access to cultural life and the arts, burdensome domestic chores and childcare responsibilities. In many countries, girls report lower levels of health and life satisfaction indicators than boys, a difference that gradually increases with age. ... States need to invest in proactive measures to promote the empowerment of girls, challenge patriarchal and other harmful gender norms and stereotyping and legal reforms in order

Accordingly, a range of policy bodies and international instruments and domestic laws alike recognise the legitimate reasons to place legislative and practice-based limits on when a child can marry. One would have thought that these reasons were sufficient to motivate reform. However, some have recently.

Is Child Marriage a Form of Child Sexual Abuse?

In 2011, the United Nations Committee on the Rights of the Child arguably provided another compelling justification for national and multilateral action, when it included forced marriage in its definition of sexual abuse. It stated that child sexual abuse includes:

(a) The inducement or coercion of a child to engage in any unlawful or psychologically harmful sexual activity;
(b) The use of children in commercial sexual exploitation;
(c) The use of children in audio or visual images of child sexual abuse;
(d) Child prostitution, sexual slavery, sexual exploitation in travel and tourism, trafficking (within and between countries) and sale of children for sexual purposes and forced marriage.

The language in the definition is slightly ambiguous, so that it is possible that this statement intended only to apply to forced marriage in the context of "trafficking … and sale of children for sexual purposes and forced marriage", rather than any and all instances of forced marriage. However, other UN Committee statements have made it clear that all forms of child marriage constitute forced marriage based on lack of consent; moreover, there is no good justification for limiting a definition of forced marriage to one subset of trafficking cases. Accordingly, the better interpretation seems to be that the definition promulgated here applies to all cases of forced marriage. On this basis, the UN Committee's 2011 definition marks something of a departure from the standard approach to child marriage. While seen broadly as a fundamental violation of human rights as shown above, child marriage has not generally been conceptualised as a form of child sexual abuse. Is it able to be characterised as a form of child sexual abuse? And if so, might this help accelerate domestic legal and practical change?

Emerging Understandings of Child Marriage as a Form of Child Sexual Abuse In March 2018, at the UN Commission on the Status of Women, a forum was convened on child early forced marriage and female genital mutilation, by UN Women, the Working Group on Girls and the Feminist Majority Foundation. There, UN Women Executive Director Phumzile Mlambo-Ngcuka declared that "child marriage—child

---

to address direct and indirect discrimination against girls, in cooperation with all stakeholders, including civil society, women and men, traditional and religious leaders and adolescents themselves. Explicit measures are needed in all laws, policies and programmes to guarantee the rights of girls on an equal basis with boys."

abuse that is sanctioned by society—curtails the potential of a girl for the rest of her life." Even more forcefully, African Union Goodwill Ambassador Nyaradzayi Gumbonzvanda declared that the term child marriage is a euphemism, stating: "It is not a marriage … There can never be a marriage of a child. It is child sexual abuse, it is exploitation, it is rape, it is abduction. It's a modern form of slavery. We need to name it appropriately" (Turcotte 2018).

To date, the UN Committee's definition and Ambassador Gumbonzvanda's declaration alike finds surprisingly little scholarly support. This may be due to the deep embedding throughout history of child marriage, of patriarchy and gender roles, and of the centrality of early marriage to family life, property, and culture. To question a widespread cultural custom, and to ask whether it constitutes a practice which is and should be broadly condemned, causes discomfort for those posing the question, offence for those receiving it. Such questions can often be dismissed as reflecting arrogance and ignorance, or as a manifestation of cultural imperialism.

Nevertheless, especially in recent years, research and advocacy bodies have engaged with the concept that child marriage – at the very least in situations where it is clearly forced – is at a minimum a kind of child sexual exploitation, or of child sexual abuse. For example, Susanne Louis Mikhail (2002) categorised child marriage as a form of sexual exploitation, noting the "extraordinary and contradictory climate where a man who sexually abuses a child can on the one hand be sentenced to death (if it is a matter of child rape or child prostitution), but on the other [be] backed up by legal instruments and social approval (if he chooses to marry the child)" (Mikhail 2002, pp. 48–49). More recently, Chaudhuri (2015) posited that child marriage can itself constitute a form of sexual abuse. Chaudhuri (2015) set out a comprehensive framework for action in response to child marriage generally. Depending on the circumstances of the case, she conceptualised any given child marriage as constituting one or more of: a channel leading to various forms of sexual violence; itself a form of sexual abuse; a form of commercial or economic exploitation.[5] For Chaudhuri, a child marriage itself constitutes a form of child sexual abuse when sufficiently closely connected to the experience of sexual abuse

[5] Chaudhuri stated (2015, p. v): At the first level, child marriage is understood as a channel leading to various forms of sexual violence against children, such as trafficking, prostitution, pornography, or exposure to high levels of vulnerability that in turn may result in sexual victimisation. The second level focuses on how underage unions themselves can be potentially regarded as a form of sexual abuse and exploitation of the underage parties involved. Prevalent domestic and sexual violence by intimate partners, early forced sexual initiation, premature onset of sexual activity, non-consensual sex, unwanted adolescent pregnancy and premature child bearing, exposure to sexually transmitted diseases and female genital mutilation are highly detrimental to married girls' health and overall protection. The final level of the framework explores how economic transactions or financial gains benefitting the adult parties involved in contracting an underage union may justify relating forms of child marriage to commercial or otherwise economic sexual exploitation of children. This includes situations in which child marriage is linked to child servitude and forced child labour, slavery and bondage, or the payment of a dowry. The three levels are interlinked insofar as their determinants are concerned, and the individual child may experience one or more of the different determinants reviewed across the model, depending on specific circumstances.

within the married relationship due to the occurrence of sexual abuse by the husband. Essentially, the relationship provides the setting within which sexual abuse occurs; the nexus between the sexual abuse of the child bride is so closely connected with the marriage state that the marriage is itself seen as constituting child sexual abuse.

Across all cases of child marriage, a balanced assessment should acknowledge that positive experiences are reported by some, especially by those girls who marry as an older adolescent minor, know their husband, and where the husband is of the same age. However, there appears widespread agreement that in a very large proportion of child marriages, the girls entering into the relationship do not or cannot provide full and free consent. Even where the element of coercion is not as clear, it is evident that a fundamental purpose of child marriage is to enable sexual relations between a girl who is not yet an adult, and a husband who is often an adult and who in a large proportion of cases is decades older than the girl. In this sense, it is difficult to escape from a conclusion that a great proportion of instances of child marriage are of their nature designed to facilitate interactions with the girl child occurring soon after the marriage, and which will likely continue, which inevitably include sexual relations, to which she either cannot or does not provide full and free consent. This applies especially to those marriage transactions (whether motivated by financial, relational, or status-related reasons, or other similar reasons) that are clearly forced, but also is arguably capable of extending to those transactions that involve a more subtle cultural, societal or familial coercion, where the girl either cannot or does not provide full and free consent.

The conceptual model proposed by Mathews and Collin-Vézina (2017), discussed earlier in Chap. 2, lends further support to this contention, at least in some cases of child marriage. That is, it is possible that at least some cases of child marriage possess the components of "child sexual abuse" on that approach, where: it involves a "child" (either or both chronologically or developmentally regarding capacity to provide consent); acts that are "sexual" (being contact or non-contact acts for the purpose of seeking or obtaining sexual gratification, whether immediate or deferred, as well as considering the child's experience fo the act); and "abuse" (the act being abusive due to its unconscionability, derived from the presence of a relationship of power, the child being in a position if inequality, the child's vulnerability being exploited to her detriment, and absence of true consent).

Efforts to End Child Marriage – A Harmful Practice, Inherently Related to Sex, and Characterised by Lack of Consent Whether one claims child marriage is itself a form of child sexual abuse, or subscribes to the less comprehensive view that child marriage provides a socially sanctioned setting in which child sexual abuse frequently occurs and otherwise violates girls and women's fundamental human rights, it is clear that efforts to eradicate child marriage will continue. These efforts will be spurred by the UN Sustainable Development Goals, adopted in 2015, which include a target to eliminate all harmful practices such as child marriage by 2030.

They will also be motivated by a growing general impulse that this practice needs to end to promote public health, social justice, and the dignity of girls and women, and of boys and men. Efforts to end child marriage continue to develop, exemplified by the World Bank Group's foundational report entitled Voice and Agency: Empowering Women and Girls for Shared Prosperity (Klugman et al. 2014). In March 2016, the United Nations Population Fund-UNICEF Global Programme to Accelerate Action to End Child Marriage was announced. This joint initiative will focus on proven strategies, including increasing girls' access to education and health services, educating parents and communities on the dangers of child marriage, increasing economic support to families, and strengthening and enforcing laws that establish 18 as the minimum age of marriage.

Female Genital Mutilation/Cutting

A Cultural Custom, Not Required by Religion Female genital mutilation or cutting (FGM/C) is a cultural practice involving the non-therapeutic physical modification of female genitalia.

FGM historically predates and has no basis in the Koran, or any other religious text (Barstow 1999; Office of the High Commissioner For Human Rights et al. 2008). Rather, it is a cultural tradition, particularly common in Islamic societies in regions of Africa, which is motivated by a patriarchal society's desire to control female bodies and lives, and their capacity for sexual enjoyment and fulfilment. The primary reason for this desire for control is to ensure virginity at marriage, thereby preserving family honour, within a patriarchal social structure where females' value as persons is intrinsically connected to, and limited to, their worth as virgin brides. Other justifications routinely offered for FGM include that it is a rite of passage into womanhood; it prevents the clitoris from growing like a penis; it restrains rampant sexual urges; it removes clitorises, which are 'dirty'; it helps attract a husband because uncircumcised women are seen as immoral; it preserves a traditional cultural practice; and that it prevents infidelity by controlling sexual desire and capacity (Barstow 1999; Joseph 1996; Obermeyer 1999, 2005; Office of the High Commissioner For Human Rights et al. 2008; Toubia 1994).

The most recent estimate from the World Health Organisation (2018) is that more than 200 million girls and women alive today have experienced FGM/C in 30 countries in Africa, the Middle East and Asia, and that three million girls are estimated to be at risk for FGM annually.

Eleven African nations have lifetime prevalence rates of FGM/C in females aged 15–49 of 70–98%. These are, in descending order, Somalia, Egypt, Guinea, Sierra Leone, Djibouti, Sudan, Eritrea, Gambia, Ethiopia, Burkina Faso and Mauritania (Office of the High Commissioner For Human Rights et al. 2008). In jurisdictions where FGM/C is less common, societies need to deal with the phenomenon due to immigrants from regions where it is customary. In 2009, in the course of making a resolution on combating female genital mutilation in the European Union, the European Parliament indicated that FGM is estimated to affect 500,000 women and girls in Europe, with 180,000 girls at risk each year (Mathews 2013).

Four Types There are considered to be four types of FGM/C (Office of the High Commissioner For Human Rights et al. 2008; Toubia 1994). Clitoridectomy (Type 1) involves partial or total removal of the visible part of the clitoris. Excision (Type 2) involves partial or total removal of the clitoris and the labia minora, and sometimes also the labia majora. Infibulation (Type 3) is the most extreme form, generally involving clitoridectomy, excision, suturing together of the raw surfaces of the labia, and narrowing of the vaginal opening, leaving only a small opening for urination and menstruation. Other less invasive non-therapeutic procedures (Type 4) involve pricks, nicks and incisions of the clitoris or labia.

Consequences Numerous studies have found myriad adverse physical and psychological effects of FGM/C. Especially when conducted in unsterile environments with rudimentary tools and without modern wound management, the risk of infection is high, and death from haemhorraging is not infrequent (Barstow 1999). An association between more extensive forms of FGM and infertility has been found (Almroth et al. 2001). The more invasive the FGM, the greater are the complications for intercourse, childbirth, menstruation, and the higher the likelihood of recurrent infections, chronic pain, and perinatal death (Adam et al. 2010; Barstow 1999). Those who are infibulated suffer re-incision to facilitate intercourse and childbirth, with higher risk for fatalities in childbirth (Office of the High Commissioner For Human Rights et al. 2008). A study of 28,393 women in six African nations found that women who have experienced FGM, especially when it is more extensive, are significantly more likely to suffer adverse obstetric outcomes such as episiotomy (surgical cuts to aid delivery), perineal tears, heavy postpartum blood loss, and longer hospital stays (WHO Study Group et al. 2006). Significant effects on longevity have also been found (Adam et al. 2010). Psychologically, the consequences of FGM commonly include post-traumatic stress disorder, depression, anxiety and fear of sexual relations (Barstow 1999). Underpinning motivations for FGM/C flow into both women's and men's understandings of and attitudes towards sex in general, intimate sexual relations, and the general relationship between wives and husbands. A study in rural and slum areas in Egypt, where FGM is almost universal in women aged 15–49, found widespread lack of women's pleasure in sex and other adverse impacts on healthy sexual relationships (Fahmy et al. 2010). Women were considered unable to reject a husband's demand for sex. Women generally did not have an independent pleasure in sex, but related 'sexual pleasure' to their situation in familial and social contentment and security.

Infibulation, the most invasive from of FGM/C, affects approximately 10% of those who have experienced FGM/C, being especially likely in Djibouti, Eritrea, Ethiopia, Somalia and the north of Sudan (Yoder and Khan 2008). Adverse consequences of infibulation include complications for menstruation and intercourse, urinary and reproductive tract infections, urinary complications, chronic pain, and lower sexual quality of life (Adam et al. 2010; Obermeyer 2005; Momoh et al. 2001; Andersson et al. 2012; Nour et al. 2006). Adverse obstetric outcomes include episiotomy, perineal tears, excessive post-partum blood loss caused by tearing of scar tissue around the vaginal opening, perinatal death, and longer hospital stays (WHO Study Group et al. 2006).[6]

Is FGM/C Child Sexual Abuse?

Depending on the definition used, it is possible that some and perhaps most manifestations of FGM/C are not properly classed as "child sexual abuse". As seen in Chap. 2, most definitions of "child sexual abuse" in international policies and epidemiological studies contain an element of sexual gratification, and or that the acts or activities are inherently "sexual". Similarly, the conceptual analysis and definition proposed in Chap. 2 and by Mathews and Collin-Vézina (2017) contains a requirement that there be an element of sexual gratification for some person, whether immediate or deferred in time and space. While FGM/C is inherently related to sex, the act itself is arguably not one that is "sexual". Many, and probably most cases of FGM/C do not contain any such element of gratification, and these may be best considered as involving a physical assault (albeit on a girl's genitalia), a serious human rights violation, and as sex-based or gender based violence which should be prohibited and sought to be eradicated. The recent social movements to eradicate FGM/C in Europe and Africa alike have frequently referred to FGM/C as a form of child abuse, but not explicitly as child sexual abuse. For example, in July 2016, the head of the UN Population Fund, Dr. Babatunde Osotimehin, described FGM as "child abuse". This is conceptually consistent, even when acknowledging that the acts occur on the child's genitalia, that consent is absent, and that effects include many similar consequences for those who experience child sexual abuse, and that effects commonly adversely affect future sexual capacity. It is also consistent with international policy definitions of CSA, including the most detailed approach in 2011 by the United Nations Committee on the Rights of the Child, as detailed in Chap. 2. While it expressly included a list of specific acts and experiences in its definition of "sexual abuse and exploitation", the Committee did not expressly include FGM/C.

However, there may be exceptions to this, meaning that some specific experiences of FGM/C may indeed be considered to constitute child sexual abuse. Some have argued that, at least in some forms, FGM/C is a kind of incest (de Mause 1998). Moreover, there are some manifestations of FGM/C which do appear to involve ritualized sexual assault involving sexual gratification (Barstow 1999,

[6] Women who have experienced infibulation can be particularly likely to present special challenges for medical practitioners, including around how to treat an infibulated patient, and whether reinfibulation after childbirth is medically, ethically and legally justified. This was the basis of the unsuccessful prosecution in England.

Toubia 1994), and these specific situations may be more persuasively considered to involve sexual abuse. In addition, the definition proposed by Mathews and Collin-Vézina (2017) acknowledged that even if the sexual gratification element of an act is not clear, an act may be both inherently related to sex and may be legitimately perceived by the child as a sexual act, whether at the time or retrospectively. So, a particular child may subjectively interpret the acts involved in her experience of FGM/C as sexual. While FGM/C takes different forms and has different sequelae, a particular individual could legitimately perceive it as a sexual act because of the manner in which it is performed, as well as its primary focus on sexual function and its impact on physical and psychological sexual capacity.

However one characterises the practice of FGM/C in its various forms, it is clear that this is a widespread custom, affecting an extremely substantial number of girls, having substantial effects on girls and women, and with these effects explicitly connected to sex. Any detailed consideration of "child sexual abuse" must at least consider the prospect that some of its manifestations either do or may be interpreted as constituting child sexual abuse, and should provide some coverage of this topic. As well, this topic is significant because it demonstrates how a long-established cultural practice of physical and sexual violence may be overturned, and how a new emerging social norm may translate into an absolute human right (Mathews 2013).

Emerging Social Norms Prohibiting FGM/C

In 1979, the WHO hosted the world's first international conference on female circumcision, and made the first formal recommendation from a major policy body for the eradication of FGM (Toubia and Sharief 2003). Since then, many nations have enacted domestic laws prohibiting FGM, and international instruments have also incorporated articles which expressly or implicitly urge States to take all necessary measures to eradicate FGM. Legislative and policy developments have proliferated in recent years to reduce and even eradicate FGM/C.

Significant gains in reducing FGM/C have occurred in recent years (UNICEF 2016). Health and human rights bodies have called for its eradication to promote girls' and women's health and human rights (World Health Organization Study Group 2006). Numerous international legal instruments have been created in diverse regions including Africa to promote its abandonment (United Nations Population Fund 2014; World Bank Group 2018). In 2012, the United Nations adopted Resolution 11,331 urging all nations to take all necessary measures to eradicate FGM/C.[7] In 2003, the African Charter on Human and Peoples' Rights; Protocol on the Rights of Women in Africa 2003 (the Maputo Protocol) imposed a ban on all forms of FGM (including medicalized FGM). The Convention on the Elimination of

[7] United Nations General Assembly, Resolution 11,331, Intensifying global efforts for the elimination of female genital mutilations, A/67/PV.60, 20 December 2012, http://www.un.org/News/Press/docs//2012/ga11331.doc.htm

All Forms of Discrimination against Women 1979 article 2(f) urges State Parties to take 'all appropriate measures, including legislation, to modify or abolish existing laws, regulations, customs and practices which constitute discrimination against women'. Further, Article 5 urges States parties to take all appropriate measures to 'modify the social and cultural patterns of conduct of men and women, with a view to achieving the elimination of prejudices and customary and all other practices which are based on the idea of the inferiority or the superiority of either of the sexes'. In 2005, in the Islamic context, the Rabat Declaration on Child Issues (art 10) established a commitment to eliminate discrimination against girls and harmful traditional practices including FGM, and in article 20 urged legislative measures to be taken to accomplish these goals. Underpinning all of these instruments is the United Nations Convention on the Rights of the Child 1989, which contains several articles relevant to this context. Article 24(3) states that States Parties 'shall take all effective and appropriate measures with a view to abolishing traditional practices prejudicial to the health of children'. The World Health Assembly passed a resolution in 2008 on the elimination of FGM, emphasizing the need for concerted action by organizations responsible for health, education, finance, justice and women's affairs, to eliminate FGM.[8] In 2008, the United Nations Commission on the Status of Women also made a resolution on ending female genital mutilation.[9] The UN Sustainable Development Goals adopted in 2015 include a target to eliminate all harmful practices such as FGM by 2030.

These norms continue to gather momentum in the broader public realm. In the UK, the End FGM Guardian Global Media Campaign, supported by the United Nations Population Fund, was launched in 2014 to respond to awareness of a growing problem. As a result of this movement, the Serious Crime Act 2015 introduced mandatory reporting of FGM in girls under 18 years by healthcare workers, teachers and social workers in the UK. In 2016, UNICEF reported data from countries where the practice is still common and not yet prohibited that two thirds of all people want the practice to end (UN News Centre 2016). In some nations, more men opposed the practice than women.

Domestic Legal Prohibitions

Domestic laws in numerous Western countries, and elsewhere including 24 countries in Africa, now prohibit FGM/C in all its forms (Mathews 2011, 2013). The World Bank Group (2018) reported that domestic legal prohibitions exist in 79 nations, including 31 countries in Africa; 5 countries in Asia and Pacific; 29 countries in Europe; 5 countries in Latin America; 7 in Northern Africa and the Middle East; and 2 countries in North America. Nations which have recently enacted their

[8] World Health Assembly, Female genital mutilation: Resolution 61.16. 24 May 2008. http://www.who.int/reproductivehealth/topics/fgm/fgm_resolution_61.16.pdf

[9] United Nations Commission on the Status of Women, Document E/CN.6/2008/L.2/Rev.1, 2008.

first groundbreaking prohibitions include Nigeria in 2015 (Topping 2015), and the Gambia in 2015 (Lyons 2015).

The Nature of Legal Prohibitions The laws prohibit all four forms of FGM/C. There are general and specific legislative provisions establishing that consent to FGM/C is not a defence. In all jurisdictions there is a general exception for medical procedures conducted for therapeutic purposes or which are necessary for the patient's health (Table 6.1).

Prosecutions Unsurprisingly, criminal prosecutions are relatively infrequent due to the clandestine nature of the acts, generally being conducted by a family member, acquaintance or community member experienced in the practice, and the reluctance of the parties involved and other members of society to disclose breaches of the criminal law. At least until 2013, there had been no prosecutions in the USA, Canada or New Zealand. In some Western nations, such as Canada, scholars have expressed concern that not enough is being done to prevent he practice in the nation or when girls return to their country of origin for holidays (Packer et al. (2015). However, the infrequency of prosecution should neither cause undue pessimism about the value of the law, nor influence prosecutions based on an impulse to show the law "works". The primary object of statutory prohibitions of FGM/C is to set fundamental social norms, and to buttress other health, policy and educational efforts to change attitudes and practices (Mgbako et al. 2010; Muteshi and Sass 2006). Secondary objects are to deter its continuance, and to allow prosecution of cases where FGM/C has either already been conducted or where preparations are being made for its conduct at home or overseas.

Prosecutions are usually facilitated by a member of a girl's family or community bringing the situation to the attention of police or other authorities. Other countries, including France, have a stronger record of prosecutions. The UNFPA-UNICEF Joint Programme on Female Genital Mutilation/Cutting (2016) reported that during 2016, 90 individuals were arrested, 253 cases of FGM/C were brought to court and 77 individuals were convicted. Several countries have recently witnessed the first prosecutions for alleged breaches of FGM/C prohibitions. In Egypt in 2015, there was a successful prosecution of a doctor (Hayoun 2015). An unsuccessful prosecution of a doctor occurred in England (Kmietowicz 2014). In the Australian state of Queensland, the first prosecution of the prohibition on FGM/C is currently proceeding, with two accused pleading not guilty to allegedly taking two girls aged nine and 12 from Queensland to Africa to undergo the procedure (Vujkovic 2018).

In Australia, in the state of New South Wales, a 2015 trial resulted in three people being convicted for conducting FGM/C on two girls, aged 6 and 7 years old (Jabour 2015).[10] This case was significant because the offence involved several parties who had played different roles in the offence, which involved cutting or nicking of the

[10] R v A2; R v KM; R v Vaziri (No. 19) [2015] NSWSC 1700. See the account of the trial in Jabour, B. (2015). Australia's first female genital mutilation trial: how a bright young girl convinced a jury. The Guardian. 13 November.

Table 6.1 Summary of legislative prohibitions regarding FGM/C and medical exceptions: the UK, Scotland, Ireland, USA, Canada, Australia and New Zealand

Jurisdiction	Legislation	Prohibition	Exceptions
UK (England, Wales, Northern Ireland)	**Female Genital Mutilation Act 2003**	**Section 1(1):** A person is guilty of an offence if he excises, infibulates or otherwise mutilates the whole or any part of a girl's labia majora, labia minora or clitoris	**Section 1(2):** But no offence is committed by an approvedpersonwhoperforms– (a) a surgical operation on a girl which is necessary for her physical or mental health, or (b) a surgical operation on a girl who is in any stage of labour, or has just given birth, for purposes connected with the labour or birth
Scotland	**Prohibition of Female Genital Mutilation (Scotland) Act 2005**	**Section 1(1):** A person who performs an action mentioned in ss (2) in relation to the whole or any part of the labia majora, labia minora, prepuce of the clitoris, clitoris or vagina of another person is guilty of an offence. (2) Those actions are- (a) excising it; (b) infibulating it; or (c) otherwise mutilating it.	**Section 1(3):** No offence is committed by an approved person who performs an action mentioned in subsection (4). (4) Those actions are- (a) a *surgical operation on another person which is necessary for that other person's physical or mental health*; or (b) a *surgical operation on another person who is in any stage of labour or has just given birth, for purposes connected with the labour or birth.*
Ireland	**Criminal Justice (Female Genital Mutilation) Act 2012**	**Section 2(1):** A person is guilty of an offence if the person does or attempts to do an act of female genital mutilation **Section 1:** "female genital mutilation" means any act the purpose of which, or the effect of which, is the excision, infibulation or other mutilation of the whole or any part of the labia majora, labia minora, prepuce of the clitoris, clitoris or vagina of a girl or woman	**Section 2(2):** A person is not guilty of an offence under subsection (1) if— (a) the act concerned is a *surgical operation performed by a registered medical practitioner on the girl or woman concerned, which is necessary for the protection of her physical or mental health*, or (b) the act is a *surgical operation performed by a registered medical practitioner or a midwife, or a person undergoing training to be a midwife, on the girl or woman concerned when she is in any stage of labour, or has just given birth, for purposes connected with the labour or birth*

(continued)

Table 6.1 (continued)

Jurisdiction	Legislation	Prohibition	Exceptions
USA	**United States Code Title 18 – Crimes and Criminal Procedure; note that many States also have legislative prohibitions**	**Section 116 – Female genital mutilation** (a) Except as provided in subsection (b), whoever knowingly circumcises, excises, or infibulates the whole or any part of the labia majora or labia minora or clitoris of another person who has not attained the age of 18 years shall be fined under this title or imprisoned not more than 5 years, or both.	**Section 116(b)**: A surgical operation is not a violation of this section if the operation is-- (1) *necessary to the health of the person on whom it is performed*, and is performed by a person licensed in the place of its performance as a medical practitioner; or (2) *performed on a person in labor or who has just given birth and is performed for medical purposes connected with that labor or birth* by a person licensed in the place it is performed as a medical practitioner, midwife, or person in training to become such a practitioner or midwife.
Canada	**Criminal Code 1985**	**Section 268(1)** Every one commits an aggravated assault who wounds, maims, disfigures or endangers the life of the complainant. … (3) "wounds" or "maims" includes to excise, infibulate or mutilate, in whole or in part, the labia majora, labia minora or clitoris	**Section 268(3)**: '…except where (a) a surgical procedure is performed, by a person duly qualified by provincial law to practise medicine, *for the benefit of the physical health of the person or for the purpose of that person having normal reproductive functions or normal sexual appearance or function…*'
New Zealand	**Crimes Act 1961**	**Section 204A** (1) female genital mutilation means the excision, infibulation, or mutilation of the whole or part of the labia majora, labia minora, or clitoris of any person (2) Subject to ss (3), every one is liable to imprisonment for a term not exceeding 7 years who performs, or causes to be performed, on any other person, any act involving female genital mutilation.	**Section 204A(3)**: Nothing in ss (2) applies to— (a) *any medical or surgical procedure* (including a sexual reassignment procedure) *that is performed* on any person— (i) *for the benefit of that person's physical or mental health*; and (ii) by a medical practitioner: (b) *any medical or surgical procedure that is performed* on any person— (i) *while that person is in labour or immediately after that person gives birth*; and (ii) *for the benefit of that person's health or the health of the child*; and (iii) by a medical practitioner

(continued)

Table 6.1 (continued)

Jurisdiction	Legislation	Prohibition	Exceptions
Australia	**Each State and Territory has its own legislation**	Australian Capital Territory: Crimes Act 1900 s 74 New South Wales: Crimes Act 1900 s 45 Northern Territory: Criminal Code s 186B Queensland: Criminal Code s 323A	In all State and Territories, a general exception permits medical procedures necessary for the patient's health, or for a genuine therapeutic purpose: Australian Capital Territory: s 76(1)-(2) New South Wales: s 45(3)-(4) Northern Territory: s 186B(3)(a) Queensland: ss 323A, 323(3)(f) South Australia: s 33(1)-(2) Tasmania: s 178C(1)(a) Victoria: ss 34(1)(a), 34A(2) Western Australia: s 306(1)(e)
		South Australia: Criminal Law Consolidation Act 1935 s 33A Tasmania: *Criminal Code* s 178A Victoria: *Crimes Act 1958* s 32 Western Australia: *Criminal Code 1913* s 306	In four jurisdictions, a specific exception permits medical procedures associated with childbirth by allowing surgical operations '*performed on a person in labour or who has just given birth, and for medical purposes or the relief of physical symptoms connected with that labour or birth*': Australian Capital Territory: s 76(2)(a) New South Wales: s 45(3)(b) Queensland: s 323A(3)(f) Victoria: s 34(1)(b)

girls' clitorises. Two of the three people convicted were the girls' mother (A2), who requested that the procedure be done, and KM, a retired former nurse and midwife; each was convicted of performing the acts. The third person, Vaziri, a senior member of the community, was convicted of being an accessory after the fact by trying to divert the police investigation. The two women were sentenced to a minimum of 11 months' home detention, while Vaziri was sentenced to a minimum 11 months' jail (Partridge 2016). The sentencing judge found that Vaziri was the religious leader of the Dawoodi Bohra community in Sydney, and exploited that position in a clear, determined and calculated manner, by directing community members to lie to police about the practice "to obstruct the police so that no successful investigation of the use of "khatna" in his own community could be achieved … [and] to defeat an investigation of FGM offences, which are difficult to detect, investigate and prosecute."

How Has Change Happened? An Approach Animated by Public Health and Human Rights

It is instructive to note the kinds of efforts that have helped to produce social change. The United Nations Populations Fund (UNFPA)–United Nations Children's Fund (UNICEF) Joint Programme on Female Genital Mutilation/Cutting (2016) emphasise the positive effects on change of community declarations of commitment to abandonment of FGM; educational efforts involving health programs; educational efforts involving religious leaders; community education sessions; and education and information via the media. Given the significance of maternal education on the practice of FGM/C, educational efforts are paramount for the entire community but with a special focus on girls and women (Asekun-Olarinmoye and Amusan 2008; Wakabi 2007; Yoder et al. 2004). Wakabi (2007) noted several such features of successful interventions: public discussion of issues around FGM; cooperation between government and nongovernment agencies, religious leaders, societal opinion leaders and health experts in educating the public about FGM; using culturally and linguistically appropriate methods of communication with the community, including theatre and role-play, to heighten awareness of the issues and catalyse self-starting cultural change; involving men and community leaders in these educational and awareness-raising efforts (including facilitating conversations between men and women who have suffered FGM); education of young girls; and promoting awareness of key human rights instruments.

The review by Muteshi and Sass (2006) drew five conclusions about the approaches generally understood to be most effective in helping to reduce FGM and to change attitudes towards it. First, some approaches are inadequate or insufficient by themselves (for example, criminal prohibition, training and conversion of circumcisers, and the health risk approach). Second, the best approaches are both multipronged and situated in a philosophy of sustained efforts to support gender equality and the empowerment of women and girls. This includes programs that improve women's health and well-being overall, as well as their liberty and autonomy and freedom from violence. Individuals and communities must commit to abandoning FGM by dialogue and collective will, and there must be safe environments for such dialogue. Efforts to encourage discussion and education are necessary. The most effective interventions are commenced and conducted by local communities, address their culture, and have long-term involvement and commitment to consensus and the empowerment of individuals and the community. They can also be considered to involve a shift in attitudes towards the concept of male honour, and what kinds of conduct are honourable and dishonourable, thereby using as a lever for social change a refined idea of personal identity and status (Appiah 2010). One can be considered strong, masculine, and honourable if one promotes and defends girls' and women's rights to bodily inviolability, rather than oppressing them. The need for an approach using multiple strategies recognizes the complex nature and reasons for the practice, as well as its deep cultural roots. Regarding this, the Women's Empowerment-Community Consensus' model by Toubia et al. (2003) is similar, in prioritizing and promoting the self-empowerment of women and girls by developing their awareness, and their decision-making capacity in matters including economic empowerment, and in building community consensus about the need to protect women's and children's rights, through means including the support of powerful social agents.

Third, for sustainability and the avoidance of stigma to 'early adopters', programs must have features supporting the changes being made and the people adopting them. Fourth, governments must support individuals and communities by facilitating these changes by adopting clear national laws and policies promoting abandonment, and appropriation of resources to intensify successful programs. Cross-sector collaboration between government departments and nongovernment agencies is essential. Fifth, donors, government and nongovernment agencies need to coordinate their efforts, and require sufficient investment to disseminate programs. These approaches clearly embody a broad public health model combining the efforts of individuals, institutions and community agencies, supported by public health law reforms promoting fundamental human rights and social justice.

Child Sex Tourism and Overseas Travel Restrictions for Child Sex Offenders

Child sex tourism occurs where adults, usually adult men, travel to other jurisdictions or destinations to gain access to children for sexual purposes. The individuals involved may or may not have a criminal record, but a substantial proportion of such persons do have a criminal record for serious child sex offences. The region where this phenomenon was first identified was Southeast Asia, in countries including Hong Kong, the Philippines, Taiwan and Thailand, with the offenders initially coming from Western nations in Europe and the USA. These traditional destinations for foreign child sex offenders still attract offenders, with other countries such as Cambodia, Indonesia and Vietnam now thought to also be prominent destinations. Most child sex offenders in these nations are still citizens, but substantial minorities are foreign nationals. Authorities report, for example, that around 10–15% of offenders in the Philippines, and around one quarter of offenders in Cambodia, are foreign nationals (ECPAT International 2016).

Trends in Geographical Areas of Concern Demographic and economic shifts strongly influence human movement and therefore the demand for sex, including sexual exploitation of children. From 2009–2013, for example, the number of outgoing Chinese tourists and travellers more than doubled. Nongovernment agencies have gathered information on areas of particular concern, and have identified changes in trends in child sex tourism (ECPAT International 2016). This data is important as it should inform national governments about the priority they should afford to efforts to respond, especially where they have not yet taken any steps to minimise the practice. ECPAT International (2016) reported, for example, that increased business travel by East Asians over the past 20 years, within and outside the region, is an important change increasing the risk of sexual exploitation of children in travel and tourism. ECPAT International (2016) also suggested that evidence indicates that after Thai citizens, Chinese men are now the largest group of travellers and tourists buying sex with adults and minors in Thailand, and other high risk areas for child sexual exploitation by Chinese men are the border areas between China's Yunnan province and Myanmar, Lao PDR, Vietnam, and Cambodia.[11]

Multinational Responses Recent developments involving national legislation and policy approaches, and international cooperation, aim to respond to child sex tourism. Many nations have enacted domestic laws specifically prohibiting sexual acts committed against children overseas.[12] Nations are also enacting preventative legislation to control the movement of individuals who are deemed dangerous to children due to their criminal records. Countries are also working together to respond to this phenomenon by harnessing intelligence from their collective law enforcement agencies and sharing this information to enable capture of those with criminal records who are travelling for sinister motives and or who are breaking the conditions of their domestic law by travelling without permission or when it is simply prohibited because of the nature of their crimes and due to the application of the relevant domestic law.

These efforts are consistent with aspects of the Optional Protocol directed at such activity. At least insofar as these prevention efforts apply to ban international travel where passports are required, these mechanisms should prove to be an effective preventative tool, either to prevent specific individuals from entering a jurisdiction in the first place, or to monitor their movements while there. While there is not information about those who evade these restrictions, data on detected offenders demonstrates substantial success. For example, in the 2015 fiscal year, the U.S. Immigration and Customs Enforcement's Homeland Security Investigations, which administers Operation Angel Watch, made over 2100 notifications to more than 90 countries.[13]

[11] ECPAT International (2016) reported on these shifts for all major regions: East Asia, Europe, Latin America, the Middle East and North Africa, North America, The Pacific, South Asia and Southeast Asia, Sub-Saharan Africa.

[12] In Australia, for example, the Criminal Code Act 1995 (Cth) sets out a range of these offences regarding sex with a child, including s 272.8 (Sexual intercourse with child outside Australia); s 272.9 (Sexual activity (other than sexual intercourse) with child outside Australia); s 272.10 (Aggravated offence—child with mental impairment or under care, supervision or authority of defendant); s 272.11 (Persistent sexual abuse of child outside Australia); s 272.14 (Procuring child to engage in sexual activity outside Australia); s 272.15 ("Grooming" child to engage in sexual activity outside Australia); s 272.18 (Benefiting from offence against this Division); s 272.19 (Encouraging offence against this Division); s 272.20 (Preparing for or planning offence against this Division); s 273.5 (Possessing, controlling, producing, distributing or obtaining child pornography material outside Australia).

[13] Angel Watch is conducted under HSI's Operation Predator, an international initiative to protect children from sexual predators. Since the launch of Operation Predator in 2003, HSI has arrested

Legal Frameworks: Passport Control, Offender Reporting and Information Sharing

In the United States, Operation Angel Watch has existed since 2007 to respond to the problem of child sex tourism. Managed by the Child Exploitation Investigations Unit of the US Immigration and Customs Enforcement ICE Cyber Crimes Center, the operation is a multi-agency initiative combining the resources and capacities of U.S. Customs and Border Protection (CBP) and the U.S. Marshals Service. In 2016, these efforts were expanded when President Obama signed the International Megan's Law to Prevent Child Exploitation and Other Sexual Crimes Through Advanced Notification of Traveling Sex Offenders (IML). This legislation prohibits the Department of State from issuing a passport to a "covered sex offender" unless it contains a unique identifier.[14] It also enables revocation of previously issued passports that do not have this identifier. This identifier is a statement which reads: "The bearer was convicted of a sex offense against a minor, and is a covered sex offender pursuant to 22 United States Code Section 212b(c)(l)."[15] The provisions apply to any "covered sex offender" which is defined as an individual who is a sex offender as defined in s 21503(f) of title 34; and who is currently required to register under the sex offender registration program of any jurisdiction.

Australia In Australia, recent developments have also strengthened the capacity of law enforcement agencies in this context. The *Passports Legislation Amendment (Overseas Travel by Child Sex Offenders) Act 2017* (Cth) commenced on 13 December 2017. The key aim of the law is to prevent Australian citizens who are listed on a State or Territory child sex offender register with reporting obligations (known as "reportable offenders") from travelling overseas to commit sexual abuse or exploitation against vulnerable children in jurisdictions where their activities are not monitored and where law enforcement frameworks may be less robust. The reforms created new provisions in the Australian Passports Act 2005 including s 12(1A), so that a competent authority – either a court, sex offender registry, or police - can request the Minister to refuse to issue a passport, or to cancel an Australian travel document, because the person is a "reportable offender". Under s 22AA, the Minister must cancel an Australian passport following such a request.

more than 14,000 individuals for crimes against children, including the production and distribution of online child pornography, traveling overseas for sex with minors, and sex trafficking of children. In fiscal year 2015, nearly 2400 individuals were arrested by HSI special agents under this initiative and more than 1000 victims identified or rescued. In addition to creating the Angel Watch Center, the new law provides the authority for the center to receive information from other countries about convicted child predators intending to travel to the United States, and it directs the Secretary of State, in coordination with the Attorney General and Secretary of Homeland Security, to seek agreements and use technical assistance with other countries so that the United States is notified in advance of incoming foreign sex offenders.

[14] Public Law 114–119 in effect October 31, 2017.

[15] https://travel.state.gov/content/travel/en/News/passports/passports-and-international-megans-law.html

Section 12(3) defines a reportable offender as a person: (a) whose name is entered on a State or Territory child protection offender register; and (b) who has reporting obligations under that entry. The reforms also created a new offence in the Criminal Code s 271A.1(1) where an Australian registered child sex offender with reporting obligations[16] travels overseas (or attempts to do so) without prior permission from the relevant competent authority.

In Parliamentary proceedings, it was acknowledged that previous measures were inadequate. In 2016, more than 770 reportable offenders travelled overseas, often without complying with obligations to notify police of their travel.[17] While an offence had existed of planning a child sex tourism offence, it had proved impossible to operationalize, partly due to the difficulty of obtaining evidence in jurisdictions where law enforcement agencies had less capacity to detect offenders. As well, the prior law had allowed cancellation, surrender or refusal of a passport on the basis of a competent authority's assessment of the offender's likelihood to cause harm, this process was so cumbersome that it was not used by any state or territory authorities.

Tension Between Rights, and a Preference for the Child's Right to Protection, Resolved in Favour of Potential Child Victims These developments are significant not only in practice, but because they reflect a theoretical preference. The individual's freedom of movement is generally a cherished right in liberal democracies, and is protected by international instruments – for example, in the ICCPR article

[16] All States and Territories have these kinds of provisions. See, e.g., in Queensland, the Child Protection (Offender Reporting and Offender Prohibition Order) Act 2004 (Qld). Section 5 defines who is a "reportable offender" and s 9 defines what constitutes a "reportable offence" by reference to a list of serious child sex offences. Section 20 requires a reportable offender to report their travel intentions to police if they intend to leave Queensland for 48 or more consecutive hours to travel elsewhere in Australia, or alternatively if they intend leaving Queensland to travel outside of Australia. Section 50 provides strong penalties. A "reportable offender" is an individual who has been sentenced for a specified serious sex crime, with a conviction recorded (there are exceptions based on the number and type of offences, the court's sentence, and the offender's age). Section 24 provides that as soon as practicable after receiving any report of a reportable offender's intention to travel outside Australia, the Police Commissioner must ensure that a copy of the report is given to the Commissioner of the Australian Federal Police; this information-sharing aims to counter child sex tourism. Under s 37, reduced reporting periods apply to children who are convicted of such offences. Section 68 requires the police commissioner to maintain a child protection register. Note that some have criticised the use of these reporting models for juvenile offenders, including on the basis that – at least informed by an analysis of subsequent officially reported criminal offending - they do not result in any subsequent prevention of offending: see, e.g., Sandler, Letourneau, Vandiver, Shields, & Chaffin, 2017). This important issue is complex, since these policies deal with different categories of offender, different kinds of offense, and have multiple purposes. It certainly merits further analysis especially as applied to juvenile offenders, who generally do require differential treatment by criminal justice systems due to their incomplete moral agency and nascent psychosocial skills; however it is beyond the scope of this chapter to explore it further.

[17] Passports Legislation Amendment (Overseas Travel by Child Sex Offenders) Bill 2017, Explanatory Memorandum, p. 2.

12 - and national laws alike. It is significant that the child's right to protection from sexual abuse is being preferred to the adult's right of freedom of movement; while many countries are yet to take steps to respond to this phenomenon, the emerging approaches reflect a newfound priority and seriousness with which sexual abuse and children's rights are perceived and prioritised.

This tension was explicitly recognised and settled recently, for example, in the Australian federal Parliament. The legislature justified these bold measures by explicitly referring to the UNCRC rights in article 3, stating that the child's best interests must be paramount, and explaining that when reportable offenders are in Australia they are monitored and subject to strict reporting requirements; however, if allowed to travel overseas they may evade these obligations, and there is a high risk of re-offending in countries where they are not monitored, where child sexual abuse is rampant, and where legal frameworks are weaker.

In addition, article 34 was expressly offered as a justification for the law: it requires States to take national and multilateral measures to protect children from sexual exploitation. Finally, to resolve the tension between the right to freedom of movement in the ICCPR art 24 and the child's right to protection from sexual abuse, the legislature noted that the right to freedom of movement may be limited where the limitation is provided by law and is necessary to protect the rights and freedom of others. This was further justified by noting that, in conformity with General Comment 27 on this right, the restriction both served the permissible purpose, was necessary to protect the purpose, and was proportional to achieve the protective function since it applied only to a specific class of high risk offenders, endured only as long as their domestic reporting obligations lasted, and included reasonable exceptions on a case-by-case basis (for example, to visit a dying relative).[18]

Technological Challenges

Some Brief Observations on Online Sexual Abuse Generally

The broad phenomenon of online sexual abuse of children is of substantial concern. As well as all the consequences associated with offline child sexual abuse, online exploitation can have unique adverse effects, given the capture of the child's image and its capacity for storage and distribution on an ongoing basis. This field is vast and complex, and has been considered by many researchers, practitioners and non-government organisations (Wortley and Smallbone 2012). Michael Seto's recent but classic work *Internet Sex Offenders* (2013) is an essential resource for a comprehensive understanding of the history, nature and scope of sexual offending against children through online means. Recent significant studies include knowledge generated

[18] Passports Legislation Amendment (Overseas Travel by Child Sex Offenders) Bill 2017, Explanatory Memorandum, p.4–5.

by the Crimes Against Children Research Center at the University of New Hampshire, including through the National Juvenile Online Victimization Project studies (e.g., Mitchell et al. 2010, 2011; Wolak et al. 2008, 2011a, b; Ybarra and Mitchell 2005).

National legal and policy responses have flourished. Domestically, jurisdictions can create legislation to punish offences committed beyond and within their geographical boundaries. In Australia, for example, the Criminal Code Act 1995 (Cth) Division 10.6 creates offences related to the use of telecommunications services for child pornography material, child abuse material, and actual online sexual activity and grooming.[19] However, these efforts remain challenged by the scale and cross-national nature of offending, the complexity of responding to advanced technological methods of keeping such offending covert, and new modes of exploiting children sexually. In some nations, poverty is one factor apparently contributing to growing parental exploitation of children for commercial gain.[20] Law enforcement work in this field requires extensive resources, specialised skills, and capacity to shoulder a unique psychological and emotional burden of exposure to extremely distressing material. Yet, within and across nations, specialised operations such as Australia's Task Force Argos have made great progress in apprehending prolific offenders and organised criminal groups, and intervening to protect children.

International Efforts Require Ongoing Support and Commitment The United Nations Optional Protocol To The Convention On The Rights Of The Child On The Sale Of Children, Child Prostitution And Child Pornography 2002 recognised multiple significant and increasing problems requiring concerted responses within and across States, and with the cooperation of the internet industry.[21] Most relevantly to the topic of child pornography, the Protocol acknowledged its growing availability on the Internet and other evolving technologies (as well as its relationship with child

---

[19] Offences in relation to "child pornography material" via telecommunications services include: s 471.16 (Using a postal or similar service for child pornography material); s 471.17 (Possessing, controlling, producing, supplying or obtaining child pornography material for use through a postal or similar service); s 474.19 (Using a carriage service for child pornography material); s 474.20 (Possessing, controlling, producing, supplying or obtaining child pornography material for use through a carriage service). Offences in relation to "child abuse material" via telecommunications services include s 471.19 (Using a postal or similar service for child abuse material); s 474.22 (Using a carriage service for child abuse material); s 474.23 (Possessing, controlling, producing, supplying or obtaining child abuse material for use through a carriage service). Offences of grooming and sexual activity via telecommunications services include s 471.24 (Using a postal or similar service to procure persons under 16); s 471.25 (Using a postal or similar service to "groom" persons under 16); s 474.25A (Using a carriage service for sexual activity with person under 16 years of age); s 474.26 (Using a carriage service to procure persons under 16 years of age); s 474.27 (Using a carriage service to "groom" persons under 16 years of age); s 474.27A (Using a carriage service to transmit indecent communication to person under 16 years of age). See also ss 272 and 273.

[20] The Philippines is a key location for organised cybersex involving children (ECPAT International 2016).

[21] Adopted and opened for signature, ratification and accession by General Assembly resolution A/RES/54/263 of 25 May 2000; entered into force on 18 January 2002.

sale, trafficking, and sex tourism), and recalled the 1999 Vienna International Conference on Combating Child Pornography on the Internet and its conclusion calling for the worldwide criminalization of the production, distribution, exportation, transmission, importation, intentional possession and advertising of child pornography.[22]

The key provisions of the Protocol should be emphasised. Most relevantly, Article 1 requires all States Parties to prohibit the sale of children, child prostitution and child pornography. Article 2(c) defines "child pornography" as "any representation, by whatever means, of a child engaged in real or simulated explicit sexual activities or any representation of the sexual parts of a child for primarily sexual purposes." This clearly includes not only any representations involving real children; it also extends to any "non-human" representation of a child. Article 3(1) then requires each State Party to ensure that the production, distribution, dissemination, import, export, offer, sale and possession of child pornography are "fully covered under its criminal or penal law, whether these offences are committed domestically or transnationally or on an individual or organized basis", that this applies to attempts and to anyone who is complicit in participation in such acts (3(2)), and that the offences should be punished by appropriate penalties that take into account their grave nature (3(3)).

From a preventative perspective, article 9 requires the adoption or strengthening of laws, administrative measures, social policies and programmes to prevent child pornography offences, and that this should include awareness-raising in the public and especially for children through education and training about the preventive measures and harmful effects of these offences. Article 9(4) requires States Parties to ensure that all child victims of these offences have access to adequate procedures to seek compensation for damages from those legally responsible. In terms of responses, article 9(3) requires States Parties to take all feasible measures to ensure all appropriate assistance to victims, including full social reintegration and physical and psychological recovery. In terms of international cooperation, Article 10 requires States Parties to take all necessary steps to strengthen multilateral, regional and bilateral arrangements (and cooperation with international non-governmental organizations and international organizations) to prevent, detect, investigate, prosecute and punish those responsible for acts involving child pornography. Article 10(3) aims to address root causes of child pornography, including poverty. Article 10(2) urges international cooperation to assist child victims in their physical and psychological recovery, social reintegration and repatriation.

The aspirations of these efforts are laudable, and in line with a public health approach to this species of child sexual abuse, nations and corporations should continue to respond to online child sexual abuse and adopt measures to prevent it. I will return to this point later in this chapter when discussing a new ethic of technology.

[22] The Protocol also acknowledged the broader environmental influences on these phenomena, including poverty, economic disparities, inequitable socio-economic structures, dysfunctioning families, lack of education, urban-rural migration, gender discrimination, irresponsible adult sexual behaviour, harmful traditional practices, armed conflicts and trafficking of children.

In the next section of this chapter, I will focus on sexting activity, with an emphasis on interactions between children and adolescents.

Sexting

Especially in developed economies, children and teenagers have become widespread consumers of technology, and have grown up with this technology as an ever present part of their lives. These so-called "digital natives" have high and growing rates of mobile phone ownership, device usage, and, significantly, a relationship with their peers and the world which is heavily dependent on both device use and personal image and status. Jean Twenge, the world authority on generational change, proposed in her book *iGen* that the most recent big generational shift was connected with technology exposure, use and dependence, and occurred for those born between 1995 and 2012 (Twenge 2017). This shift – unprecedented in nature - was influenced by the advent of smartphones with internet access like the iPhone in 2007, access to Facebook in 2006 for anyone over 13 in 2012, and the emergence of other new social media platforms including Snapchat and Instagram. Twenge (2017) noted device dependence among youth, and highlighted usage trends from the US Monitoring the Future 2013–2015 Report. She related that the average estimated use for high school seniors as two and quarter hours per day texting, another 2 h on the internet, one and a half hours gaming and half an hour on video chat, with patterns for eight graders not dissimilar. These trends are not limited to the USA. In many societies, digital communication through texting and social media has become a dominant method of interaction amongst children and teenagers, and is also common between children and teenagers and adults online.

It can only be expected that children and teenagers will want to behave in roughly the same way as their peers do in participating in the digital world, will be conscious of the image they present of themselves to their peer group, and will crave acceptance and endorsement. These impulses are natural from both developmental perspectives and as a method of survival in the social world. Technological advances enable both positive opportunities for communication and engagement, as well as potential dangers. In recent years, and especially with smartphones enabling the capture and transmission of photos and videos, and other social media enabling communications via text and image, the phenomenon of "sexting" has become possible, and a subject of community concern, scholarly enquiry and legal regulation. Coined by Chalfen (2009), the term sexting generally refers to communications of a sexual nature, including both text messages and a nude/semi-nude images, sent via mobile phones and other electronic means such as social networking sites. Sexting can occur between children – usually, between teenagers - or it can involve adults. In an environment where the use of smartphones, social media and the internet is so pervasive, where children's psychosocial skills are still forming, where social expectations of girls and boys are heavily gendered, and where relationships are negotiated and status secured through digital communications and profiles, many complex issues arise for parents, educational systems,[23] social systems and regulatory bodies. Here, I will briefly consider two broad domains of sexting activity that must be considered by legal systems and policy responses.

Experimental Sexting and Aggravated Sexting: Consent vs Coercion What kinds of sexting exist? Wolak and Finkelhor (2011) analysed over 550 cases obtained from a national survey of law enforcement agencies to identify different categories of behaviour involving youth-produced sexual images,[24] and considered differential levels of harm. They identified two broad categories of sexting behaviour. First, there is "experimental" sexting. This involves conduct between youths, either in the context of an established romantic relationship, to generate romantic interest, or for other reasons such as attention-seeking. These cases do not involve criminal behaviour.

Second, there is "aggravated sexting". Here, the behaviour can involve an adult, in which case the behaviour will normally involve adults considerably older than the child, but which may also involve a very young adult, and an adolescent. Most of these adult-involved cases will involve criminal conduct, but not necessarily all, depending on the ages of the parties involved, and the circumstances of the behaviour. As well, aggravated sexting can involve only youths, where there is either intent to harm, or reckless misuse of the technology. This can constitute criminal or abusive behaviour, occurring through sexual abuse, extortion, threats; malicious conduct arising from interpersonal conflicts; or creation or sending or showing of images without the knowledge or against the will of a minor who was pictured.

This approach is supported by the systematic review by Cooper et al. (2016). Cooper et al. (2016) considered the motivational, lifestyle and personality factors influencing adolescent sexting practices. They found that sexting is widely varied in context, meaning and intention, and includes consensual and non-consensual acts. They concluded that while sexting can be a means of flirting and enhancing a sexual relationship, it can also lead to victimisation and participation in risky sexual practices. Accordingly, there are activities that are consensual, playful, innocuous, beneficial and pleasurable, occurring between equals without exploitation or harm. In contrast, there are other activities that are coercive, threatening and harmful, occurring in exploitative and unequal circumstances.

Prevalence While prevalence estimates of sexting behaviour have varied widely depending on definitions and methodologies used by different studies, it is not uncommon and may be more frequent in some settings and amongst older youth. Studies with school-based samples with older youth respondents find higher rates. In a study in Texas, Temple et al. (2012) found that 68% of girls and 42% of boys had been asked to send a sexting image, although this figure is elevated due to

[23] One major issue, which cannot be considered further here, is whether schools should allow children to use mobile phones during school hours or on school premises, and related issues regarding sexual victimisation at school, cyberbullying, and liability of educational authorities. This is a substantial issue worthy of extensive analysis.

[24] This was the authors' preferred terminology rather than "sexting".

respondents being aged 14–19. In a study in one school, Strassberg et al. (2013) found nearly 20% of all participants reported they had ever sent a sexually explicit image of themselves using a cell phone. This did not vary by sex, with 18.3% of males and 17.3% of females reporting sending such an image. Almost half of the males (49.7%) and one third of the females (30.9%) reported receiving a sexually explicit picture. Of those who had received such a picture, over one quarter said they had distributed it to others. Rates for sending and receiving images were substantially higher amongst older youth. Significantly, 8.4% reported that they had ever sent a sexually explicit picture that they took of someone else to a third party, with males significantly more likely to report having done so than females.

A study with 800 respondents aged 12 to 17 found 4% of youths reported sending nude or partially nude sexually suggestive pictures (Lenhart 2009). Mitchell et al. (2012) analysed data from a national telephone survey of 1560 young people aged 10–17. Across this age group, they found that 2.5% of young participants had appeared in nude or nearly nude pictures or videos, and 1.8% had self-produced an image. When the definition was restricted to only include images that were sexually explicit (i.e., showed naked breasts, genitals, or bottoms), prevalence was only 1.3%. Slightly more young people (7%) reported receiving nude or nearly nude images of others; and 6% of participants said the image received was sexually explicit. However, few youth reported distributing these images. As could be expected, Wolak et al. (2012) found that studies of adolescent samples show increased sexting prevalence with increasing age.

Consequences The literature does not clearly establish a trend of significant adverse health and behavioural consequences as a result merely of participating in sexting behaviour conceived broadly. This could be expected, especially when considering that much of this activity is consensual and relatively minor. However, the consequences for those who are subjected to aggravated sexting, and especially those whose images are distributed without their consent (or even where this is threatened) can be extremely substantial.

In addition, even for sexting activity construed broadly, there may be some contextually significant outcomes. Sevcikova (2016) analysed data from 17,016 participants aged 11–16 from 25 European countries to examine adverse outcomes for boys and girls, stratified by earlier and later adolescence. It was found that irrespective of age and gender, sexting was associated with emotional problems and alcohol use. These effects generally decreased in later adolescence, but emotional difficulties remained relatively high in older boys. Vaginal sex was associated with sexting in both younger and older boys while, in girls, the association was observed only in the older group. Younger boys with higher self-efficacy were more likely to send sexts than those with lower self-efficacy. Temple et al. (2014) examined whether adolescents who report sexting exhibit more psychosocial health problems, compared to their non-sexting counterparts. Participants were 937 ethnically diverse male and female adolescents from high schools in Texas. Measures included self-report of sexting, impulsivity, alcohol and drug use, and depression and anxiety symptoms. Teen sexting was significantly associated with symptoms of depression, impulsivity, and substance use. However, after adjusting for prior sexual behavior and other demographic variables, sexting was only related to impulsivity and substance use. These results were broadly consistent with a study of 800 young adults aged 18–25 by Benotsch et al. (2013, who found that those who engaged in sexting were more likely to report recent substance use and high-risk sexual behaviors, including unprotected sex and sex with multiple partners.

Coercive Practices Between Teenagers

Choi et al. (2016) found that offline sexual coercion was significantly associated with sending and being asked for a naked image, as well as receiving a naked image without giving permission. The results suggest that sexting could function as an online extension of offline forms of sexual coercion. These findings are consistent with those from a comprehensive study by Wood et al. (2015). The authors analysed data from 4564 young people aged between 14 and 17 in schools across Bulgaria, Cyprus, England, Italy and Norway. They found significant differences in sexting experience by location and gender. However, they found that in general, sexting was associated with positive impacts that were also mutually reciprocal, except for girls in England, who experienced more mixed outcomes.

Wood et al. (2015) urged a nuanced and appropriate response in policy and practice, which recognised this generally positive nature of the phenomenon. However, they also found that in England, Italy and Norway, about half of girls reported a negative impact after sending a sexual image, and twice as many girls reported negative outcomes compared with boys. The study also found that those who reported some form of interpersonal violence and abuse were over twice as likely to have sent or received a sexual image. Also significantly, over a quarter of girls in England who sent a sexual image had been pressured by a partner to send it, and almost half had sent an image to demonstrate their commitment to the partner. In addition, in some countries, substantial proportions of those who had sent an image reported that the image had been distributed to others by their partner. This was experienced by 42% of girls who shared an image in England and 27% of girls in Norway; in both countries these figures substantially exceeded those for boys (13% of boys in England and 12% of boys in Norway). These findings indicate that there are aspects of coercion and lack of consent in both the pressured sending of an image, and in its subsequent distribution to others, especially in these two countries, and that these experiences are significantly gendered.

Sextortion Another coercive practice in this context, whether between teenagers themselves, or between a minor and an adult, occurs where the minor is subjected to a threat to expose their sexual images. Such threats are often termed "sextortion" due to the intention to extort additional pictures, actual sex, or other benefits from the child, based on the threatened outcome should the child refuse. As found by

Wolak and Finkelhor (2016), these experiences manifest in two kinds of situation. First, where after an actual romantic or sexual relationship within which sexual images were taken or shared, an aggrieved partner threatens to disseminate images either to force reconciliation or to embarrass or humiliate the respondent. Second, where a perpetrator who meets a child online uses a sexual image obtained from her (or less often, him) or from another source to demand more images or sexual activity.

Wolak et al. (2018) found that such experiences are not uncommon, and should be understood as serious victimizations. Wolak et al. (2018) examined the experiences of minors aged under 18, and young adults aged 18–25. They found the vast majority (91%) of minor victims were female, and 75% were aged 16 or 17 when the threats began. Over half knew the offenders personally, often as romantic partners, and the experiences often co-occurred with teen dating violence. Three quarters of these victims knowingly provided images to offenders, with two thirds feeling pressured to do so. The threats were serious: approximately one-third were threatened with physical assaults and were menaced for over 6 months. Offenders who were extorting from minors were more likely to pressure victims into producing initial sexual images, demand additional images, threaten victims for over 6 months, and urge victims to harm themselves. About half of the minors did not disclose the experience to anyone. Wolak and Finkelhor (2016) found that these experiences often exact an extremely severe personal and psychological toll on the extorted child. They found that 24% of respondents saw a medical or mental health practitioner, and 12% had to move house. They also found that threats are frequently carried out, especially where the parties had previously interacted in person. Threats were carried out or harm was actually caused in approximately 45% of cases, and images were distributed in about 30% of cases.

Criminal Legal Prohibitions and Their Application to Sexting

There is inevitably a time lag between the appearance of a new social phenomenon and the creation of laws to regulate it. Sexting is a prime example of this, and jurisdictions need to take prompt yet careful steps to design adequate legal prohibitions, as well as policy and preventative responses. In the context of sexting, many jurisdictions do not have appropriate, customised criminal prohibitions, and instead either have no adequate prohibitions, or rely problematically on other prohibitions not intended for this specific activity. For example, in the US, prosecutions for sextortion often rely on other criminal statutes, such as those against hacking, child pornography, harassment, extortion, stalking, and privacy violations (Wolak and Finkelhor 2016). Similarly, in responding to sexting generally, current legal frameworks are generally in need of reform. Key issues include the identification of what kinds of activity should and should not be prohibited, and how provisions that prohibit certain kinds of activity should be designed to adequately capture the proscribed behaviours while including appropriate exceptions for permissible activity.

Consensus on the Appropriate Nature of Legal Regulation There is broad acceptance that legal systems should not criminalise consensual sexting that does not involve otherwise criminal behaviour. This conclusion has been reached through arguments premised on child development (Thomas and Cauffman 2013), and on the basis that this activity is properly regarded as being within the scope of children's human rights, including freedom of expression in genuinely consensual circumstances, privacy, and sexual autonomy (Crofts et al. 2015; Gillespie 2013; Shariff 2015; Simpson 2013; Spooner and Vaughn 2016; Villacampa 2017; Wolak and Finkelhor 2011). Instead, criminal prohibitions should be restricted to cases of non-consensual or "aggravated" sexting on Wolak and Finkelhor's typology, including sextortion.

Problems in Existing Laws Against Child Pornography Being Used for Consensual Sexting Laws have been created in many jurisdictions to respond to the staggering scale of child pornography and online child sexual abuse generally (Akdeniz, 2008; McGlynn and Rackley 2017; Thomas and Cauffman 2014; Wortley and Smallbone 2012). In Australia, for example, Commonwealth and State laws regulate and respond to material considered to be either child pornography material, child exploitation material, or child abuse material, and the use of new technological means to store, create and distribute it. State and Territory criminal laws contain numerous provisions prohibiting the possession, distribution, and creation of "child exploitation material", or "child pornography", or "child abuse material". Some jurisdictions have a single definition section in which these various concepts are contained, which then connect with the various prohibitions, while others have separate definitions provisions and more detailed discrete prohibitions.[25] For example, in New South Wales, the *Crimes Act 1900* s 91H(2) prohibits the production, dissemination, and possession of child abuse material. "Child abuse material" is defined in s 91FB as:

> material that depicts or describes, in a way that reasonable persons would regard as being, in all the circumstances, offensive:
>
> (a) a person who is, appears to be or is implied to be, a child as a victim of torture, cruelty or physical abuse, or
> (b) a person who is, appears to be or is implied to be, a child engaged in or apparently engaged in a sexual pose or sexual activity (whether or not in the presence of other persons), or
> (c) a person who is, appears to be or is implied to be, a child in the presence of another person who is engaged or apparently engaged in a sexual pose or sexual activity, or
> (d) the private parts of a person who is, appears to be or is implied to be, a child.

[25] See, e.g., Crimes Act 1900 (ACT) ss 64–65; Crimes Act 1900 (NSW) s 91H, 91FA-FB; Criminal Code (NT) s 125B; Criminal Code 1899 (Qld) ss 228A-E; Criminal Law Consolidation Act 1935 (SA) ss 62–63; Criminal Code 1924 (Tas) s 1A; ss130-130G; Crimes Act 1958 (Vic) ss 51C, 51D, 51G; Criminal Code Act 1913 (WA) ss 217-221A.

(2) The matters to be taken into account in deciding whether reasonable persons would regard particular material as being, in all the circumstances, offensive, include:
(a) the standards of morality, decency and propriety generally accepted by reasonable adults, and
(b) the literary, artistic or educational merit (if any) of the material, and
(c) the journalistic merit (if any) of the material, being the merit of the material as a record or report of a matter of public interest, and
(d) the general character of the material (including whether it is of a medical, legal or scientific character).
(3) Material that depicts a person or the private parts of a person includes material that depicts a representation of a person or the private parts of a person (including material that has been altered or manipulated to make a person appear to be a child or to otherwise create a depiction referred to in subsection (1)).

Notably, the definition encompasses not only real human persons, and any "representation" of a person. Similarly, at the federal level, legislation commenced in 2005 prohibiting the use of postal services, carriage services, mobile phones, and other technology to possess, control, produce, supply or obtain material defined as "child pornography material" or "child abuse material".[26]

---

[26] Criminal Code Act 1995 (Cth) Chapter 10—National infrastructure; Part 10.6 Telecommunications Services: Division 474—Telecommunications offences - Subdivision D—Offences relating to use of carriage service for child pornography material or child abuse material. The provisions make it an offence to use a carriage service for child pornography material (s 474.19) or for child abuse material (474.22); and to possess, control, produce, supply or obtain child pornography material (s 474.20) or child abuse material (474.23) for use through a carriage service. The definitions of "child abuse material" and "child pornography material" are as follows:

"Child abuse material" is defined by s 73.1 as: (a) material that depicts a person, or a representation of a person, who: (i) is, or appears to be, under 18 years of age; and (ii) is, or appears to be, a victim of torture, cruelty or physical abuse; and does this in a way that reasonable persons would regard as being, in all the circumstances, offensive; or (b) material that describes a person who: (i) is, or is implied to be, under 18 years of age; and (ii) is, or is implied to be, a victim of torture, cruelty or physical abuse; and does this in a way that reasonable persons would regard as being, in all the circumstances, offensive.

"Child pornography material" is defined by s 73.1 as: (a) material that depicts a person, or a representation of a person, who is, or appears to be, under 18 years of age and who: (i) is engaged in, or appears to be engaged in, a sexual pose or sexual activity (whether or not in the presence of other persons); or

(ii) is in the presence of a person who is engaged in, or appears to be engaged in, a sexual pose or sexual activity; and does this in a way that reasonable persons would regard as being, in all the circumstances, offensive; or (b) material the dominant characteristic of which is the depiction, for a sexual purpose, of:

(i) a sexual organ or the anal region of a person who is, or appears to be, under 18 years of age; or (ii) a representation of such a sexual organ or anal region; or (iii) the breasts, or a representation of the breasts, of a female person who is, or appears to be, under 18 years of age; in a way that reasonable persons would regard as being, in all the circumstances, offensive; or (c) material that describes a person who is, or is implied to be, under 18 years of age and who: (i) is engaged in, or is implied to be engaged in, a sexual pose or sexual activity (whether or not in the presence of other persons); or (ii) is in the presence of a person who is engaged in, or is implied to be engaged in, a sexual pose or sexual activity; and does this in a way that reasonable persons would regard as being, in all the circumstances, offensive; or (d) material that describes: (i) a sexual organ or the anal region of a person who is, or is implied to be, under 18 years of age; or (ii) the breasts of a female person who is, or is implied to be, under 18 years of age; and does this in a way that reasonable persons would regard as being, in all the circumstances, offensive.

These laws were created, rightly, to respond to child pornography material and child abuse material. They were not developed to regulate consensual behaviour between adolescents engaging in self-regarding sexual activity or genuinely consensual peer-to-peer sexual activity. Laws created to prohibit and respond to child pornography have not been updated to clearly exclude consensual sexting behaviour, which may be either merely self-regarding material created by young people (e.g. taking a photo/video of yourself and not distributing it) or is genuinely consensual private material created by and for young people involved in romantic relationships (e.g., one partner sending an image of themselves to a partner, or one or both partners sharing images of both parties together).

As an example, in South Australia, the Criminal Law Consolidation Act 1935 s 63A makes it an offence to possess child exploitation material. Section 63 makes it an offence to produce or disseminate child exploitation material. It states:

> A person who: (a) produces, or takes any step in the production of, child exploitation material knowing of its pornographic nature; or (b) disseminates, or takes any step in the dissemination of, child exploitation material knowing of its pornographic nature, is guilty of an offence.
>
> Maximum penalty: (a) for a basic offence—imprisonment for 10 years; (b) for an aggravated offence—imprisonment for 12 years.

Section 62 defines "child exploitation material" as material:

> (a) that—
> (i) describes or depicts a child under, or apparently under, the age of 17 years engaging in sexual activity; or
> (ii) consists of, or contains, the image of (or what appears to be the image of) a child under, or apparently under, the age of 17 years, or of the bodily parts of such a child, or in the production of which such a child has been or appears to have been involved; and
> (b) that is of a pornographic nature;
>
> "disseminate"—a person disseminates child exploitation material if the person—
> (a) sends, supplies, exhibits, transmits or communicates it to another, or enters into an agreement or arrangement to do so; or
> (b) makes it available for access by another (including access by means of a computer) or enters into an agreement or arrangement to do so;
>
> "material" includes—
> (a) any written or printed material; or
> (b) any picture, painting or drawing; or
> (c) any carving, sculpture, statue or figure; or
> (d) any photographic, electronic or other information or data from which an image or representation may be produced or reproduced; or
> (e) any film, tape, disc, or other object or system containing any such information or data;
>
> "pornographic nature"—material is of a pornographic nature for the purposes of this Division if the material is intended or apparently intended—
> (a) to excite or gratify sexual interest; or
> (b) to excite or gratify a sadistic or other perverted interest in violence or cruelty;
> Note—See also section 63C(1).[27]

[27] Section 63C(1) states that in determining whether material to which a charge of an offence relates is of a pornographic nature, the circumstances of its production and its use or intended use

"private act" means—
(a) a sexual act; or
(b) an act involving an intimate bodily function such as using a toilet; or
(c) an act or activity involving undressing to a point where the body is clothed only in undergarments; or
(d) an activity involving nudity or exposure or partial exposure of sexual organs, pubic area, buttocks or female breasts;

"prurient purpose"—a person acts for a prurient purpose if the person acts with the intention of satisfying his or her own desire for sexual arousal or gratification or of providing sexual arousal or gratification for someone else.

These laws may apply appropriately to cases of aggravated sexting, although even here, arguably the laws need to be amended to properly accommodate the kinds of behaviour engaged in, and to respond to the harms done (McGlynn and Rackley 2017; Najdowski 2017). McGlynn and Rackley (2017), who have called the non-consensual creation and/or distribution of private sexual images "image-based sexual abuse", argue that the current approach in most jurisdictions fails victim survivors, potential defendants and society as a whole. They have identified a problem that many criminal law responses aimed, for example, at revenge pornography as a form of aggravated sexting, do not adequately accommodate the range of behaviour warranting prohibition. For example, current provisions may require an intention to cause distress or harm, and many instances of damaging behaviour may not have that specific intent, but nevertheless need to be prohibited. They may be distributed, for example, for financial gain, social bonding, status elevation, or amusement.

However, just as problematically, because of the way the laws are framed, they may in some instances also technically apply to consensual sexting activity. It is highly problematic that despite the consensus in the literature about the appropriate non-punitive response to consensual sexting, criminal prosecutions for consensual sexting have been brought under the standard, generic prohibitions against child pornography in many jurisdictions. These laws were clearly, and appropriately, designed to respond to non-consensual exploitative child pornography, and should be used in those cases. However, they should not be used against children and teenagers who are acting in either purely self-regarding conduct, or in consensual relationships with a peer. This stance is endorsed by Wolak and Finkelhor (2011), who recommended a nuanced approach depending on the circumstances and whether the conduct involved the kinds of features they described in the aggravated category of case, as reflected in some US state laws.

An example of inappropriate prosecution can be seen in a South Australian case. In November 2017, a 16 year old boy was prosecuted for taking photographs of his own genitals and sending them to his girlfriend. He was charged with two counts of

may be taken into account, but no such circumstance can deprive material that is inherently pornographic of that character. Section 63C(2)–(4) set out circumstances under which dealing with child exploitation material is lawful, including actions required for the administration of justice, good faith actions done to advance legal, medical or scientific knowledge, and actions for genuine artistic purposes.

producing child exploitation material, pleaded guilty, and was placed on a 12 month supervised obligation order. The boy's relationship had broken down acrimoniously, and his former girlfriend then distributed the images on social media, which ultimately brought his actions to the attention of police (Prosser 2017).

This is a paradigm case of inappropriate technical application of the law, and inappropriate prosecution. These provisions were clearly not intended by Parliament to apply to consensual sexual activity between youth. Prosecutions for such activity are an unsound response. In this South Australian case, there was greater justification for charging the individual who engaged in "revenge porn" by maliciously distributing the images without consent, and who urged their further distribution. In this case, the former girlfriend was referred to a diversionary family conference. Police have extensive powers and discretion about methods of proceeding in response to a complaint. Factors relevant to prosecution decisions include the availability of evidence, the public interest, and the fact that the person is under 18 years old will weigh against a prosecution and will favour less intrusive responses such as warnings and cautions. Furthermore, in South Australia, s 63C(1) states that "In determining whether material to which a charge of an offence relates is of a pornographic nature, the circumstances of its production and its use or intended use may be taken into account but no such circumstance can deprive material that is inherently pornographic of that character." This provision should be capable of guiding police and prosecutors in making appropriate decisions in dealing with consensual sexting images. However, if it is not a sufficiently clear and express protection, then appropriate legislative amendments are required.

New Provisions Some jurisdictions have responded to these problems and have created new laws to fill these conceptual and practical gaps. In the Australian state of Victoria, provisions enacted in 2016 in the Crimes Act 1958 confer protections on children taking images of themselves for their own purposes, or for private, consensual romantic purposes.[28] Section 51 M, for example, states that if a child takes a photo of herself and stores it on her mobile phone, she does not commit an offence against other provisions regarding child abuse material namely s 51B (involving a

[28] Crimes Act 1958 (Vic), Division 8D Child abuse material, ss 51A-51Y inserted by Act 47 of 2016. Section 51A defines "child abuse material" as "material that—

(a) depicts or describes—

(i) a person who is, or who appears or is implied to be, a child—

(A) as a victim of torture, cruelty or physical abuse (whether or not the torture, cruelty or abuse is sexual); or

(B) as a victim of sexual abuse; or (C) engaged in, or apparently engaging in, a sexual pose or sexual activity (whether or not in the presence of another person); or (D) in the presence of another person who is engaged in, or apparently engaged in, a sexual pose or sexual activity; or

(ii) the genital or anal region of a person who is, or who appears or is implied to be, a child; or

(iii) the breast area of a person who is, or who appears or is implied to be, a female child; and

(b) reasonable persons would regard as being, in the circumstances, offensive".

See also Victorian Parliament, Hansard (Legislative Assembly), Second Reading of the Crimes Amendment (Sexual Offences) Bill 2016, 9 June 2016 (Martin Pakula, Attorney-General), pp. 2439–2442.

child in its production), s 51C (production), s 51D (distribution), s 51G (possession) or s 51H (accessing). Section 51P provides a defence to charges for these same offences if the accused who produces or possesses the image, or who distributes it only to the person in the image, is not more than 2 years older than a 16 or 17 year old child who is in the image, acts with the child's consent (or reasonably believes this), and does not distribute the image to any person other than the child.

Similarly, in 2017, the Australian Capital Territory enacted the Crimes (Intimate Image Abuse) Amendment Act 2017, which inserts a new division of offences in the Crimes Act 1900. Part 3A (ss 72A-72I), headed "Intimate image abuse", creates offences of distributing intimate images without consent (s 72D), and of threatening to capture or distribute intimate images (s 72E). Detailed definitions of the concepts of "intimate images" and "distribution" and are set out in ss 72A and 72B respectively. The meaning of "consent" is set out in s 72C(1) as meaning free and voluntary agreement to the distribution of the image, and must be expressed or communicated by the person to the other person. Under s 72C(3), consent is negated if:

(a) the person is under 16 years old;
(b) the person does not have the capacity to consent, whether as a result of cognitive incapacity or otherwise;
(c) the person does not have an opportunity to consent because the person is unconscious, asleep, or otherwise physically helpless;
(d) the person consents because of actual or threatened violence, force or terror directed at the person or someone else; or
(e) the person consents because the person is unlawfully detained.

Moreover, under s 72C(2), clear exceptions to consent are set out, so that a person who consents to the distribution of an image on a particular occasion must not, by reason only of that consent, be taken to have consented to the distribution of the image or any other image on another occasion. As well, a person who consents to the distribution of an image to a particular person or in a particular way must not, by reason only of that consent, be taken to have consented to the distribution of the image or any other image to another person or in another way. Finally, a person who distributes an image of themself is not, by reason only of the distribution, to be regarded as having consented to any other distribution of the image.

Laws Responding to Non-consensual Distribution of Images and "Revenge Pornography" As has been noted (Henry and Powell 2016; McGlynn and Rackley 2017), in the context of sexting generally, as applied to both adults and children, most jurisdictions have not yet taken specific legislative action to respond to these new behaviors. Where laws have been enacted, they may still raise questions due to conceptual ambiguity, and appropriate conceptual and operational scope.

In the context of so-called "revenge pornography", Henry and Powell (2016) noted these legislative developments in many countries, and identified challenges confronting legislators. In the Australian state of Victoria, for example, legislative development occurred in 2014 to prohibit the actual or threatened malicious distribution of intimate images of another person without their consent (Summary Offences Act 1966 ss 41DA, 41DB). Section 41DA(1) ("Distribution of intimate image") provides that a person commits an offence if he or she intentionally distributes an intimate image of a person to another person, and the distribution of the image is contrary to community standards of acceptable conduct. In s 40, an "intimate image "is defined as a moving or still image that depicts a person engaged in sexual activity; or a person in a manner or context that is sexual; or the genital or anal region of a person or, in the case of a female, the breasts". "Consent" is defined as "free agreement". The concept of "community standards of acceptable conduct" is defined as standards of conduct having regard to:

(a) the nature and content of the image;
(b) the circumstances in which the image was captured;
(c) the circumstances in which the image was distributed;
(d) the age, intellectual capacity, vulnerability or other relevant circumstances of a person depicted in the image;
(e) the degree to which the distribution of the image affects the privacy of a person depicted in the image.

Henry and Powell (2016) observed the challenges in identifying when an image is in fact "intimate" or sexual; in applying the acceptable conduct standard; challenges proving malice; and normative questions about the scope of the concept of distribution. Someand perhaps all of these questions are far more easily resolvable in the case of images of children. Nevertheless, legislatures need to carefully consider these questions and ensure the nature and scope of the legal prohibitions is sufficiently strong and precise.

McGlynn and Rackley (2017) recommend that coherent criminal provisions prohibiting image-based sexual abuse should be guided by several requirements. In their view, the scope should be determined by the terms 'private and sexual', which the authors posit are preferable to formulations such as 'intimate' or 'sexually explicit'. A reasonableness standard should be included to provide flexibility to deal with the range of offenders' actions of perpetrators. The prohibition should apply wherever there is an intention to create and/or distribute private sexual images without consent, regardless of the presence of malice. The prohibition must cover threats to distribute images without consent, as well as actual distribution. Due to the range of technological capacities to create and distribute images, the law must cover the non-consensual creation and distribution of private sexual images by any relevant means, including through manipulation of images.

Finally, the offences should be framed as sexual offences, not as communication offences, to appropriately reflect the harms done and the broader social context, which are vital to discharge the law's role in establishing social norms through its expressive function. These recommendations are sound and apply generally to cases involving minors. In addition, I would suggest that there should be clear exceptions to demarcate permissible behaviour, and to recognise the gendered experience of females and males, there should be clear and robust definitions and requirements for consent, as exemplified by the provisions referred to above. In addition, there must be clear guidelines to police and prosecutors defining which kinds of case warrant prosecution.

All these developments would refine the criminal law, and ideally should be accompanied by an appropriate remedy in civil law. Those who suffer harm from such actions can experience extensive psychological injuries, damage to reputation, lost schooling and employment, and may endure other costs such as having to relocate. Especially in these cases, injured individuals need to be able to obtain compensation for injuries. While some existing common law remedies may provide compensation in some circumstances, McGlynn and Rackley (2017) are correct in asserting that this context may call for a new specific statutory civil action for image-based sexual abuse, providing access to injunctions and compensation.

Prevention Considerations and Education of Children and Adolescents

Technological advances have placed in children's hands the capacity to enjoy new forms of communication and consensual sexual behaviour, but have also created a vehicle through which they can be exposed to new kinds of harm and themselves inflict these harms. A public health approach to prevention that is consistent with social justice and developmental norms must first ensure that children and adolescents are never inappropriately punished for either purely self-regarding behaviour, or for genuinely consensual behaviour. The appropriate target of the criminal law should only be on non-consensual behaviour, or aggravated sexting on Wolak & Finkelhor's model, including the distribution of images to a third party without consent; and even here, the full range of criminal law responses should be considered and applied appropriately after consideration of all the circumstances. There is strong support in the literature for this conclusion (Barrense-Dias et al. 2017; Harris et al. 2013; McGlynn and Rackley 2017; Thomas and Cauffman 2014).

The second major priority of such an approach must be a focus on education to build children's capabilities in the multiple dimensions connected with technology use and access to information (Nussbaum 2011). A meta-analysis of standard child sexual abuse prevention programs showed that they do have benefits in improving children's knowledge, self-protective behaviors, and disclosures (Walsh et al. 2015). It seems plausible that well-designed prevention programs directed towards responsible and safe use of technology, perhaps aligned with comprehensive education in sex and relationships, can have positive effects. The strong attachment to such devices and the awareness of the prevalence of sexting activity should provide children and adolescents with a self-serving motivation to engage with such efforts.

Harris et al. (2013) proposed a prevention framework based on developmental science, and a public health approach integrating families, peers, and the community rather than harsh disciplinary actions or legal prosecution. Villacampa (2017) urged education to prevent particularly harmful expressions of sexting to aim to ensure that where sexting does occur, it is safe and consensual, and that teenagers are aware of potential risks and strategies to adopt to maximise safety. Such education should also include making youths aware that coercive behaviour related to sexting is a type of intimate partner aggression, and is unethical, and may breach the jurisdiction's criminal law. Finally, for such educational programmes to be effective, both parents and teachers must also receive equally reliable information and training on this phenomenon, to complement that offered to the teenagers.

In their study of sextortion, Wolak et al. (2018) considered prevention programs as an avenue for addressing sextortion, teen dating violence, and related problems. They noted that several specific programs aimed at middle and high school students are effective at reducing teen dating violence and other forms of youth interpersonal violence. These programs - Safe Dates, Green Dot, and The Fourth R - do not directly address sextortion, but Wolak et al. (2018) posited that they include elements that can help potential victims by teaching adolescents to recognize unhealthy relationships and develop skills to deal with pressurised situations, and educate bystanders about how to intervene. As noted by Wolak et al. (2018), some of these programs also address the underlying gender inequality serving to facilitate dating violence and threats of sextortion (Lundgren and Amin 2014). Similarly, in the context of sextortion, Wolak and Finkelhor (2016) recommended increased public awareness to promote disclosure and victim support; prevention curricula in the education system; bystander mobilization to stop perpetration of the activity and support victims; and, importantly, involving the technology industry to develop interventions, respond effectively to those disclosing online; implementing practical methods to prohibit sextortion; and enhancing law enforcement's capacity to respond appropriately to sextortion cases.

A New Ethic of Technology

All such efforts through legal, educational and health systems to deal with these varied manifestations of online child sexual abuse may be conceived as an essential part of a movement towards a new ethic of technology. Given the rapid and unstoppable progression of the digital revolution and the ubiquity of communication through technological devices, the need to advance our understanding and improve our responses to the regulation and consumption of technology is pressing and will only become more significant. The number of mobile phone users in the world is expected to pass five billion by 2019, and most market growth is attributable to consumption of smartphones; by 2018, the proportion of smartphone use within all mobile phone use was 50% and growing, and the number of smartphone users in the world is expected to reach 2.7 billion by 2019 (Statista 2018).[29]

[29] In 2016, an estimated 62.9% of the population worldwide already owned a mobile phone. The mobile phone penetration is forecasted to continue to grow, rounding up to 67% by 2019. China

The use of these technologies can be addictive, and especially for those whose psychosocial skills are still developing, the capacity to resist compulsive consumption can be compromised. Children and teenagers with smartphones have the ability to access the internet at any time, with great frequency, and the material to which they can now be exposed and the level and immediacy of exposure is arguably different to that previously available in any human society throughout history. Society has a responsibility to support and educate children so that they may become skilled and safe consumers of this technology; children's capabilities in this regard must be promoted and safeguarded at the same time. There are many areas of activity that have tangential connections with child sexual abuse, and which warrant comprehensive separate treatment.

These include, for example, whether and to what extent exposure to online pornography, and especially to violent pornography, affects boys' understandings of sex, expectations about sex, and actual sexual behaviour in relation to themselves and others, and if so, what can and should be done to remedy the problem. Regarding general population studies not limited to recorded sex offenders, the meta-analysis by Wright et al. (2016) found that, for both adolescents and younger adults, pornography consumption is positively correlated with actual acts of sexual aggression, with strongest associations for verbal than physical sexual aggression. In addition, results overall indicated that violent content may be an exacerbating factor. The meta-analysis by Seto and Lalumiere (2010) also found that male adolescent sex offenders reported more early exposure to sex or pornography and atypical sexual interests than non-offenders. Rodenhizer and Edwards (2017) found that dating violence and sexual violence are widespread among adolescents and emerging adults. Their systematic review of literature on the impact of exposure to sexually explicit media and sexually violent media on domestic violence and sexual violence attitudes and behaviors made several significant findings. First, exposure to sexually explicit media and sexually violent media was positively related to DV and SV myths and more accepting attitudes toward DV and SV. Second, exposure to sexually explicit media and sexually violent media is positively related to actual and anticipated domestic violence and sexual violence victimization, perpetration, and bystander non-intervention. Third, sexually explicit media and sexually violent media more strongly affect males' attitudes and behaviors regarding domestic violence and sexual violence. Fourth, pre-existing attitudes to domestic violence and sexual violence and media preferences moderated the relationship between exposure to sexually explicit media and sexually violent media, and attitudes and behaviors to domestic violence and sexual violence.

Individual Liberty, Corporate Responsibility, and Appropriate Regulation This new ethic of technology raises serious questions about the permissible boundaries of individual liberty, the ethical responsibilities of technology manufacturers, and

was predicted to have just over 1.4 billion mobile connections in 2017, while India was forecast to reach over one billion. By 2019, China is expected to reach almost 1.5 billion mobile connections and India almost 1.1 billion. Samsung and Apple are leading smartphone vendors, with about 18% of the market share each.

the legitimate scope of regulatory bodies when pursuing public health and social justice. Clearly, children and adults alike have rights to freedom of expression, privacy, and access to technology. However, as with all rights and freedoms, legitimate restraints can be placed on certain activity when it is judged to produce a greater cost compared to its benefits. In addition, conditions can be placed on the exercise of such rights and freedoms, exemplified, for example, by laws about the age at which an individual can consume certain kinds of sexually explicit material. Agreements about the nature of legitimate restraints are ideally best supported by theoretical arguments, ethical principles and empirical evidence. Thus, laws in their expressive function set social norms, marking the boundary at which otherwise protected rights and freedoms can justifiably be fettered.

The question of the nature and scope of the legal liability of technology corporations is not straightforward: under what circumstances is it justifiable to hold the creator of a social media platform legally liable for harm occasioned to children who use it? Notwithstanding technical difficulties in such a regulatory response using existing common law principles, legislators may be justified in creating new legislative frameworks which compel the entities responsible for creating vehicles of risk or potential harm to not only provide adequate recompense for injuries due to the inherent risks created through such a powerful means of communication. In addition, legislators may be justified in creating new legislative frameworks which require these entities to take reasonably practicably actions to reduce risk and safeguard those who are most vulnerable to misuse. In this sense, law can exercise its expressive function to impose on those who reap enormous financial benefits from the voracious use of these platforms a concomitant duty to protect those users who are especially vulnerable to misuse.

Governmental regulation of technology through various public health law measures, educational efforts, and cooperation with technology creators and companies appear to have great untapped capacity to increase preventive protections in the fields of online child exploitation. Are there better methods to minimise the likelihood of the creation and sharing of sexual images of children? Can new protections be created to control children and adolescents from accessing material that can be considered harmful, undignified or at least not yet able to be handled by a psychosexually undeveloped person? Given the difficulty of reliance on parental education, can and should schools play a particularly significant role in this regard, and what consequences do these concerns and the digital age this have for the teaching profession and current approaches to the curriculum? A new ethic of technology should educate children from early childhood onwards about their obligations towards themselves and others when using it, and should create new protections for children from harm occasioned by misuse. A new ethic of technology should also be embedded within educational systems, given the plain fact that parents may be either unwilling or unable to perform this function. This new ethic should also be directed towards the community as a whole, and should involve major public policy bodies and corporations. Given the likelihood that consumption of these technologies is only growing in all countries, this obligation will only assume more prominence.

Finally in this part of the chapter, some brief observations are warranted concerning an new emerging technological phenomenon, since it is gaining increasing attention, presents difficult questions, and is likely to attain greater prominence. This development is the creation of child-like robots for sexual purposes.

Robotics

The technology used to manufacture life-like robots created for the purpose of sexual interaction has rapidly developed in recent years. While most such endeavours are directed towards making adult-like robots, in recent years some companies in China and Japan have begun designing child-like robots, also for the purpose of sexual interaction. Robotics companies are now selling child-like robots to appeal to adults wishing to have sex with a child, or at least with a child-like simulacra (Sharkey et al. 2017; Torjesen 2017).[30]

Because of their child-like nature, the creation, distribution, purchase and use of these objects possesses singular dimensions of ethical concern, and presents important regulatory challenges. In 2017, an Editorial in Nature urged research to generate evidence regarding the "social, legal and moral implications" of sex with robots (Nature 2017). As reported by Sharkey et al. (2017), some have proposed child robots could be used to treat paedophilia and reduce crime. However, others have pointed to the absence of any empirical evidence that this would have therapeutic effects and not produce adverse effects, and have urged the use of the "precautionary principle" so that until there is sufficient evidence of benefit that it should not be permitted (Cox-George and Bewley 2018). In addition, others have argued that in any case, use of such representations of children is degrading and objectifying, and constitutes its own category of sexual violence (Facchina et al. 2017; Sparrow 2017). There is little doubt that this development marks a new ethical frontier of robotics (Sharkey 2008).

Legislative Prohibitions Are General, Not Specific Few, if any, nations have legislated specifically to respond to this new phenomenon. As briefly outlined below, in nations such as the UK, Canada and Australia, prosecutions tend to rely on existing legislation prohibiting possession and importation of pornographic material or child abuse material. However, this enables a person charged with such an offence to dispute this characterisation and claim these robots are not in fact "pornographic" or "child abuse material", including on the basis that the object is neither a real child, nor depicts a real child. Another argument made by defendants is that the rights to freedom of expression and privacy safeguard these actions and places them beyond the legitimate boundaries of legal regulation.

[30] In Australia, a nation of only 25 million people, Australian authorities seized 126 child sex dolls in the period from 2013 to 2017 (The Herald Sun 2017), and the manufacture of these objects is likely to grow.

United Kingdom In the United Kingdom, the Customs Consolidation Act 1876 s 42 prohibits the importation of indecent and obscene material. This provision prohibits indecent or obscene prints, paintings, photographs, books, cards, lithographic or other engravings, or other indecent or obscene articles. It is an offence under the Customs and Excise Management Act 1979 s 170(2) to be knowingly concerned in attempting to evade the prohibition on indecent and obscene articles imposed by section 42 of the Customs Consolidation Act 1876. The offence can be tried under either provision. The Customs Consolidation Act 1876 does not define the terms "indecent" or "obscene" and so it is necessary to rely on principles of statutory interpretation, dictionary definitions and the changing standards of society as reflected in contemporary court decisions. The maximum term of imprisonment on summary conviction is 6 months. On indictment the maximum is 7 years imprisonment.

In 2017, two British men were convicted and given custodial sentences for the "Importation of Indecent and Obscene Materials" under s 42 *Customs Consolidation Act 1876* and s 170(2) *Customs and Excise Management Act 1979* in relation to the importation of child sex dolls. Both men were also sentenced for other child sex offences (National Crime Agency 2017a, 2017b). These were not the first convictions in the UK, but were notable because offenders in previous prosecutions for importing the dolls have all pleaded guilty. A landmark judgment was delivered in July 2017, when a court found that a child sex doll was "indecent or obscene". This interpretation underpinned a finding that David Turner, aged 72, was found guilty of importing a child sex doll. In June, Turner had admitted possessing indecent images of children (over 34,000 images) but declined to plead over the doll, in the hope the court would rule it was not indecent or obscene. Turner was sentenced on 8 September 2017 to 16 months imprisonment.

Canada In Canada, the Customs Tariff prohibits the importation of any goods referred to in tariff item 9899.00.00, which includes "Books, printed paper, drawings, paintings, prints, photographs or representations of any kind that (a) are deemed to be obscene under subsection 163(8) of the Criminal Code…". Subsection 163(8) of the Criminal Code 1985 states that "any publication a dominant characteristic of which is the undue exploitation of sex, or of sex and any one or more of the following subjects, namely, crime, horror, cruelty and violence, shall be deemed to be obscene."

In 2018, Kenneth Harrison will stand trial for ordering a child sex doll from Japan. Harrison has pleaded not guilty to one count each of possessing child pornography and mailing obscene matter, and charges under the federal customs act of smuggling and possessing prohibited goods. In April 2018, a court rejected his application to dismiss the case (Bradbury 2018). He argued that his civil rights to freedom from discrimination under the Canadian Charter of Rights and Freedoms protected his right to procure and possess the doll. Article 15 of the Charter protects Canadians against discrimination based on race, national or ethnic origin, colour, religion, sex, age, or mental or physical disability. Judge Pike accepted that pedophilia can be defined as a mental disorder for some medical purposes, but concluded "pedophiles are not a member of a group analogous to those enumerated in Section 15". The court ruled that child pornography legislation does not discriminate against pedophiles since it applies to everyone equally. The court acknowledged a 2001 ruling in the Supreme Court of Canada, which concluded that simple possession of child pornography is in fact a form of expression protected by the Charter in Canada. However, the court ruled the risk of harm to children, and therefore society at large, outweighed that protection.

Australia In Australia, as discussed earlier in this Chapter, federal, State and Territory criminal legislation prohibits the importation, production, dissemination, and possession of material considered to be either child pornography material, child exploitation material, or child abuse material. In this context, as an example of a prosecution under these provisions, Zhiguo Miao was convicted in 2016 of two offences of possession of child abuse material, including a child sex doll.[31] He was convicted of breaching the *Crimes Act 1900* (NSW) s 91H(2), which prohibits the production, dissemination, and possession of child abuse material. Because the definition of "child abuse material" is defined broadly in s 91FB(3)[32] to include not only material depicting a human child, but a *representation* of a human child, the scope of this provision is broad enough - and in my opinion appropriately so - to cover non-human representations or simulacra of children. Miao was sentenced to 2 years imprisonment, with a non-parole period of 12 months. The sentencing judge acknowledged that no child was directly harmed by his possession of the doll, but held that "any normalisation of sexual acts committed upon children is capable of increasing the likelihood that children will be abused in that way." James Friess was the person who sold Miao the doll, and he was convicted of dissemination of child abuse material under s 91H(2), and was sentenced to 9 months imprisonment.

However, it is at federal level that importation of child sex robots from overseas jurisdictions is more likely to be policed. There a range of offences under Australian federal law, and while none expressly applies to child sex robots, the existing provisions would apply to these objects. The *Customs (Prohibited Imports) Regulations 1956* regs 4A and 4A(1A) prohibit importation of "objectionable goods", including any goods that:

> *(a) describe, depict, express or otherwise deal with matters of sex, drug misuse or addiction, crime, cruelty, violence or revolting or abhorrent phenomena in such a way that they*

[31] R v Miao [2016] NSWDC 181. He was also convicted of the offence of use of a carriage service to access child pornography (s 474.19(1)(a)(i) of the *Criminal Code 1995* (Cth). On the federal offence, the applicant received a term of 1 year and 3 months. Thus, the sentences were accumulated by 3 months, resulting in a total sentence of 2 years and 3 months with a non-parole period of 1 year and 3 months. Miao appealed his sentence but the appeal was denied: Miao v R [2017] NSWCCA 89.

[32] See the full definition as detailed above: ss (3) states: "Material that depicts a person or the private parts of a person includes material that depicts a representation of a person or the private parts of a person (including material that has been altered or manipulated to make a person appear to be a child or to otherwise create a depiction referred to in subsection (1))".

> *offend against the standards of morality, decency and propriety generally accepted by reasonable adults to the extent that they should not be imported; or*
> *(b) describe or depict in a way that is likely to cause offence to a reasonable adult, a person who is, or who appears to be, a child under 18 (whether the person is engaged in sexual activity or not)...*

Section 233BAB of the *Customs Act 1901 (Cth)* makes it a special offence to import tier 2 goods, including items of child pornography or of child abuse material (s 233BAB(h)). The maximum penalty is imprisonment for 10 years or 2500 penalty units, or both. The Customs Act definition of child pornography material includes a representation of a child, and the interpretation of this should include a child-like robot.[33]

Conflicting Values and the Prospect of Prohibition However, the challenges made in trials in the UK and Canada indicate specific legislative prohibitions may be required, both to resolve any doubt about the scope of the legal prohibitions, and as a means of employing law's capacity to set social norms. This context is a site of values that may conflict. Should an individual be free to buy and use such products? Should a corporation be free to create, market and sell them? Some will assert that an individual's right to freedom of expression and privacy means they should have the right to buy and use such items, and will claim no harm is caused to any real person. Others will claim they should have the right to create such products and sell them, in the absence of evidence of harm. Others will argue that in the absence of solid empirical evidence, there may be some circumstances legitimising their use, especially if it is shown to reduce the sexual abuse of human children. These arguments are challenging and on their surface they are difficult to easily defeat. Danaher (2017) considered whether criminalisation of such activity is warranted, and did not arrive at a clear conclusion, although he accepted that a legitimate function of the criminal law is to demarcate the boundaries of moral behavior, even where that behavior is "extrinsically harmless" or does not have any "direct" victim.

---

[33] The Australian Department of Immigration and Border Protection has published further guidance on importing prohibited, including pornography and other objectionable goods, and this advice specifically mentions child sex dolls (but not robots), as follows (Australian Government Department of Home Affairs 2018): "Objectionable goods include material that describes, depicts, expresses or otherwise deals with matters of sex, drug misuse or addiction, crime, cruelty, violence or revolting or abhorrent phenomena in a way that would offend a reasonable adult. It also includes goods that depict children under 18 years of age in a way that would offend a reasonable adult ... The determination of whether goods are objectionable will take into account the overall context of the goods in addition to certain specific characteristics. In relation to dolls manufactured for a sexual purpose, if the doll appears to be a depiction of a child under 18 years of age, the doll is considered to be objectionable and prohibited under Regulation 4A. Any accessories and instructional or descriptive material (including the marketing of the product) accompanying the doll, will be taken into consideration when the age depiction of the doll is determined...Where the goods are considered to be commercial importations of child pornography and child abuse material, more serious penalties apply including significant fines and/or imprisonment.

A counter-argument based on public health and dignity may provide firm grounds to legitimately circumscribe individual privacy and rights, and the principle of the free market.

As humanity enters a new epoch of artificial intelligence and social robotics, societies must embrace advances in technological capability while preserving human dignity and freedom from violence. Individual liberty, freedom of expression and privacy are not untrammelled rights. There are some types of human conduct which are sufficiently repugnant to fundamental concepts of human dignity and freedom from bodily inviolability and objectification that they may and should be legitimately be prohibited. The use of such representations of children is degrading and objectifying, and constitutes its own category of sexual violence (Facchina et al. 2017; Sparrow 2017). Employing Foster's concept of dignity (Foster 2014), it is against the interests of society as a whole, children as a group, and the individual consumer himself, to engage in sexual acts with child-like robots and other child-like simulacra. This is not to say that those with such impulses should not be able to seek and receive therapeutic assistance and healthier, more dignified outlets for their impulses. A sound public health response that promotes social justice and individual human rights to health and dignity can and should place appropriate controls on behavior while advancing other public policy goals.

References

Adam, T., Bathija, H., Bishai, D., Bonnenfant, Y., Darwish, M., Huntington, D., et al. (2010). Estimating the obstetric costs of female genital mutilation in six African countries. *Bulletin of the World Health Organization, 88*, 281–288.

Almroth, L., Almroth-Berggren, V., Hassanein, O., El Hadi, N., Al-Said, S., Hasan, U., Lithell, B., & Bergstrom, S. (2001). A community based study on the change of practice of female genital mutilation in a Sudanese Village. *International Journal of Gynecology & Obstetrics, 74*, 179–185.

Andersson, S., Rymer, J., Joyce, D., Momoh, C., & Gayle, C. (2012). Sexual quality of life in women who have undergone female genital mutilation: A case–control study. *BJOG, 119*, 1606–1611.

Appiah, K. (2010). *The honor code: How moral revolutions happen*. New York: W.W. Norton.

Asekun-Olarinmoye, E., & Amusan, O. (2008). The impact of health education on attitudes towards female genital mutilation (FGM) in a rural Nigerian community. *The European Journal of Contraception and Reproductive Health Care, 13*(3), 289–297.

Australian Government Department of Home Affairs. (2018). *Importing prohibited and restricted goods*. https://www.border.gov.au/Trav/Impo/Proh

Aziz, S. (2017). Indian court rules sex with minor wife is rape. *Al Jazeera*. 11 October.

Barrense-Dias, Y., Berchtold, A., Surís, J., & Akre, C. (2017). Sexting and the definition issue. *Journal of Adolescent Health, 61*, 544–554.

Barstow, D. G. (1999). Female genital mutilation: The penultimate gender abuse. *Child Abuse & Neglect, 23*, 501–510.

Beaumont, P. (2018). Teenager who killed husband after he raped her is sentenced to death in Sudan. *The Guardian*. 11 May.

Benotsch, E. G., Snipes, D. J., Martin, A. M., & Bull, S. S. (2013). Sexting, substance use, and sexual risk behavior in young adults. *Journal of Adolescent Health, 52*, 307–313.

Bradbury, T. (2018). St. John's judge denies request for dismissal of sex-doll case. *The Telegraph*. 23 April 2018.

Chalfen, R. (2009). It's only a picture: Sexting, smutty snapshots and felony charges. *Visual Studies, 24*, 258–268.

Chaudhuri, E. (2015). *Unrecognised sexual abuse and exploitation of children in child, early and forced marriage*. Bangkok: ECPAT International.

Choi, H., Van Ouytsel, J., & Temple, J. (2016). Association between sexting and sexual coercion among female adolescents. *Journal of Adolescence, 53*, 164–168.

Clark, S., Bruce, J., & Dude, A. (2006). Protecting young women from HIV/AIDS: The case against child and adolescent marriage. *International Family Planning Perspectives, 32*, 79–88.

Cooper, K., Quayle, E., Jonsson, L., & Svedin, C. (2016). Adolescents and self-taken sexual images: A review of the literature. *Computers in Human Behavior, 55*, 706–716.

Cox-George, C., & Bewley, S. (2018). I, sex robot: The health implications of the sex robot industry. *BMJ Sexual & Reproductive Health, 358*, j3353.

Crofts, T., Lee, M., McGovern, A., & Milivojevic, S. (2015). *Sexting and young people*. London: Palgrave Macmillan.

Danaher, J. (2017). Robotic rape and robotic child sexual abuse: Should they be criminalised? *Criminal Law and Philosophy, 11*, 71–95.

de Mause, L. (1998). The history of child abuse. *The Journal of Psychohistory, 25*(3).

ECPAT International. (2016). *Global study on sexual exploitation of children in travel and tourism*. http://www.ecpat.org/resources/global-study-sexual-exploitation-children-travel-tourism-country-specific-reports/

Facchina, F., et al. (2017). Sex robots: The irreplaceable value of humanity. *BMJ, 15*, 358.

Fahmy, A., El-Mouelhy, M., & Ragab, A. (2010). Female genital mutilation/cutting and issues of sexuality in Egypt. *Reproductive Medicine, 18*(36), 181–190.

Foster, C. (2014). Dignity and the ownership and use of body parts. *Cambridge Quarterly of Healthcare Ethics, 23*, 417–430.

Gillespie, A. (2013). Adolescents, sexting and human rights. *Human Rights Law Review, 13*(4), 623–643.

Harris, A., Davidson, J., Letourneau, E., Paternite, C., Miofsky, K. (2013). *Building a prevention framework to address teen "sexting" behaviors*. Office of Juvenile Justice and Delinquency Prevention. National Criminal Justice Reference Service.

Hayoun, M. (2015). Egypt court jails doctor in 'historic' FGM prosecution. *Al Jazeera America*. January 26.

Henry, A., & Powell, N. (2016). Sexual violence in the digital age: The scope and limits of criminal law. *Social & Legal Studies, 25*, 397–418.

International Center for Research on Women. (2005). *Development initiative on supporting health adolescents project. Analysis of quantitative baseline survey data conducted in 2004*. Washington, DC: International Center for Research on Women.

Jabour, B. (2015). Australia's first female genital mutilation trial: How a bright young girl convinced a jury. *The Guardian*. 13 November.

Jain, S., & Kurz, K. (2007). *New insights on preventing child marriage: A global analysis of factors and programs*. Washington, DC: ICRW.

Jenson, R., & Thornton, R. (2003). Early female marriage in the developing world. *Gender and Development, 11*, 9–19.

Joseph, C. (1996). Compassionate accountability: An embodied consideration of female gender mutilation. *The Journal of Psychohistory, 24*, 2–17.

Khanna, T., Verma, R., & Weiss, E. (2013). *Child marriage in South Asia: Realities, responses and the way forward*. Bangkok: UNFPA Asia Pacific Regional Office.

Kidman, R. (2017). Child marriage and intimate partner violence: A comparative study of 34 countries. *International Journal of Epidemiology, 46*, 662–675.

Klugman, J., Hanmer, L., Twigg, S., Hasan, T., & McCleary-Sills, J. (2014). *Voice and agency: Empowering women and girls for shared prosperity*. Washington, DC: The World Bank.

Kmietowicz, Z. (2014). Doctor one of two people to face first UK prosecutions for female genital mutilation. *British Medical Journal, 348*, 2313.
Lenhart, A. (2009). *Teens and sexting: How and why minor teens are sending sexually suggestive nude or nearly nude images via text messaging*. Washington, DC: Pew Internet & American Life Project.
Louis Mikhail, S. (2002). Child marriage and child prostitution: Two forms of sexual exploitation. *Gender and Development, 10*, 43–49.
Lundgren, R., & Amin, A. (2014). Addressing intimate partner violence and sexual violence among adolescents: Emerging evidence of effectiveness. *Journal of Adolescent Health, 56*, 42–50.
Lyons, K. (2015). The Gambia bans female genital mutilation. *The Guardian*. 25 November.
Mathews, B. (2011). Female genital mutilation: Australian law, policy and practical challenges for doctors. *Medical Journal of Australia, 194*(3), 139–141.
Mathews, B. (2013). Legal, cultural and practical developments in responding to female genital mutilation: Can an absolute human right emerge? In C. Sampford, R. Maguire, & B. Lewis (Eds.), *Human rights and shifting global powers* (pp. 207–227). London: Routledge.
Mathews, B., & Collin-Vézina, D. (2017). Child sexual abuse: Toward a conceptual model and definition. *Trauma, Violence, & Abuse, 21*, 1–18.
Mathur, S., Greene, M., & Malhotra, A. (2003). *Too young to wed: The lives, rights and health of young married girls*. Washington, DC: International Center for Research on Women.
McGlynn, C., & Rackley, E. (2017). Image-based sexual abuse. *Oxford Journal of Legal Studies, 37*(3), 534–561.
Mgbako, C., Saxena, M., Cave, A., Farjad, N., & Shin, H. (2010). Penetrating the silence in Sierra Leone: A blueprint for the eradication of female genital mutilation. *Harvard Human Rights Journal, 23*, 111–140.
Mitchell, K., Finkelhor, D., Jones, L., & Wolak, J. (2010). Use of social networking sites in online sex crimes against minors: An examination of national incidence and means of utilization. *Journal of Adolescent Health, 47*, 183–190.
Mitchell, K., Jones, L., Finkelhor, D., & Wolak, J. (2011). Internet-facilitated commercial sexual exploitation of children: Findings from a nationally representative sample of law enforcement agencies in the United States. *Sexual Abuse: A Journal of Research and Treatment, 23*, 43–71.
Mitchell, K., Finkelhor, D., Jones, L., & Wolak, J. (2012). Prevalence and characteristics of youth sexting: A national study. *Pediatrics, 129*, 13–20.
Momoh, C., Ladhani, S., Lochrie, D., & Rymer, J. (2001). Female genital mutilation: Analysis of the first twelve months of a Southeast London specialist clinic. *BJOG, 108*(2), 186–191.
Muteshi, J., & Sass, J. (2006). *Female genital mutilation in Africa: A current analysis of current abandonment approaches*. Nairobi: PATH.
Najdowski, C. (2017). Legal responses to nonconsensual pornography: Current policy in the United States and future directions for research. *Psychology, Public Policy, and Law, 23*(2), 154–165.
National Crime Agency (2017a). *Ex-school governor and church warden jailed after losing landmark child sex doll ruling*. 8 September.
National Crime Agency. (2017b). *Ex-school governor and church warden guilty in landmark child sex doll ruling*. 31 July.
Nature. (2017). AI love you: We cannot pretend that humans won't have sex with robots. *Nature, 547*(7662), 138.
Nour, N., Michels, K., & Bryant, A. (2006). Defibulation to treat female genital cutting: Effect on symptoms and sexual function. *Obstetrics and Gynaecology, 108*(1), 55–60.
Nussbaum, M. (2011). *Creating capabilities*. Cambridge, MA: Harvard University Press.
Obermeyer, C. (1999). Female genital surgeries: The known, the unknown, and the unknowable. *Medical Anthropology Quarterly, 13*(1), 79–106.
Obermeyer, C. (2005). The consequences of female circumcision for health and sexuality: An update on the evidence. *Culture, Health & Sexuality, 7*(5), 443.

Office of the High Commissioner For Human Rights, Joint United Nations Programme on HIV/AIDS, United Nations Development Programme, United Nations Economic Commission for Africa, United Nations Educational, Scientific and Cultural Organisation, United Nations Population Fund et al. (2008). *Eliminating female genital mutilation: an interagency statement.* http://www.who.int/reproductivehealth/publications/fgm/9789241596442/en/

Packer, C., Runnels, V., & Labonte, R. (2015). Canada's response to female genital mutilation: Are we failing our girls? *Canadian Medical Association Journal, 187*(6), 188–189.

Parsons, J., Edmeades, J., Kes, A., Petroni, S., Sexton, M., & Wodon, Q. (2015). Economic impacts of child marriage: A review of the literature. *The Review of Faith & International Affairs, 13*, 12–22.

Partridge, E. (2016). First person to be imprisoned over female genital mutilation in Australia. *Sydney Morning Herald*. 14 June.

Peterman, A., Bleck, J., & Palermo, T. (2015). Age and intimate partner violence: An analysis of global trends among women experiencing victimization in 30 developing countries. *Journal of Adolescent Health, 57*, 624–630.

Prosser, C. (2017). Instagram picture of genitalia lands teenager in court, but no conviction recorded. *ABC News*. 10 November.

Rodenhizer, K., & Edwards, K. (2017). The impacts of sexual media exposure on adolescent and emerging adults' dating and sexual violence attitudes and Behaviors: A critical review of the literature. *Trauma, Violence, & Abuse*, 1–14.

Rumble, L., Peterman, A., Irdiana, N., Triyana, M., & Minnick, E. (2018). An empirical exploration of female child marriage determinants in Indonesia. *BMC Public Health, 18*, 407.

Sandler, J., Letourneau, E., Vandiver, D., Shields, R., & Chaffin, M. (2017). Juvenile sexual crime reporting rates are not influenced by juvenile sex offender registration policies. *Psychology, Public Policy, and Law, 23*, 131–140.

Scolaro, E., Blagojevic, A., Filion, B., Chandra-Mouli, V., Say, L., Svanemyr, J., & Temmerman, M. (2015). Child marriage legislation in the Asia-Pacific region. *The Review of Faith & International Affairs, 13*(3), 23–31.

Sengupta, S. (2017). One by one, Marry-your-rapist laws are falling in the Middle East. *The New York Times*. 22 July.

Seto, M. (2013). *Internet sex offenders*. Washington, DC: American Psychological Association.

Seto, M., & Lalumiere, M. (2010). What is so special about male adolescent sexual offending? A review and test of explanations through metaanalysis. *Psychological Bulletin, 136*(4), 526–575.

Sevcikova, A. (2016). Girls' and boys' experience with teen sexting in early and late adolescence. *Journal of Adolescence, 51*, 156–162.

Shariff, S. (2015). *Sexting and cyberbullying. Defining the line for digitally empowered kids*. New York: Cambridge University Press.

Sharkey, N. (2008). The ethical frontiers of robotics. *Science, 322*(5909), 1800–1801.

Sharkey, N., et al. (2017). *Our sexual future with robots*. The Hague: Foundation for Responsible Robotics.

Simpson, B. (2013). Challenging childhood, challenging children: Children's rights and sexting. *Sexualities, 16*(5/6), 690–709.

Sparrow, R. (2017). Robots, rape, and representation. *International Journal of Social Robotics, 9*, 465–477.

Spooner, K., & Vaughn, M. (2016). Youth sexting: A legislative and constitutional analysis. *Journal of School Violence, 15*(2), 213–233.

Statista (2018). *Number of mobile phone users worldwide from 2013 to 2019* (in billions). https://www.statista.com/statistics/274774/forecast-of-mobile-phone-users-worldwide/

Strassberg, D., McKinnon, R., Sustaíta, M., & Rullo, J. (2013). Sexting by high school students: An exploratory and descriptive study. *Archives of Sexual Behavior, 42*, 15–21.

Temple, J. R., Paul, J. A., van den Berg, P., Le, V. D., McElhany, A., & Temple, B. W. (2012). Teen sexting and its association with sexual behaviors. *Archives of Pediatrics & Adolescent Medicine, 166*, 828–833.

Temple, J., Le, V., van den Berg, P., Ling, Y., Paul, J., & Temple, B. (2014). Brief report: Teen sexting and psychosocial health. *Journal of Adolescence, 37*, 33–36.

The Herald Sun. (2017). *How Australia became the mail order capital for sick, full-sized child dolls for sex*. 25 September.

Thomas, A., & Cauffman, E. (2014). Youth sexting as child pornography: Developmental science supports less harsh sanctions for juvenile sexters. *New Criminal Law Review, 17*, 631–651.

Topping, A. (2015). Nigeria's female genital mutilation ban is important precedent, say campaigners. *The Guardian*. 30 May.

Torjesen, I. (2017). Society must consider risks of sex robots. *BMJ, 358*, j3267.

Toubia, N. (1994). Female circumcision as a public health issue. *New England Journal of Medicine, 331*(11), 712–716.

Toubia, N., & Sharief, E. (2003). Female genital mutilation: Have we made progress? *International Journal of Gynaecology and Obstetrics, 82*, 251–261.

Turcotte, M. (2018). Where maternal health and child marriage intersect. *Ms Magazine*. 11 April.

Twenge, J. M. (2017). *iGen: Why today's super-connected kids are growing up less rebellious, more tolerant, less happy and completely unprepared for adulthood* and what that means for the rest of us*. New York: Simon & Schuster.

UN News Centre. (2016). *Majority oppose female genital mutilation in countries where practice persists – UN agency*. 15 July.

UNFPA. (2013). *State of the world population 2013: Motherhood in childhood: Facing the challenge of adolescent pregnancy*. New York: UNFPA.

UNFPA-UNICEF Joint Programme on Female Genital Mutilation/Cutting. (2016). *Accelerating change: By the numbers – Annual report of the UNFPA–UNICEF joint programme on female genital mutilation/cutting*.

UNICEF. (2005). *Early marriage: A harmful traditional practice: A statistical exploration*. New York: UNICEF.

UNICEF. (2014). *Ending child marriage: Progress and prospects*. New York: UNICEF.

UNICEF. (2016). *Female genital mutilation/cutting: A global concern*. New York: UNICEF.

UNICEF Indonesia. (2016). *Child marriage in Indonesia: Progress on pause*. Jakarta: UNICEF.

United Nations General Assembly. (2012). *Resolution 11331, Intensifying global efforts for the elimination of female genital mutilations*. 20 December, New York.

United Nations Human Rights Council. (2014). *Preventing and eliminating child, early and forced marriage: Report of the office of the united nations high commissioner for human rights*. United Nations General Assembly Document A/HRC/26/22.

United Nations Population Fund. (2014). *Implementation of the international and regional human rights framework for the elimination of female genital mutilation*.

Villacampa, C. (2017). Teen sexting: Prevalence, characteristics and legal treatment. *International Journal of Law, Crime and Justice, 49*, 10–21.

Vujkovic, M. (2018). First criminal prosecution of female genital mutilation in Queensland goes to trial. *ABC News*. 21 May.

Wakabi, W. (2007). Africa battles to make female genital mutilation history. *The Lancet, 69*, 1069–1070.

Walsh, K., Zwi, K., Woolfenden, S., & Shlonsky, A. (2015). School-based education programmes for the prevention of child sexual abuse (Review). *The Cochrane Library, 2015*, 1–121.

Wolak, J., & Finkelhor, D. (2011). *Sexting: A typology*. https://scholars.unh.edu/ccrc/48/

Wolak, J., & Finkelhor, D. (2016). *Sextortion: Findings from a survey of 1,631 victims*. Durham: Crimes against Children Research Center, University of New Hampshire.

Wolak, J., Finkelhor, D., Mitchell, K., & Ybarra, M. (2008). Online "predators" and their victims: Myths, realities, and implications for prevention and treatment. *American Psychologist, 63*, 111–128.

Wolak, J., Finkelhor, D., & Mitchell, K. (2011a). Child pornography possessors: Trends in offender and case characteristics. *Sexual Abuse: A Journal of Research and Treatment, 23*, 22–42.

Wolak, J., Finkelhor, D., Mitchell, K., & Jones, L. (2011b). Arrests for child pornography production: Data at two time points from a national sample of U.S. law enforcement agencies. *Child Maltreatment, 16*, 184–195.

Wolak, J., Finkelhor, D., & Mitchell, K. (2012). *Trends in law enforcement responses to technology-facilitated child sexual exploitation crimes: The Third National Juvenile Online Victimization Study (NJOV-3)*. Durham: Crimes against Children Research Center.

Wolak, J., Finkelhor, D., Walsh, W., & Treitman, L. (2018). Sextortion of minors: Characteristics and dynamics. *Journal of Adolescent Health, 62*, 72–79.

Wood, M., Barter, C., Stanley, N., Aghtaie, N., & Larkins, C. (2015). Images across Europe: The sending and receiving of sexual images and associations with interpersonal violence in young people's relationships. *Children and Youth Services Review, 59*, 149–160.

World Bank Group. (2018). *Compendium on international and national legal frameworks on female genital mutilation*. Washington, DC: World Bank.

World Health Assembly. (2008). Female genital mutilation: Resolution 61.16. www.who.int/reproductivehealth/topics/fgm/fgm_resolution_61.16.pdf

World Health Organization. (2018). Female genital mutilation fact sheet. http://www.who.int/news-room/fact-sheets/detail/female-genital-mutilation

World Health Organization Study Group on Female Genital Mutilation and Obstetric Outcome. (2006). Female genital mutilation and obstetric outcome: WHO collaborative prospective study in six African countries. *Lancet, 367*, 1835–1841.

Wortley, R., & Smallbone, S. (2012). *Internet child pornography: Causes, investigation and prevention*. Santa Barbara: Praeger.

Wright, P., Tokunaga, R., & Kraus, A. (2016). A meta-analysis of pornography consumption and actual acts of sexual aggression in general population studies. *Journal of Communication, 66*, 183–205.

Ybarra, M., & Mitchell, K. (2005). Exposure to internet pornography among children and adolescents: A national survey. *Cyberpsychology & Behavior, 8*, 473–486.

Yoder, P., & Khan, S. (2008). *Numbers of women circumcised in Africa: The production of a total*. Calverton: Macro International.

Yoder, P., Abderrahim, N., & Zhuzhuni, A. (2004). *Female genital cutting in the demographic health surveys a critical and comparative analysis*. Calverton: Macro International.

Part IV
Conclusion: Future Directions

Chapter 7
Future Directions

Abstract This Chapter closes the book with words of caution and hope. The scale of child sexual abuse can seem overwhelming, and its connection to deeply embedded contributing factors can make it appear an insoluble problem. Yet, progress has been made and can continue. The Chapters in this book have noted multiple aspects of progress, focusing on legal and policy reforms, and social progress. In this chapter, I make concluding remarks, informed by material already covered in this book, but moving beyond it to indicate what we may perhaps aspire to in the next couple of generations.

Keywords Child sexual abuse · Future policy priorities and possibilities · Prevention efforts · Schools · Education · Changing concepts of masculinity · Sexual literacy · Empathy and psychosocial skills · Organisational reforms · A manifesto for the Vatican · Political reforms · Promoting children's rights · Developing children's capabilities

Prevention efforts generally – Some thoughts on education, culture, masculinity, sexual literacy, empathy and psychosocial skills – A manifesto for the Vatican – Political changes.

The scale and severity of child sexual abuse can seem overwhelming, and its connection to deep social, environmental, and individual factors can make it appear to be an insoluble problem. Certainly, child sexual abuse remains a significant problem worldwide, and there are some particularly intractable problems and challenging new phenomena to deal with. Yet, progress has been made and can continue to be made. There is cause for cautious hope, which can nurture an ongoing commitment to seek further improvements. The Chapters in this book have noted multiple aspects of progress, focusing on legal and policy reforms. We should also consider ongoing research and proliferating, sustained advocacy efforts at local, national and international levels to themselves constitute progress. It is easy to forget how only a couple of generations ago, none of this work had happened. Here, I will make a few brief concluding remarks, informed by the material already covered in this book, but moving beyond it to indicate what we may perhaps aspire to in the next couple of generations.

B. Mathews, *New International Frontiers in Child Sexual Abuse*,
Child Maltreatment 7, https://doi.org/10.1007/978-3-319-99043-9_7

Prevention Efforts Generally

As a precondition of a sound public health approach to child sexual abuse, prevention efforts must continue, must continue to be refined, and must be prioritised. In 2009, David Finkelhor concluded that school-based prevention programs were the most promising form of prevention program, and should continue to receive investment. The Cochrane Review by Walsh et al. (2015) also found some encouraging results, with this meta-analysis of standard child sexual abuse prevention programs showing that these efforts do have benefits in improving children's knowledge, retention of knowledge, self-protective behaviors, and disclosures. The use of schools as a locus for prevention programs is clearly the most appropriate strategy, arguably exceeding even programs aimed at parents, given reasons of practicability. Recent work is aiming to develop primary prevention with adolescents (Letourneau et al. 2017), and this also appears essential given a significant proportion of child sexual offending is inflicted by adolescents, whether within or beyond dating relationships.

Finkelhor (2009) also recommended continued efforts to minimize harm as well as to reduce the occurrence of sexual abuse, to minimise some of the personal and social costs caused by sexual abuse associated with its legacy of mental health, physical health, and interpersonal problems. The provision of therapeutic assistance to children who have experienced abuse is essential, as a human right, and possibly to reduce the salience of the abuse as a risk factor for subsequent abuse. Based on the insights from experts such as Herman (1997) and Miller (1998), societies should take steps to ensure survivors of child sexual abuse have access to a supportive and empathic trusted listener. This is so that if they wish, they can engage in actions assisting recovery, namely to express their experience in a way they are comfortable with, to know it was not their fault, and to learn to cope. The impediments to disclosure are myriad (Alaggia et al. 2017) and the silencing of sexual abuse has caused untold pain and facilitated continued trauma and victimisation. The benefits of telling of one's experience may be immense, and there could be innovative ways of providing such supports to facilitate disclosure, in person, online, or through other ethical means. Similarly, laws requiring those who know of cases of child sexual abuse to bring them to the attention of legal or welfare agencies play a role in interrupting ongoing cases and preventing further abuse.

On Education, Culture, Masculinity, Sexual Literacy, Empathy and Psychosocial Skills

The role of education more broadly about sex, gender and violence is central to all attempts to reduce violence against children, and especially girls. The reframing of culture and conceptions of masculinity is vital. Robust research has shown the adverse effects of a sense of sexual entitlement, empathy deficits, poorly developed socio-emotional skills, atypical sexual interests, and a construction of masculinity emphasising dominance. Education has traditionally focused on cognitive skills rather than affective skills, and it is likely that relatively little progress has been made in these domains. Perhaps it is time for a greater focus on education in emotional literacy, in sexual literacy and developing healthier attitudes towards sex and relationships, in empathy, and in sexual and technological ethics, beginning in primary school and continuing throughout school with particular attention on key themes at critical developmental stages. Due to normal stages of brain growth, psychosocial development naturally will continue to occur through adolescence (Casey et al. 2008), yet such efforts may assist in tempering impulses towards violence and attitudes that justify it. This normal process of psychosocial development also indicates we need appropriate criminal justice responses for serious young offenders that focus on treatment and rehabilitation (Cauffman and Steinberg 2000), and this should occur as early as possible and be sustained. Both researchers and contemporary feminists alike suggest we need a new approach to teaching both boys and girls (Adichie 2017). These themes are not radical; they have been shown for some time to be necessary to deal with entrenched cultural practices prejudicial to children's bodily integrity and sexual wellbeing, as seen in the efforts to reduce FGM/C. However, a modified approach to masculinity in particular, reconceptualising honour, duty, strength and responsibility may still be in its infancy.

A Manifesto for the Vatican

The Roman Catholic Church is an immensely large and powerful organisation. It has been the locus of widespread child sexual abuse, despite its core professed purpose to be a place of virtue. The Church has been the institution most strongly criticised in this context, and not without reason. There is no need to repeat the figures already discussed earlier in this book.

Because of its nature as a religious body, the Church has a clear moral obligation to behave ethically in its dealings with survivors and in its efforts to prevent future abuse. Moreover, even setting aside its unenviable record, the Vatican has a clear moral obligation to adopt optimal practices because it plays a global role in setting norms of conduct for institutions and even nation states. In addition, the Vatican must now be considered to possess more than sufficient knowledge about the likely level of existing abuse and ongoing risk within its jurisdiction. Any continued failure to take the steps now known to be required could readily be interpreted as knowingly facilitating continued sexual abuse.

The question now is: what will the Vatican do about this? There are, in essence, three options. The first is to do nothing. The second is to make inadequate piecemeal efforts. The third is to make substantial efforts to properly deal with those who have already experienced abuse, and to enhance prevention. The third option is the only ethical route. It may cause short-term institutional cost, but it may also produce long-term benefits. The choices made will determine whether in another 20 years,

Table 7.1 Countries with the highest Catholic population (2015), and proportion aged 0–14 (2017)

Country	Number of baptized Catholics[a]	Total population (2015)[b]	0–14 years old (est 2017)[c]
Brazil	172.2 million	205,962,108	22.33%
Mexico	110.9 million	125,890,949	26.93%
Philippines	83.6 million	101,716,359	33.39%
USA	72.3 million	320,896,618	18.73%
Italy	58 million	60,730,582	13.65%
France	48.3 million	66,624,068	18.53%
Colombia	45.3 million	48,228,697	24.22%
Spain	43.3 million	46,447,697	15.38%
Democratic Rep. of the Congo	43.2 million	76,196,619	41.74%
Argentina	40.8 million	43,417,765	24.59%

[a]The Pontifical Yearbook. (2017); Annuarium Statisticum Ecclesiae (2015). https://press.vatican.va/content/salastampa/en/bollettino/pubblico/2017/04/06/170406e.html
[b]World Bank http://databank.worldbank.org/data/reports.aspx?Code=USA&id=556d8fa6&report_name=Popular_countries&populartype=country&ispopular=y
[c]CIA Factbook. (2017). https://www.cia.gov/library/publications/the-world-factbook/fields/2010.html#ar

we will be lauding the Vatican for global leadership in responding to child sexual abuse, or continuing to track an appalling record of malfeasance. This is particularly apposite given that in the nations with the largest Catholic population – including vast numbers of children – inquiries of the nature of those in Ireland and Australia are yet to occur, and the rule of law is weaker (Table 7.1).

While internal political difficulties may compromise quick fixes to canon law, these should still be pursued and it should nevertheless be within the Vatican's financial and logistical power to make substantial efforts elsewhere. At a minimum, the Vatican should, for example, take the following steps. First, it should immediately remove known offenders from ministry and exposure to children. Second, it should take all reasonable steps to enhance prevention and appropriate responses, especially in locations of highest risk. This should include taking whatever steps are necessary to revoke the 1962 Crimen Sollicitationis rules of secrecy, so that there is instead a new organisational requirement to report known cases of child sexual abuse both internally and to police in all jurisdictions, whether or not there is a domestic law requiring such a report. Third, it should implement redress schemes with the participation and oversight of domestic governments. Fourth, it should self-fund redress and other compensation through its own resources. Fifth, it should work with policy bodies, researchers and practitioners, domestic governments and law enforcement authorities to increase knowledge mobilisation, accountability and transparency. Sixth, it should involve the Catholic laity in building awareness of all these efforts, and should create mechanisms through which it is accountable to them through regular transparent reports on progress.

Political Changes

Finally, are there developments in political structures that may help to catalyse broader cultural change? Progress in women's rights, for example, only gathered substantial momentum with suffrage and representation in Parliament. Political power and the ability to mobilise as a group is required for stakeholders to exert greater pressure for policy change. Might future generations exist in a context where more individuals we now class as children are able to vote? Are 16 year olds, or at least 17 year olds, not sufficiently cognitively developed to be able to vote? If so, might there be more political attention paid to children's issues generally, including to their experience of sexual abuse? Perhaps the responsibility and accountability of institutions and governments would be elevated if more children were able to exert such pressure. Whether such advances occur or not, governments could still choose to take the issue of child sexual abuse more seriously, through steps such as having Ministers for Children, and developing policy statements for children, and reporting on progress. These may be avenues through which societies can capitalise on the progress made to date in prevention, identification and responding to child sexual abuse, and make continued efforts to promote children's rights and capabilities.

References

Adichie, C. N. (2017). *Dear Ijeawele, or A Feminist Manifesto in Fifteen Suggestions*. London: 4th Estate.

Alaggia, R., Collin-Vézina, D., & Lateef, R. (2017). Facilitators and barriers to child sexual abuse (CSA) disclosures: A research update (2000-2016). Trauma, Violence & Abuse, 21, 1–26.

Casey, B., Jones, R., & Hare, T. (2008). The adolescent brain. *Annals of the New York Academy of Science, 1124*, 111–126.

Cauffman, E., & Steinberg, L. (2000). (Im)maturity of judgment in adolescence: Why adolescents may be less culpable than adults. Behavioral Sciences and the Law, 18(6), 741-760.

Finkelhor, D. (2009). The prevention of childhood sexual abuse. *The Future of Children., 19*(2), 169–194.

Herman, J. L. (1997). *Trauma and recovery*. New York: Basic Books.

Letourneau, E., Schaeffer, C., Bradshaw, C., & Feder, K. (2017). Preventing the onset of child sexual abuse by targeting young adolescents with universal prevention programming. *Child Maltreatment, 22*(2), 100–111.

Miller, A. (1998). *Thou shalt not be aware*. New York: Farrar, Straus and Giroux.

Walsh, K., Zwi, K., Woolfenden, S., & Shlonsky, A. (2015). School-based education programmes for the prevention of child sexual abuse (Review). *The Cochrane Library, 2015*, 1–121.

Glossary

Adolescent An older child, here used to refer to an individual still aged under 18, although some approaches extend the age of adolescence beyond 18.

Capabilities Approach A species of a human rights approach advocated by Martha Nussbaum, focused on ensuring that as a matter of public policy, each individual should have a minimum amount of ten core capabilities necessary for a life of sufficient equality, dignity, autonomy and freedom.

Child A person aged under 18.

CYSO A child and youth serving organisation, being any organisation whose purpose is wholly or partially to provide education, religious, health, welfare, recreation, sports, cultural, arts or other services to children.

Child marriage Considered to take place whenever one party is aged under 18. Child marriage is considered to be a form of forced marriage, given that one or both parties have not expressed full, free and informed consent.

Child sexual abuse Includes a broad spectrum of contact and non-contact sexual acts inflicted on a child. The definition adopted here I follows that proposed by Mathews and Collin-Vézina (2017), namely that child sexual abuse will exist when: (1) the person is a child (from either or both developmental and legal standpoints); (2) there is no true consent (due either to lack of capacity to provide consent, or presence of capacity but lack of consent in fact); (3) the acts are sexual (being contact or non-contact acts done to seek or obtain physical or mental sexual gratification, whether immediate or deferred in time or space, or otherwise legitimately experienced by the child as a sexual act); and (4) the acts constitute abuse (due to the presence of a relationship of power, the child's position of inequality, and the exploitation of the child's vulnerability).

Child protection law Law within a nation generally aimed at protecting a child within the family environment; but may also extend to law's approach to protecting children more generally, especially in the case of child sexual abuse

Civil law That part of a nation's legislation and common law dealing with civil rights of action that can be brought by an individual citizen who has suffered injury.

B. Mathews, *New International Frontiers in Child Sexual Abuse*,
Child Maltreatment 7, https://doi.org/10.1007/978-3-319-99043-9

Consent The condition required to legitimise any sexual interaction. To be valid, consent is generally understood as only valid if it is informed, and is freely and fully given to the specific act at the specific time, by an individual who is cognitively able to understand the nature of the acts, and where the consent is not otherwise vitiated.

Criminal law That part of a nation's legislation and common law dealing with criminal offending and sentencing for crimes. Actions are brought by the state.

Culpability Blameworthiness. Can be distinguished from accountability: children who inflict sexual abuse on other children should always be held accountable, but not always culpable, depending on their moral agency.

Dignity Objective human flourishing or thriving, as advocated by Charles Foster. Relevant to any analysis of the normative justifiability of an experience is the dignity of not only the subject person, but also of the other actors (e.g., those exploiting or acting in relation to the subject person), and society as a whole.

Disclosure The term generally used in the literature for how children tell others about their experience of child sexual abuse. Non-disclosure and delayed disclosure refer to these connected phenomena.

Domestic law A nation's legislation and common law.

Family law That part of a nation's legislation and common law dealing only with relationships between children and their parents or caregivers

FGM/C Female genital mutilation/cutting, a cultural custom (not a religious one), which can take any one of four forms.

Human rights The broad body of rights recognised by international law, and or by political theory.

International law Law contained in international conventions and treaties. Ratification by a nation of an international convention may or may not mean the convention has domestic force depending on a nation's other domestic laws about the effect of ratification.

Law The entire body of law in a jurisdiction, comprising legislation, common law (law made by courts), and international law.

Legislation Laws enacted by Parliament, also referred to as statutes.

Mandatory reporting laws Laws enacted by Parliament imposing on designated persons an obligation to report known or suspected cases of child sexual abuse. Not to be confused with other kinds of legal or occupational policy-based reporting duty.

Prevalence/incidence Prevalence studies of child sexual abuse identify the extent of the experience within a group across the entire span of childhood; incidence normally refers to the occurrence of the experience within a shorter period, most often one year

Public health The collective actions of society, including laws, policies, practices, and activities, that have the primary purpose of protecting and improving the health of the public

Public health law On Larry Gostin's conception, the study of the legal powers and duties of the state to ensure the conditions for people to be healthy, to identify, prevent, and meliorate risks to health in the population, and of the limitations on the power of the state to constrain for the common good individual autonomy, privacy, liberty, proprietary and other interests

Sexual harassment A technical term used to refer to a broad spectrum of sexual violations in employment or workplace law.

UNCRC The United Nations Convention on the Rights of the Child.

Vicarious liability A legal principle through which an employer is deemed liable for the acts of its employees or agents. Since the employer has created the opportunity to profit through the activities of the organisation, it should also bear the risk of wrongdoing. Vicarious liability is a vehicle of distributive justice.

Victims/survivors Those who have experienced child sexual abuse. Generally, the preferred term is survivors.

The manufacturer's authorised representative in the EU is Springer Nature Customer Service Centre GmbH, Europaplatz 3, 69115 Heidelberg, Germany. If you have any concerns regarding our products, please contact ProductSafety@springernature.com

Printed and bound by CPI Group (UK) Ltd, Croydon, CR0 4YY
05/10/2026
02228135-0013